NEGIMA! 3

Ken Akamatsu

TRANSLATED BY
Douglas Varenas

ADAPTED BY
Peter David and Kathleen O'Shea David

LETTERED BY
Steve Palmer

LONDON

Published in the United Kingdom by Tanoshimi in 2006

1 3 5 7 9 10 8 6 4 2

Copyright © 2004 by Ken Akamatsu

All rights reserved

Ken Akamatsu has asserted his right under the Copyright, Designs and Patents Act,
1988 to be identified as the author of this work.

This is a work of fiction. Names, characters, places and incidents are the products of the
author's imagination or are used fictitiously. Any resemblance to actual events, locales or
persons, living or dead, is entirely coincidental.

This book is sold subject to the condition that it shall not, by way of trade or otherwise, be lent,
resold, hired out, or otherwise circulated without the publisher's prior consent in any form of
binding or cover other than that in which it is published and without a similar condition including
this condition being imposed on the subsequent purchaser.

First published in serial form by Shonen Magazine comics and subsequently published in book form by
Kodansha Ltd., Tokyo in 2003. Copyright © 2003 by Ken Akamatsu.

Published by arrangement with Kodansha Ltd., Tokyo and with Del Rey,
an imprint of Random House Inc., New York

Tanoshimi
The Random House Group Limited
20 Vauxhall Bridge Road, London, SW1V 2SA

Random House Australia (Pty) Limited
20 Alfred Street, Milsons Point, Sydney
New South Wales 2061, Australia

Random House New Zealand Limited
18 Poland Road, Glenfield
Auckland 10, New Zealand

Random House (Pty) Limited
Isle of Houghton, Corner of Boundary Road & Carse O'Gowrie
Houghton 2198, South Africa

Random House Publishers India Private Limited
301 World Trade Tower, Hotel Intercontinental Grand Complex,
Barakhamba Lane, New Delhi 110 001, India

Random House Group Limited Reg. No. 954009

www.tanoshimi.tv
www.randomhouse.co.uk

A CIP catalogue record for this book is available from the British Library

Papers used by Random House
are natural, recyclable products made from wood grown in sustainable forests.
The manufacturing processes conform to the environmental regulations of the country of origin.

ISBN 9780099504177 (from Jan 2007)
ISBN 0 09 950417 0

Printed and bound in Germany by GGP Media GmbH, Pößneck

Translator — Douglas Varenas
Adaptor — Peter David and Kathleen O'Shea David
Lettering and Text Design — Steve Palmer
Cover Design — David Stevenson

A Word from the Author

Here it is, Volume 3 of *Negima!* Volume 3 is the first *Negima!* that uses a whole volume for a single story. It's called the "Evangeline Edition."

How in the world will Negi-kun, who as an honor student who graduated top of the class from a magic school, and has yet to run into any particularly serious barriers, continue to grow up when he encounters new formidable enemies and friends he comes to depend on? What is the secret of the Thousand Master who pursues Negi!? And what is the partner binding system!?

Usually there are only nine chapters in a volume but, this time, we've packed in ten, so there's plenty to enjoy. Well then, take your time and enjoy (ha ha)!

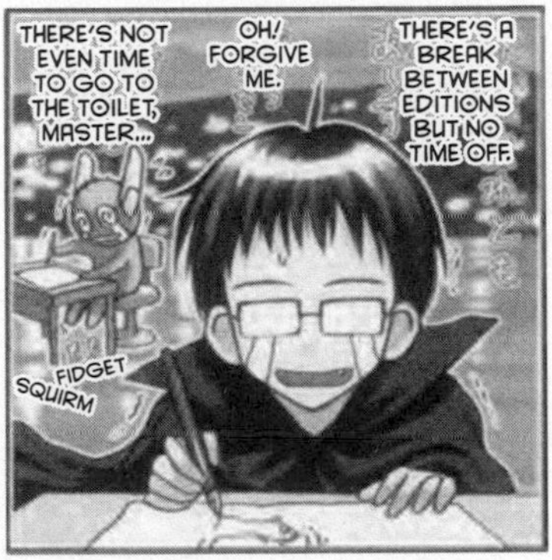
THERE'S A BREAK BETWEEN EDITIONS BUT NO TIME OFF.
OH! FORGIVE ME.
THERE'S NOT EVEN TIME TO GO TO THE TOILET, MASTER...
FIDGET SQUIRM

For more information, please check out the official site below. You can also access it from your mobile phone. I update my blog every day.

Ken Akamatsu
http://www.ailove.net

Honorifics

Throughout the Tanoshimi Manga books, you will find Japanese honorifics left intact in the translations. For those not familiar with how the Japanese use honorifics, and more important, how they differ from English honorifics, we present this brief overview.

Politeness has always been a critical facet of Japanese culture. Ever since the feudal era, when Japan was a highly stratified society, use of honorifics — which can be defined as polite speech that indicates relationship or status — has played an essential role in the Japanese language. When addressing someone in Japanese, an honorific usually takes the form of a suffix attached to one's name (example: "Asuna-san"), or as a title at the end of one's name or in place of the name itself (example: "Negi-sensei," or simply "Sensei!").

Honorifics can be expressions of respect or endearment. In the context of manga and anime, honorifics give insight into the nature of the relationship between characters. Many translations into English leave out these important honorifics, and therefore distort the "feel" of the original Japanese. Because Japanese honorifics have nuances that English honorifics lack, it is our policy at Tanoshimi not to translate them. Here, instead, is a guide to some of the honorifics you may encounter in Tanoshimi Manga.

-*san:*   This is the most common honorific, and is equivalent to Mr., Miss, Ms., Mrs., etc. It is the all-purpose honorific and can be used in any situation where politeness is required.

-*sama:* This is one level higher than -*san*. It is used to confer great respect.

-*dono:* This comes from the word *tono*, which means *lord*. It is an even higher level than *sama*, and confers utmost respect.

-kun: This suffix is used at the end of boys' names to express familiarity or endearment. It is also sometimes used by men among friends, or when addressing someone younger or of a lower station.

-chan: This is used to express endearment, mostly toward girls. It is also used for little boys, pets, and even among lovers. It gives a sense of childish cuteness.

Bozu: This is an informal way to refer to a boy, similar to the English term "kid".

Sempai: This title suggests that the addressee is one's "senior" in a group or organization. It is most often used in a school setting, where underclassmen refer to their upperclassmen as *sempai*. It can also be used in the workplace, such as when a newer employee addresses an employee who has seniority in the company.

Kohai: This is the opposite of *sempai*, and is used toward underclassmen in school or newcomers in the workplace. It connotes that the addressee is of lower station.

Sensei: Literally meaning "one who has come before," this title is used for teachers, doctors, or masters of any profession or art.

-[blank]: Usually forgotten in these lists, but perhaps the most significant difference between Japanese and English. The lack of honorific means that the speaker has permission to address the person in a very intimate way. Usually, only family, spouses, or very close friends have this kind of permission. Known as *yobisute*, it can be gratifying when someone who has earned the intimacy starts to call one by one's name without an honorific. But when that intimacy hasn't been earned, it can also be very insulting.

tanoshimi

Look out for these fantastic series coming your way in 2006

xxxHolic
Tsubasa: RESERVoir CHRoNiCLE
Negima!
Basilisk
Ghost Hunt
Guru Guru Pon-chan
Air Gear

Coming soon in 2007

School Rumble
Mamotte!Lollipop

As well as other brilliant new titles

Visit www.tanoshimi.tv for up to the minute news
about forthcoming new books and exclusive previews

www.tanoshimi.tv

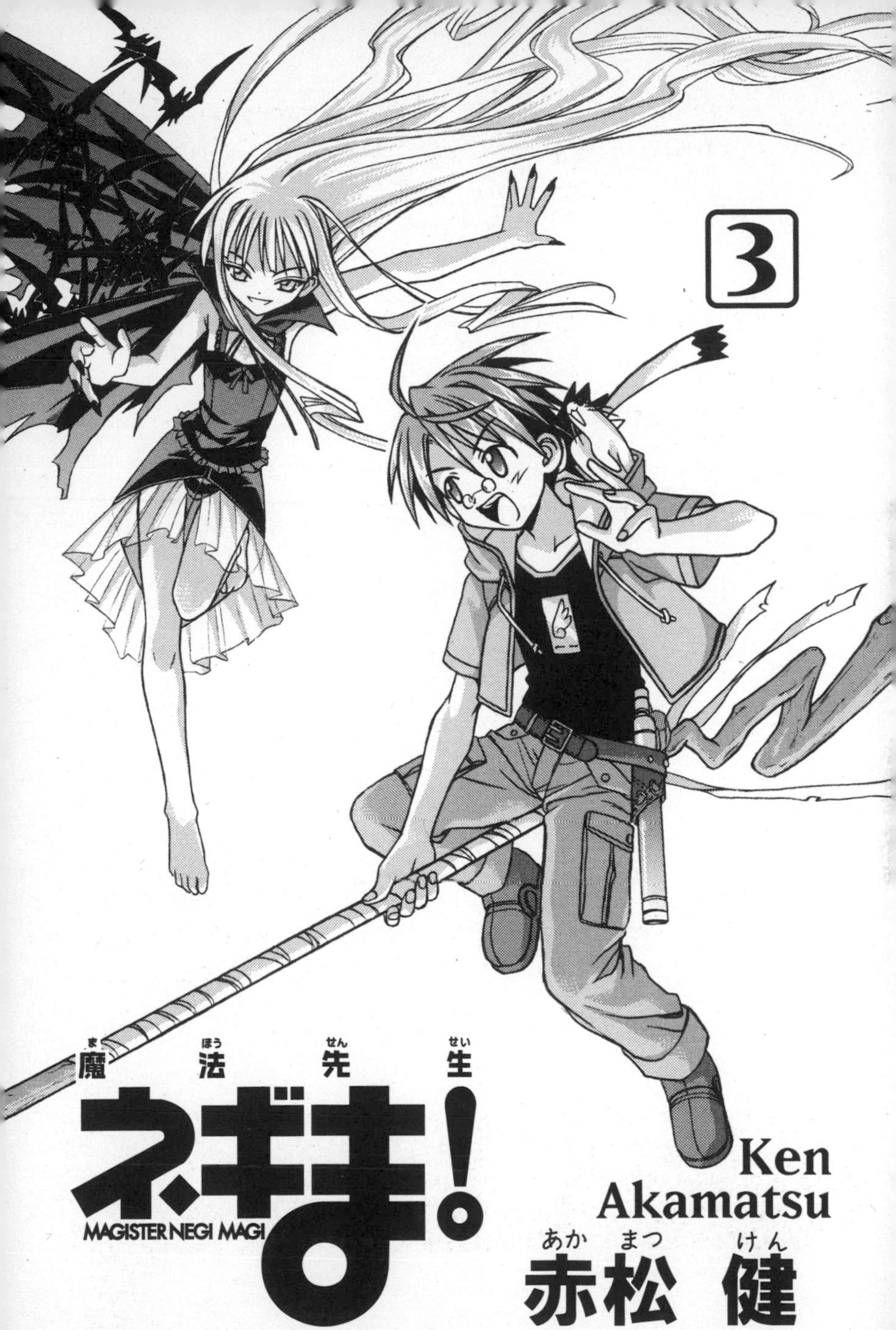

3

魔法先生ネギま!

MAGISTER NEGI MAGI

Ken Akamatsu

あかまつ けん
赤松 健

WRITTEN APPOINTMENT. NEGI SPRINGFIELD.
APRIL 2, 2003. APPOINTMENT OF TEACHER,
JUNIOR HIGH DEPARTMENT MAHORA ACADEMY.

HEADMASTER, MAHORA ACADEMY.
麻帆良学園学園長　近衛近右衛門

CONTENTS

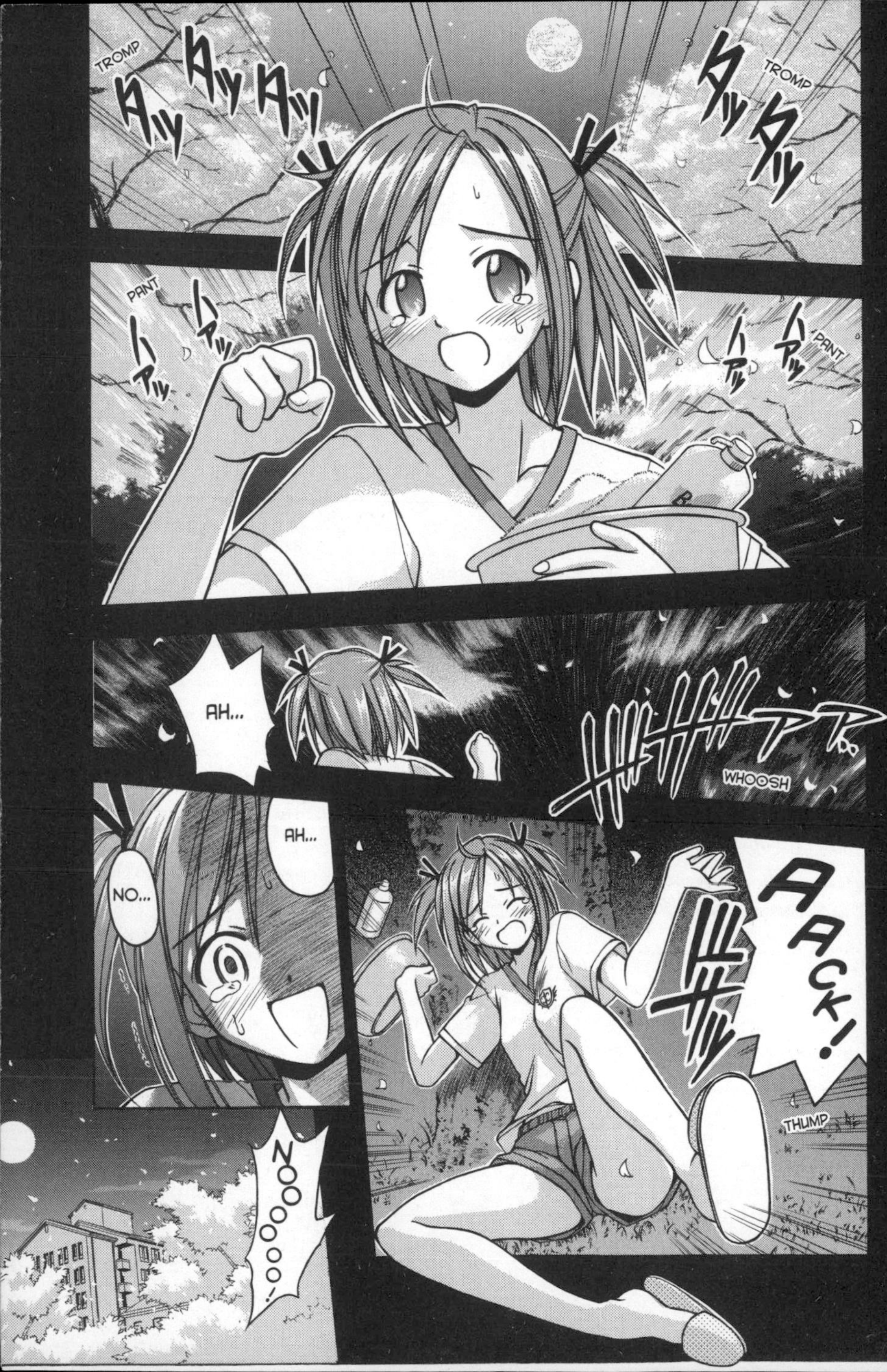
TROMP
TROMP
PANT
PANT
WHOOSH
AH...
AACK!
THUMP
AH...
NO...
NOOOOOOO!

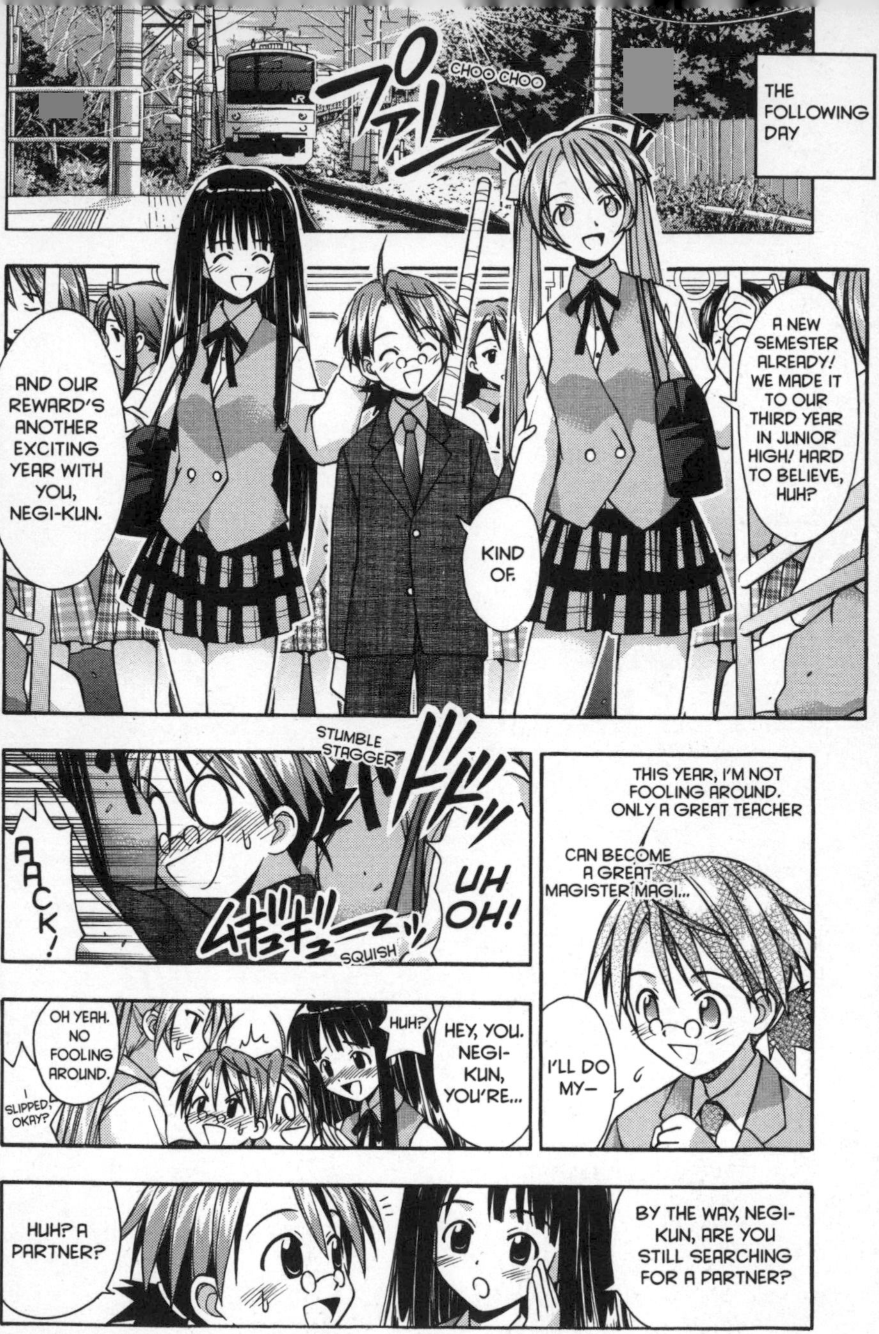
THE FOLLOWING DAY
CHOO CHOO
A NEW SEMESTER ALREADY! WE MADE IT TO OUR THIRD YEAR IN JUNIOR HIGH! HARD TO BELIEVE, HUH?
KIND OF.
AND OUR REWARD'S ANOTHER EXCITING YEAR WITH YOU, NEGI-KUN.
THIS YEAR, I'M NOT FOOLING AROUND. ONLY A GREAT TEACHER
CAN BECOME A GREAT MAGISTER MAGI...
I'LL DO MY—
STUMBLE STAGGER
UH OH!
AACK!
SQUISH
HEY, YOU. NEGI-KUN, YOU'RE...
HUH?
OH YEAH. NO FOOLING AROUND.
I SLIPPED, OKAY?
BY THE WAY, NEGI-KUN, ARE YOU STILL SEARCHING FOR A PARTNER?
HUH? A PARTNER?

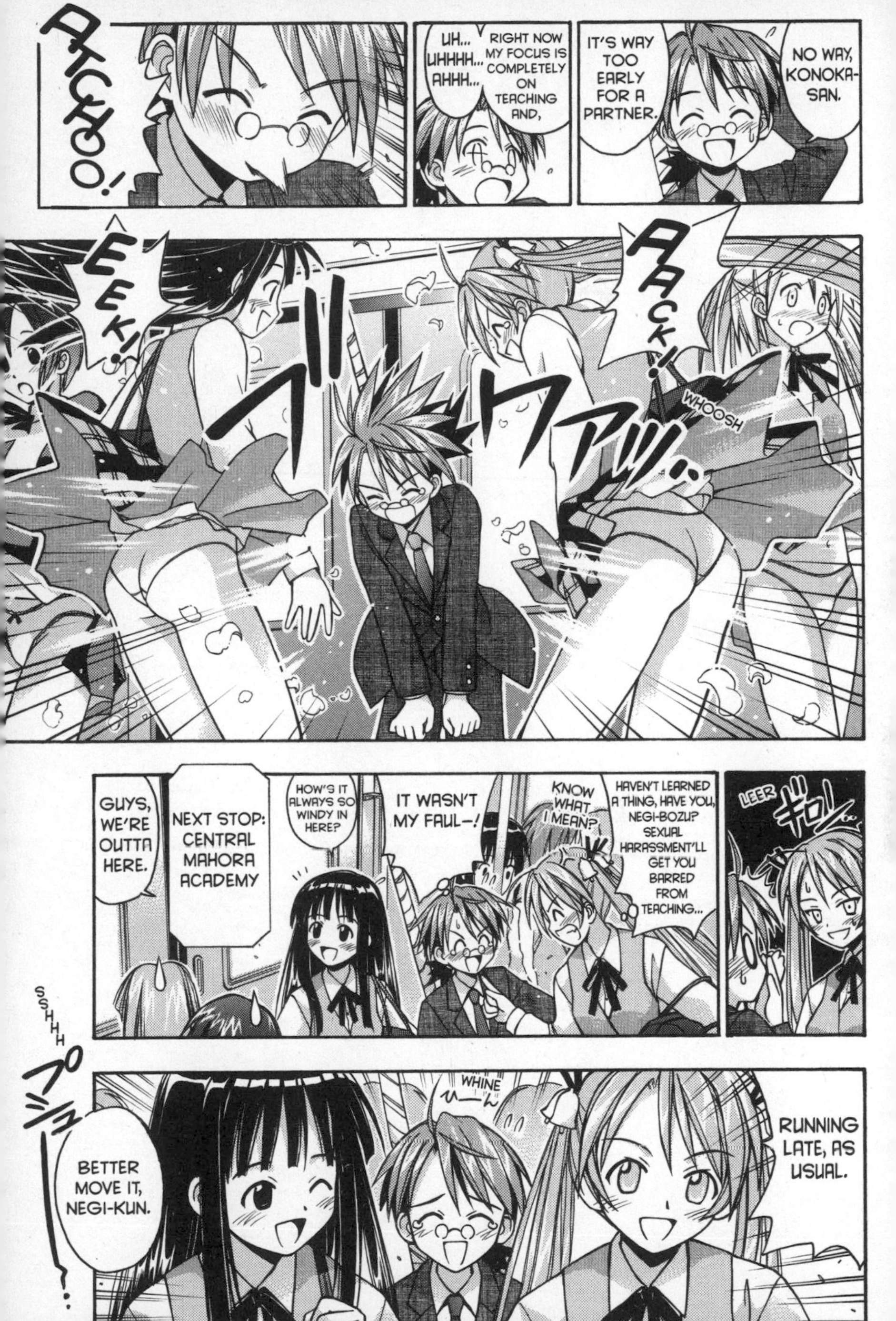
NO WAY, KONOKA-SAN.
IT'S WAY TOO EARLY FOR A PARTNER.
RIGHT NOW MY FOCUS IS COMPLETELY ON TEACHING AND,
UH... UHHHH... AHHH...
ATCHOO!
AACK!!
WHOOSH
ブワァッ
ÊEEK!
LEER
ギロッ
HAVEN'T LEARNED A THING, HAVE YOU, NEGI-BOZU? SEXUAL HARASSMENT'LL GET YOU BARRED FROM TEACHING...
KNOW WHAT I MEAN?
IT WASN'T MY FAUL—!
HOW'S IT ALWAYS SO WINDY IN HERE?
NEXT STOP: CENTRAL MAHORA ACADEMY
GUYS, WE'RE OUTTA HERE.
RUNNING LATE, AS USUAL.
WHINE
ひーん
BETTER MOVE IT, NEGI-KUN.
SSHHH
プシュー

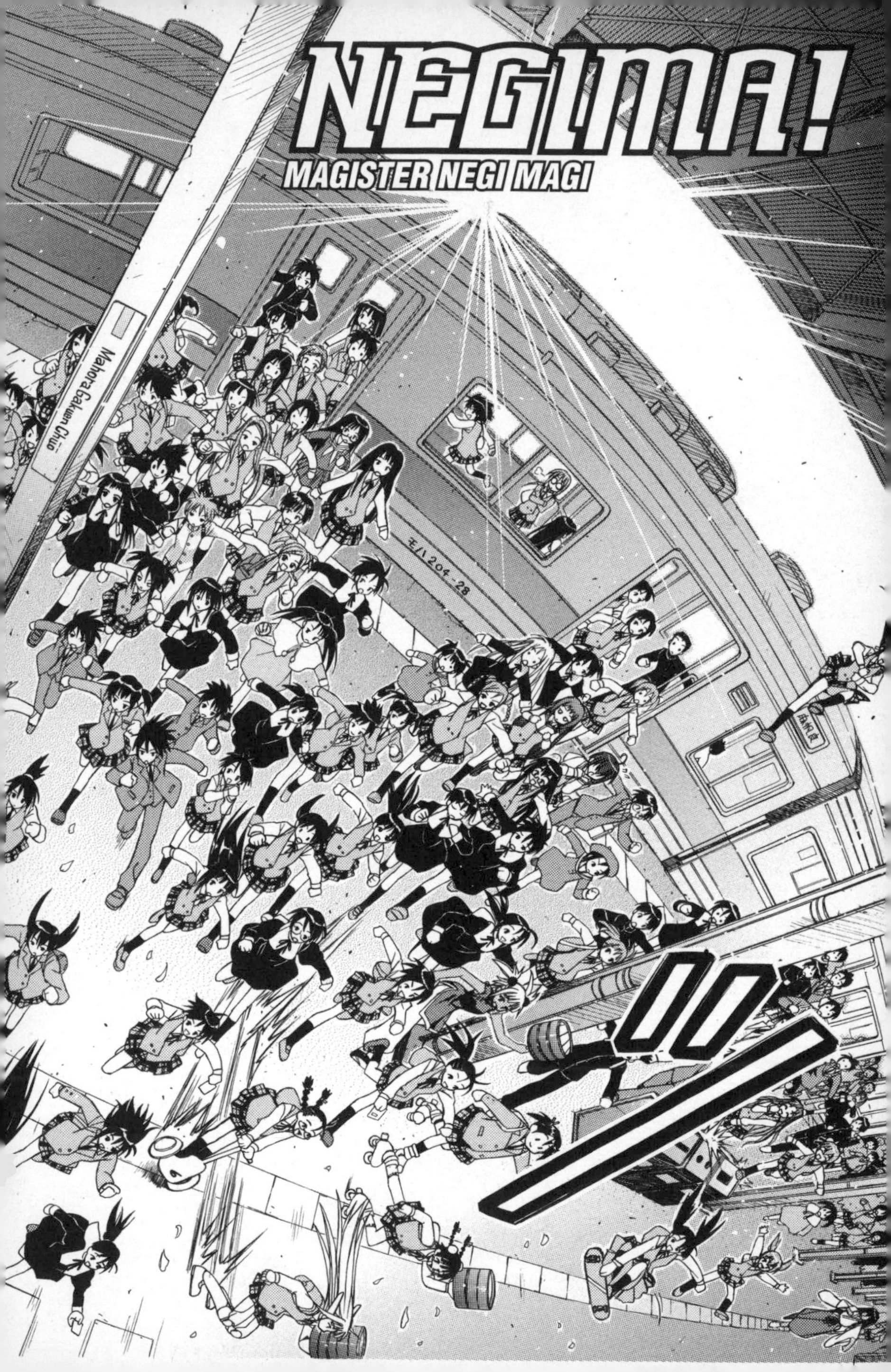
NEGIMA!
MAGISTER NEGI MAGI
Mahora Gakuen Chūō
モハ 204-28
00

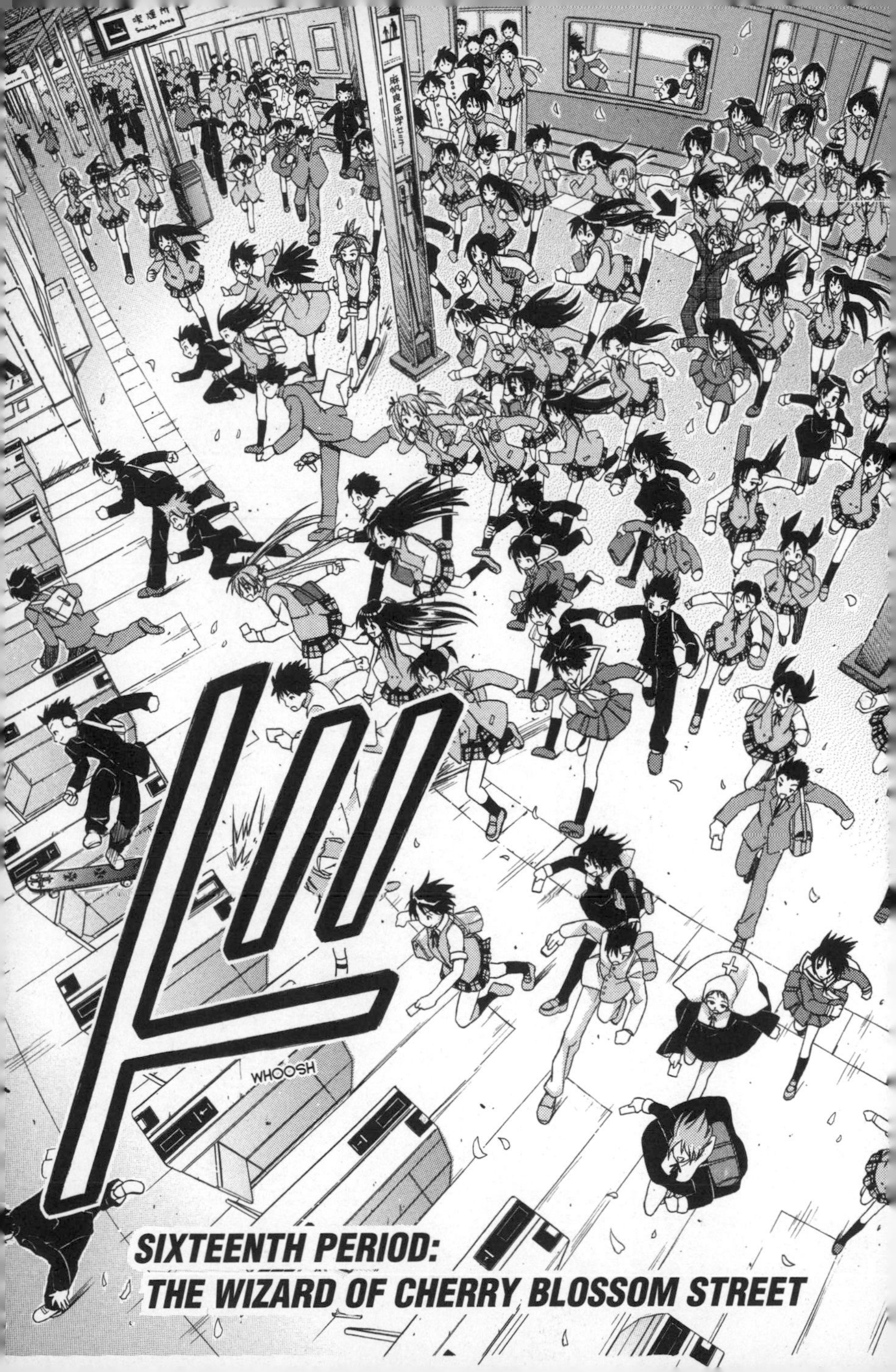
WHOOSH

SIXTEENTH PERIOD: THE WIZARD OF CHERRY BLOSSOM STREET

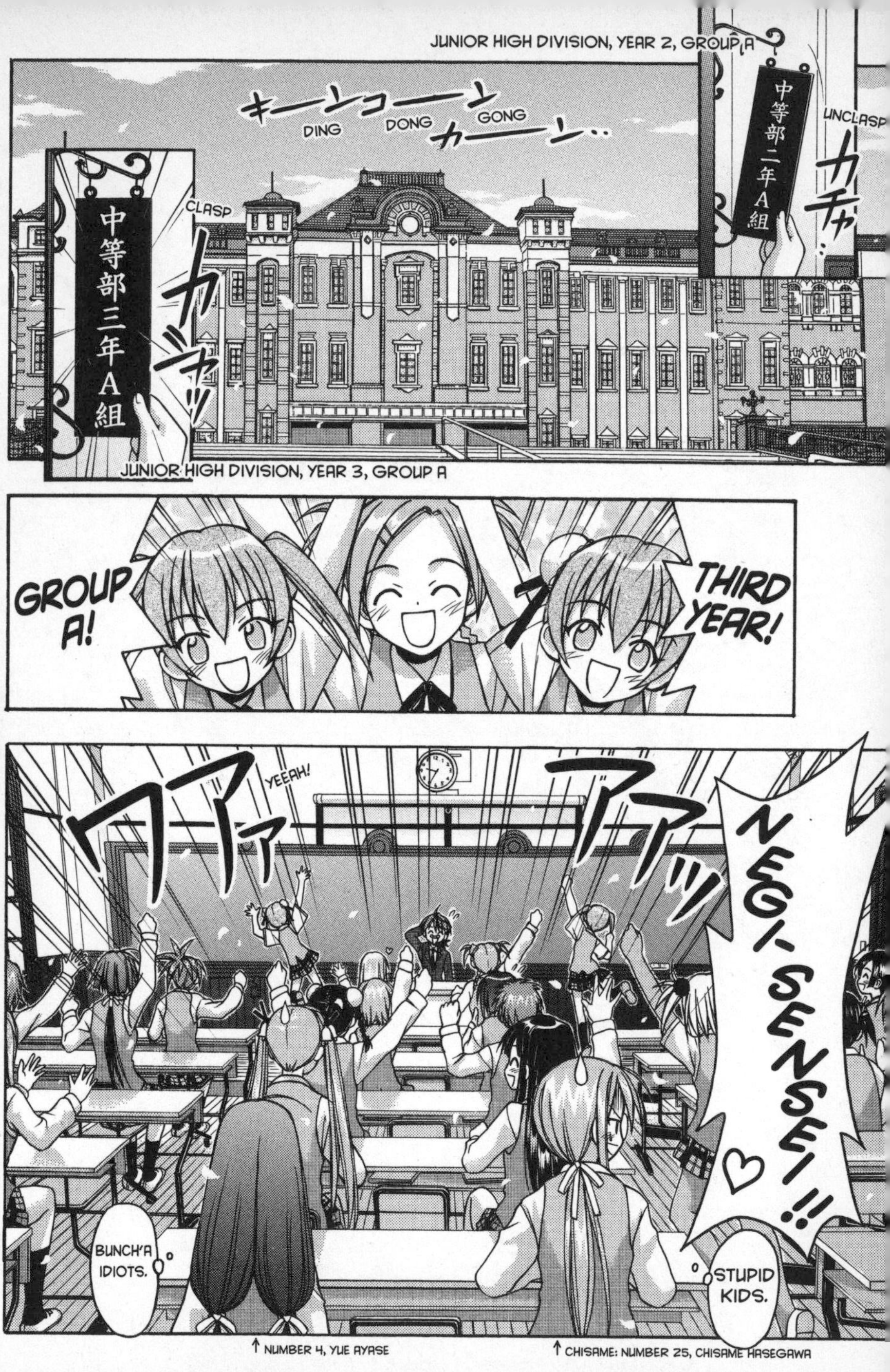
JUNIOR HIGH DIVISION, YEAR 2, GROUP A
中等部二年A組
UNCLASP
カチャ
キーンコーン
DING
DONG
GONG
カーン..
中等部三年A組
CLASP
カシャッ
JUNIOR HIGH DIVISION, YEAR 3, GROUP A
THIRD YEAR!
GROUP A!
NEGI-SENSEI ♡ !!!
アアッ
YEEAH!
ワァァ
STUPID KIDS.
BUNCH'A IDIOTS.

↑ NUMBER 4, YUE AYASE

↑ CHISAME: NUMBER 25, CHISAME HASEGAWA

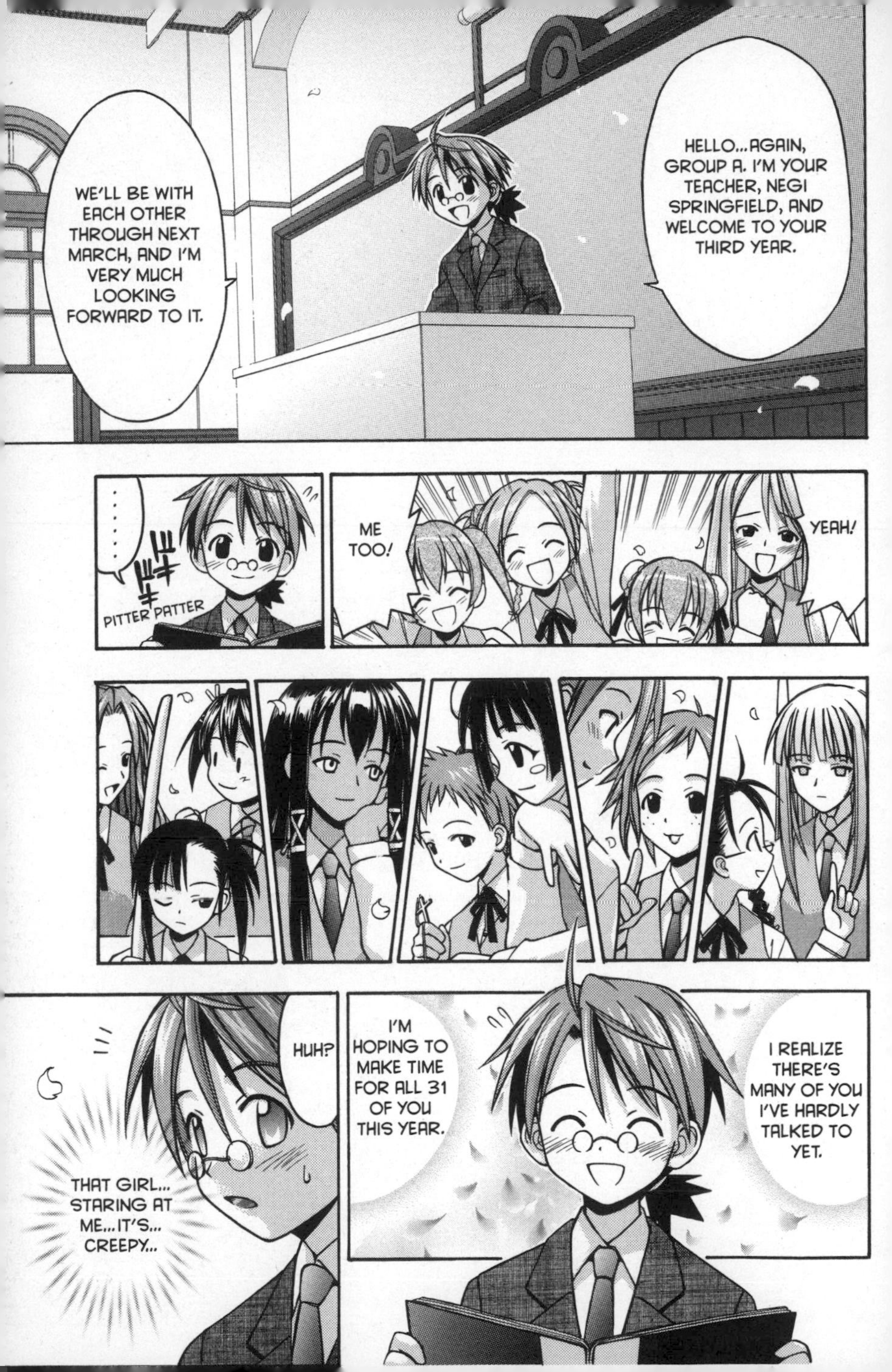
HELLO...AGAIN, GROUP A. I'M YOUR TEACHER, NEGI SPRINGFIELD, AND WELCOME TO YOUR THIRD YEAR.
WE'LL BE WITH EACH OTHER THROUGH NEXT MARCH, AND I'M VERY MUCH LOOKING FORWARD TO IT.
YEAH!
ME TOO!
......
PITTER PATTER
I REALIZE THERE'S MANY OF YOU I'VE HARDLY TALKED TO YET.
I'M HOPING TO MAKE TIME FOR ALL 31 OF YOU THIS YEAR.
HUH?
THAT GIRL... STARING AT ME...IT'S... CREEPY...

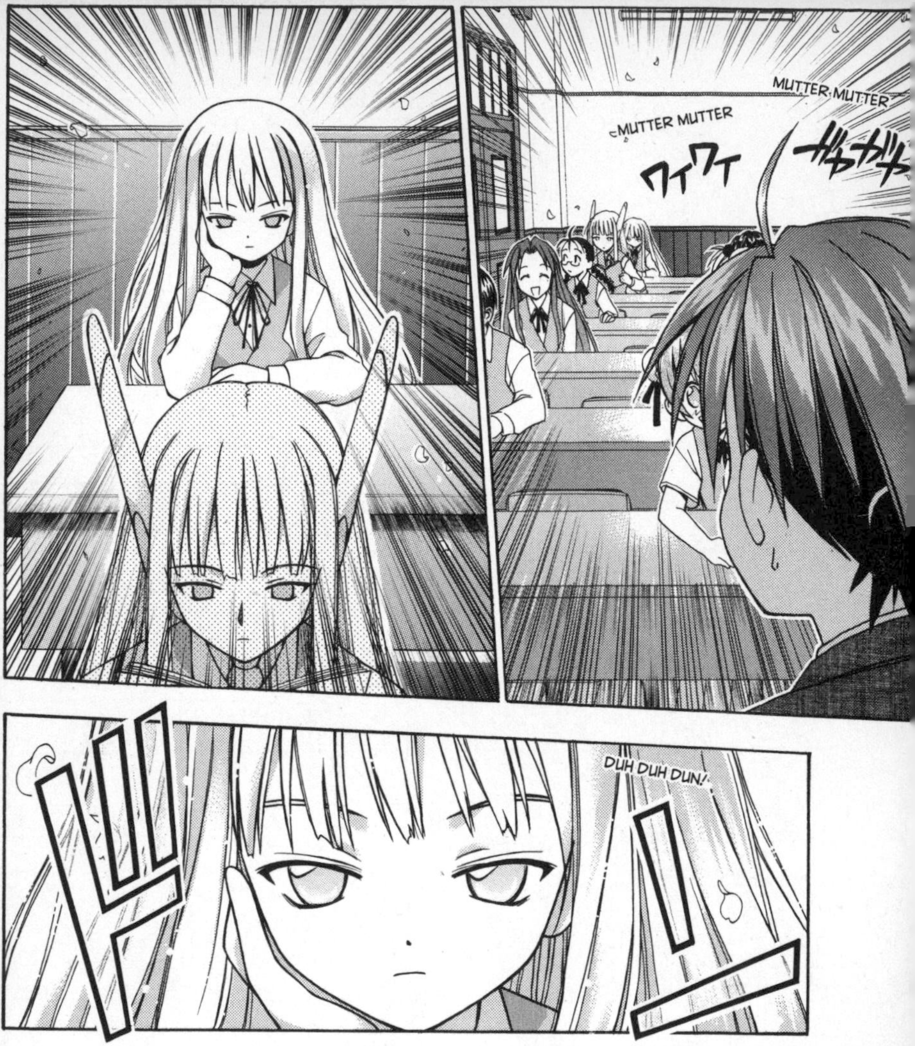

MUTTER MUTTER
MUTTER MUTTER
ワイワイ
DUH DUH DUN!
ワイワイ…
CHATTER
CHILL
WHO IS SHE?!
STUDENT NUMBER 26, EVANGELINE A.K. MCDOWELL-SAN.
GO CLUB AND TEA CEREMONY CLUB!?
TAKAMICHI WROTE I SHOULD CONSULT HER WHEN I HAVE ANY PROBLEMS.
26.Evangeline.A.K.McDowell
囲碁部
茶道部
困った時に相談しなさい

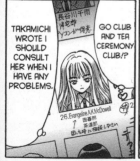

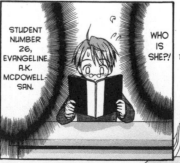

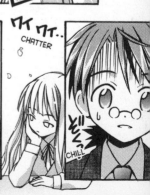

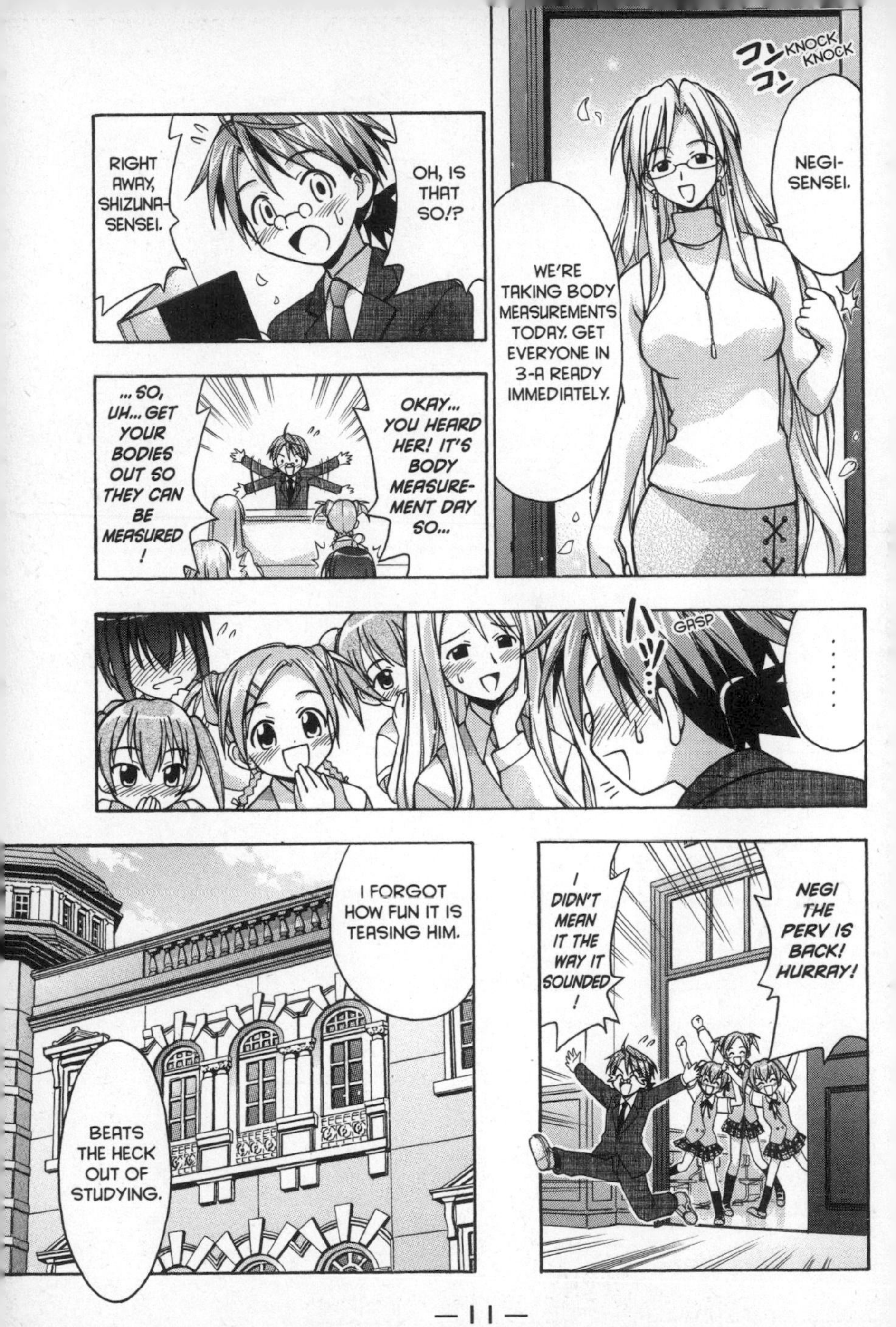
コンコン KNOCK KNOCK
NEGI-SENSEI.
WE'RE TAKING BODY MEASUREMENTS TODAY. GET EVERYONE IN 3-A READY IMMEDIATELY.
OH, IS THAT SO!?
RIGHT AWAY, SHIZUNA-SENSEI.
OKAY... YOU HEARD HER! IT'S BODY MEASUREMENT DAY SO...
...SO, UH... GET YOUR BODIES OUT SO THEY CAN BE MEASURED!
......
GASP
NEGI THE PERV IS BACK! HURRAY!
I DIDN'T MEAN IT THE WAY IT SOUNDED!
I FORGOT HOW FUN IT IS TEASING HIM.
BEATS THE HECK OUT OF STUDYING.

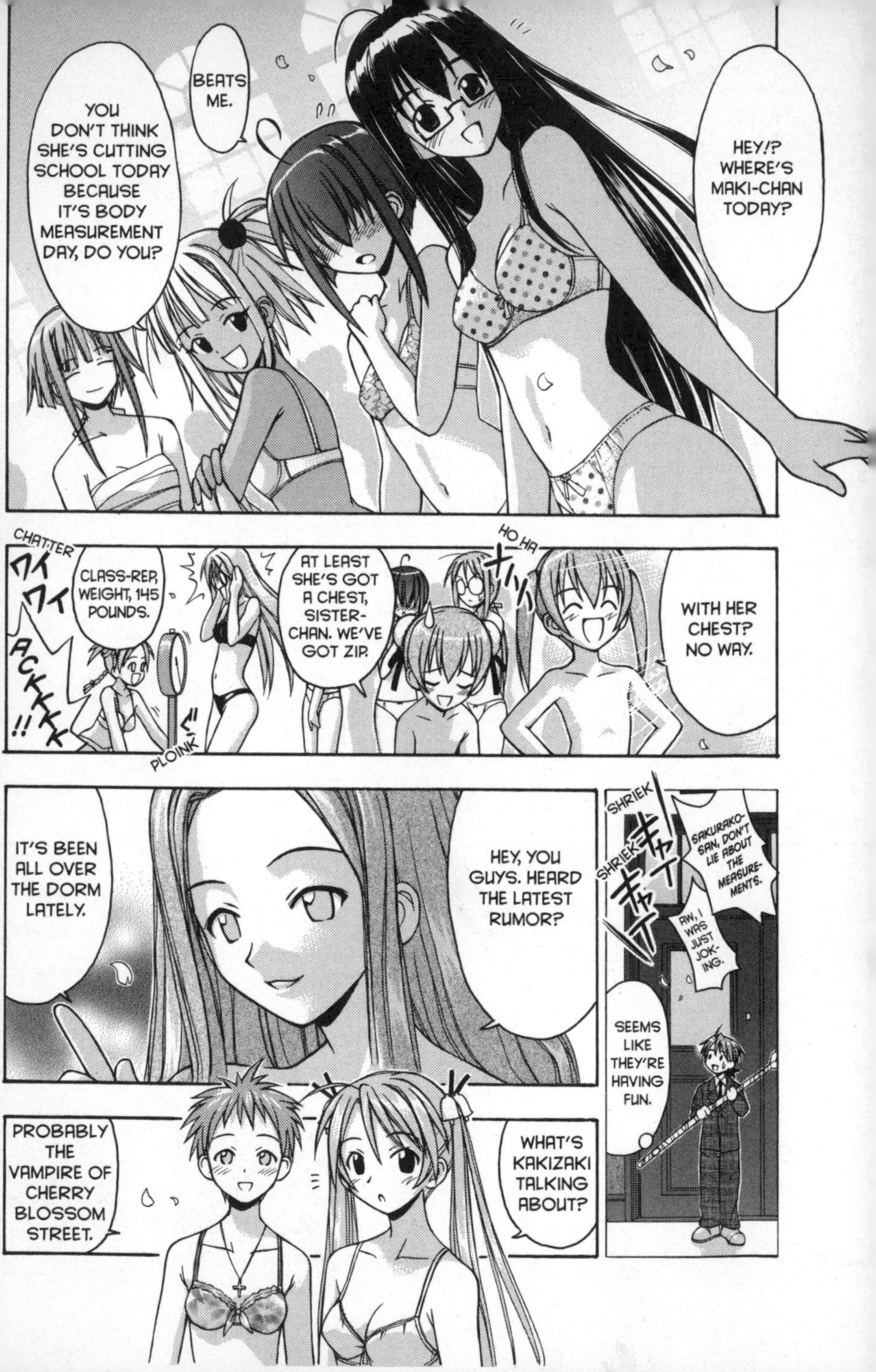
HEY!? WHERE'S MAKI-CHAN TODAY?
BEATS ME.
YOU DON'T THINK SHE'S CUTTING SCHOOL TODAY BECAUSE IT'S BODY MEASUREMENT DAY, DO YOU?
WITH HER CHEST? NO WAY.
HO HA
AT LEAST SHE'S GOT A CHEST, SISTER-CHAN. WE'VE GOT ZIP.
CLASS-REP, WEIGHT, 145 POUNDS.
CHATTER
ACKKKKK!!
PLOINK
SHRIEK
SHRIEK
SAKURAKO-SAN, DON'T LIE ABOUT THE MEASUREMENTS.
AW, I WAS JUST JOKING.
SEEMS LIKE THEY'RE HAVING FUN.
HEY, YOU GUYS. HEARD THE LATEST RUMOR?
IT'S BEEN ALL OVER THE DORM LATELY.
WHAT'S KAKIZAKI TALKING ABOUT?
PROBABLY THE VAMPIRE OF CHERRY BLOSSOM STREET.

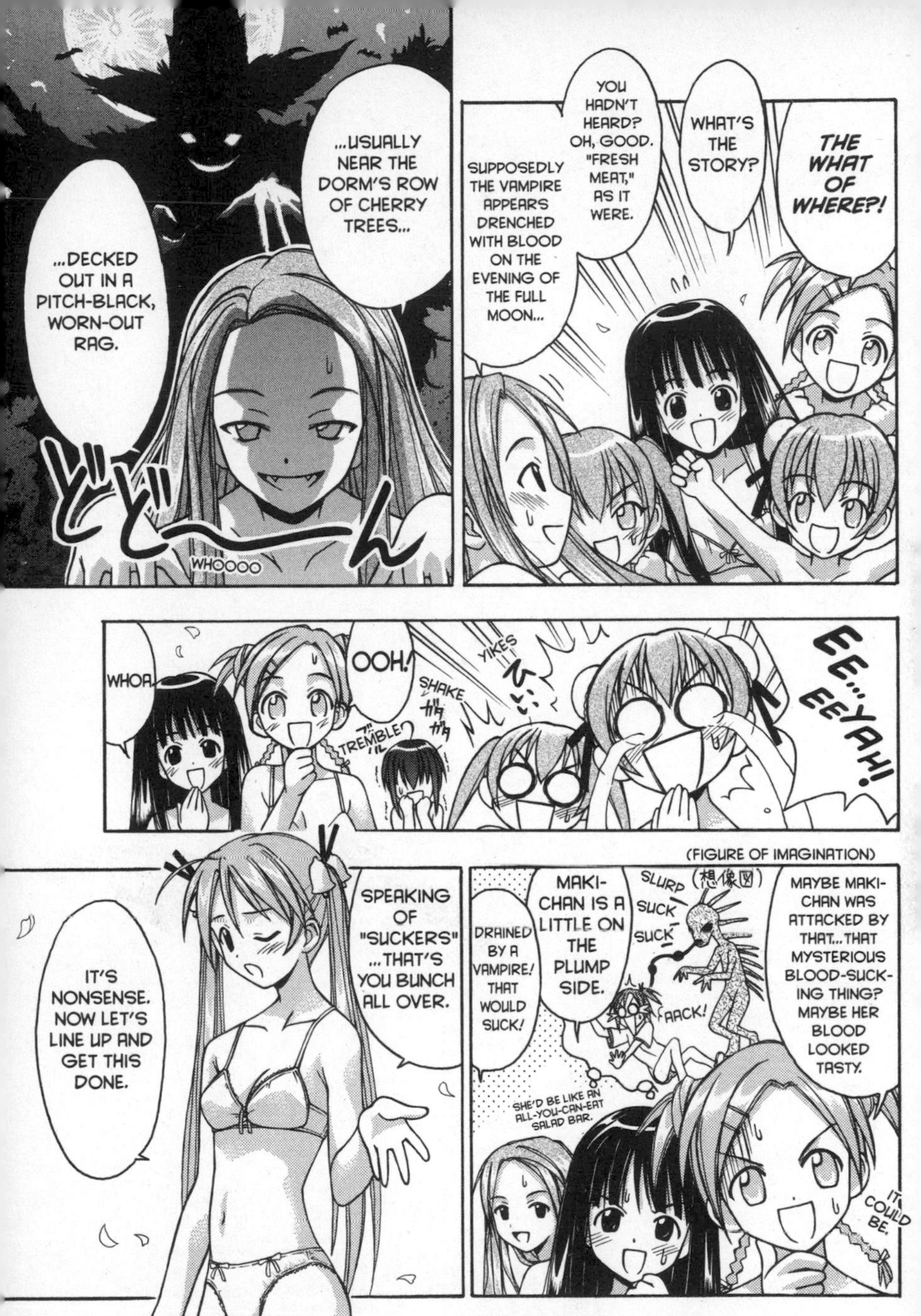
THE WHAT OF WHERE?!
WHAT'S THE STORY?
YOU HADN'T HEARD? OH, GOOD. "FRESH MEAT," AS IT WERE.
SUPPOSEDLY THE VAMPIRE APPEARS DRENCHED WITH BLOOD ON THE EVENING OF THE FULL MOON...
...USUALLY NEAR THE DORM'S ROW OF CHERRY TREES...
...DECKED OUT IN A PITCH-BLACK, WORN-OUT RAG.
どど～ん
WHOOOO
EE... EEYAH!
YIKES
SHAKE
TREMBLE
OOH!
WHOA.
(FIGURE OF IMAGINATION)
(想像図)
MAYBE MAKI-CHAN WAS ATTACKED BY THAT... THAT MYSTERIOUS BLOOD-SUCKING THING? MAYBE HER BLOOD LOOKED TASTY.
SLURP
SUCK
SUCK
MAKI-CHAN IS A LITTLE ON THE PLUMP SIDE.
DRAINED BY A VAMPIRE! THAT WOULD SUCK!
AACK!
SHE'D BE LIKE AN ALL-YOU-CAN-EAT SALAD BAR.
IT COULD BE.
SPEAKING OF "SUCKERS" ...THAT'S YOU BUNCH ALL OVER.
IT'S NONSENSE. NOW LET'S LINE UP AND GET THIS DONE.

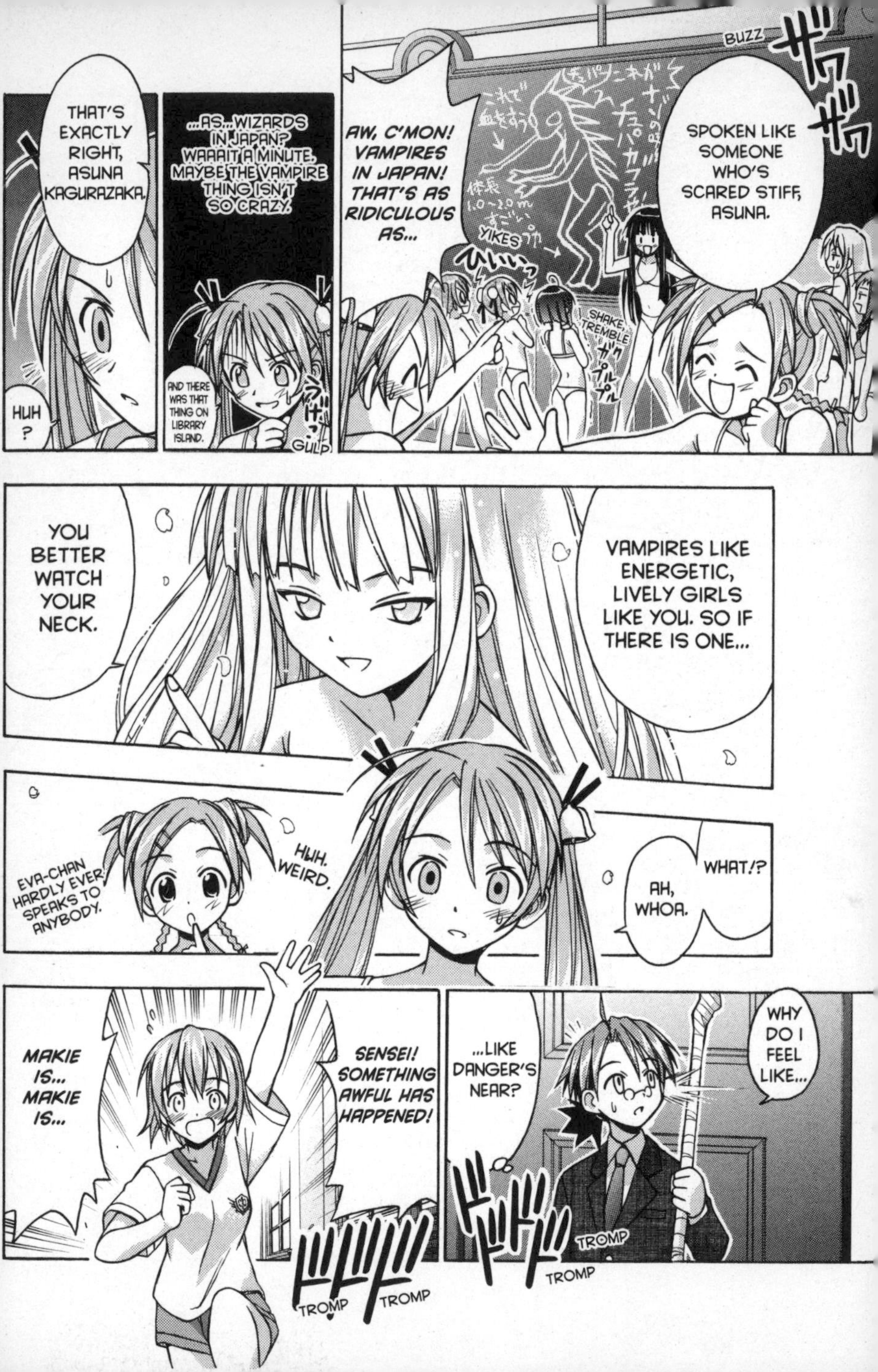
BUZZ
ザワザワ
SPOKEN LIKE SOMEONE WHO'S SCARED STIFF, ASUNA.
AW, C'MON! VAMPIRES IN JAPAN! THAT'S AS RIDICULOUS AS...
YIKES
SHAKE, TREMBLE
...AS...WIZARDS IN JAPAN? WAAAIT A MINUTE, MAYBE THE VAMPIRE THING ISN'T SO CRAZY.
AND THERE WAS THAT THING ON LIBRARY ISLAND.
GULP
THAT'S EXACTLY RIGHT, ASUNA KAGURAZAKA.
HUH ?
VAMPIRES LIKE ENERGETIC, LIVELY GIRLS LIKE YOU. SO IF THERE IS ONE...
YOU BETTER WATCH YOUR NECK.
WHAT!?
AH, WHOA.
HUH. WEIRD.
EVA-CHAN HARDLY EVER SPEAKS TO ANYBODY.
WHY DO I FEEL LIKE...
...LIKE DANGER'S NEAR?
TROMP
TROMP
SENSEI! SOMETHING AWFUL HAS HAPPENED!
MAKIE IS... MAKIE IS...
TROMP
TROMP

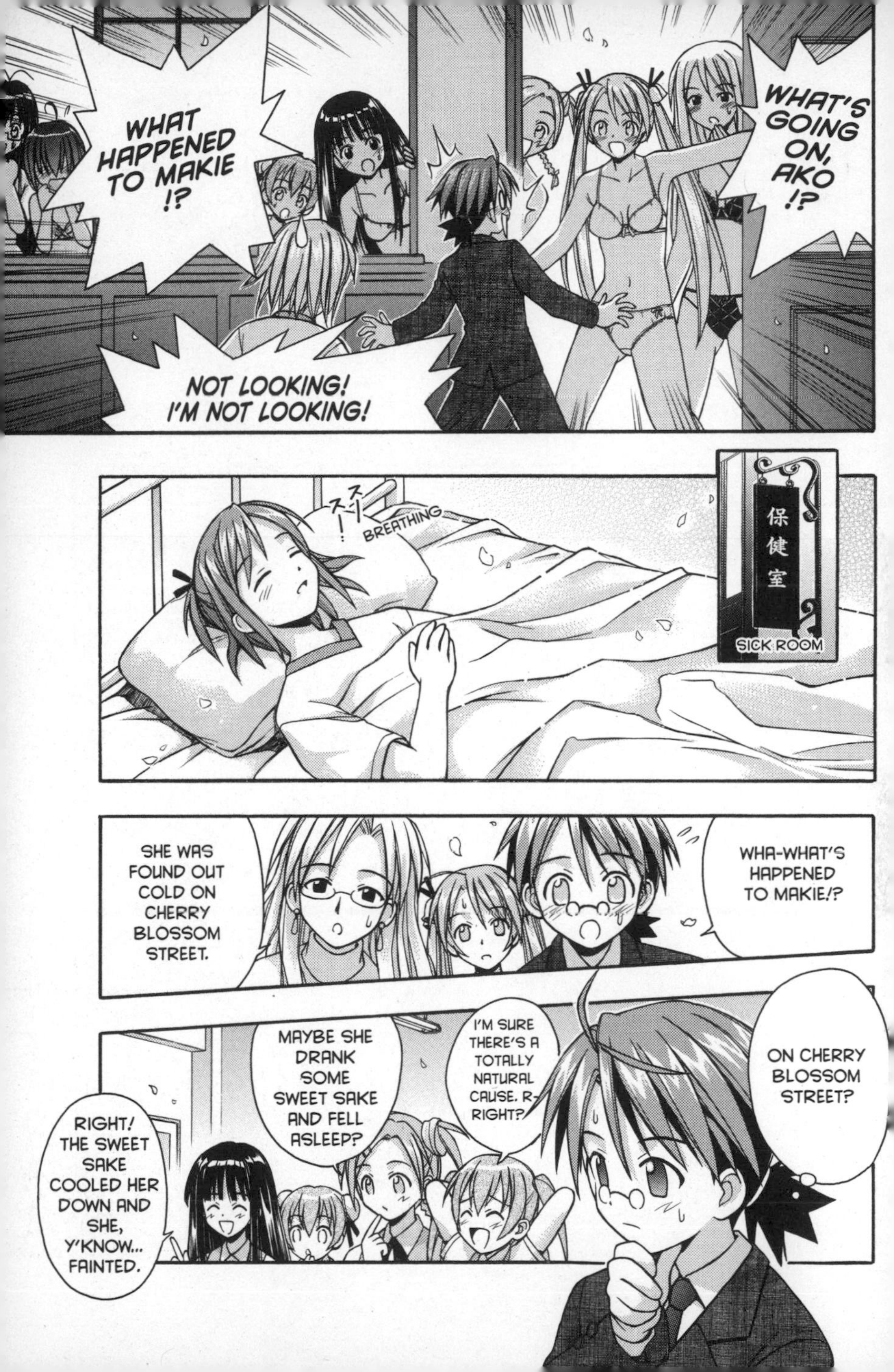
WHAT'S GOING ON, AKO!?
WHAT HAPPENED TO MAKIE!?
NOT LOOKING! I'M NOT LOOKING!
保健室
SICK ROOM
スー スー
BREATHING
WHA-WHAT'S HAPPENED TO MAKIE!?
SHE WAS FOUND OUT COLD ON CHERRY BLOSSOM STREET.
ON CHERRY BLOSSOM STREET?
I'M SURE THERE'S A TOTALLY NATURAL CAUSE. R-RIGHT?
MAYBE SHE DRANK SOME SWEET SAKE AND FELL ASLEEP?
RIGHT! THE SWEET SAKE COOLED HER DOWN AND SHE, Y'KNOW... FAINTED.

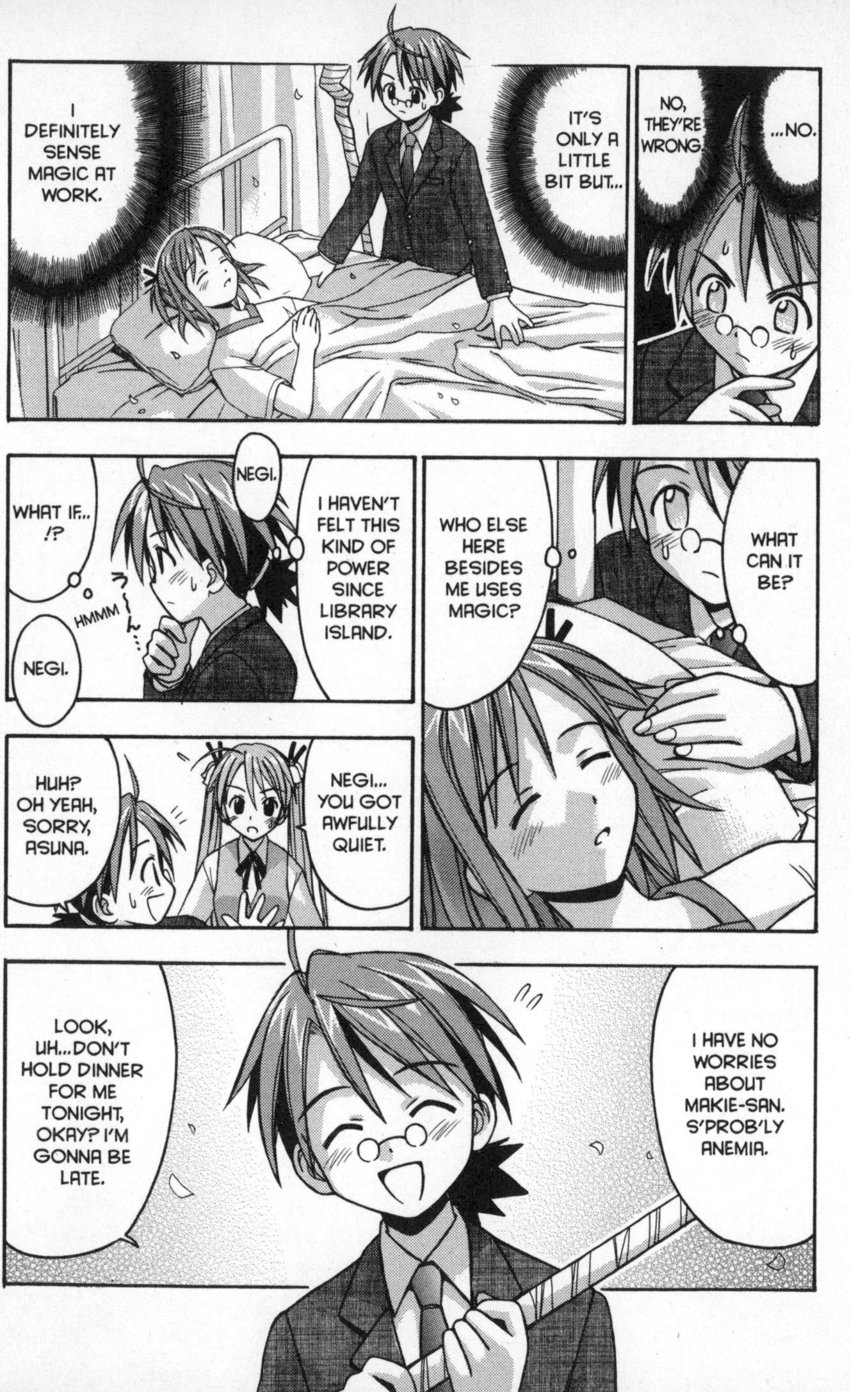
...NO.
NO, THEY'RE WRONG.
IT'S ONLY A LITTLE BIT BUT...
I DEFINITELY SENSE MAGIC AT WORK.
WHAT CAN IT BE?
WHO ELSE HERE BESIDES ME USES MAGIC?
I HAVEN'T FELT THIS KIND OF POWER SINCE LIBRARY ISLAND.
NEGI.
WHAT IF.. !?
HMMM
NEGI.
NEGI... YOU GOT AWFULLY QUIET.
HUH? OH YEAH, SORRY, ASUNA.
I HAVE NO WORRIES ABOUT MAKIE-SAN. S'PROB'LY ANEMIA.
LOOK, UH...DON'T HOLD DINNER FOR ME TONIGHT, OKAY? I'M GONNA BE LATE.

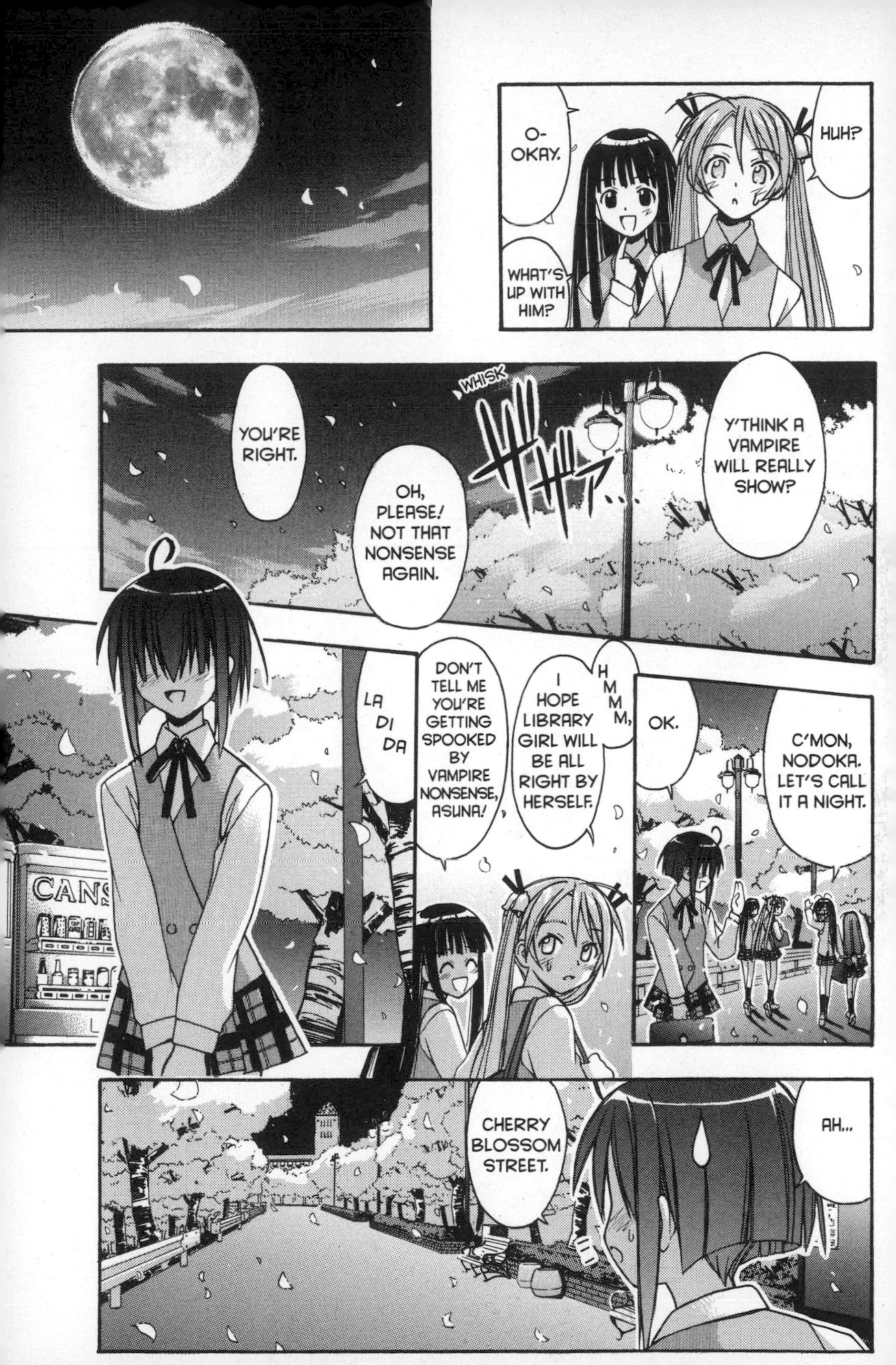
HUH?
O-OKAY.
WHAT'S UP WITH HIM?
Y'THINK A VAMPIRE WILL REALLY SHOW?
WHISK
OH, PLEASE! NOT THAT NONSENSE AGAIN.
YOU'RE RIGHT.
C'MON, NODOKA. LET'S CALL IT A NIGHT.
OK.
HMMM,
I HOPE LIBRARY GIRL WILL BE ALL RIGHT BY HERSELF.
DON'T TELL ME YOU'RE GETTING SPOOKED BY VAMPIRE NONSENSE, ASUNA!
LA DI DA
CANS
AH...
CHERRY BLOSSOM STREET.

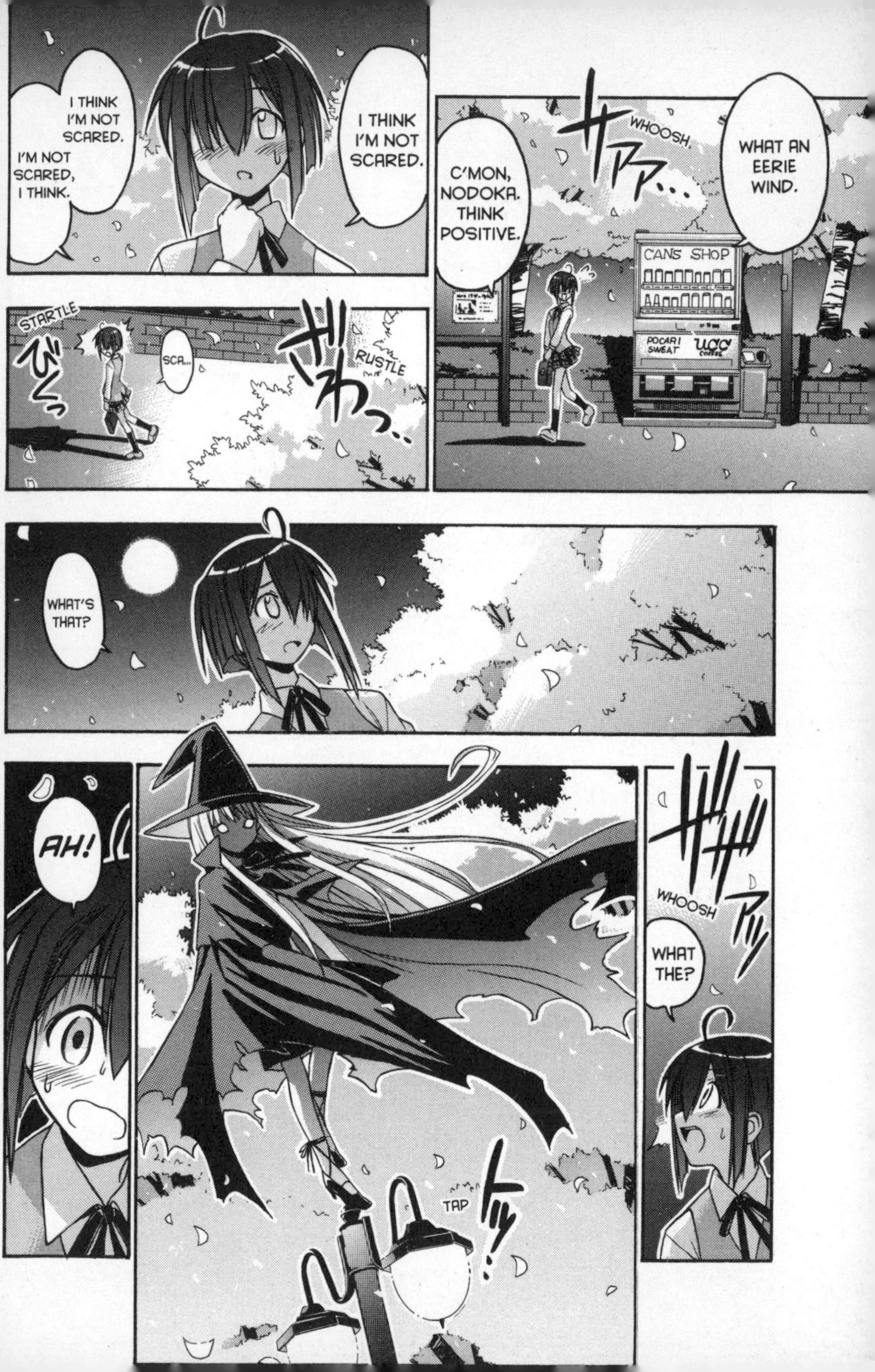
WHAT AN EERIE WIND.
WHOOSH
C'MON, NODOKA. THINK POSITIVE.
CANS SHOP
POCARI SWEAT
UCC COFFEE
I THINK I'M NOT SCARED.
I THINK I'M NOT SCARED.
I'M NOT SCARED, I THINK.
RUSTLE
SCA...
STARTLE
WHAT'S THAT?
WHOOSH
WHAT THE?
TAP
AH!

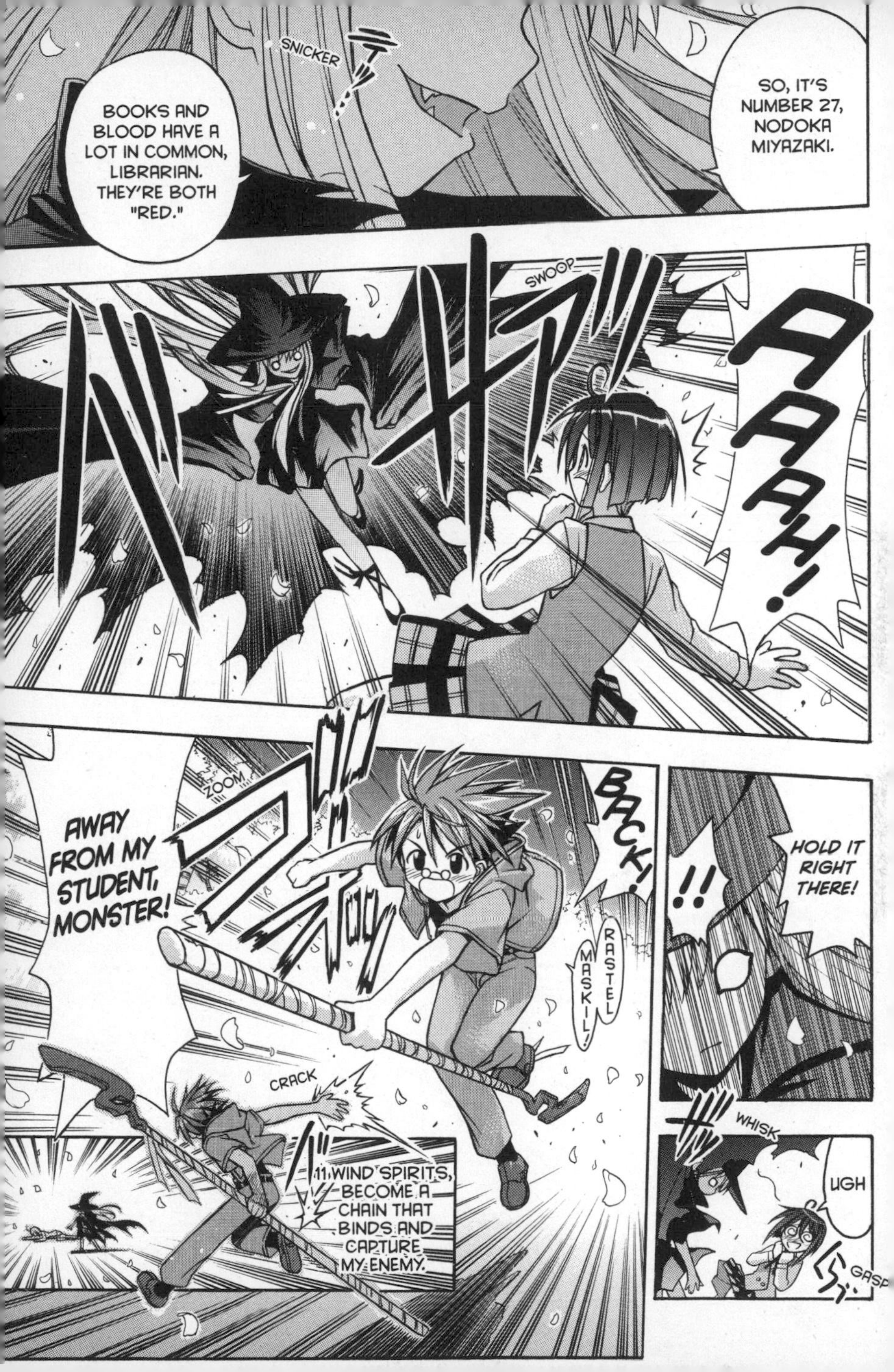
SO, IT'S NUMBER 27, NODOKA MIYAZAKI.
SNICKER
BOOKS AND BLOOD HAVE A LOT IN COMMON, LIBRARIAN. THEY'RE BOTH "RED."
AAAAH!!
SWOOP
HOLD IT RIGHT THERE!
!!
WHISK
UGH
GASP
BACK!
ZOOM
AWAY FROM MY STUDENT, MONSTER!
RASTEL MASKIL!
CRACK
11 WIND SPIRITS, BECOME A CHAIN THAT BINDS AND CAPTURE MY ENEMY.

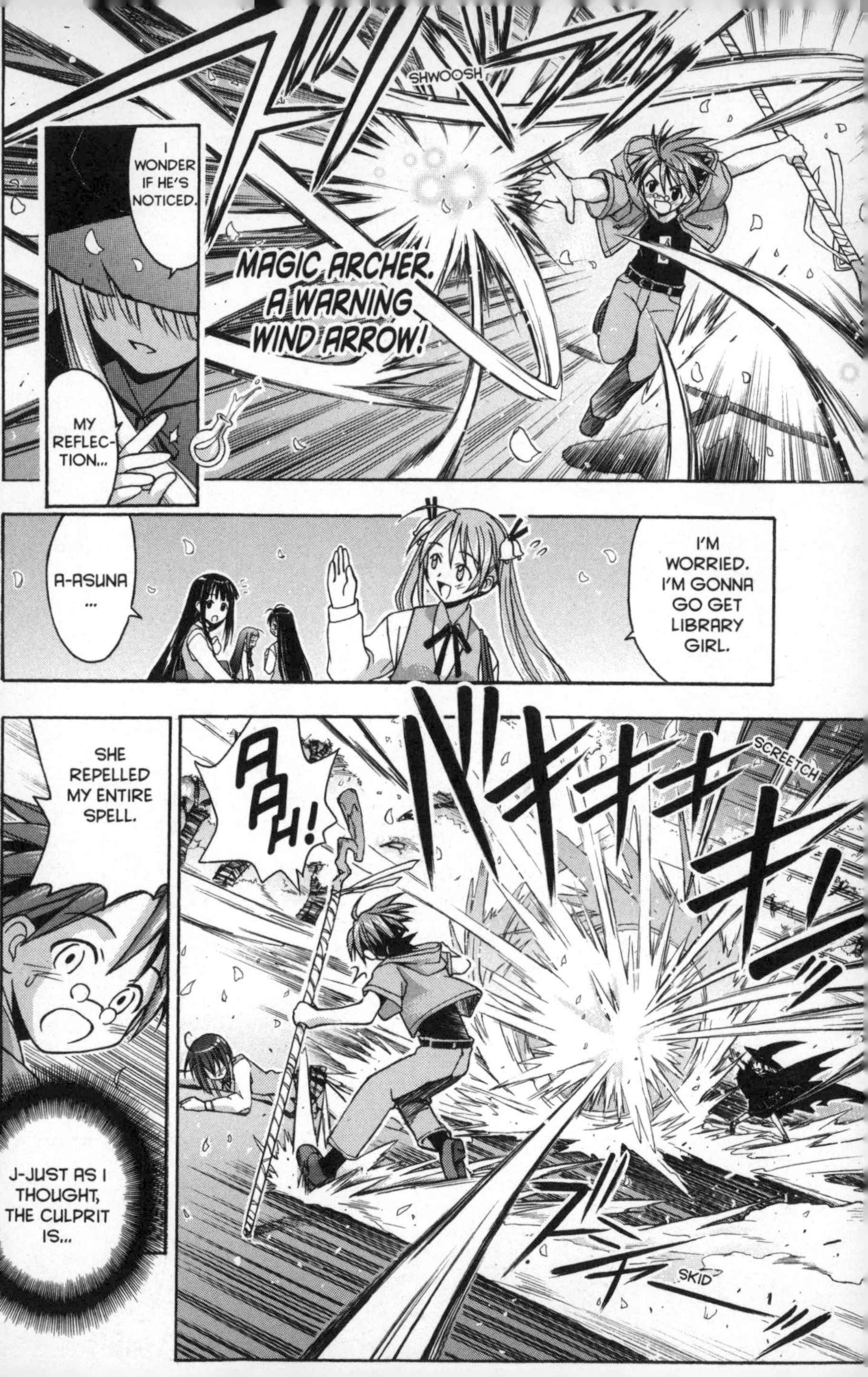
SHWOOSH
MAGIC ARCHER. A WARNING WIND ARROW!
I WONDER IF HE'S NOTICED.
MY REFLECTION...
I'M WORRIED. I'M GONNA GO GET LIBRARY GIRL.
A-ASUNA ...
SCREETCH
AAH!
SKID
SHE REPELLED MY ENTIRE SPELL.
J-JUST AS I THOUGHT, THE CULPRIT IS...

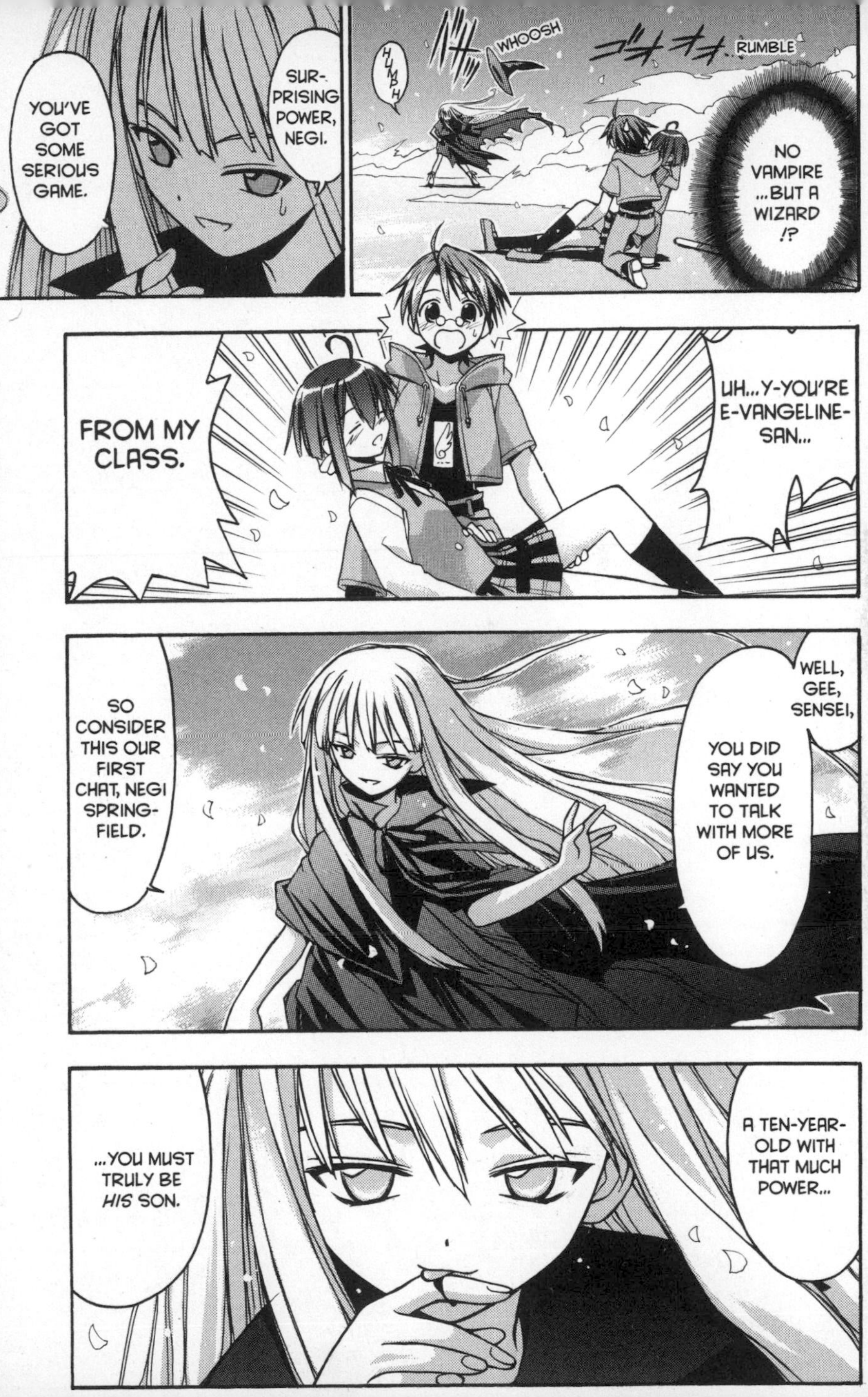
RUMBLE
NO VAMPIRE ...BUT A WIZARD!?
WHOOSH
HUMPH
SUR-PRISING POWER, NEGI.
YOU'VE GOT SOME SERIOUS GAME.
UH...Y-YOU'RE E-VANGELINE-SAN...
FROM MY CLASS.
WELL, GEE, SENSEI,
YOU DID SAY YOU WANTED TO TALK WITH MORE OF US.
SO CONSIDER THIS OUR FIRST CHAT, NEGI SPRING-FIELD.
A TEN-YEAR-OLD WITH THAT MUCH POWER...
...YOU MUST TRULY BE *HIS* SON.

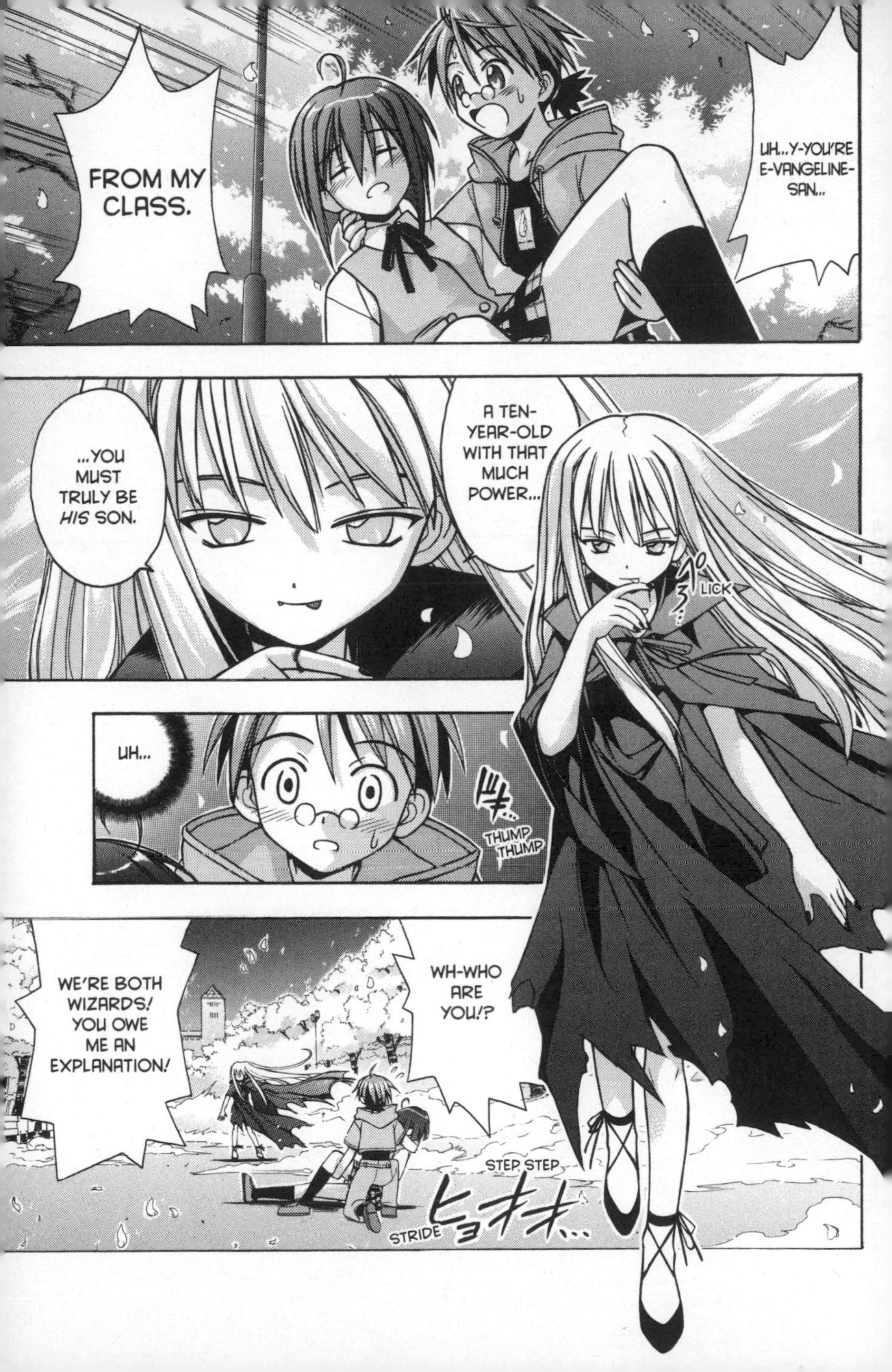
UH...Y-YOU'RE E-VANGELINE-SAN...
FROM MY CLASS.
A TEN-YEAR-OLD WITH THAT MUCH POWER...
LICK
...YOU MUST TRULY BE HIS SON.
UH...
THUMP THUMP
WH-WHO ARE YOU!?
WE'RE BOTH WIZARDS! YOU OWE ME AN EXPLANATION!
STEP STEP
STRIDE

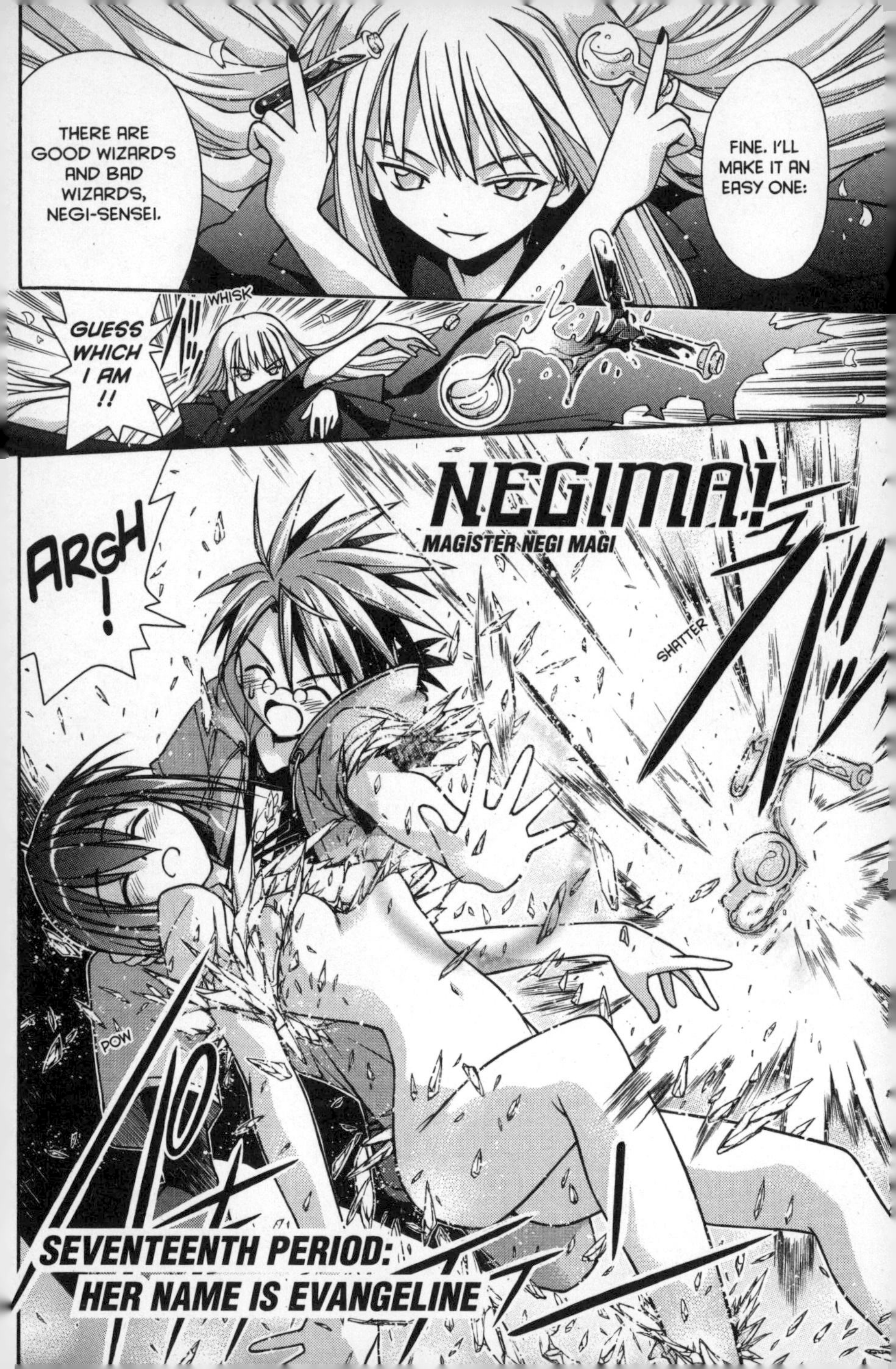
FINE. I'LL MAKE IT AN EASY ONE:
THERE ARE GOOD WIZARDS AND BAD WIZARDS, NEGI-SENSEI.
WHISK
GUESS WHICH I AM !!
NEGIMA!
MAGISTER NEGI MAGI
SHATTER
ARGH !
POW
SEVENTEENTH PERIOD:
HER NAME IS EVANGELINE

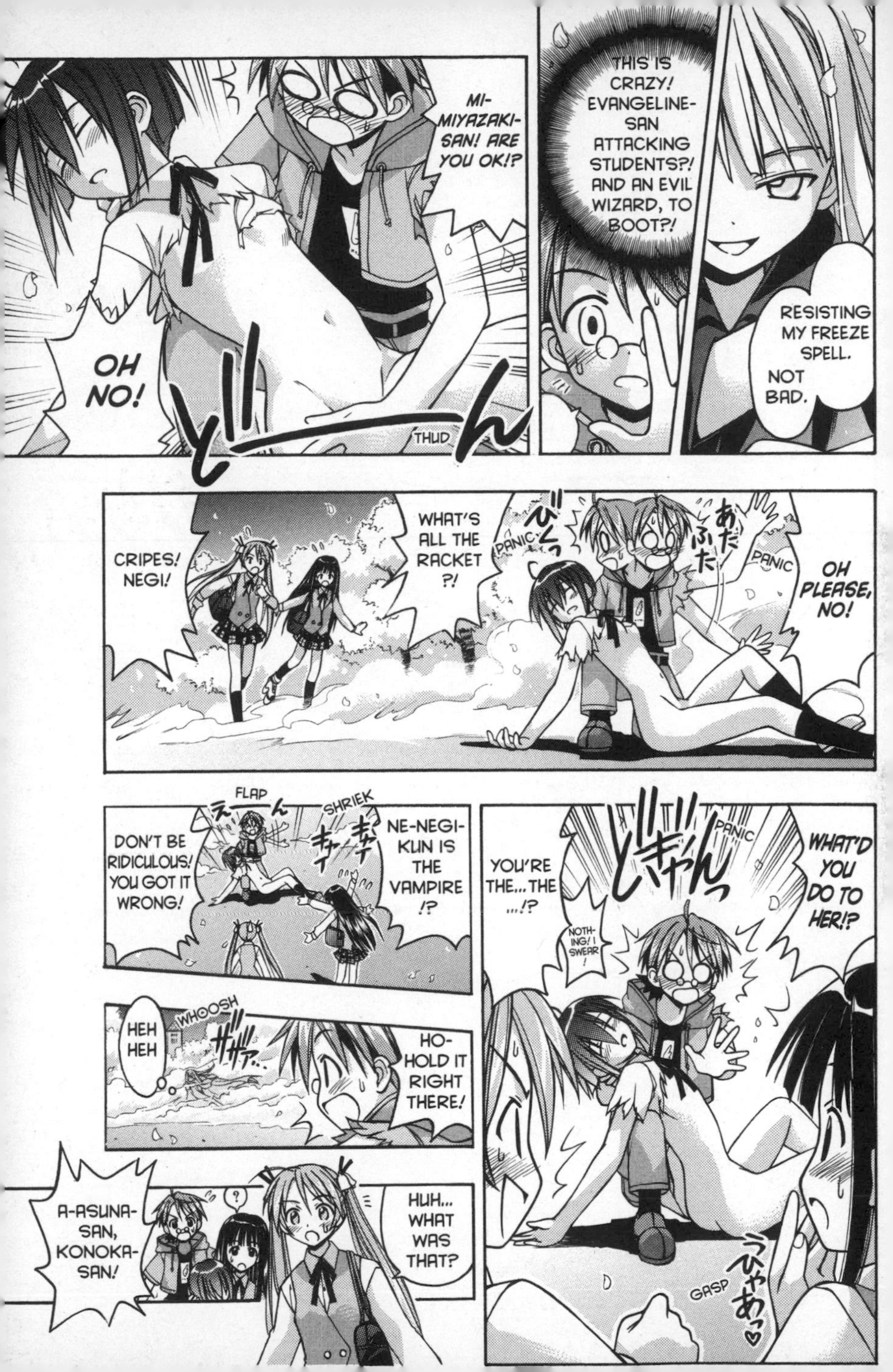
THIS IS CRAZY! EVANGELINE-SAN ATTACKING STUDENTS?! AND AN EVIL WIZARD, TO BOOT?!
RESISTING MY FREEZE SPELL.
NOT BAD.
MI-MIYAZAKI-SAN! ARE YOU OK!?
OH NO!
THUD
OH PLEASE, NO!
PANIC
あたふた
びくっ
PANIC
WHAT'S ALL THE RACKET?!
CRIPES! NEGI!
WHAT'D YOU DO TO HER!?
PANIC
どぎゃんっ
YOU'RE THE... THE ...!?
NOTHING! I SWEAR!
GASP
うひゃあっ♡
NE-NEGI-KUN IS THE VAMPIRE!?
SHRIEK
FLAP
DON'T BE RIDICULOUS! YOU GOT IT WRONG!
HO-HOLD IT RIGHT THERE!
WHOOSH
HEH HEH
HUH... WHAT WAS THAT?
?
A-ASUNA-SAN, KONOKA-SAN!

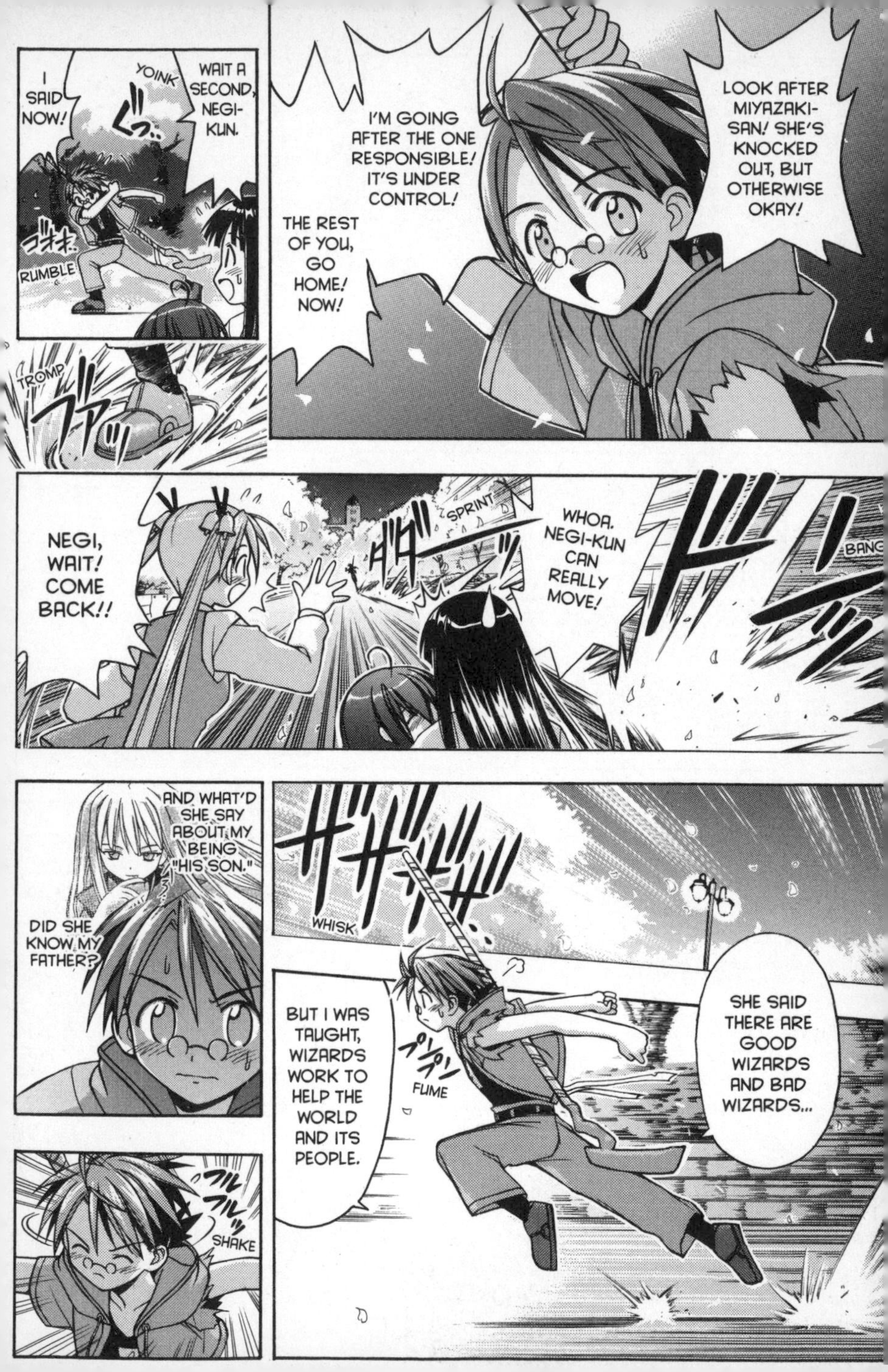
LOOK AFTER MIYAZAKI-SAN! SHE'S KNOCKED OUT, BUT OTHERWISE OKAY!
I'M GOING AFTER THE ONE RESPONSIBLE! IT'S UNDER CONTROL!
THE REST OF YOU, GO HOME! NOW!
WAIT A SECOND, NEGI-KUN.
YOINK
I SAID NOW!
RUMBLE
TROMP
BANG
WHOA. NEGI-KUN CAN REALLY MOVE!
SPRINT
NEGI, WAIT! COME BACK!!
WHISK
SHE SAID THERE ARE GOOD WIZARDS AND BAD WIZARDS...
FUME
BUT I WAS TAUGHT, WIZARDS WORK TO HELP THE WORLD AND ITS PEOPLE.
AND WHAT'D SHE SAY ABOUT MY BEING "HIS SON."
DID SHE KNOW MY FATHER?
SHAKE

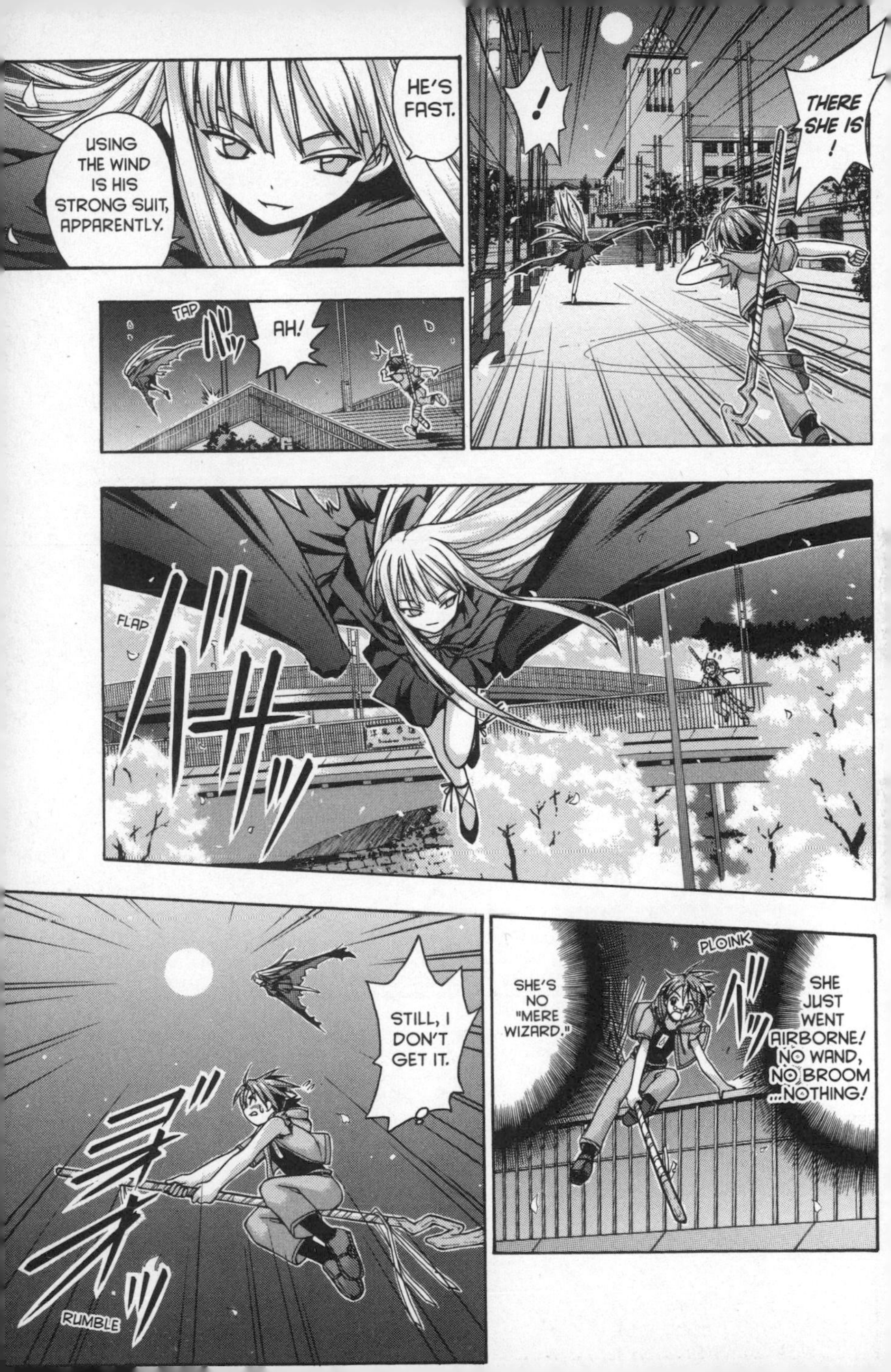
THERE SHE IS!
!
HE'S FAST.
USING THE WIND IS HIS STRONG SUIT, APPARENTLY.
TAP
AH!
FLAP
PLOINK
SHE JUST WENT AIRBORNE! NO WAND, NO BROOM ...NOTHING!
SHE'S NO "MERE WIZARD."
STILL, I DON'T GET IT.
RUMBLE

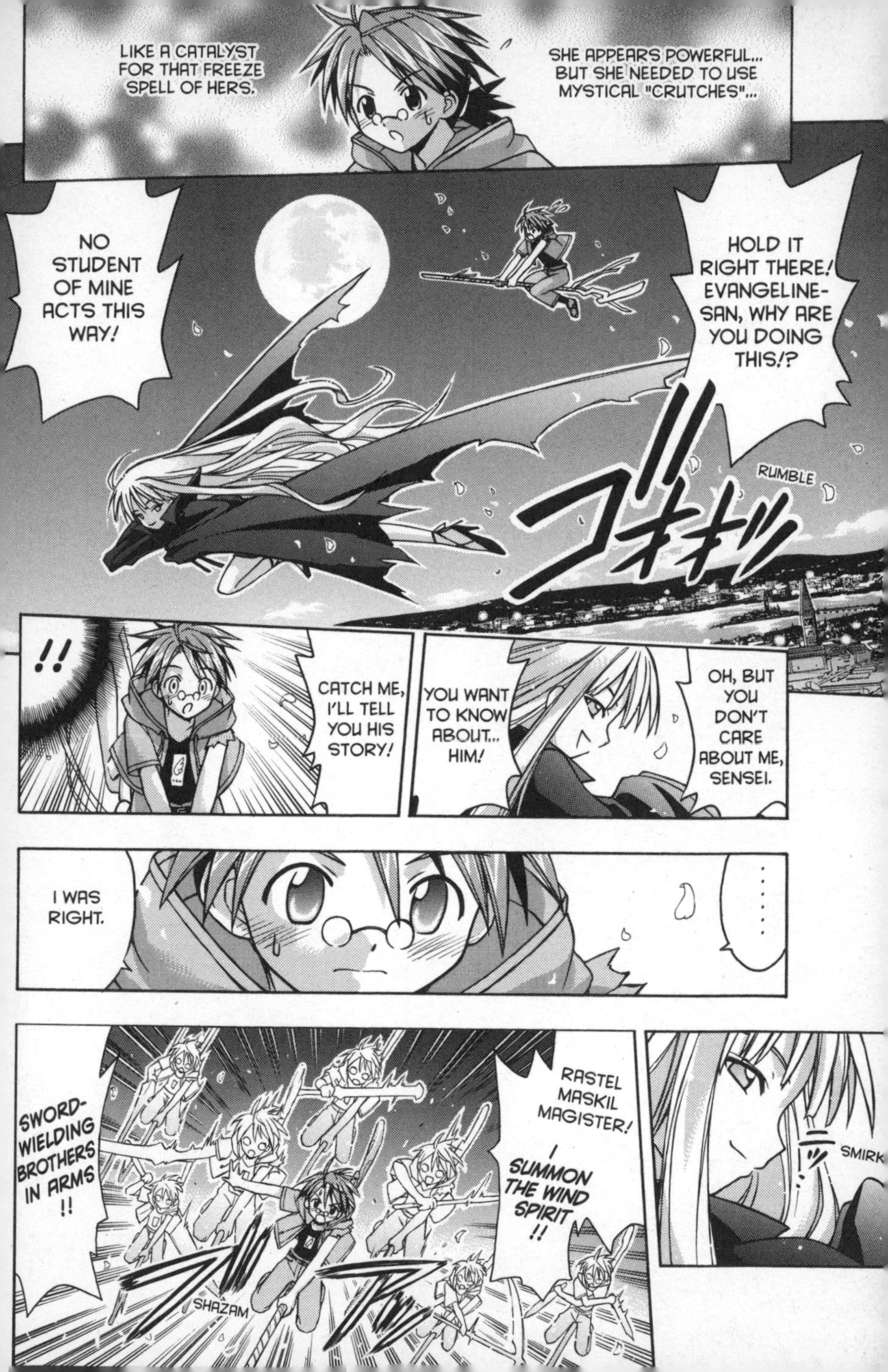
SHE APPEARS POWERFUL... BUT SHE NEEDED TO USE MYSTICAL "CRUTCHES"...
LIKE A CATALYST FOR THAT FREEZE SPELL OF HERS.
HOLD IT RIGHT THERE! EVANGELINE-SAN, WHY ARE YOU DOING THIS!?
RUMBLE
NO STUDENT OF MINE ACTS THIS WAY!
OH, BUT YOU DON'T CARE ABOUT ME, SENSEI.
YOU WANT TO KNOW ABOUT... HIM!
CATCH ME, I'LL TELL YOU HIS STORY!
!!
......
I WAS RIGHT.
SMIRK
RASTEL MASKIL MAGISTER!
I SUMMON THE WIND SPIRIT !!
SWORD-WIELDING BROTHERS IN ARMS !!
SHAZAM

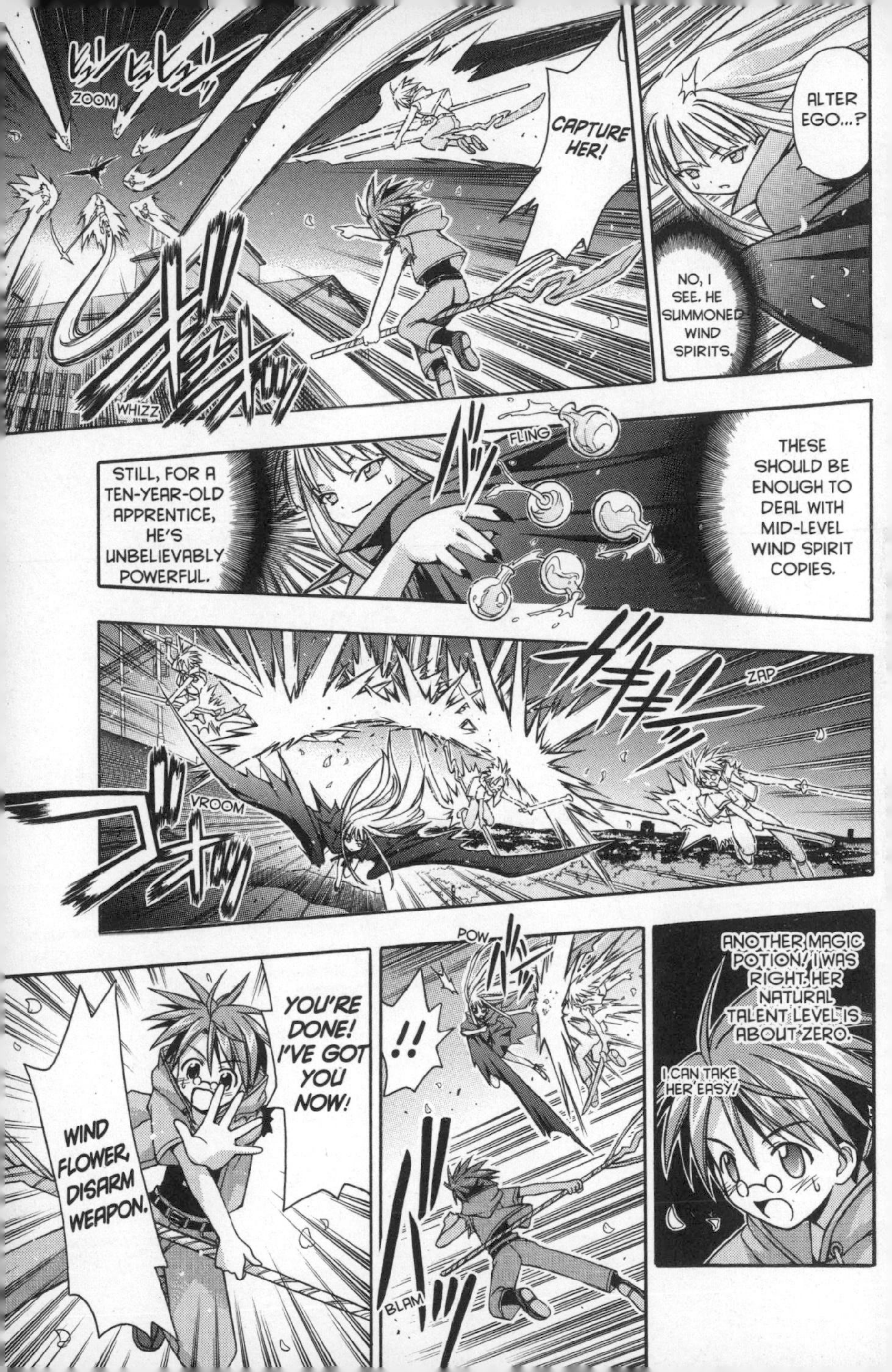
ALTER EGO...?
NO, I SEE. HE SUMMONED WIND SPIRITS.
CAPTURE HER!
ZOOM
WHIZZ
THESE SHOULD BE ENOUGH TO DEAL WITH MID-LEVEL WIND SPIRIT COPIES.
FLING
STILL, FOR A TEN-YEAR-OLD APPRENTICE, HE'S UNBELIEVABLY POWERFUL.
ZAP
VROOM
ANOTHER MAGIC POTION! I WAS RIGHT. HER NATURAL TALENT LEVEL IS ABOUT ZERO.
I CAN TAKE HER EASY!
POW
!!
BLAM
YOU'RE DONE! I'VE GOT YOU NOW!
WIND FLOWER, DISARM WEAPON.

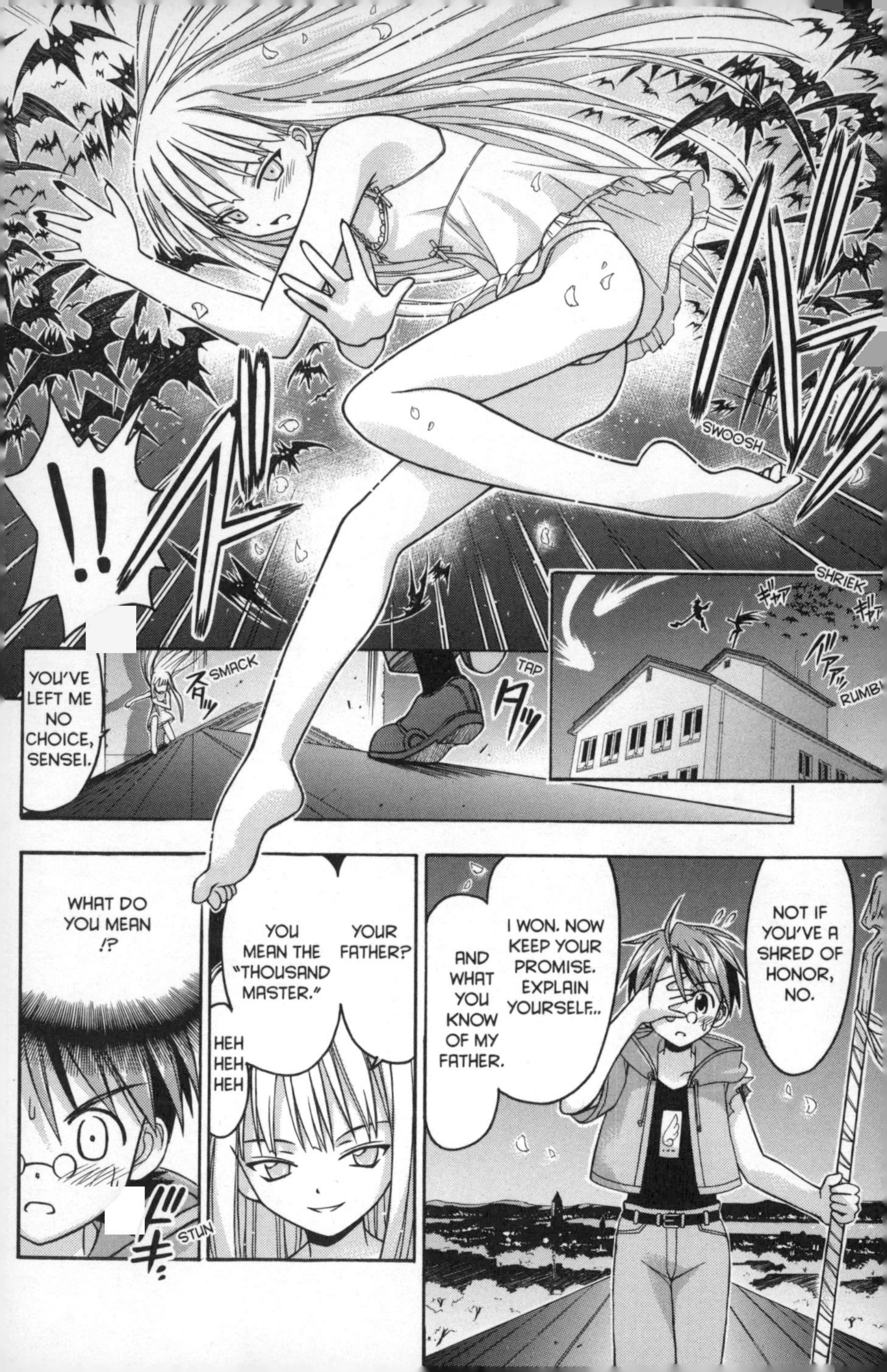
SWOOSH
!!
SHRIEK
RUMB
TAP
SMACK
YOU'VE LEFT ME NO CHOICE, SENSEI.
NOT IF YOU'VE A SHRED OF HONOR, NO.
I WON. NOW KEEP YOUR PROMISE. EXPLAIN YOURSELF...
AND WHAT YOU KNOW OF MY FATHER.
YOUR FATHER?
YOU MEAN THE "THOUSAND MASTER."
HEH HEH HEH
WHAT DO YOU MEAN !?
STUN

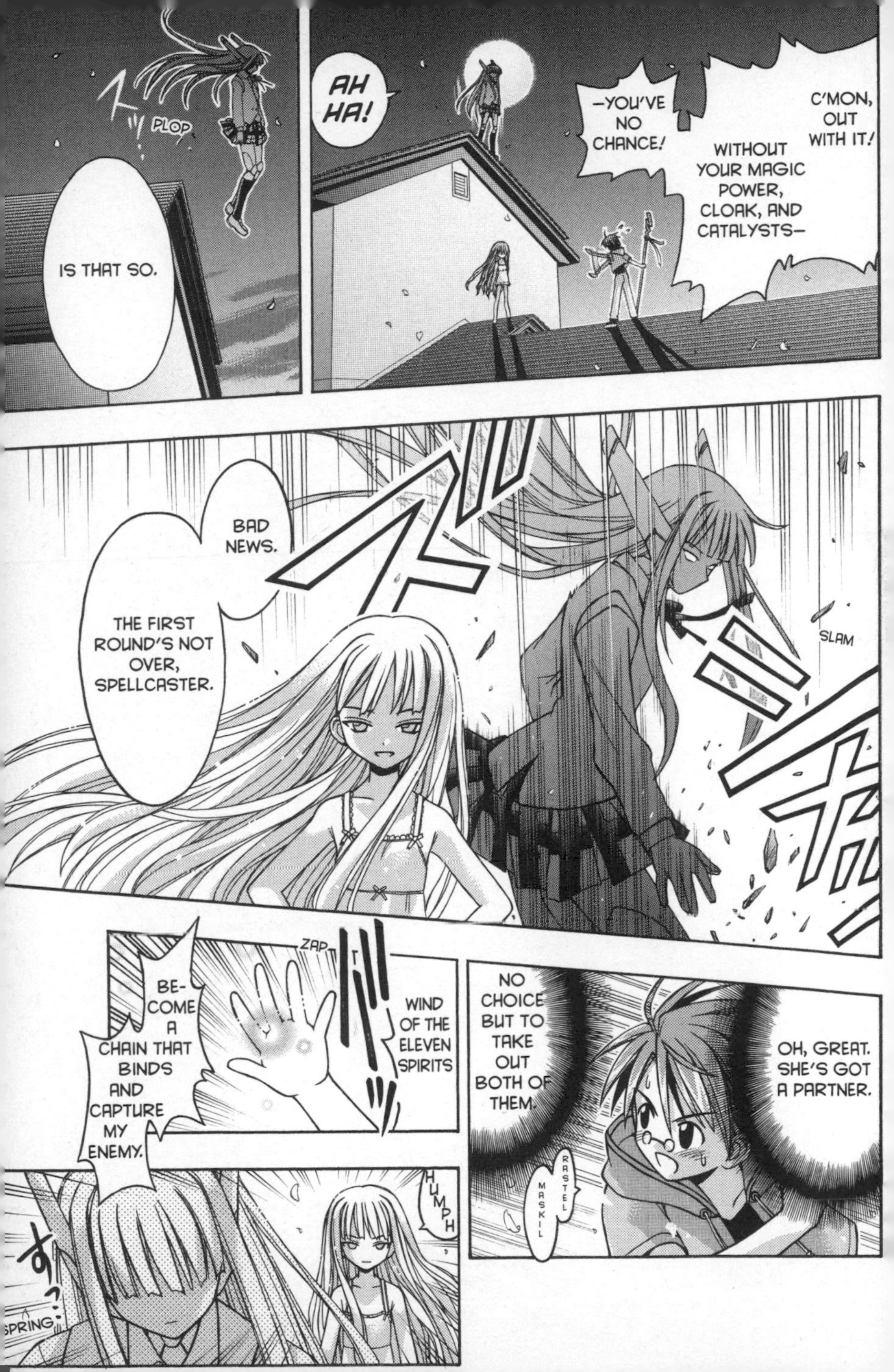
C'MON, OUT WITH IT!
WITHOUT YOUR MAGIC POWER, CLOAK, AND CATALYSTS—
—YOU'VE NO CHANCE!
AH HA!
PLOP
IS THAT SO.
SLAM
BAD NEWS.
THE FIRST ROUND'S NOT OVER, SPELLCASTER.
OH, GREAT. SHE'S GOT A PARTNER.
NO CHOICE BUT TO TAKE OUT BOTH OF THEM.
RASTEL MASKIL
ZAP
WIND OF THE ELEVEN SPIRITS
BE-COME A CHAIN THAT BINDS AND CAPTURE MY ENEMY.
HUMPH
SPRING

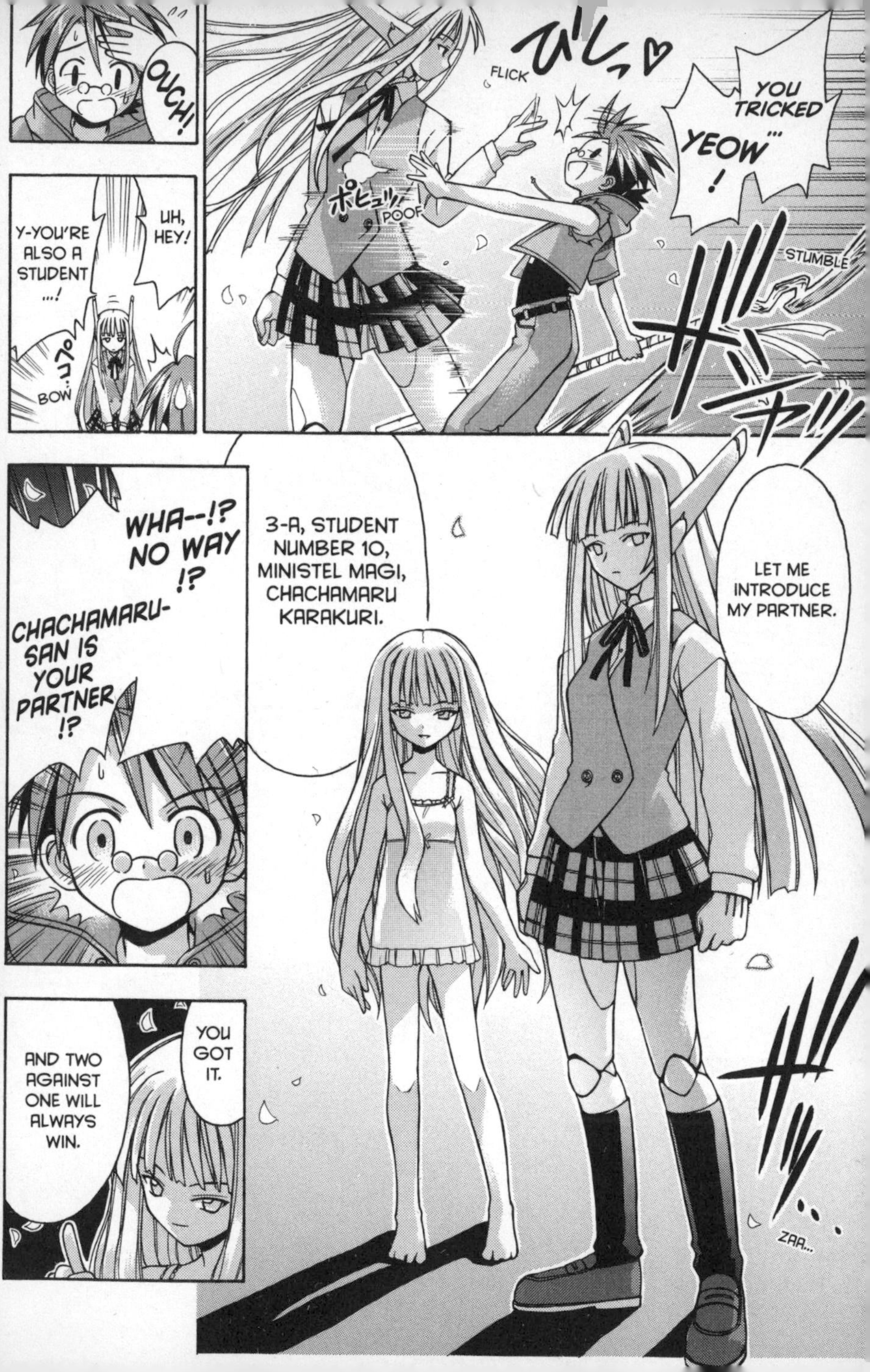
FLICK
YOU TRICKED
YEOW...!
POOF
STUMBLE
OUCH!
UH, HEY!
Y-YOU'RE ALSO A STUDENT ...!
BOW
LET ME INTRODUCE MY PARTNER.
3-A, STUDENT NUMBER 10, MINISTEL MAGI, CHACHAMARU KARAKURI.
ZAA...
WHA--!? NO WAY !?
CHACHAMARU-SAN IS YOUR PARTNER !?
YOU GOT IT.
AND TWO AGAINST ONE WILL ALWAYS WIN.

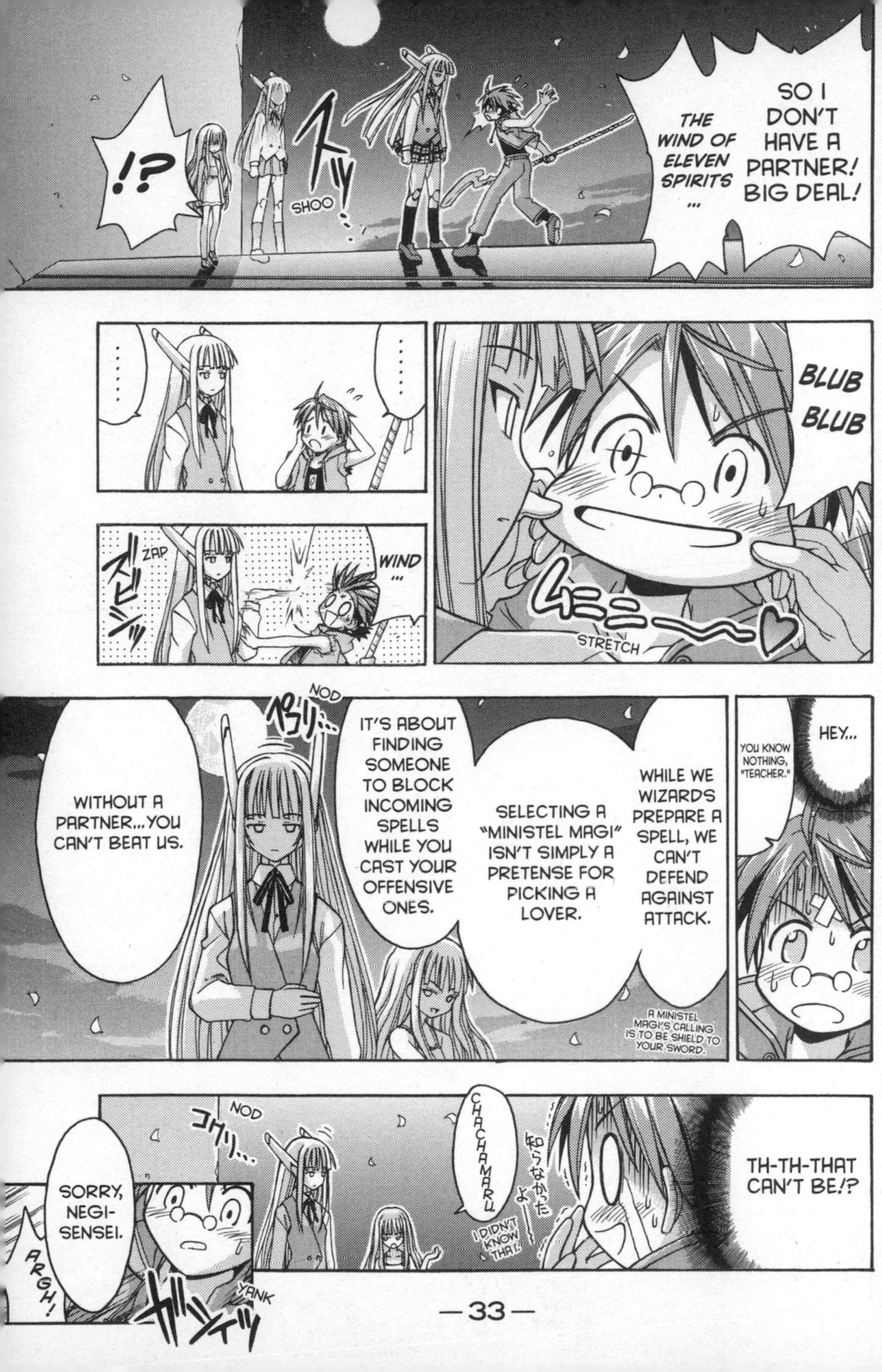
SO I DON'T HAVE A PARTNER! BIG DEAL!
THE WIND OF ELEVEN SPIRITS ...
SHOO
!?
BLUB BLUB
STRETCH
......
......
WIND ...
ZAP
HEY...
YOU KNOW NOTHING, "TEACHER."
WHILE WE WIZARDS PREPARE A SPELL, WE CAN'T DEFEND AGAINST ATTACK.
SELECTING A "MINISTEL MAGI" ISN'T SIMPLY A PRETENSE FOR PICKING A LOVER.
IT'S ABOUT FINDING SOMEONE TO BLOCK INCOMING SPELLS WHILE YOU CAST YOUR OFFENSIVE ONES.
NOD
WITHOUT A PARTNER...YOU CAN'T BEAT US.
A MINISTEL MAGI'S CALLING IS TO BE SHIELD TO YOUR SWORD.
TH-TH-THAT CAN'T BE!?
I DIDN'T KNOW THAT!
CHACHAMARU
NOD
SORRY, NEGI-SENSEI.
YANK
ARGH!

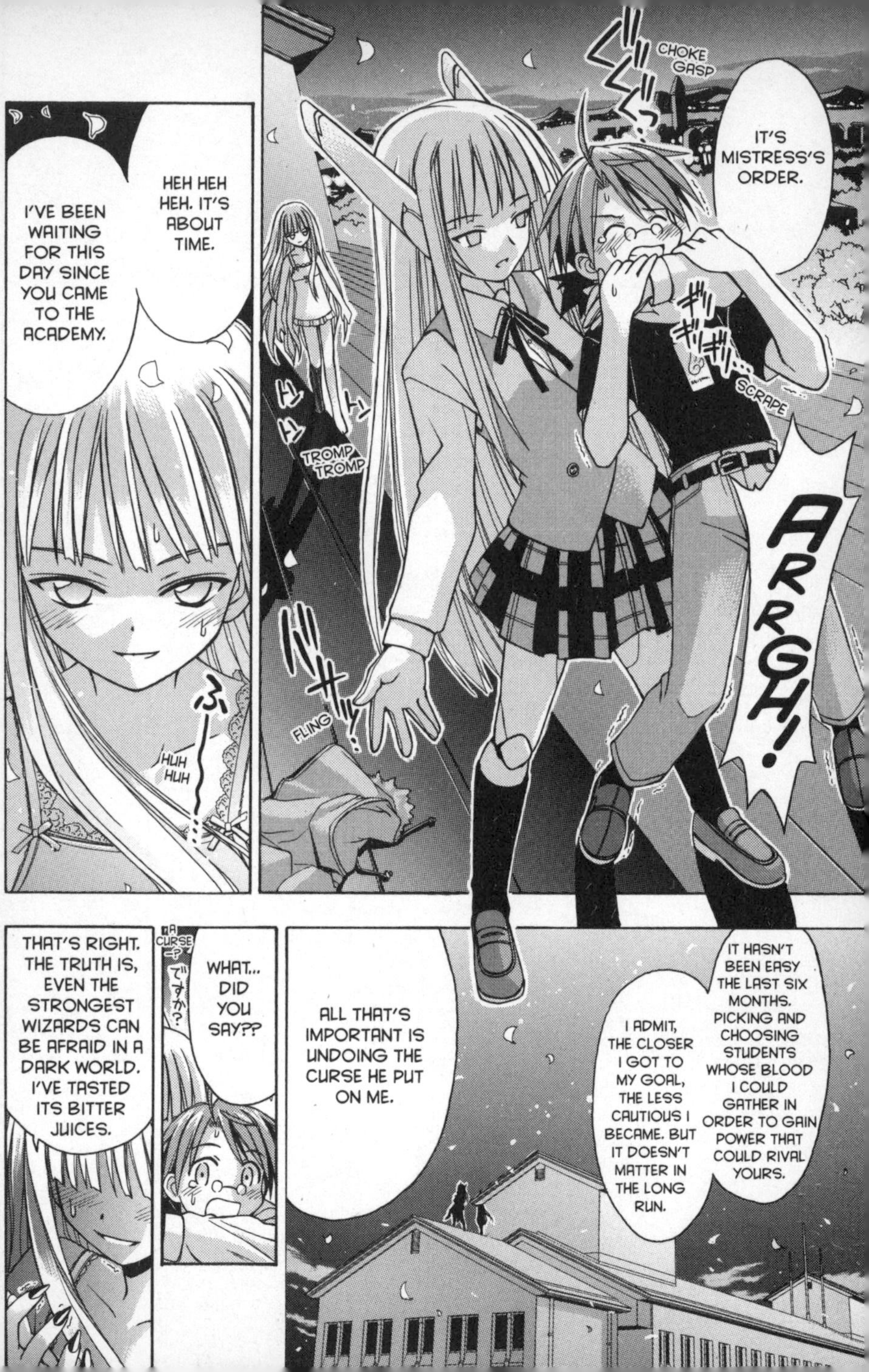
CHOKE GASP
IT'S MISTRESS'S ORDER.
SCRAPE
TROMP TROMP
ARRGH!
FLING
HEH HEH HEH. IT'S ABOUT TIME.
I'VE BEEN WAITING FOR THIS DAY SINCE YOU CAME TO THE ACADEMY.
HUH HUH
IT HASN'T BEEN EASY THE LAST SIX MONTHS. PICKING AND CHOOSING STUDENTS WHOSE BLOOD I COULD GATHER IN ORDER TO GAIN POWER THAT COULD RIVAL YOURS.
I ADMIT, THE CLOSER I GOT TO MY GOAL, THE LESS CAUTIOUS I BECAME. BUT IT DOESN'T MATTER IN THE LONG RUN.
ALL THAT'S IMPORTANT IS UNDOING THE CURSE HE PUT ON ME.
A CURSE—?
ですか?
WHAT... DID YOU SAY??
THAT'S RIGHT. THE TRUTH IS, EVEN THE STRONGEST WIZARDS CAN BE AFRAID IN A DARK WORLD. I'VE TASTED ITS BITTER JUICES.

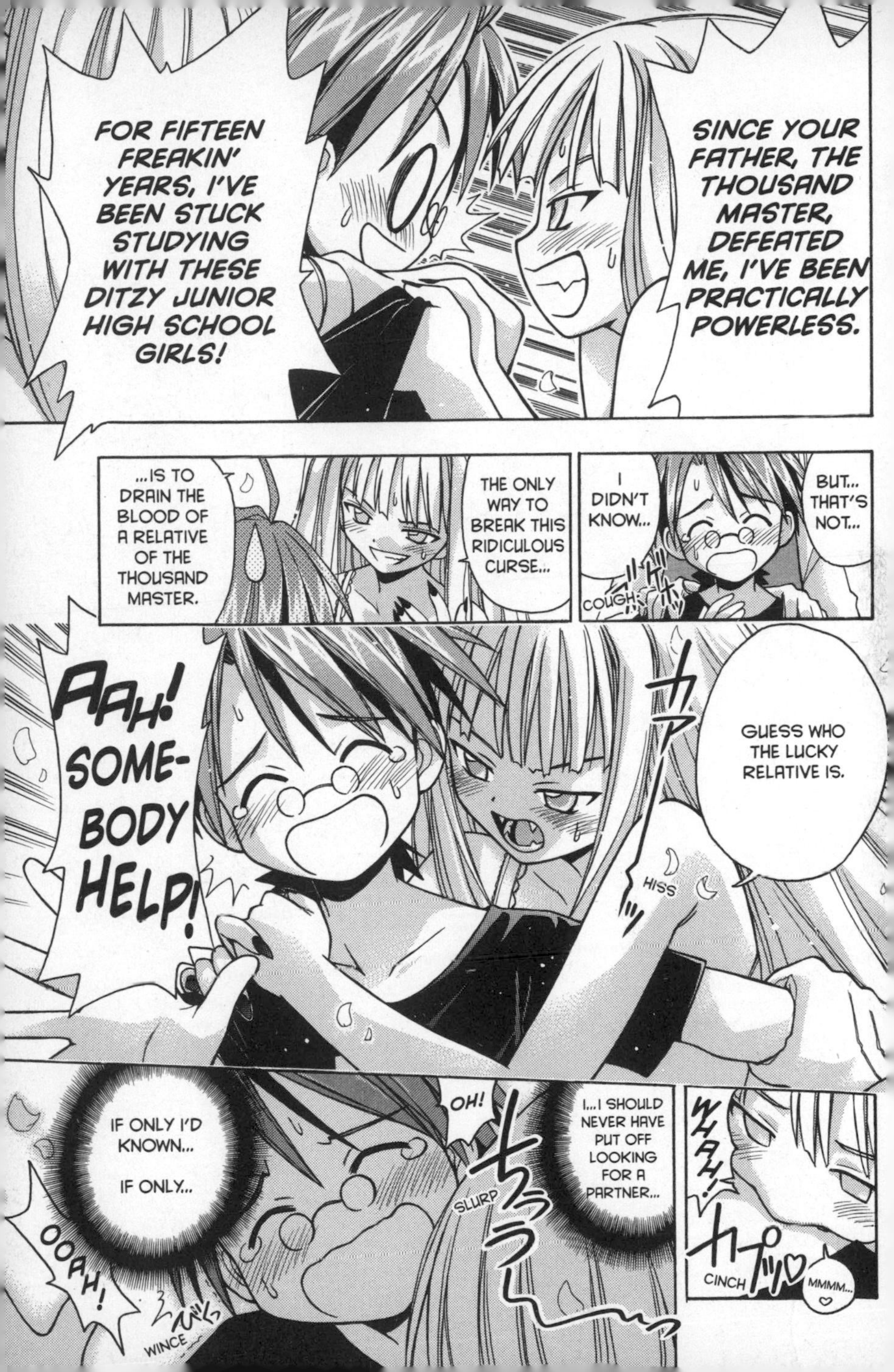

SINCE YOUR FATHER, THE THOUSAND MASTER, DEFEATED ME, I'VE BEEN PRACTICALLY POWERLESS.
FOR FIFTEEN FREAKIN' YEARS, I'VE BEEN STUCK STUDYING WITH THESE DITZY JUNIOR HIGH SCHOOL GIRLS!
BUT... THAT'S NOT...
I DIDN'T KNOW...
COUGH
THE ONLY WAY TO BREAK THIS RIDICULOUS CURSE...
...IS TO DRAIN THE BLOOD OF A RELATIVE OF THE THOUSAND MASTER.
GUESS WHO THE LUCKY RELATIVE IS.
HISS
AAH! SOMEBODY HELP!
WHAP!
CINCH
MMMM...
I...I SHOULD NEVER HAVE PUT OFF LOOKING FOR A PARTNER...
OH!
SLURP
IF ONLY I'D KNOWN...
IF ONLY...
OOAH!
WINCE

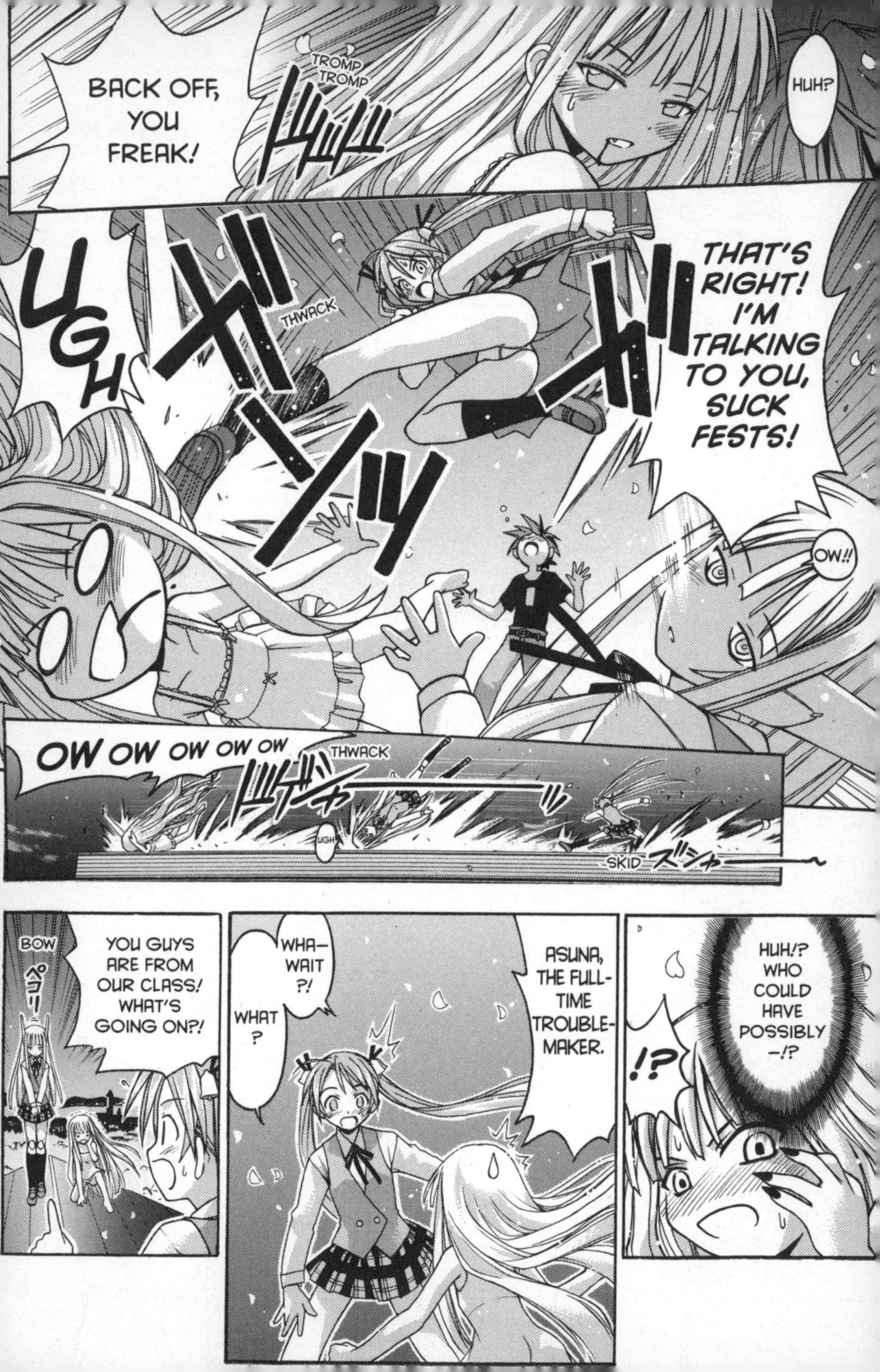
HUH?
TROMP TROMP
BACK OFF, YOU FREAK!
THAT'S RIGHT! I'M TALKING TO YOU, SUCK FESTS!
OW!!
THWACK
UGH
SKID
UGH
THWACK
OW OW OW OW OW
HUH!? WHO COULD HAVE POSSIBLY—!?
!?
ASUNA, THE FULL-TIME TROUBLE-MAKER.
WHA— WAIT?!
WHAT?
YOU GUYS ARE FROM OUR CLASS! WHAT'S GOING ON?!
BOW

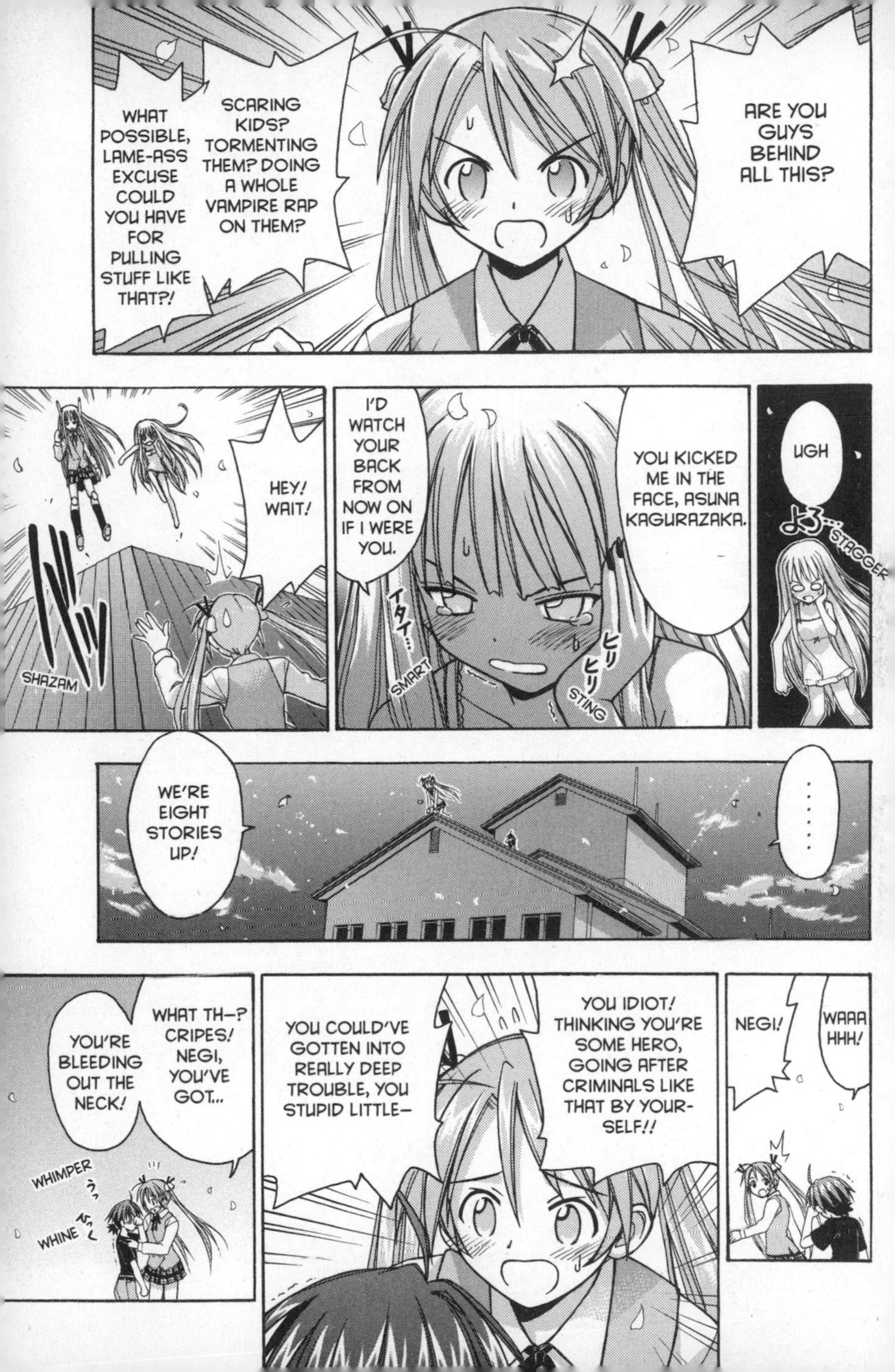
ARE YOU GUYS BEHIND ALL THIS?
SCARING KIDS? TORMENTING THEM? DOING A WHOLE VAMPIRE RAP ON THEM?
WHAT POSSIBLE, LAME-ASS EXCUSE COULD YOU HAVE FOR PULLING STUFF LIKE THAT?!
UGH
よろ…
STAGGER
YOU KICKED ME IN THE FACE, ASUNA KAGURAZAKA.
I'D WATCH YOUR BACK FROM NOW ON IF I WERE YOU.
ヒリヒリ
STING
イタイ…
SMART
HEY! WAIT!
SHAZAM
......
WE'RE EIGHT STORIES UP!
WAAAHHH!
NEGI!
YOU IDIOT! THINKING YOU'RE SOME HERO, GOING AFTER CRIMINALS LIKE THAT BY YOUR-SELF!!
YOU COULD'VE GOTTEN INTO REALLY DEEP TROUBLE, YOU STUPID LITTLE—
WHAT TH—? CRIPES! NEGI, YOU'VE GOT...
YOU'RE BLEEDING OUT THE NECK!
WHIMPER
WHINE

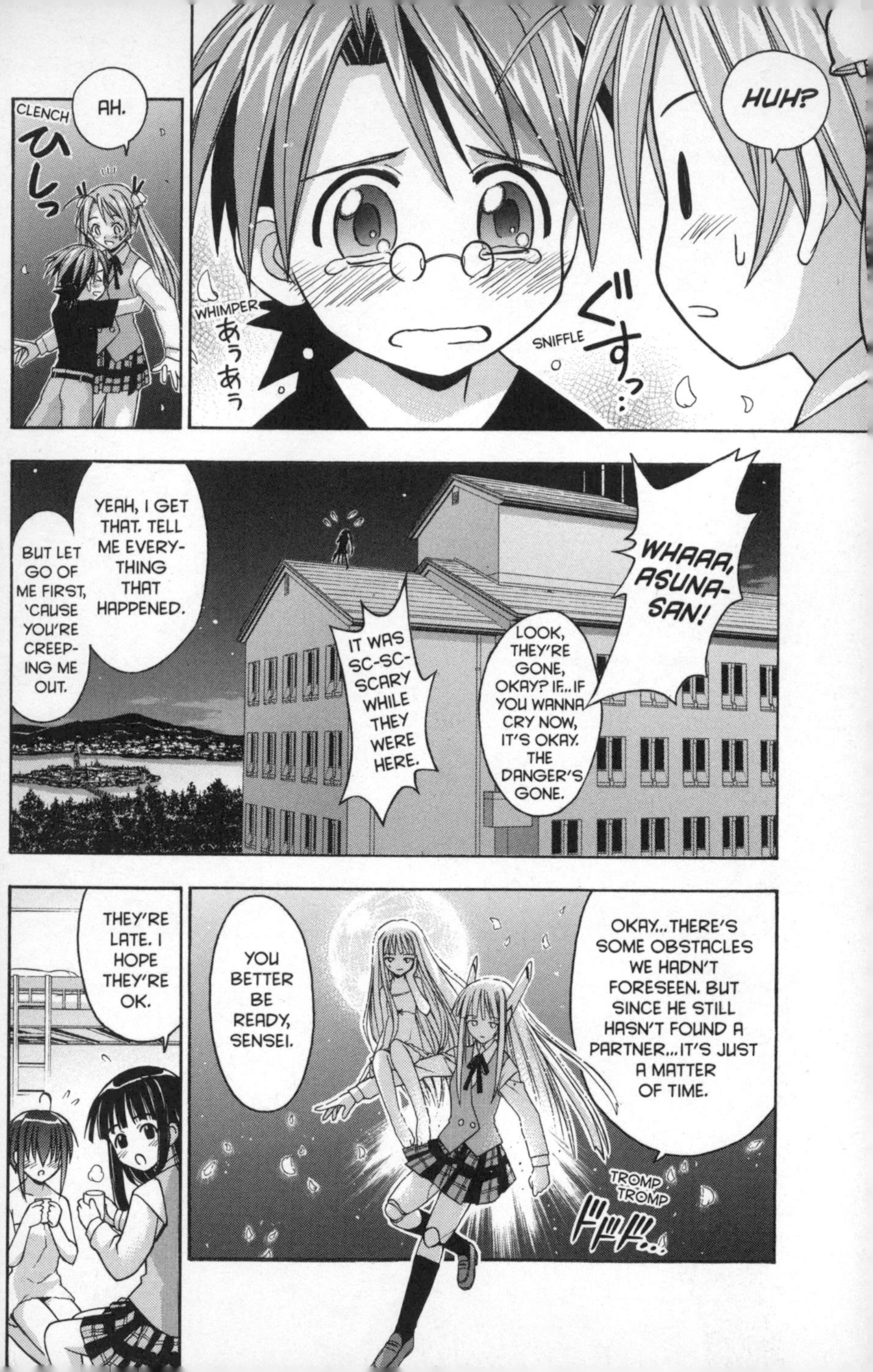
HUH?
SNIFFLE
ぐすっ…
WHIMPER
あぅあぅ
CLENCH
ひしっ
AH.
WHAAA, ASUNA-SAN!
LOOK, THEY'RE GONE, OKAY? IF...IF YOU WANNA CRY NOW, IT'S OKAY. THE DANGER'S GONE.
IT WAS SC-SC-SCARY WHILE THEY WERE HERE.
YEAH, I GET THAT. TELL ME EVERY-THING THAT HAPPENED.
BUT LET GO OF ME FIRST, 'CAUSE YOU'RE CREEP-ING ME OUT.
OKAY...THERE'S SOME OBSTACLES WE HADN'T FORESEEN. BUT SINCE HE STILL HASN'T FOUND A PARTNER...IT'S JUST A MATTER OF TIME.
TROMP TROMP
ドッドッ…
YOU BETTER BE READY, SENSEI.
THEY'RE LATE. I HOPE THEY'RE OK.

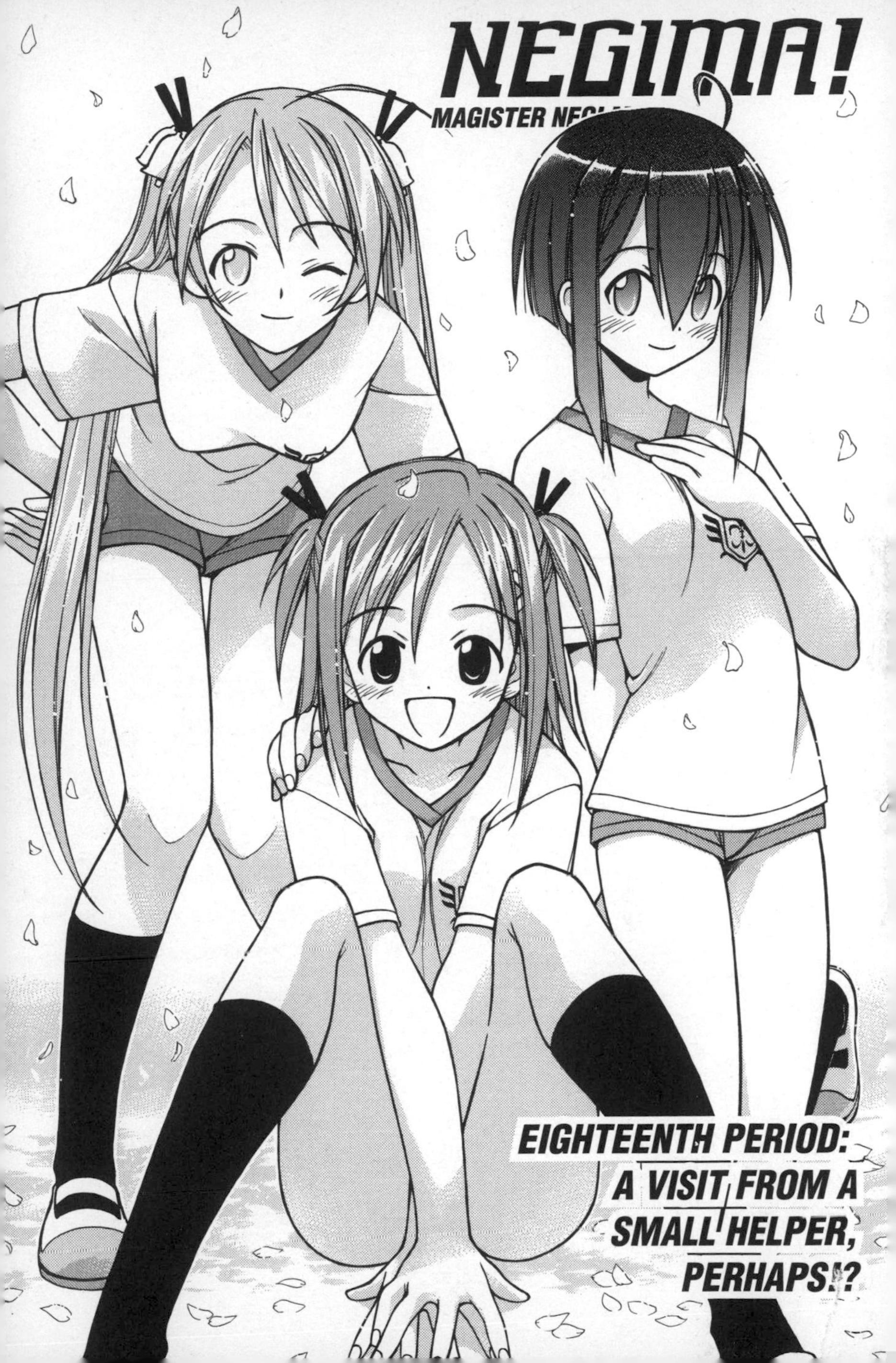
NEGIMA!
MAGISTER NEGI
EIGHTEENTH PERIOD:
A VISIT FROM A
SMALL HELPER,
PERHAPS!?

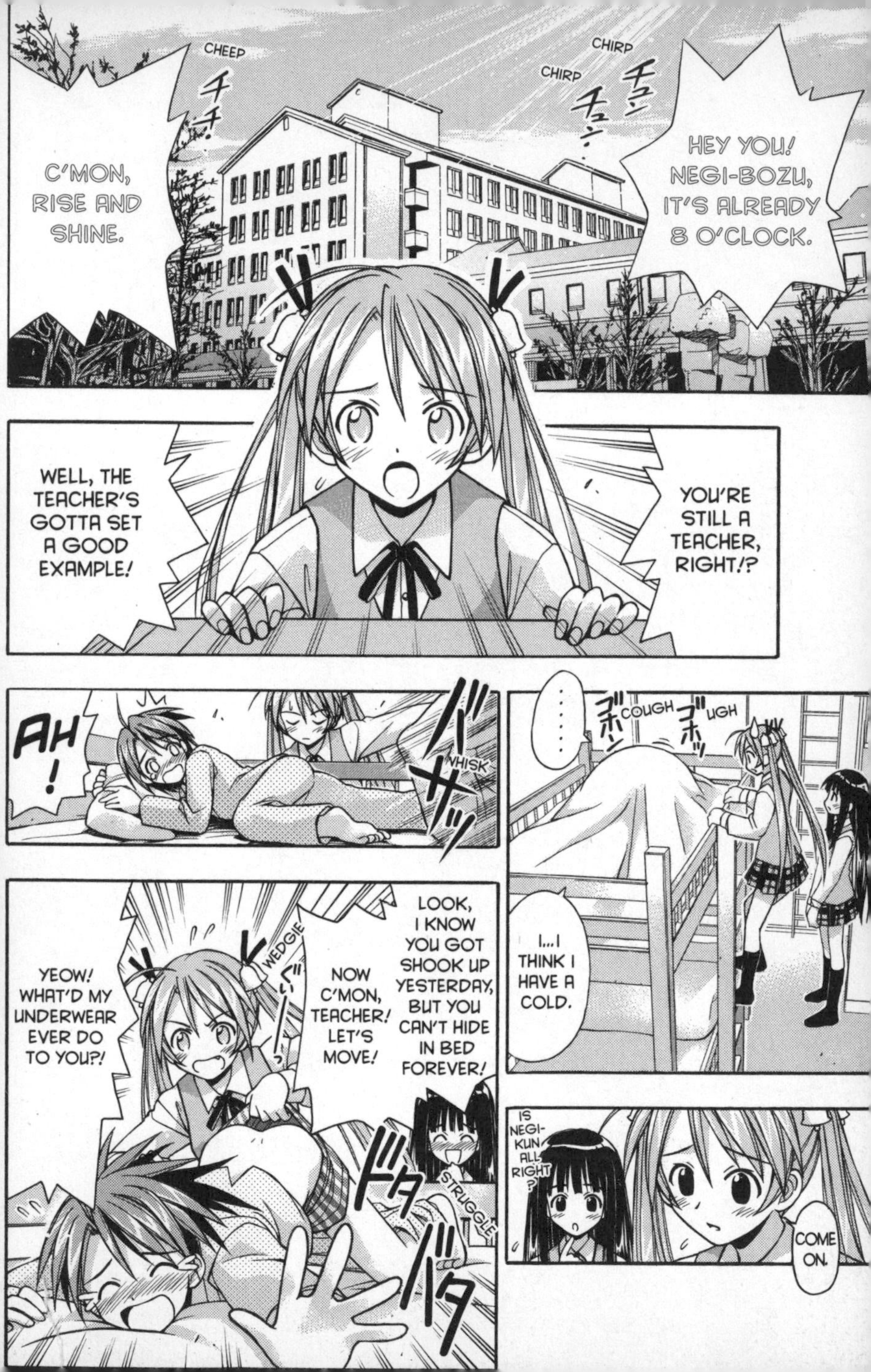
HEY YOU! NEGI-BOZU, IT'S ALREADY 8 O'CLOCK.
CHIRP
CHIRP
CHEEP
C'MON, RISE AND SHINE.
YOU'RE STILL A TEACHER, RIGHT!?
WELL, THE TEACHER'S GOTTA SET A GOOD EXAMPLE!
......
COUGH
UGH
I...I THINK I HAVE A COLD.
IS NEGI-KUN ALL RIGHT?
COME ON.
WHISK
AH!
LOOK, I KNOW YOU GOT SHOOK UP YESTERDAY, BUT YOU CAN'T HIDE IN BED FOREVER!
NOW C'MON, TEACHER! LET'S MOVE!
WEDGIE
YEOW! WHAT'D MY UNDERWEAR EVER DO TO YOU?!
STRUGGLE

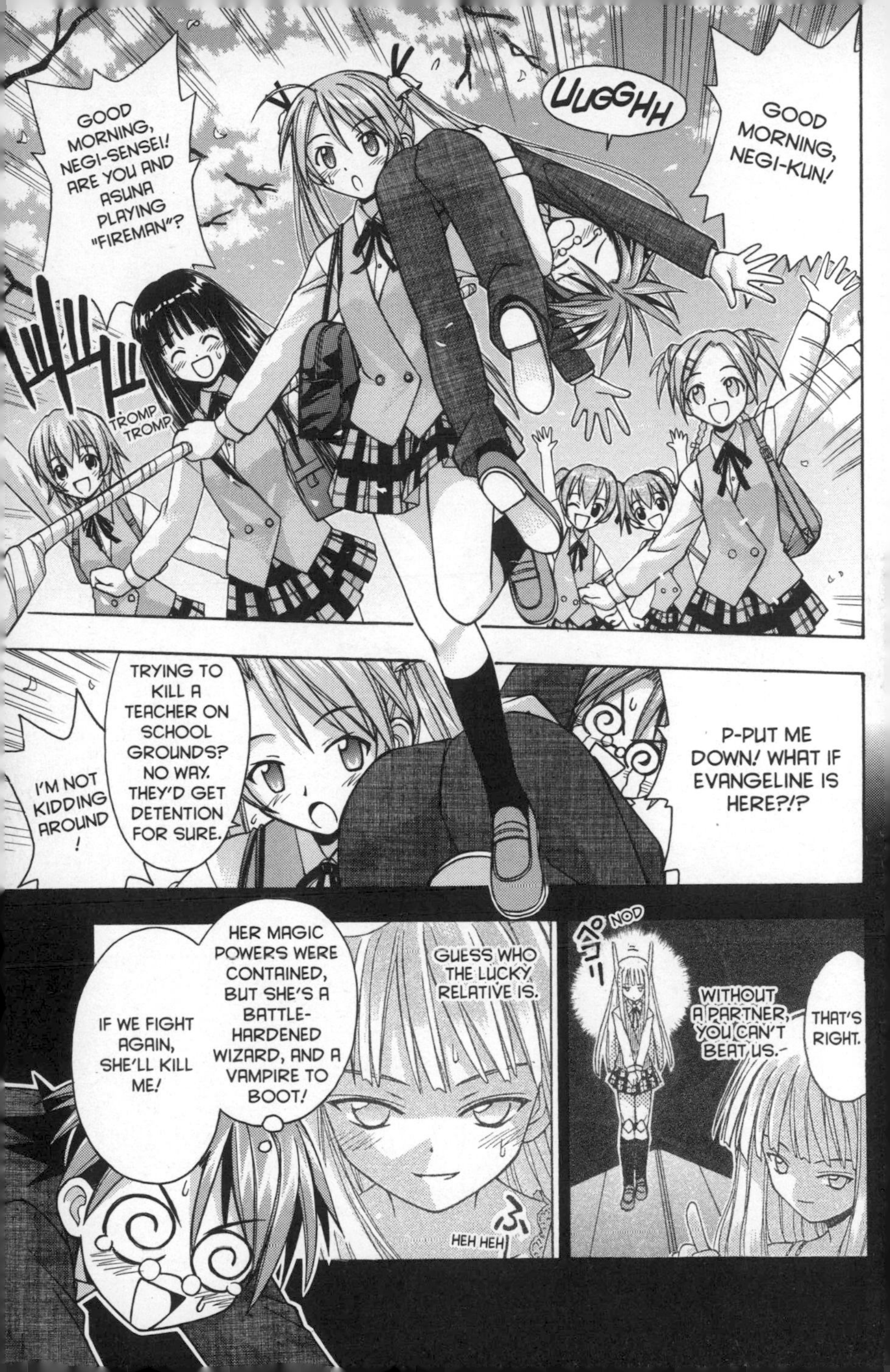
GOOD MORNING, NEGI-KUN!
UUGGHH
GOOD MORNING, NEGI-SENSEI! ARE YOU AND ASUNA PLAYING "FIREMAN"?
TROMP TROMP
P-PUT ME DOWN! WHAT IF EVANGELINE IS HERE?!?
TRYING TO KILL A TEACHER ON SCHOOL GROUNDS? NO WAY. THEY'D GET DETENTION FOR SURE.
I'M NOT KIDDING AROUND!
NOD
THAT'S RIGHT.
WITHOUT A PARTNER, YOU CAN'T BEAT US.
GUESS WHO THE LUCKY RELATIVE IS.
HER MAGIC POWERS WERE CONTAINED, BUT SHE'S A BATTLE-HARDENED WIZARD, AND A VAMPIRE TO BOOT!
IF WE FIGHT AGAIN, SHE'LL KILL ME!
HEH HEH

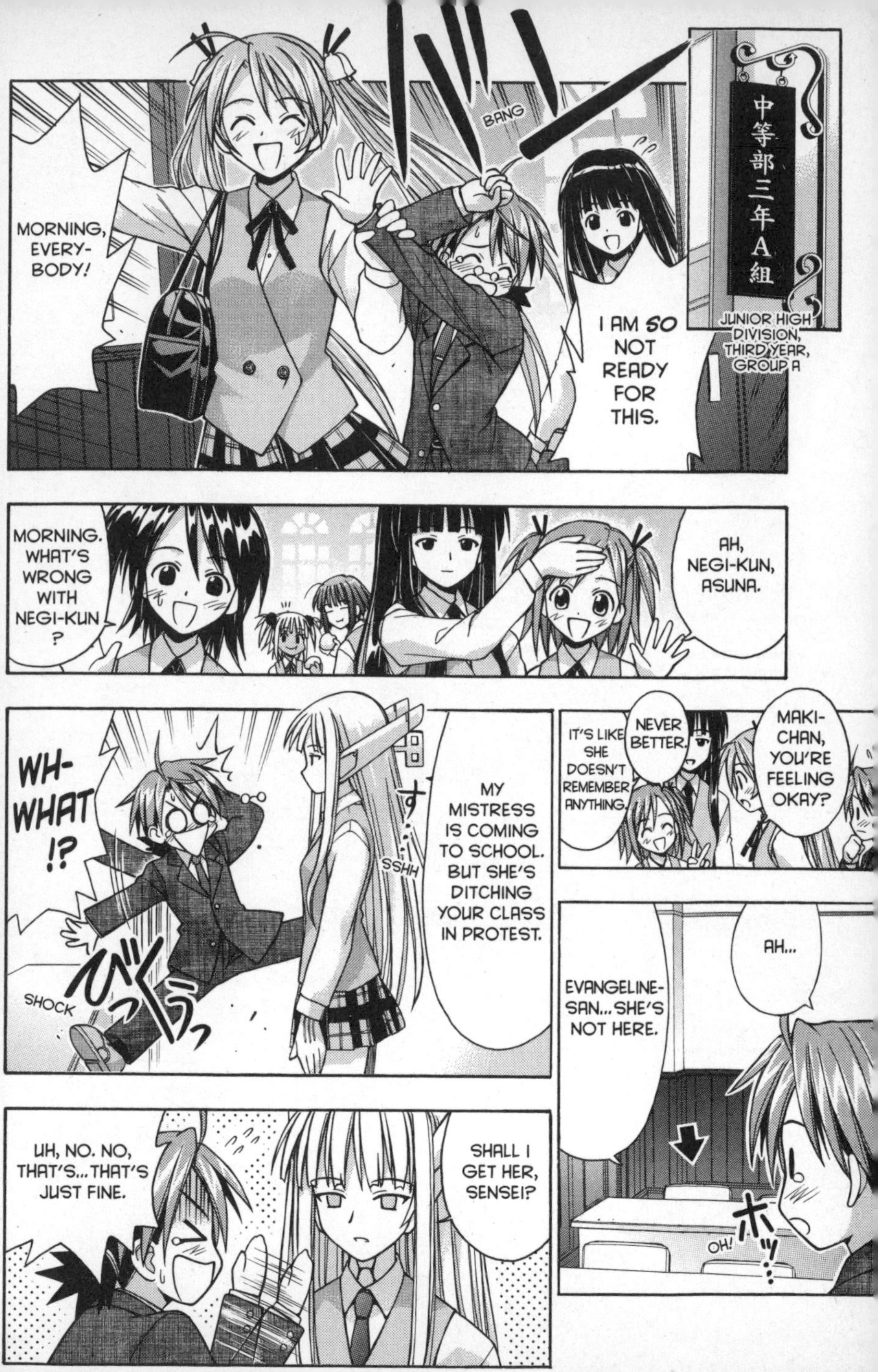
中等部三年A組
BANG
JUNIOR HIGH DIVISION, THIRD YEAR, GROUP A
MORNING, EVERY-BODY!
I AM SO NOT READY FOR THIS.
AH, NEGI-KUN, ASUNA.
MORNING. WHAT'S WRONG WITH NEGI-KUN?
MAKI-CHAN, YOU'RE FEELING OKAY?
NEVER BETTER.
IT'S LIKE SHE DOESN'T REMEMBER ANYTHING.
AH...
EVANGELINE-SAN... SHE'S NOT HERE.
ポッ
OH!
MY MISTRESS IS COMING TO SCHOOL. BUT SHE'S DITCHING YOUR CLASS IN PROTEST.
す…
SSHH
WH-WHAT!?
びっくう
SHOCK
SHALL I GET HER, SENSEI?
UH, NO. NO, THAT'S... THAT'S JUST FINE.

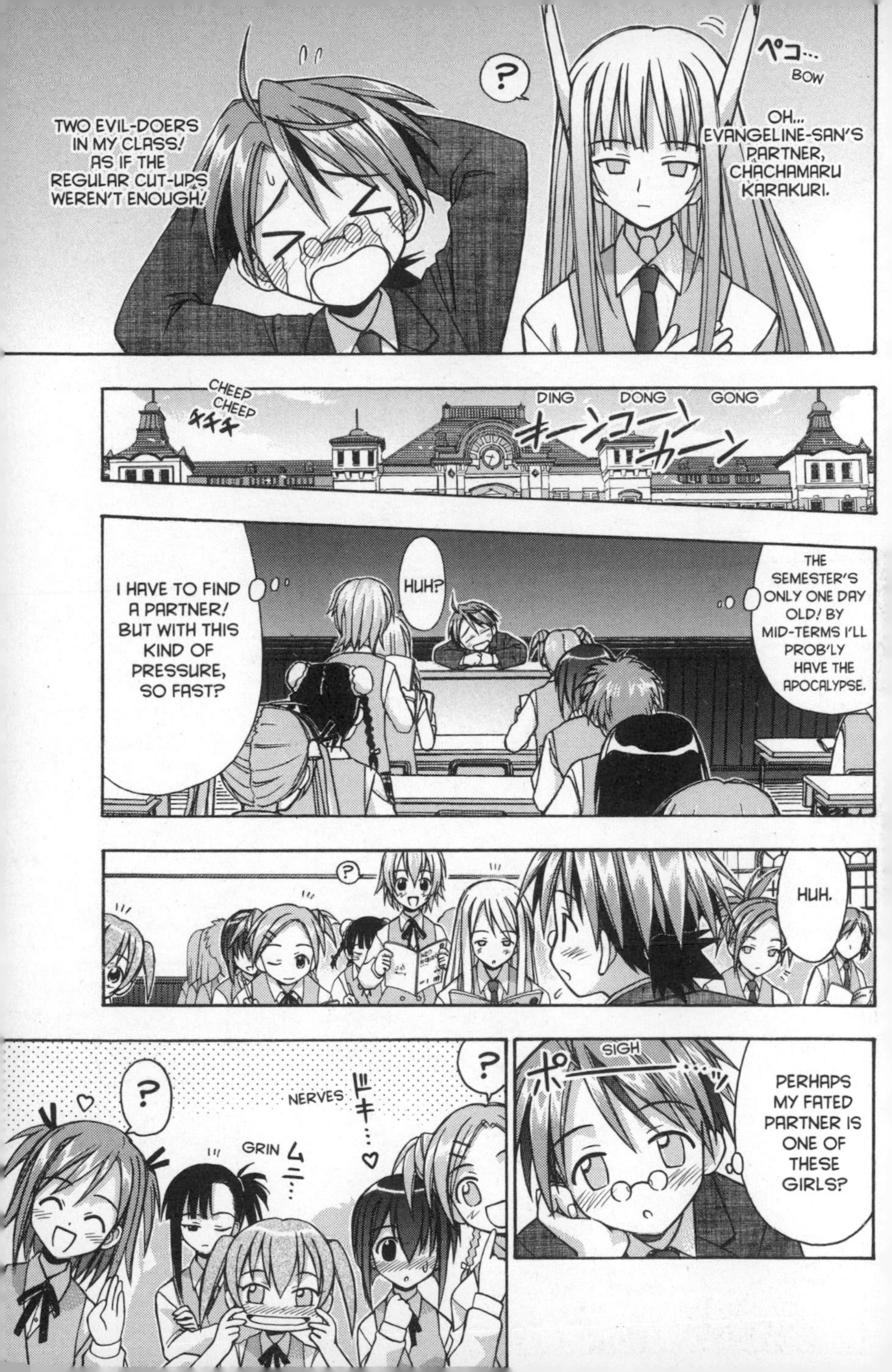
ペコ…
BOW
OH... EVANGELINE-SAN'S PARTNER, CHACHAMARU KARAKURI.
?
TWO EVIL-DOERS IN MY CLASS! AS IF THE REGULAR CUT-UPS WEREN'T ENOUGH!
キーンコーンカーン
DING DONG GONG
チチチ
CHEEP CHEEP
THE SEMESTER'S ONLY ONE DAY OLD! BY MID-TERMS I'LL PROB'LY HAVE THE APOCALYPSE.
HUH?
I HAVE TO FIND A PARTNER! BUT WITH THIS KIND OF PRESSURE, SO FAST?
HUH.
?
ポーーッ
SIGH
PERHAPS MY FATED PARTNER IS ONE OF THESE GIRLS?
?
ドキ…♡
NERVES
ムニ…
GRIN
?

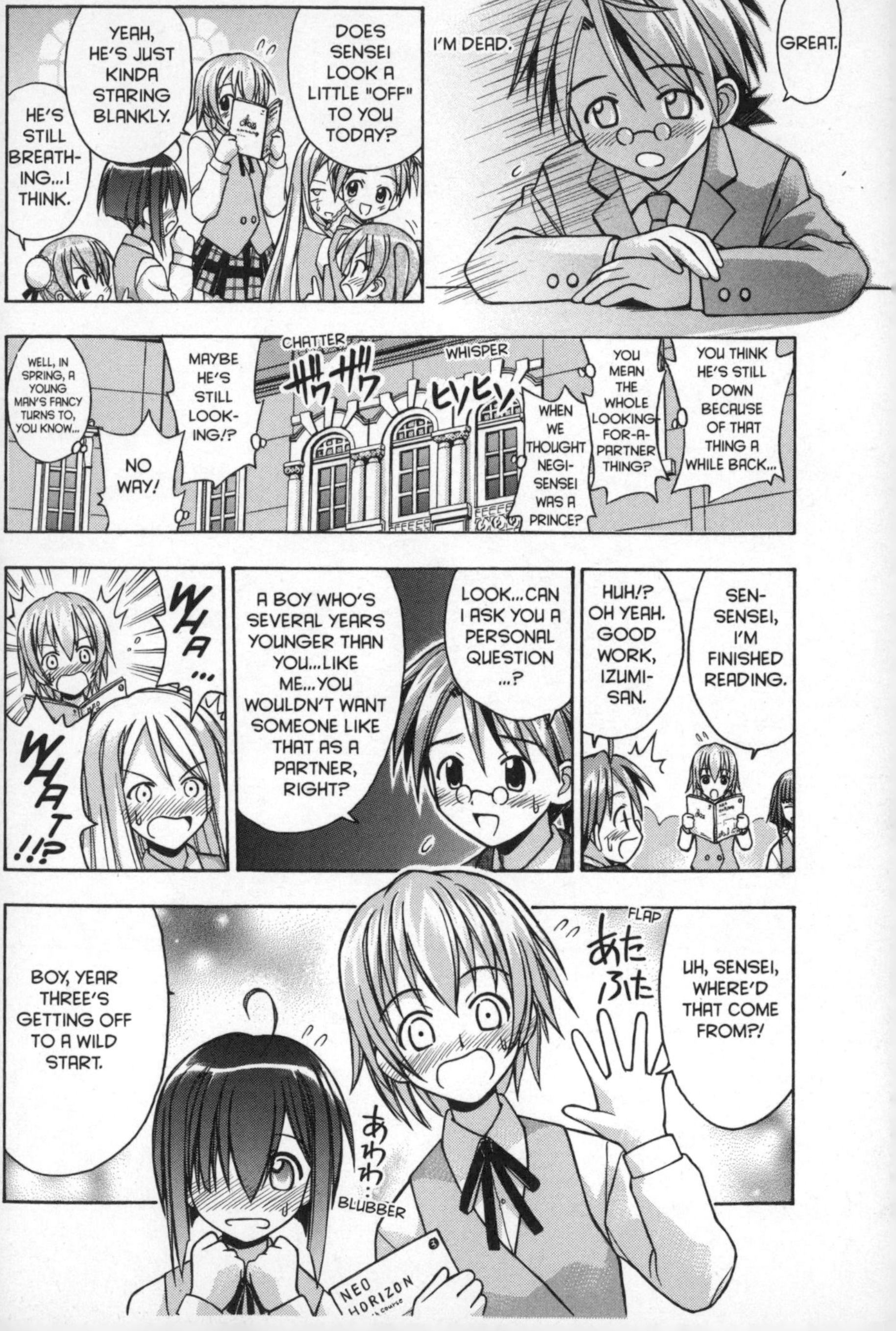
GREAT.
I'M DEAD.
DOES SENSEI LOOK A LITTLE "OFF" TO YOU TODAY?
YEAH, HE'S JUST KINDA STARING BLANKLY.
HE'S STILL BREATH-ING...I THINK.
YOU THINK HE'S STILL DOWN BECAUSE OF THAT THING A WHILE BACK...
YOU MEAN THE WHOLE LOOKING-FOR-A-PARTNER THING?
WHEN WE THOUGHT NEGI-SENSEI WAS A PRINCE?
WHISPER
ヒソヒソ
CHATTER
ザワザワ
MAYBE HE'S STILL LOOK-ING!?
NO WAY!
WELL, IN SPRING, A YOUNG MAN'S FANCY TURNS TO, YOU KNOW...
SEN-SENSEI, I'M FINISHED READING.
HUH!? OH YEAH. GOOD WORK, IZUMI-SAN.
LOOK...CAN I ASK YOU A PERSONAL QUESTION ...?
A BOY WHO'S SEVERAL YEARS YOUNGER THAN YOU...LIKE ME...YOU WOULDN'T WANT SOMEONE LIKE THAT AS A PARTNER, RIGHT?
WHA...
WHAT!!?
UH, SENSEI, WHERE'D THAT COME FROM?!
FLAP
あたふた
BOY, YEAR THREE'S GETTING OFF TO A WILD START.
あわわ…
BLUBBER
NEO HORIZON

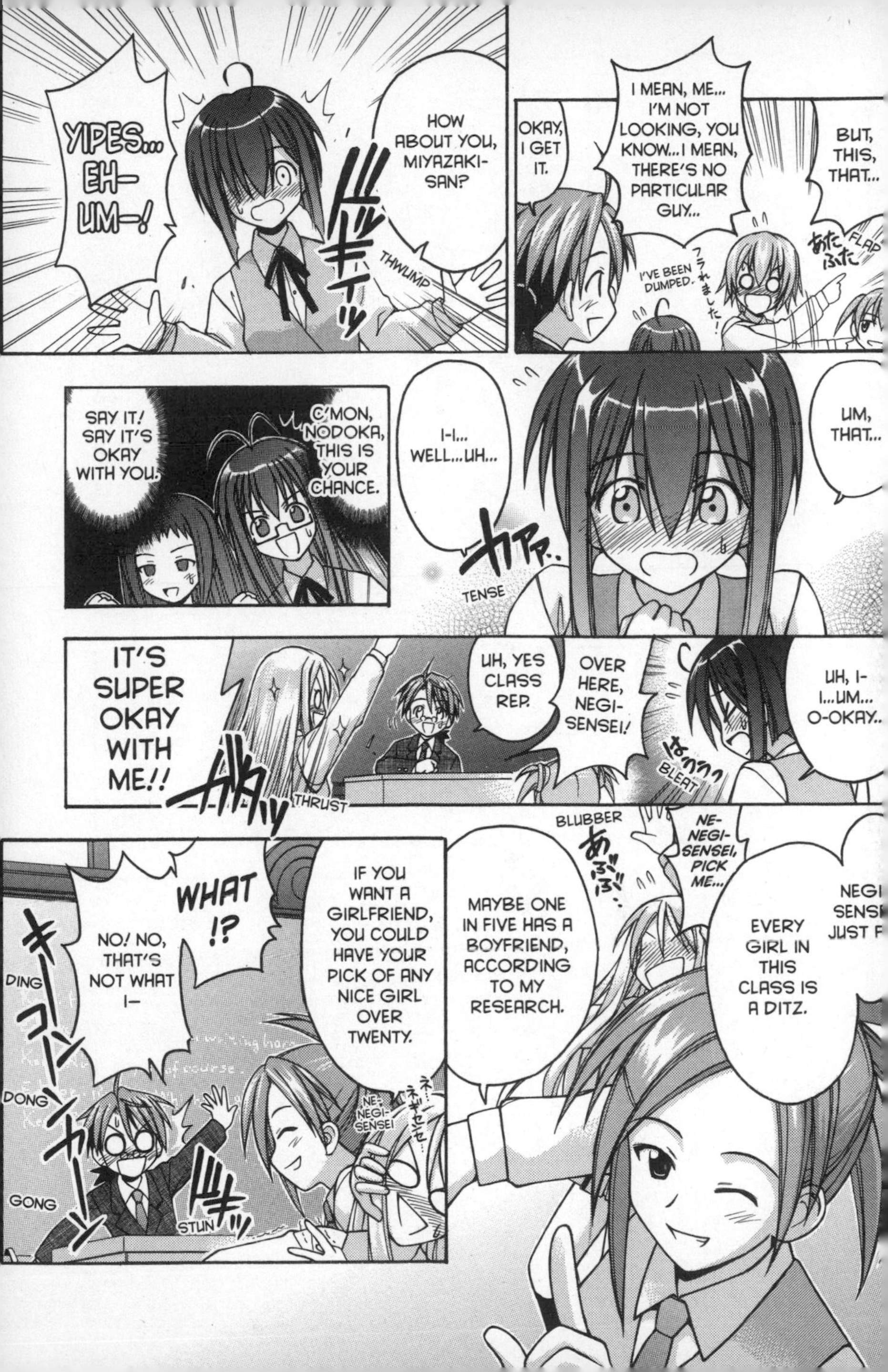
BUT, THIS, THAT...
I MEAN, ME... I'M NOT LOOKING, YOU KNOW...I MEAN, THERE'S NO PARTICULAR GUY...
OKAY, I GET IT.
あたふた FLAP
フラれました！ I'VE BEEN DUMPED.
HOW ABOUT YOU, MIYAZAKI-SAN?
THWUMP
YIPES... EH-UM-!
UM, THAT...
I-I... WELL...UH...
TENSE
C'MON, NODOKA, THIS IS YOUR CHANCE.
SAY IT! SAY IT'S OKAY WITH YOU.
UH, I- I...UM... O-OKAY..
BLEAT
OVER HERE, NEGI-SENSEI!
UH, YES CLASS REP.
THRUST
IT'S SUPER OKAY WITH ME!!
NEGI SENS JUST
EVERY GIRL IN THIS CLASS IS A DITZ.
NE-NEGI-SENSEI, PICK ME...
BLUBBER
MAYBE ONE IN FIVE HAS A BOYFRIEND, ACCORDING TO MY RESEARCH.
IF YOU WANT A GIRLFRIEND, YOU COULD HAVE YOUR PICK OF ANY NICE GIRL OVER TWENTY.
ネ…ネギセンセ… NE-NEGI-SENSEI
WHAT !?
NO! NO, THAT'S NOT WHAT I—
STUN
DING
DONG
GONG

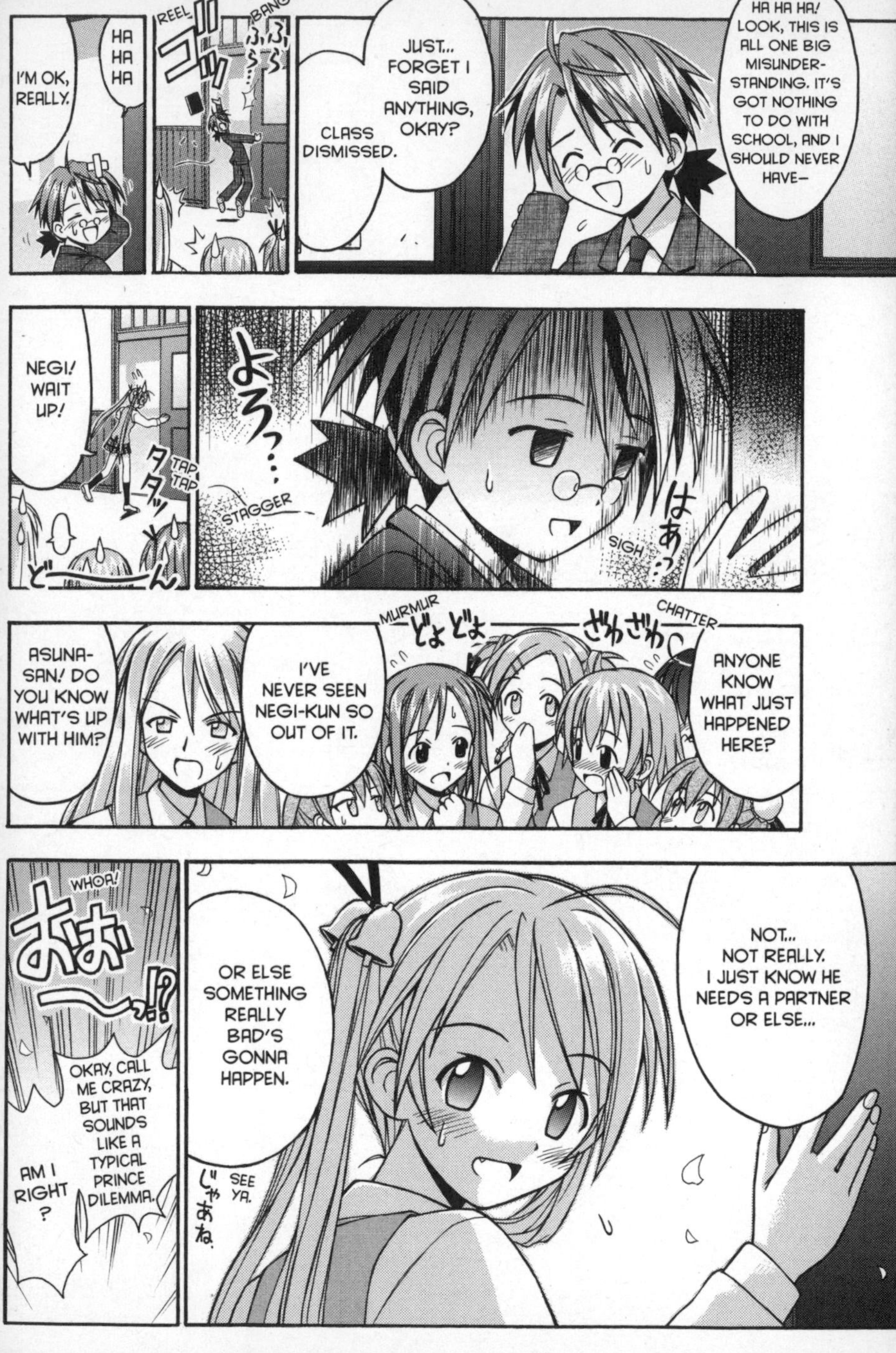
HA HA HA! LOOK, THIS IS ALL ONE BIG MISUNDER-STANDING. IT'S GOT NOTHING TO DO WITH SCHOOL, AND I SHOULD NEVER HAVE—
JUST... FORGET I SAID ANYTHING, OKAY?
CLASS DISMISSED.
BANG
REEL
ゴッ
HA HA HA
I'M OK, REALLY.
よろっ...
STAGGER
はあっ...
SIGH
NEGI! WAIT UP!
タタッ
TAP TAP
どーーん
ANYONE KNOW WHAT JUST HAPPENED HERE?
ざわざわ
CHATTER
どよどよ
MURMUR
I'VE NEVER SEEN NEGI-KUN SO OUT OF IT.
ASUNA-SAN! DO YOU KNOW WHAT'S UP WITH HIM?
NOT... NOT REALLY. I JUST KNOW HE NEEDS A PARTNER OR ELSE...
OR ELSE SOMETHING REALLY BAD'S GONNA HAPPEN.
じゃあね
SEE YA.
おおーーっ!?
WHOA!
OKAY, CALL ME CRAZY, BUT THAT SOUNDS LIKE A TYPICAL PRINCE DILEMMA.
AM I RIGHT?

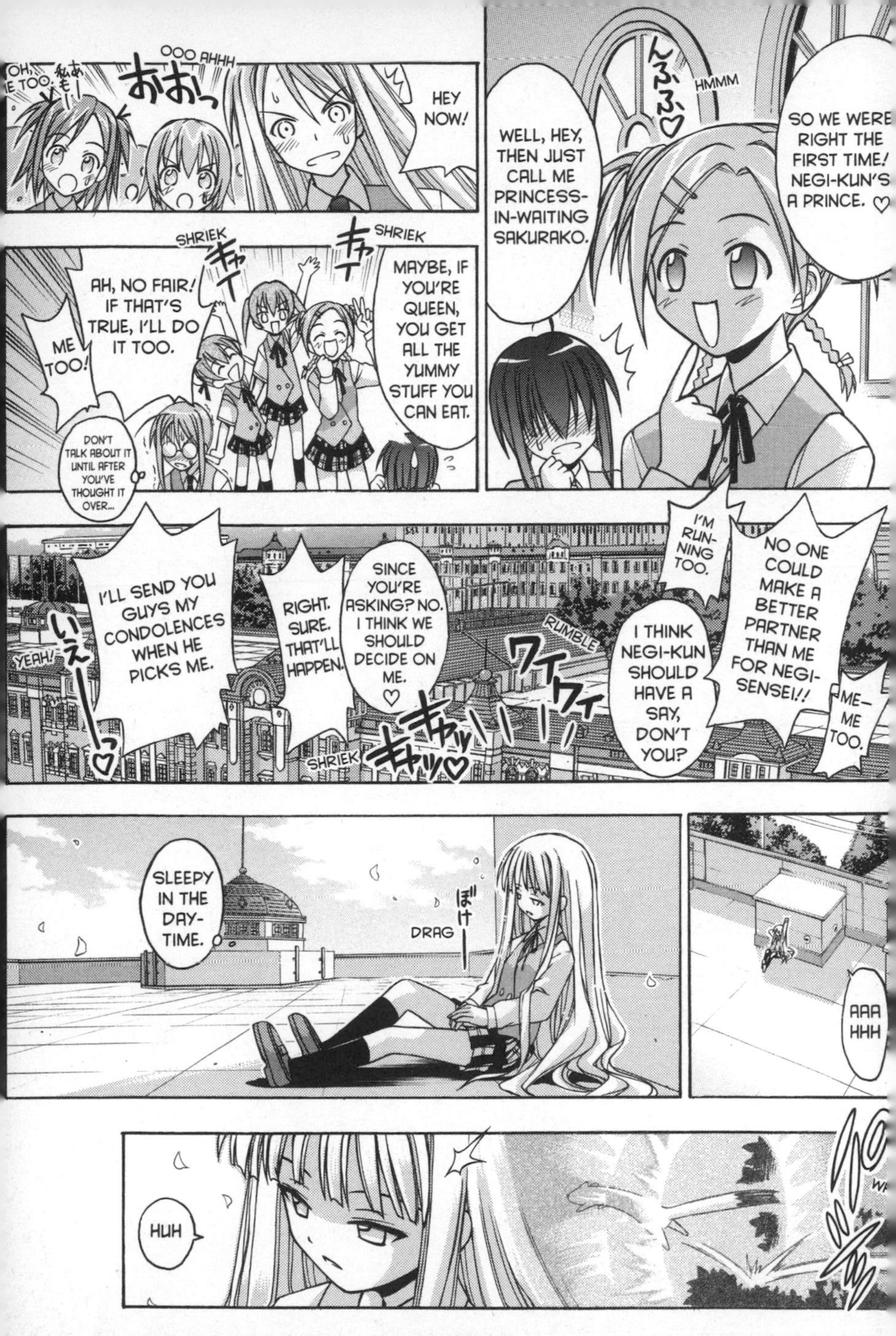
SO WE WERE RIGHT THE FIRST TIME! NEGI-KUN'S A PRINCE. ♡
んふふ♡
HMMM
WELL, HEY, THEN JUST CALL ME PRINCESS-IN-WAITING SAKURAKO.
HEY NOW!
おおっ
OOO AHHH
私も
OH,
E TOO.
MAYBE, IF YOU'RE QUEEN, YOU GET ALL THE YUMMY STUFF YOU CAN EAT.
キャ
SHRIEK
キャ
SHRIEK
AH, NO FAIR! IF THAT'S TRUE, I'LL DO IT TOO.
ME TOO!
DON'T TALK ABOUT IT UNTIL AFTER YOU'VE THOUGHT IT OVER...
ME—ME TOO.
NO ONE COULD MAKE A BETTER PARTNER THAN ME FOR NEGI-SENSEI!!
I'M RUNNING TOO.
I THINK NEGI-KUN SHOULD HAVE A SAY, DON'T YOU?
ワイワイー
RUMBLE
キャッキャッ♡
SHRIEK
SINCE YOU'RE ASKING? NO. I THINK WE SHOULD DECIDE ON ME. ♡
RIGHT. SURE. THAT'LL HAPPEN.
I'LL SEND YOU GUYS MY CONDOLENCES WHEN HE PICKS ME.
いえーっ♡
YEAH!
AAA HHH
ぼけー
DRAG
SLEEPY IN THE DAY-TIME.
HUH

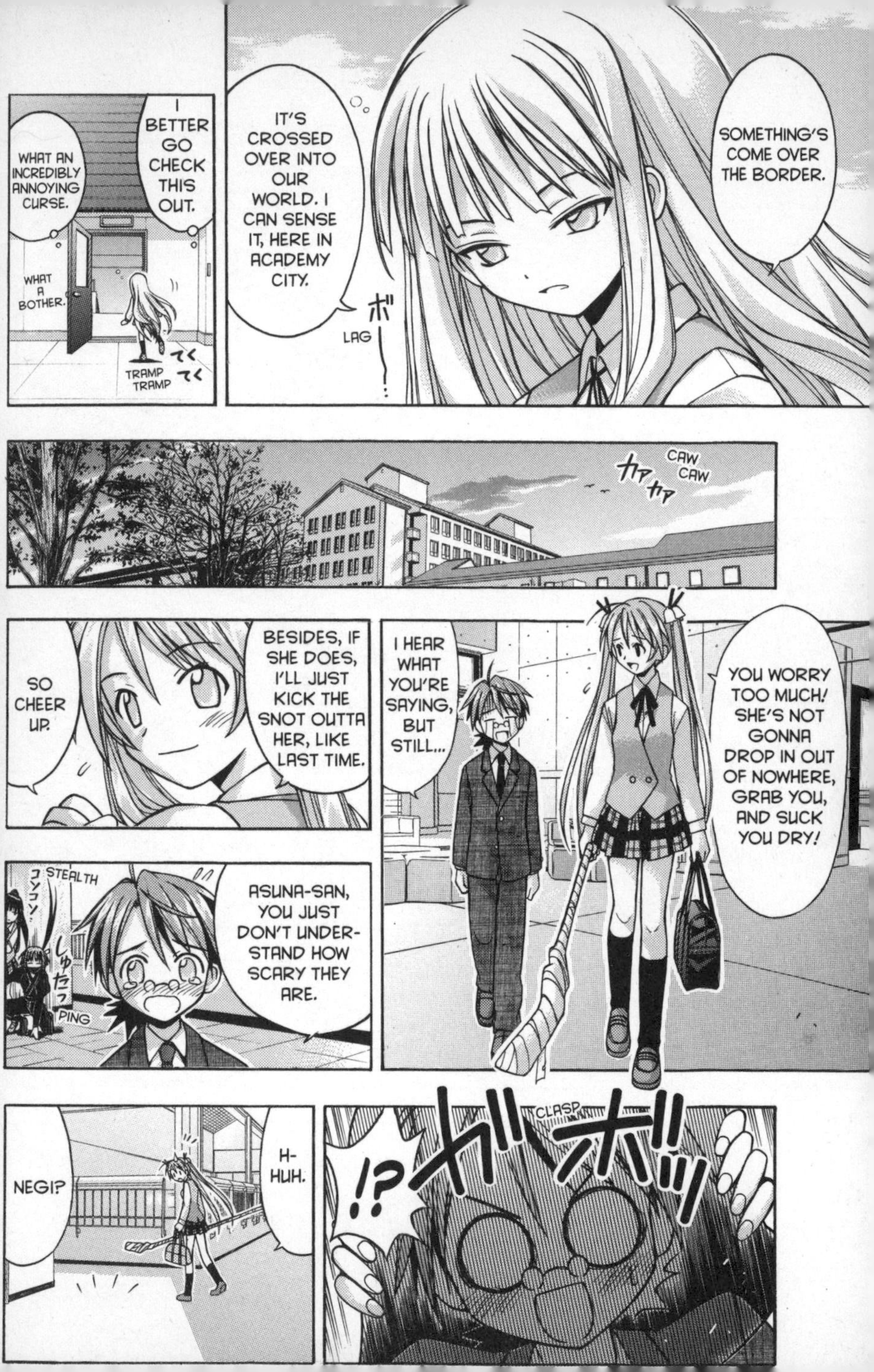
SOMETHING'S COME OVER THE BORDER.
IT'S CROSSED OVER INTO OUR WORLD. I CAN SENSE IT, HERE IN ACADEMY CITY.
ボー
LAG
I BETTER GO CHECK THIS OUT.
WHAT AN INCREDIBLY ANNOYING CURSE.
WHAT A BOTHER.
てくてく
TRAMP TRAMP
カァ カァ
CAW CAW
YOU WORRY TOO MUCH! SHE'S NOT GONNA DROP IN OUT OF NOWHERE, GRAB YOU, AND SUCK YOU DRY!
I HEAR WHAT YOU'RE SAYING, BUT STILL...
BESIDES, IF SHE DOES, I'LL JUST KICK THE SNOT OUTTA HER, LIKE LAST TIME.
SO CHEER UP.
ASUNA-SAN, YOU JUST DON'T UNDER-STAND HOW SCARY THEY ARE.
コソコソ
STEALTH
しゅたっ
PING
ガバッ
CLASP
!?
H-HUH.
NEGI?

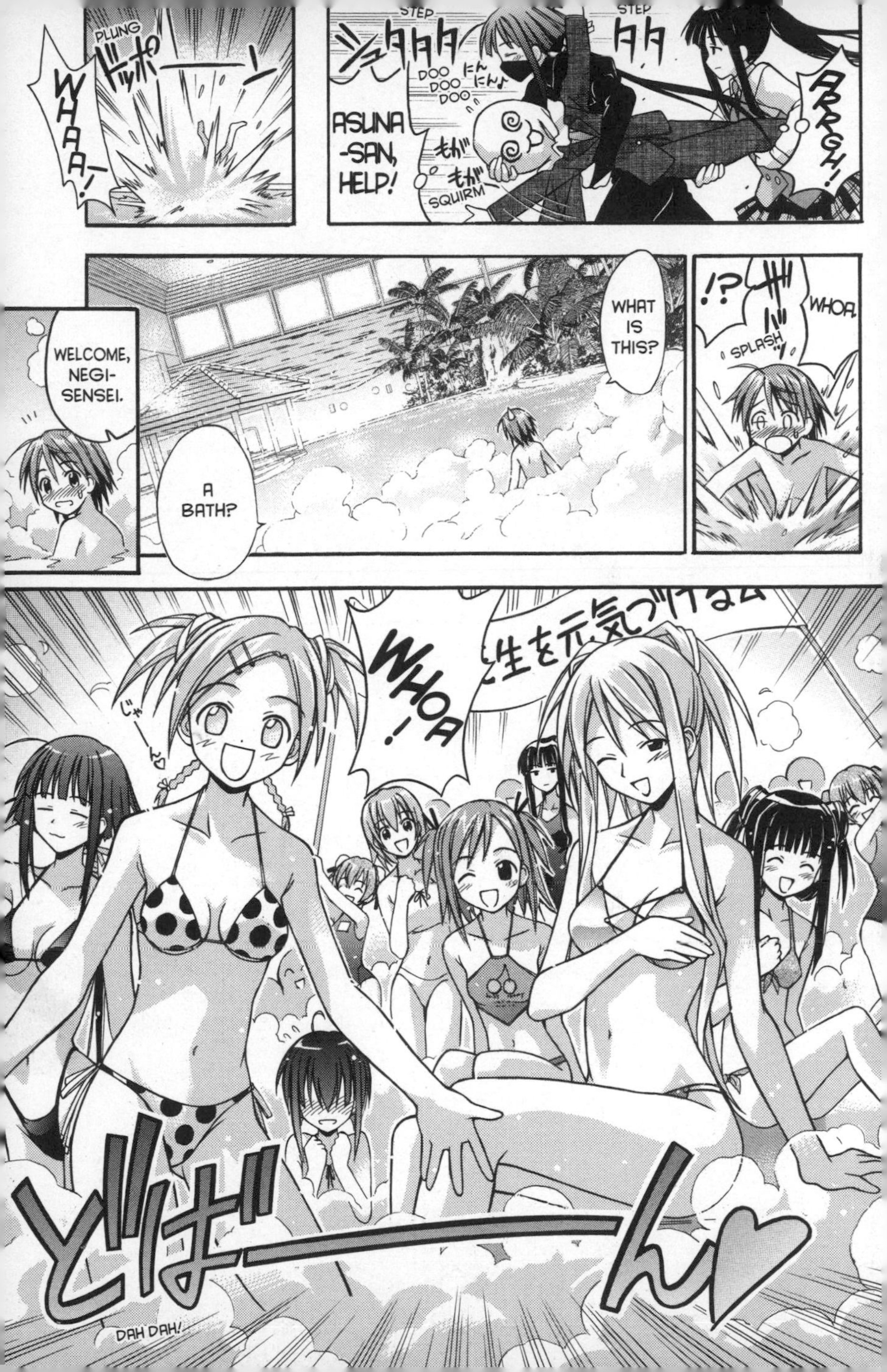
STEP
STEP
DOO DOO DOO
ARRGH!
ASUNA-SAN, HELP!
SQUIRM
PLUNG
WHAAA!
!?
WHOA
SPLASH
WHAT IS THIS?
A BATH?
WELCOME, NEGI-SENSEI.
WHOA!
DAH DAH!

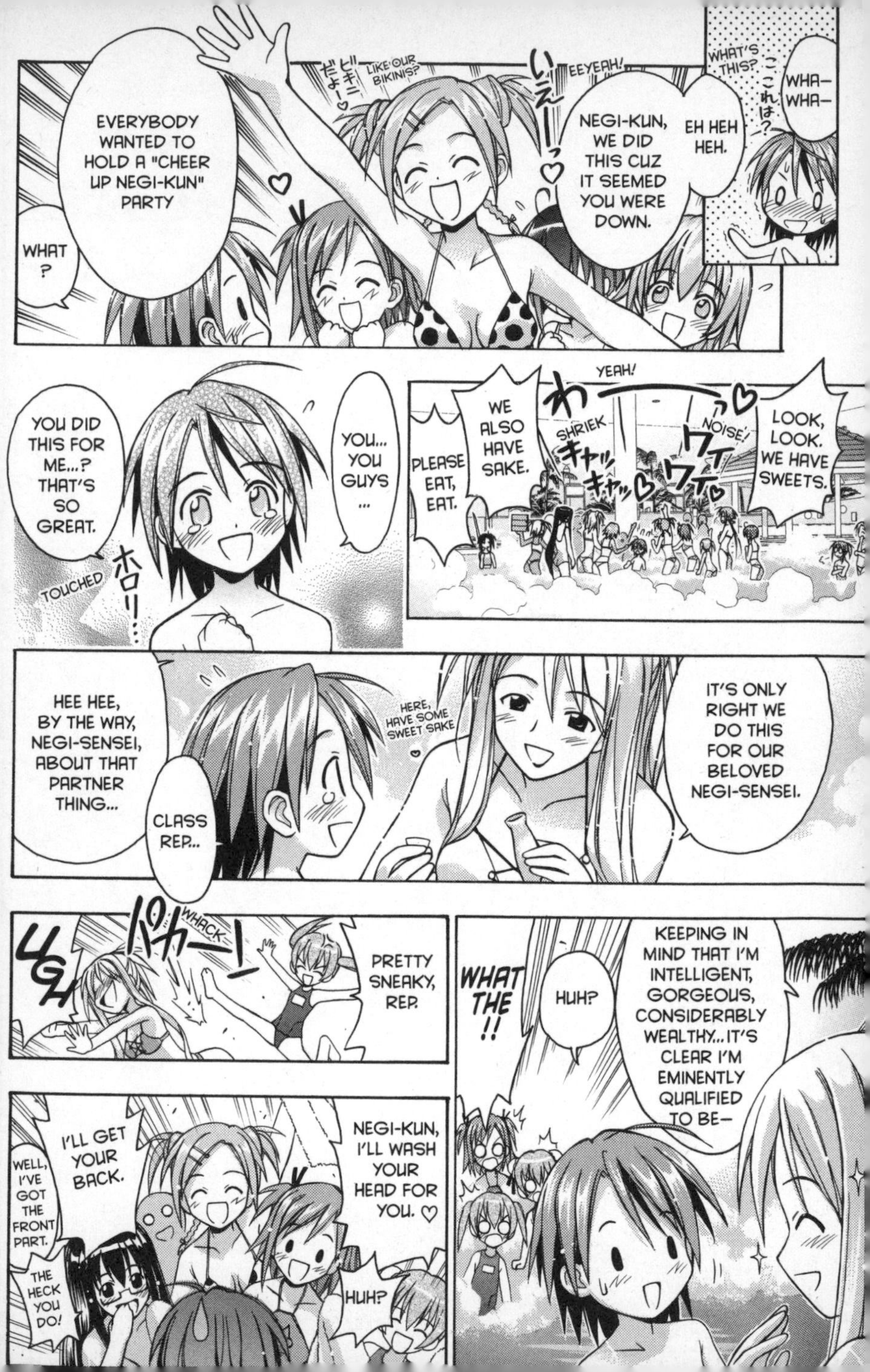
WHA- WHA-
WHAT'S THIS?
これは？
NEGI-KUN, WE DID THIS CUZ IT SEEMED YOU WERE DOWN.
EH HEH HEH.
いえーっ
EEYEAH!
ビキニだよー
LIKE OUR BIKINIS?
EVERYBODY WANTED TO HOLD A "CHEER UP NEGI-KUN" PARTY
WHAT?
LOOK, LOOK. WE HAVE SWEETS.
ワイワイ
NOISE!
わーっ
YEAH!
キャッキャッ
SHRIEK
WE ALSO HAVE SAKE.
PLEASE EAT, EAT.
YOU... YOU GUYS ...
YOU DID THIS FOR ME...? THAT'S SO GREAT.
ホロリ…
TOUCHED
IT'S ONLY RIGHT WE DO THIS FOR OUR BELOVED NEGI-SENSEI.
HERE, HAVE SOME SWEET SAKE
CLASS REP...
HEE HEE, BY THE WAY, NEGI-SENSEI, ABOUT THAT PARTNER THING...
KEEPING IN MIND THAT I'M INTELLIGENT, GORGEOUS, CONSIDERABLY WEALTHY...IT'S CLEAR I'M EMINENTLY QUALIFIED TO BE—
HUH?
WHAT THE !!
PRETTY SNEAKY, REP.
パカー!
WHACK
UGH
NEGI-KUN, I'LL WASH YOUR HEAD FOR YOU. ♡
HUH?
I'LL GET YOUR BACK.
WELL, I'VE GOT THE FRONT PART.
THE HECK YOU DO!

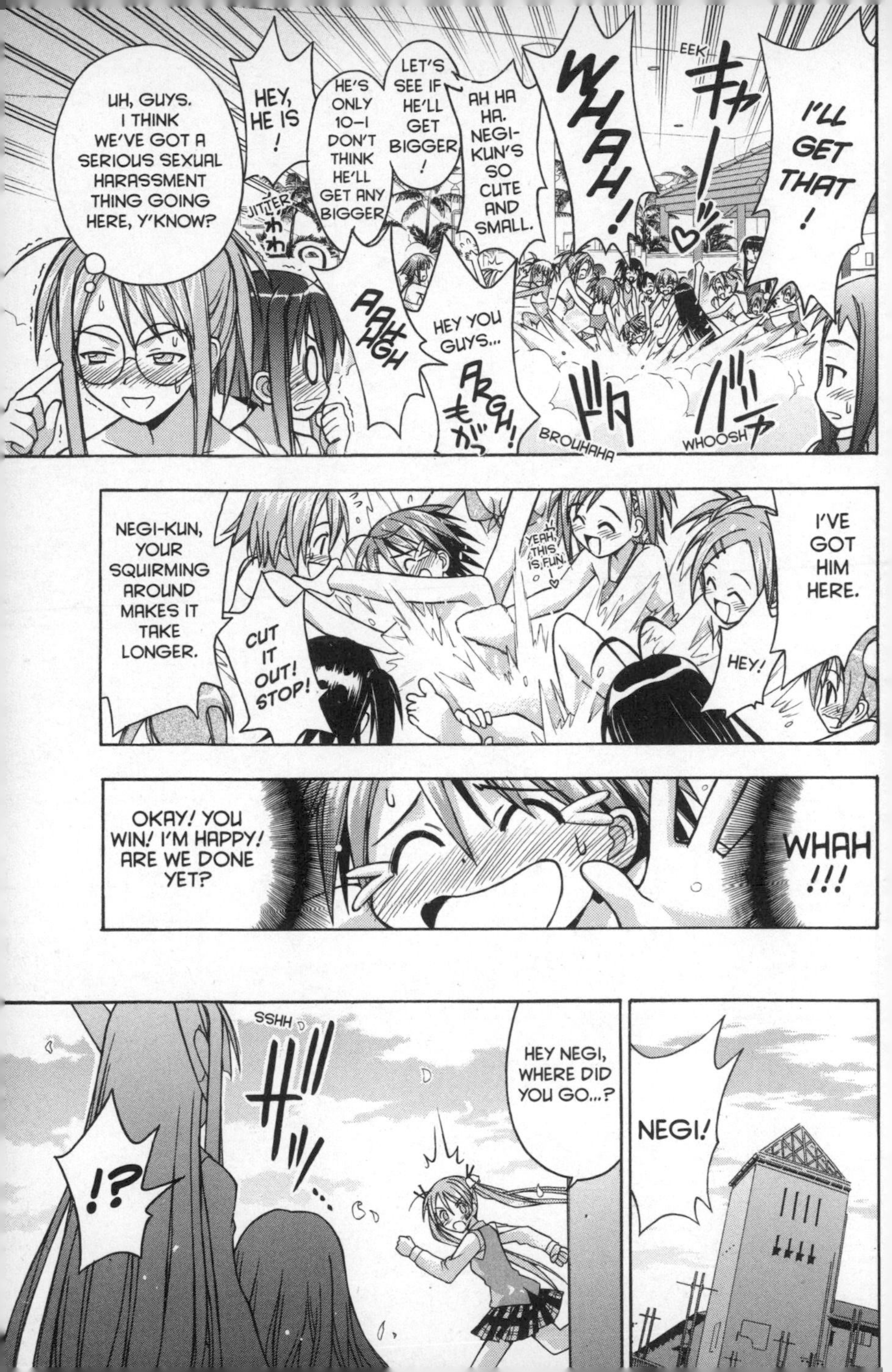
I'LL GET THAT!
EEK
WHAH!
AH HA HA. NEGI-KUN'S SO CUTE AND SMALL.
LET'S SEE IF HE'LL GET BIGGER!
HE'S ONLY 10—I DON'T THINK HE'LL GET ANY BIGGER
HEY, HE IS!
UH, GUYS. I THINK WE'VE GOT A SERIOUS SEXUAL HARASSMENT THING GOING HERE, Y'KNOW?
JITTER
WHOOSH
BROUHAHA
ARGH!
HEY YOU GUYS...
AAHHGH
I'VE GOT HIM HERE.
HEY!
YEAH, THIS IS FUN!
NEGI-KUN, YOUR SQUIRMING AROUND MAKES IT TAKE LONGER.
CUT IT OUT! STOP!
WHAH!!!
OKAY! YOU WIN! I'M HAPPY! ARE WE DONE YET?
NEGI!
HEY NEGI, WHERE DID YOU GO...?
SSHH
!?

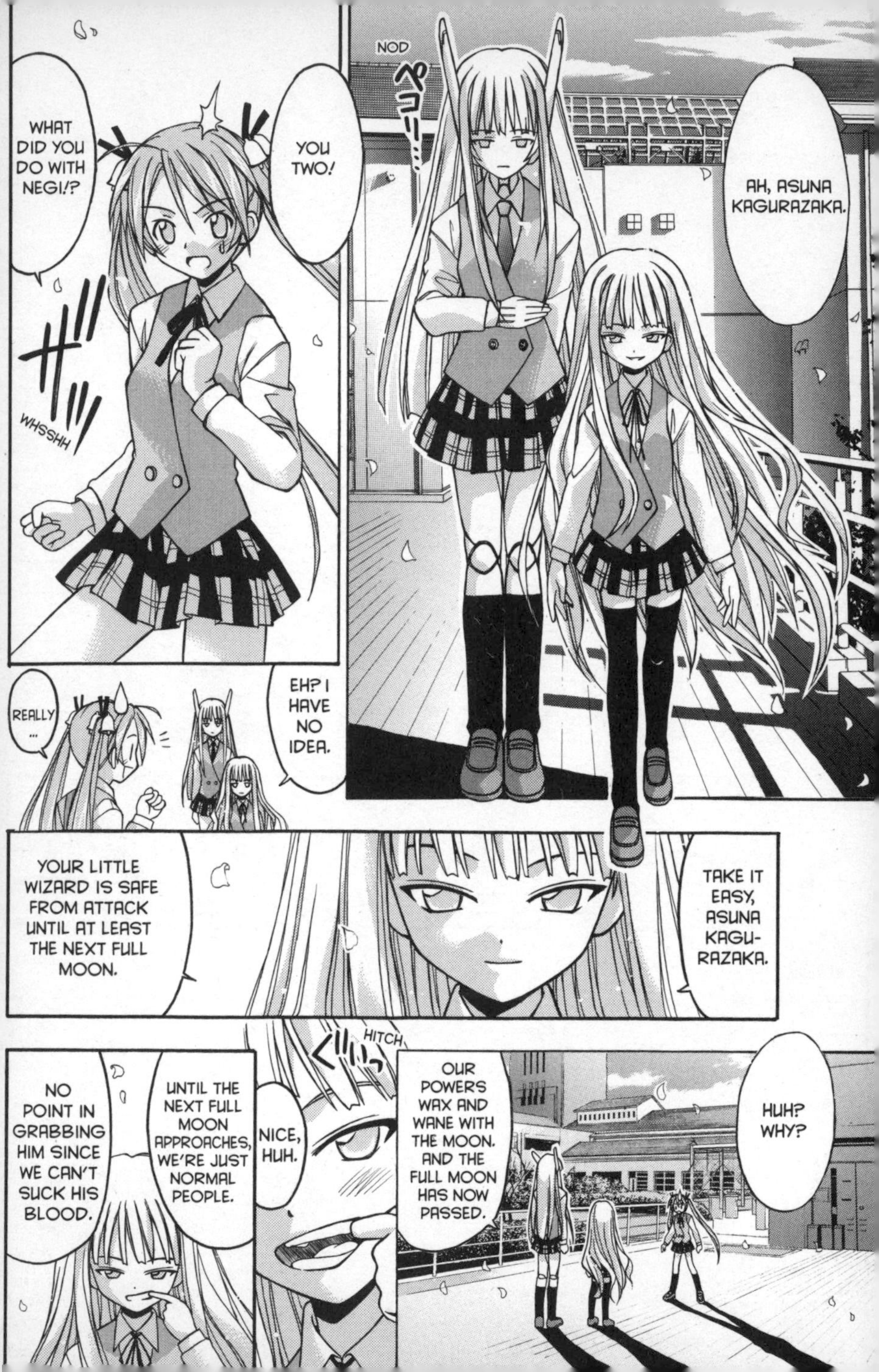
NOD
ペコリ…
AH, ASUNA KAGURAZAKA.
YOU TWO!
WHAT DID YOU DO WITH NEGI!?
WHSSHH
EH? I HAVE NO IDEA.
REALLY ...
TAKE IT EASY, ASUNA KAGURAZAKA.
YOUR LITTLE WIZARD IS SAFE FROM ATTACK UNTIL AT LEAST THE NEXT FULL MOON.
HUH? WHY?
OUR POWERS WAX AND WANE WITH THE MOON. AND THE FULL MOON HAS NOW PASSED.
HITCH
NICE, HUH.
UNTIL THE NEXT FULL MOON APPROACHES, WE'RE JUST NORMAL PEOPLE.
NO POINT IN GRABBING HIM SINCE WE CAN'T SUCK HIS BLOOD.

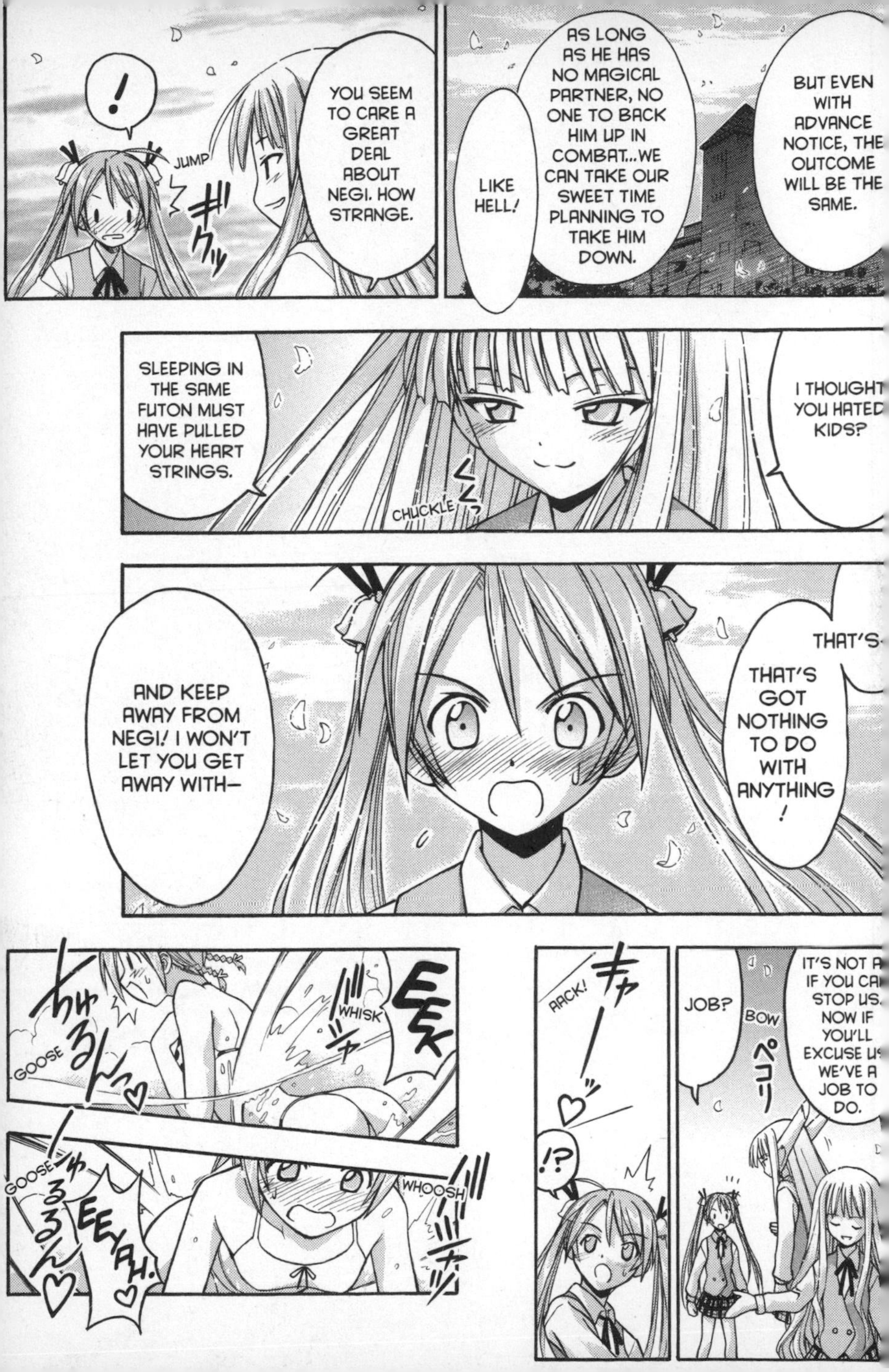
BUT EVEN WITH ADVANCE NOTICE, THE OUTCOME WILL BE THE SAME.
AS LONG AS HE HAS NO MAGICAL PARTNER, NO ONE TO BACK HIM UP IN COMBAT...WE CAN TAKE OUR SWEET TIME PLANNING TO TAKE HIM DOWN.
LIKE HELL!
YOU SEEM TO CARE A GREAT DEAL ABOUT NEGI. HOW STRANGE.
!
JUMP
I THOUGHT YOU HATED KIDS?
SLEEPING IN THE SAME FUTON MUST HAVE PULLED YOUR HEART STRINGS.
CHUCKLE
THAT'S–
THAT'S GOT NOTHING TO DO WITH ANYTHING!
AND KEEP AWAY FROM NEGI! I WON'T LET YOU GET AWAY WITH–
IT'S NOT A IF YOU CA STOP US. NOW IF YOU'LL EXCUSE US WE'VE A JOB TO DO.
JOB?
BOW
RACK!
!?
EEK
WHISK
GOOSE
WHOOSH
EEYAH!
GOOSE

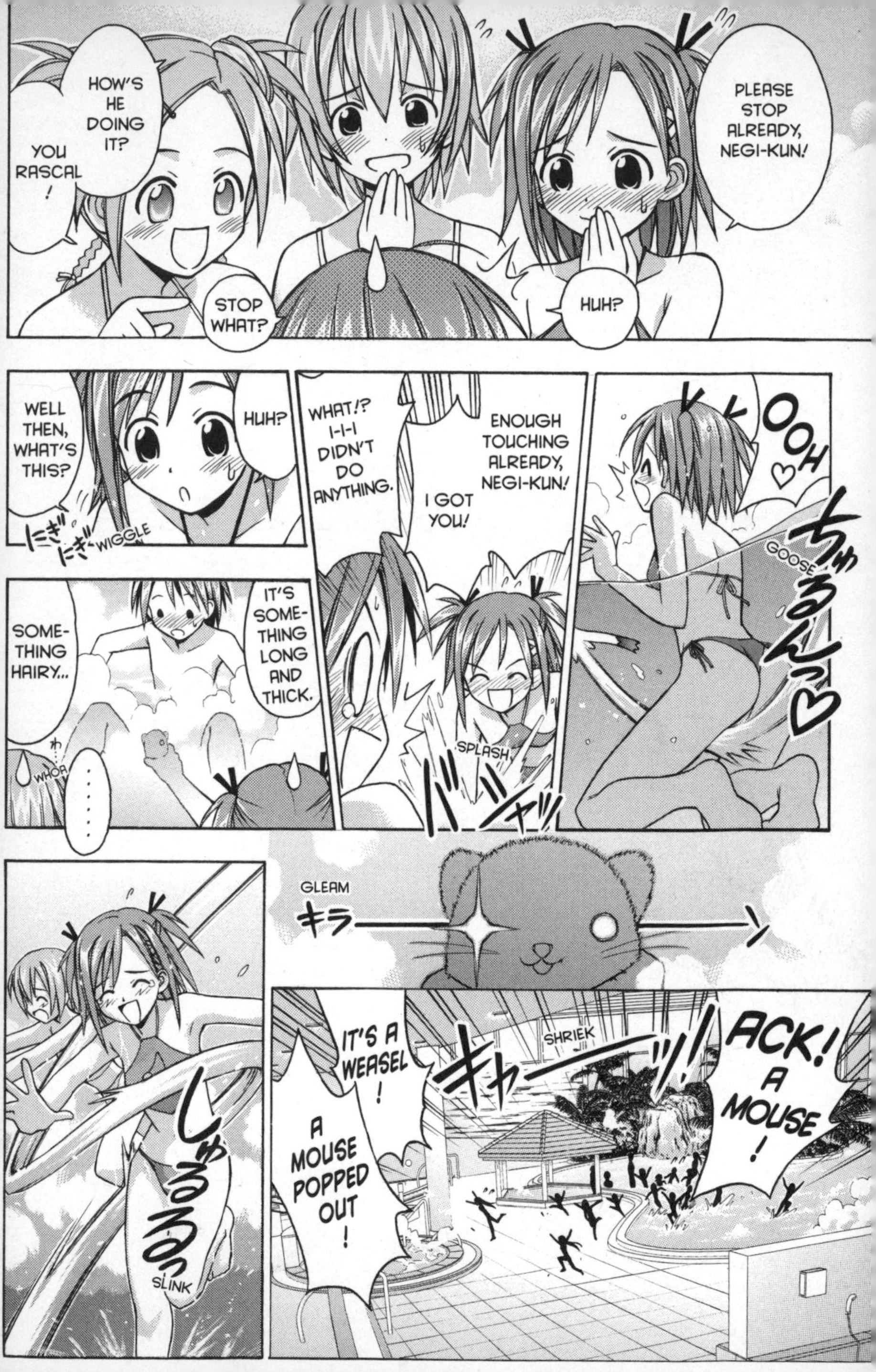
PLEASE STOP ALREADY, NEGI-KUN!
HOW'S HE DOING IT?
YOU RASCAL!
HUH?
STOP WHAT?
OOH ♥
ちゅるんっ♥
GOOSE
ENOUGH TOUCHING ALREADY, NEGI-KUN!
WHAT!? I-I-I DIDN'T DO ANYTHING.
I GOT YOU!
SPLASH
バシャ
HUH?
WELL THEN, WHAT'S THIS?
にぎ にぎ WIGGLE
IT'S SOMETHING LONG AND THICK.
SOMETHING HAIRY...
......
わ WHOA
GLEAM
キラ
ACK! A MOUSE!
SHRIEK
キャーッ!
IT'S A WEASEL!
A MOUSE POPPED OUT!
しゅるるっ
SLINK

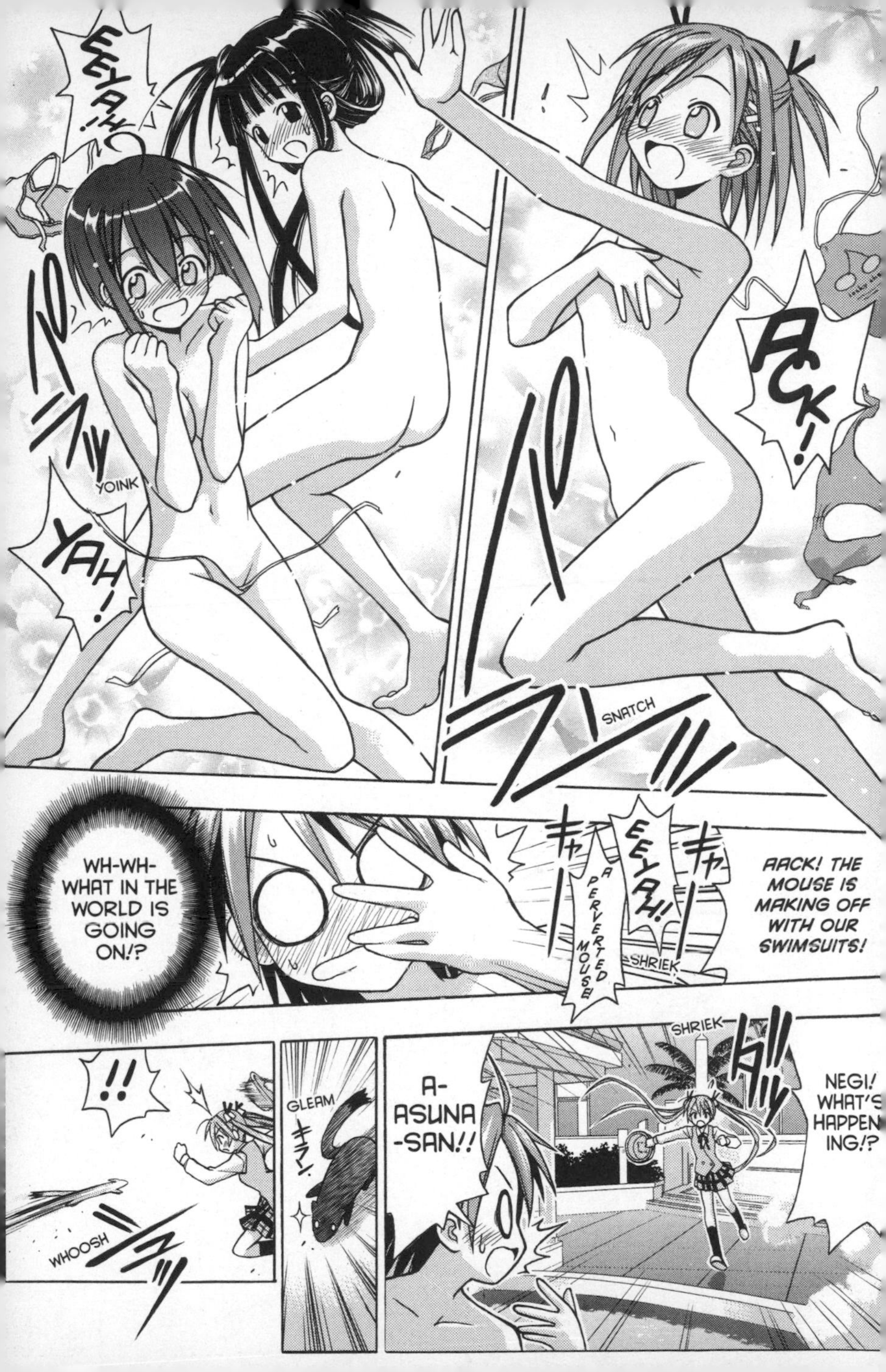
AACK!
EEYAH!!
YOINK
YAH!
SNATCH
AACK! THE MOUSE IS MAKING OFF WITH OUR SWIMSUITS!
EEYAH!!
A PERVERTED MOUSE!!
SHRIEK
WH-WH-WHAT IN THE WORLD IS GOING ON!?
NEGI! WHAT'S HAPPENING!?
SHRIEK
A-ASUNA-SAN!!
GLEAM
!!
WHOOSH

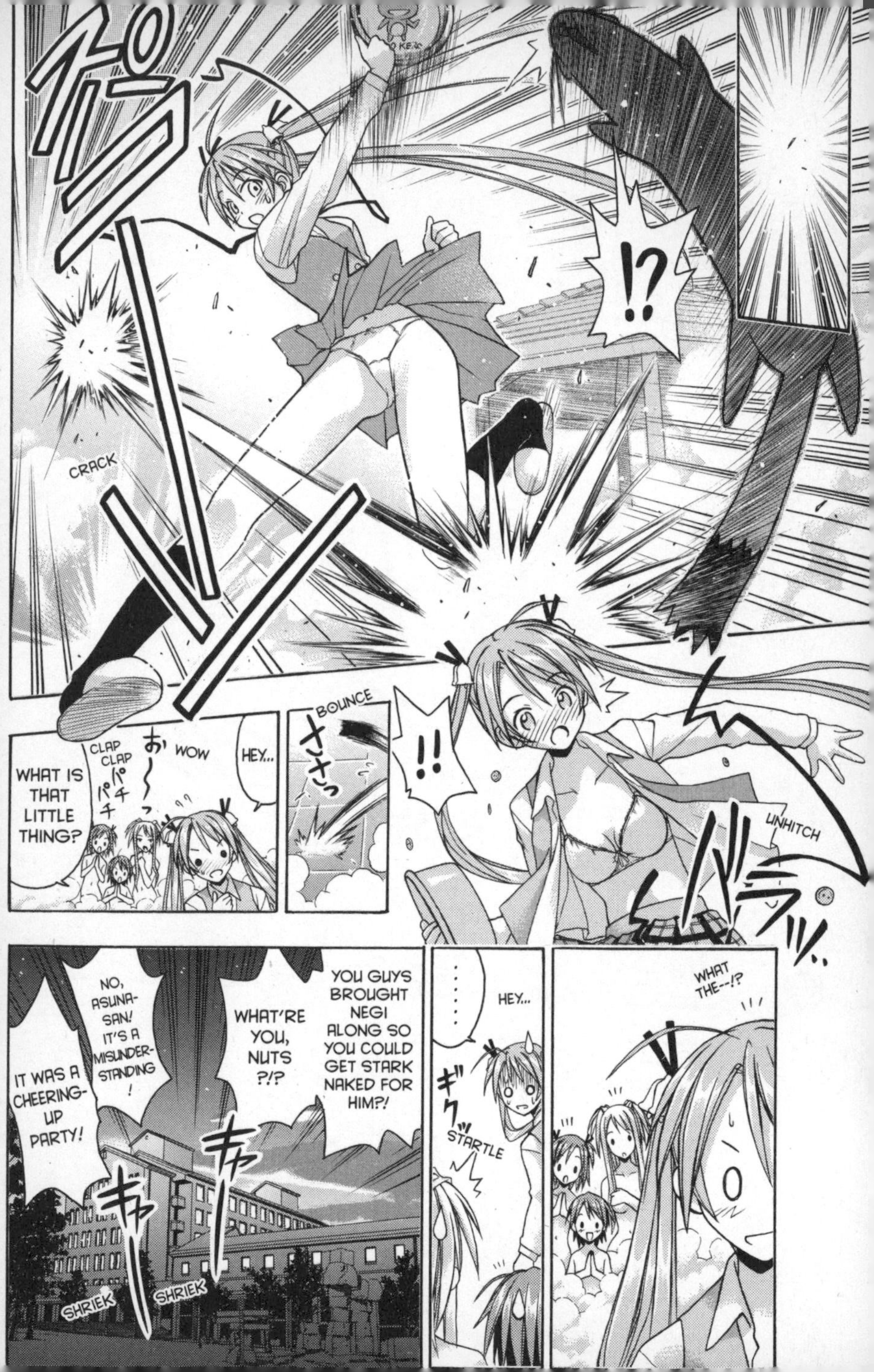
!?
CRACK
!!
UNHITCH
BOUNCE
HEY...
WOW
CLAP CLAP
WHAT IS THAT LITTLE THING?
WHAT THE--!?
......
HEY...
STARTLE
YOU GUYS BROUGHT NEGI ALONG SO YOU COULD GET STARK NAKED FOR HIM?!
WHAT'RE YOU, NUTS?!?
NO, ASUNA-SAN! IT'S A MISUNDERSTANDING!
IT WAS A CHEERING-UP PARTY!
SHRIEK
SHRIEK

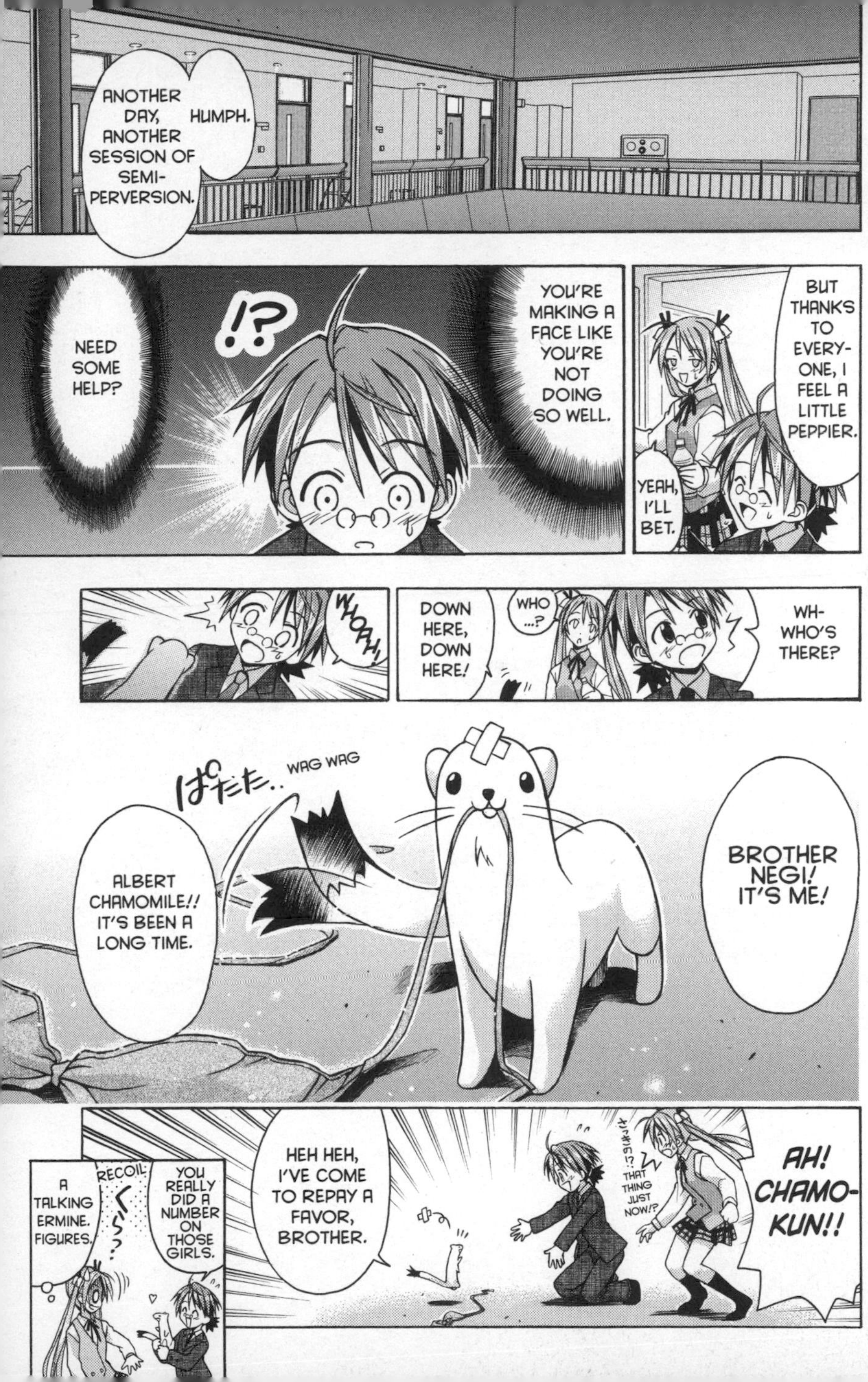
HUMPH.
ANOTHER DAY, ANOTHER SESSION OF SEMI-PERVERSION.
BUT THANKS TO EVERYONE, I FEEL A LITTLE PEPPIER.
YEAH, I'LL BET.
YOU'RE MAKING A FACE LIKE YOU'RE NOT DOING SO WELL.
!?
NEED SOME HELP?
WH-WHO'S THERE?
WHO ...?
DOWN HERE, DOWN HERE!
BROTHER NEGI! IT'S ME!
WAG WAG
ALBERT CHAMOMILE!! IT'S BEEN A LONG TIME.
AH! CHAMO-KUN!!
THAT THING JUST NOW!?
HEH HEH, I'VE COME TO REPAY A FAVOR, BROTHER.
YOU REALLY DID A NUMBER ON THOSE GIRLS.
RECOIL
A TALKING ERMINE. FIGURES.

STUDENT NUMBER 10
CHACHAMARU KARAKURI

ACTIVATED: APRIL 1, 2001
POWERS: SPRING-BASED (JUST AFTER
    COMPLETION AN OUTSIDE POWER SOURCE
    WAS USED)
LIKES: SERVING TEA, HAVING HER SPRINGS WOUND
DISLIKES: NOTHING IN PARTICULAR.
AFFILIATIONS: GO CLUB, TEA CEREMONY CLUB

STUDENT NUMBER 26
EVANGELINE A.K. MCDOWELL

DATE OF BIRTH: UNKNOWN
BLOOD TYPE: UNKNOWN
LIKES: TEA PREPARED BY CHACHAMARU,
    SCENERY OF JAPAN, GO
DISLIKES: GARLIC AND LEEKS, CLASS
AFFILIATIONS: GO CLUB, TEA CEREMONY CLUB

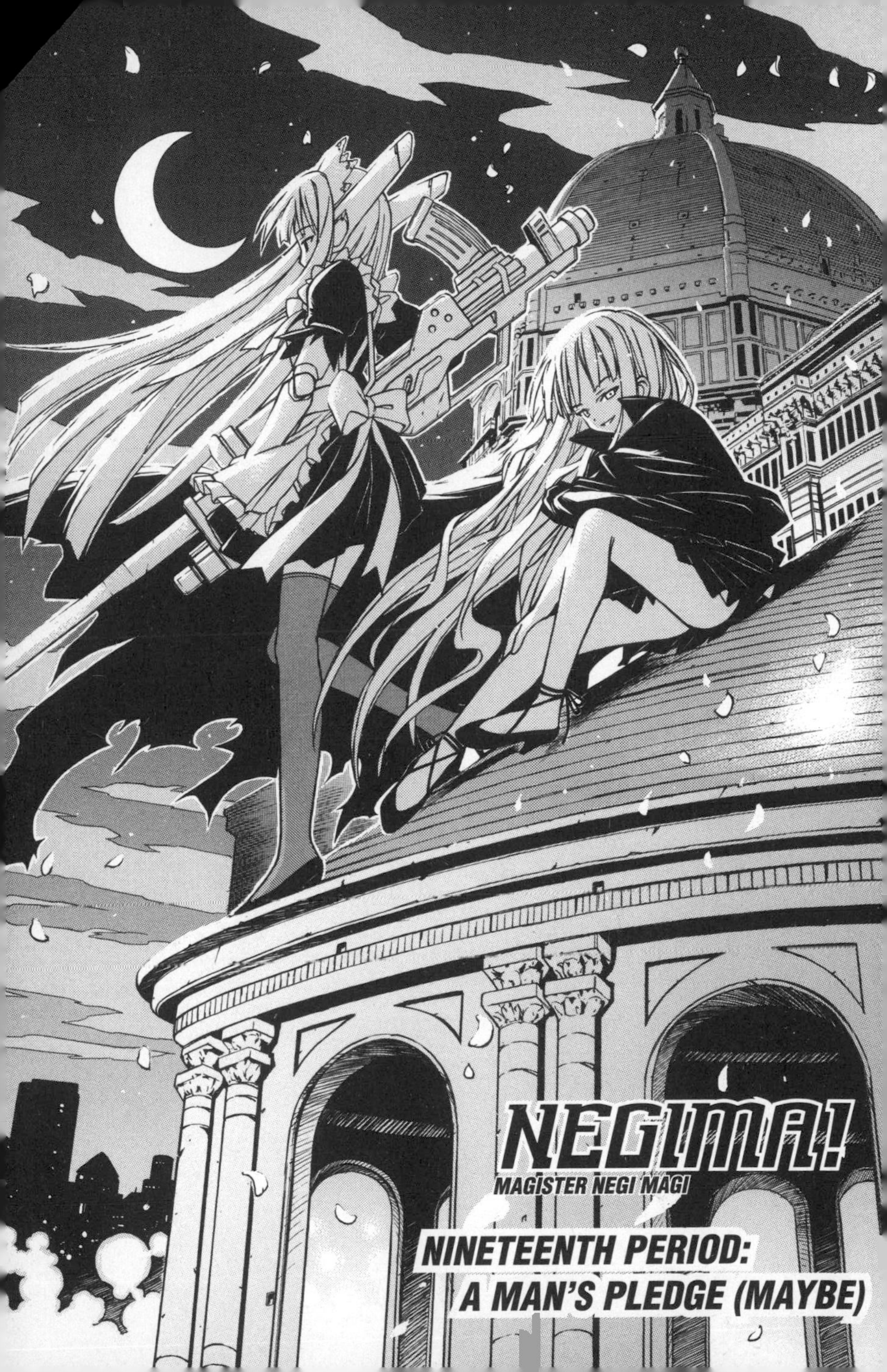
NEGIMA!
MAGISTER NEGI MAGI
NINETEENTH PERIOD:
A MAN'S PLEDGE (MAYBE)

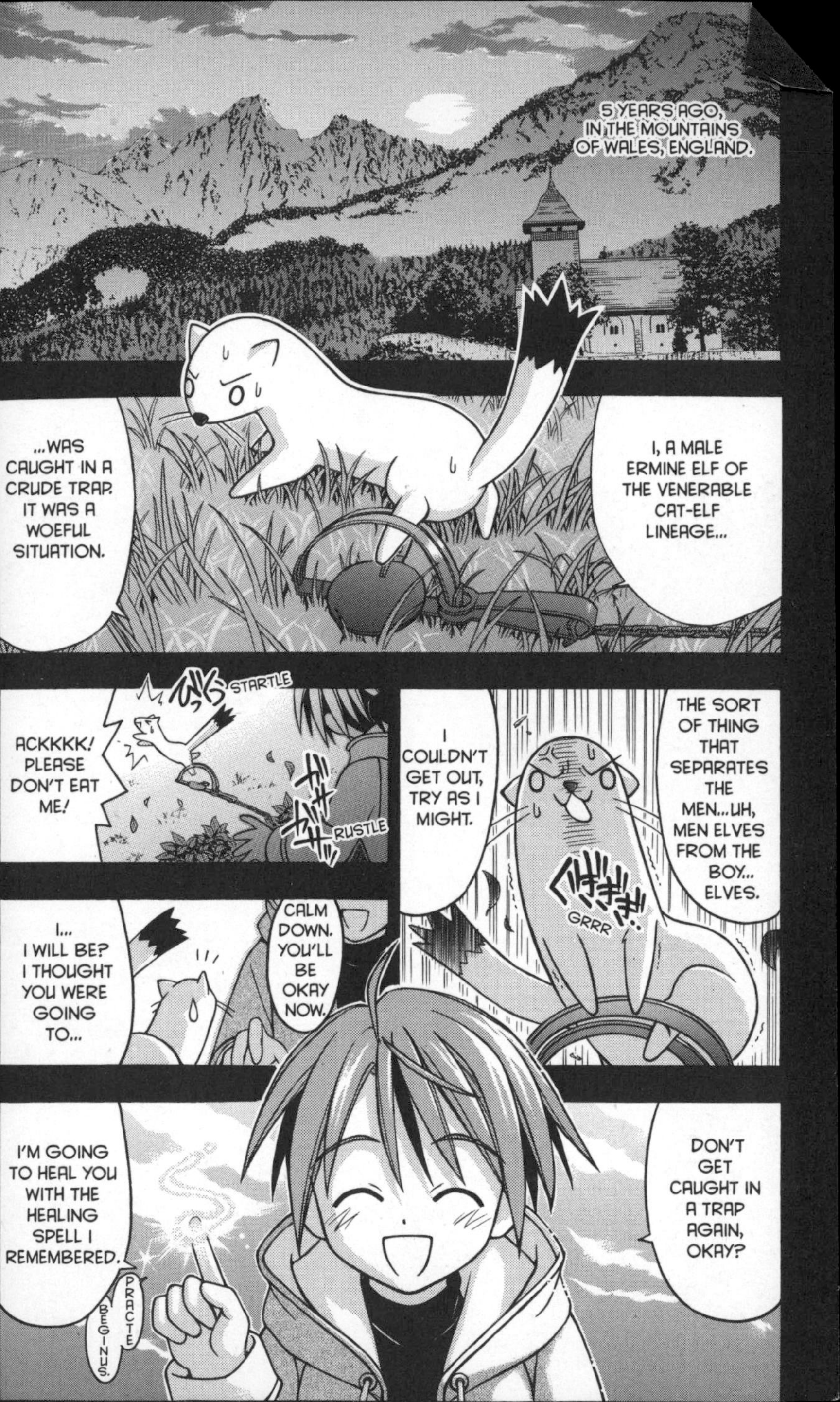
5 YEARS AGO, IN THE MOUNTAINS OF WALES, ENGLAND.
I, A MALE ERMINE ELF OF THE VENERABLE CAT-ELF LINEAGE...
...WAS CAUGHT IN A CRUDE TRAP. IT WAS A WOEFUL SITUATION.
THE SORT OF THING THAT SEPARATES THE MEN...UH, MEN ELVES FROM THE BOY... ELVES.
I COULDN'T GET OUT, TRY AS I MIGHT.
GRRR
STARTLE
RUSTLE
ACKKKK! PLEASE DON'T EAT ME!
CALM DOWN. YOU'LL BE OKAY NOW.
I... I WILL BE? I THOUGHT YOU WERE GOING TO...
DON'T GET CAUGHT IN A TRAP AGAIN, OKAY?
I'M GOING TO HEAL YOU WITH THE HEALING SPELL I REMEMBERED.
PRACTE BEGINUS.

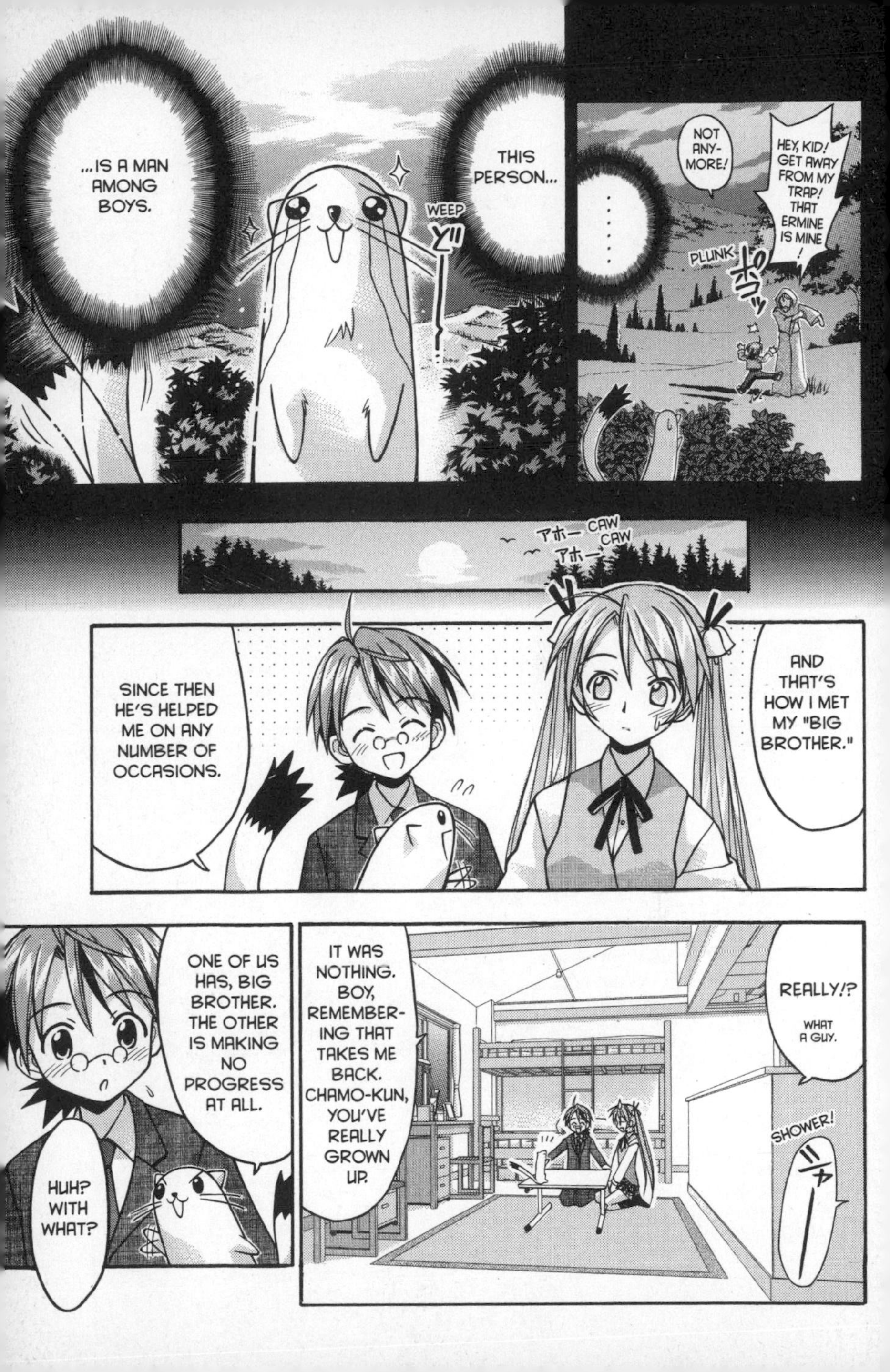

HEY, KID! GET AWAY FROM MY TRAP! THAT ERMINE IS MINE!
NOT ANY-MORE!
PLUNK
ポコッ
......
THIS PERSON...
WEEP
...IS A MAN AMONG BOYS.
アホー CAW
アホー CAW
AND THAT'S HOW I MET MY "BIG BROTHER."
SINCE THEN HE'S HELPED ME ON ANY NUMBER OF OCCASIONS.
REALLY!?
WHAT A GUY.
SHOWER!
IT WAS NOTHING. BOY, REMEMBER-ING THAT TAKES ME BACK. CHAMO-KUN, YOU'VE REALLY GROWN UP.
ONE OF US HAS, BIG BROTHER. THE OTHER IS MAKING NO PROGRESS AT ALL.
HUH? WITH WHAT?

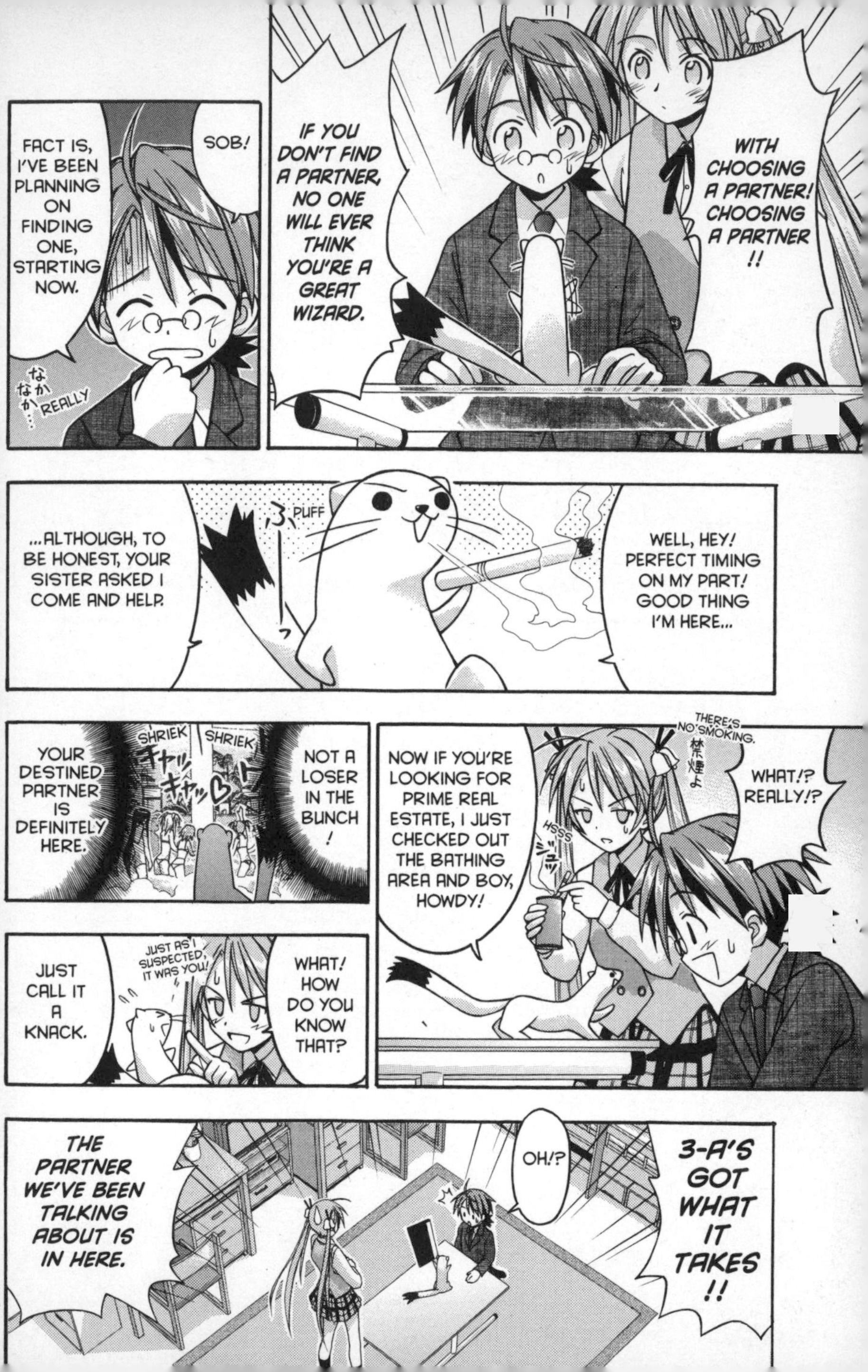
WITH CHOOSING A PARTNER! CHOOSING A PARTNER !!
IF YOU DON'T FIND A PARTNER, NO ONE WILL EVER THINK YOU'RE A GREAT WIZARD.
SOB!
FACT IS, I'VE BEEN PLANNING ON FINDING ONE, STARTING NOW.
なかなか… REALLY
WELL, HEY! PERFECT TIMING ON MY PART! GOOD THING I'M HERE...
PUFF
...ALTHOUGH, TO BE HONEST, YOUR SISTER ASKED I COME AND HELP.
WHAT!? REALLY!?
THERE'S NO SMOKING.
禁煙よ
HSSS
NOW IF YOU'RE LOOKING FOR PRIME REAL ESTATE, I JUST CHECKED OUT THE BATHING AREA AND BOY, HOWDY!
NOT A LOSER IN THE BUNCH!
SHRIEK
SHRIEK
YOUR DESTINED PARTNER IS DEFINITELY HERE.
WHAT! HOW DO YOU KNOW THAT?
JUST AS I SUSPECTED, IT WAS YOU!
JUST CALL IT A KNACK.
3-A'S GOT WHAT IT TAKES !!
OH!?
THE PARTNER WE'VE BEEN TALKING ABOUT IS IN HERE.

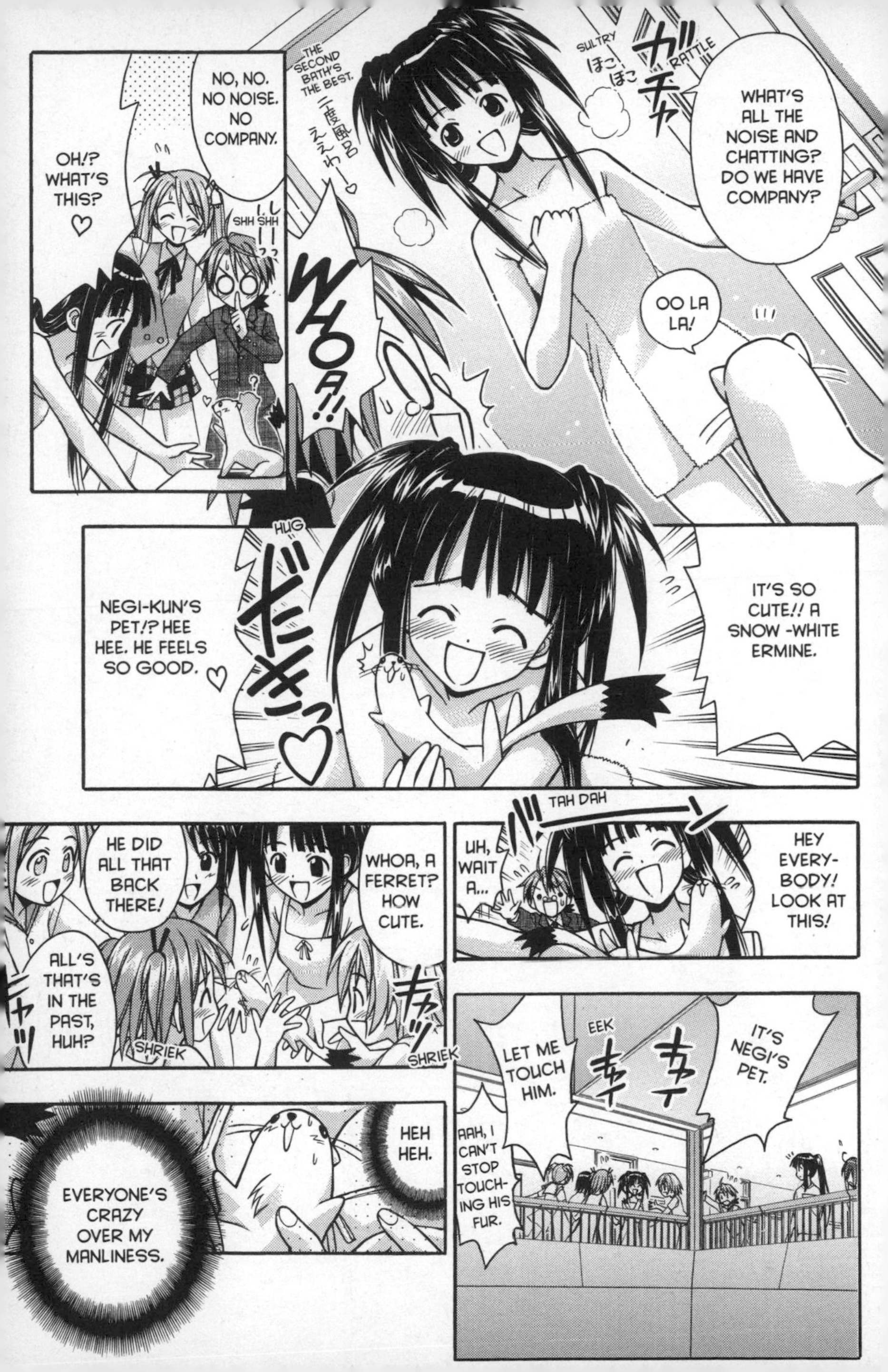
SULTRY
ほこ ほこ
RATTLE
WHAT'S ALL THE NOISE AND CHATTING? DO WE HAVE COMPANY?
THE SECOND BATH'S THE BEST.
二度風呂ええわ～♡
OO LA LA!
WHOA!!
NO, NO. NO NOISE. NO COMPANY.
OH!? WHAT'S THIS? ♡
SHH SHH
IT'S SO CUTE!! A SNOW -WHITE ERMINE.
HUG
NEGI-KUN'S PET!? HEE HEE. HE FEELS SO GOOD. ♡
HEY EVERY-BODY! LOOK AT THIS!
TAH DAH
UH, WAIT A...
WHOA, A FERRET? HOW CUTE.
HE DID ALL THAT BACK THERE!
ALL'S THAT'S IN THE PAST, HUH?
SHRIEK
SHRIEK
IT'S NEGI'S PET.
EEK
LET ME TOUCH HIM.
AAH, I CAN'T STOP TOUCHING HIS FUR.
HEH HEH.
EVERYONE'S CRAZY OVER MY MANLINESS.

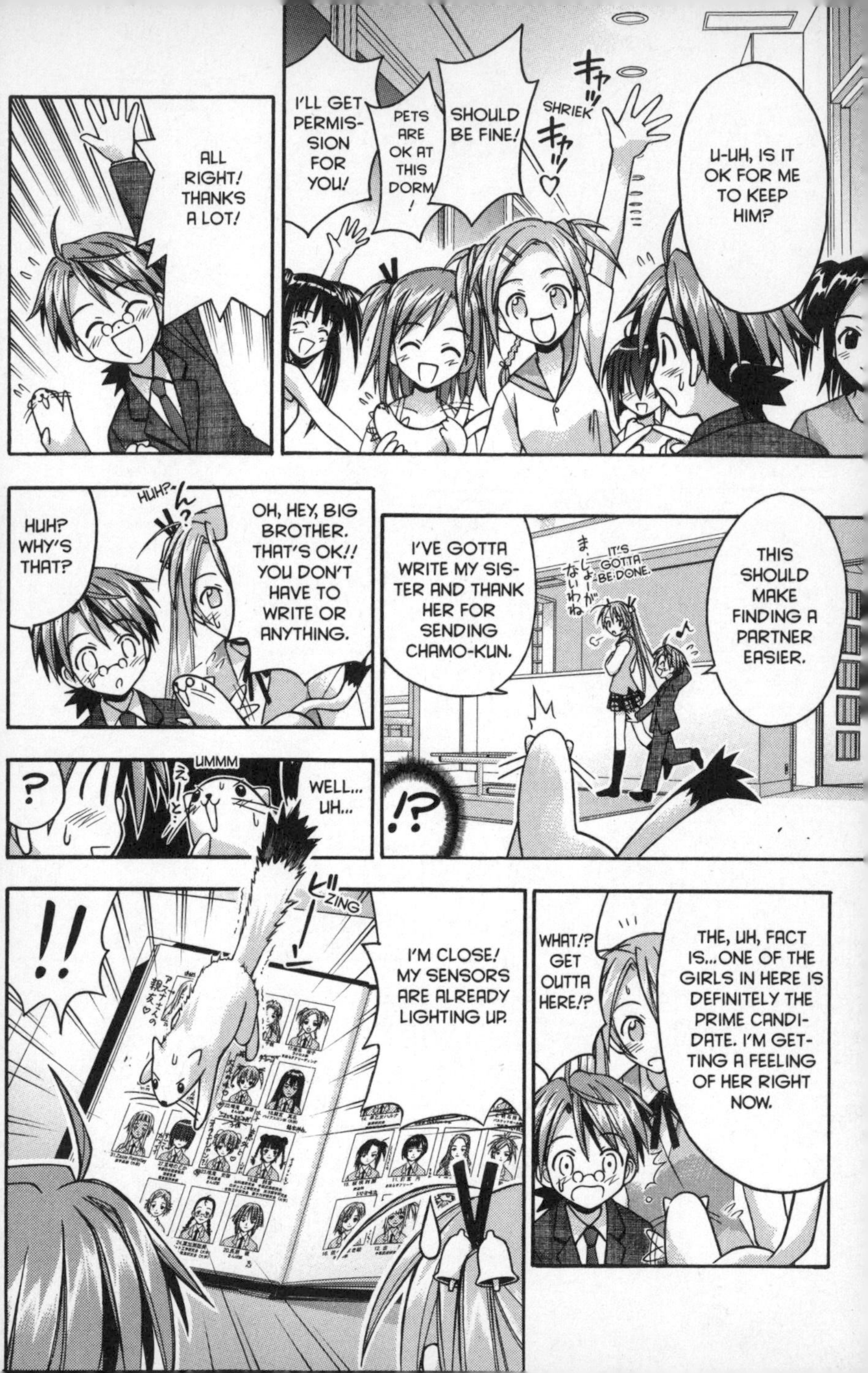
U-UH, IS IT OK FOR ME TO KEEP HIM?
キャッ
SHRIEK
キャッ
SHOULD BE FINE!
PETS ARE OK AT THIS DORM!
I'LL GET PERMISSION FOR YOU!
ALL RIGHT! THANKS A LOT!
THIS SHOULD MAKE FINDING A PARTNER EASIER.
ま、しょーがないわね
IT'S GOTTA BE DONE.
I'VE GOTTA WRITE MY SISTER AND THANK HER FOR SENDING CHAMO-KUN.
!?
OH, HEY, BIG BROTHER. THAT'S OK!! YOU DON'T HAVE TO WRITE OR ANYTHING.
ん?
HUH?
HUH? WHY'S THAT?
WELL... UH...
えーと
UMMM
?
THE, UH, FACT IS...ONE OF THE GIRLS IN HERE IS DEFINITELY THE PRIME CANDIDATE. I'M GETTING A FEELING OF HER RIGHT NOW.
WHAT!? GET OUTTA HERE!?
I'M CLOSE! MY SENSORS ARE ALREADY LIGHTING UP.
ビッ
ZING
!!

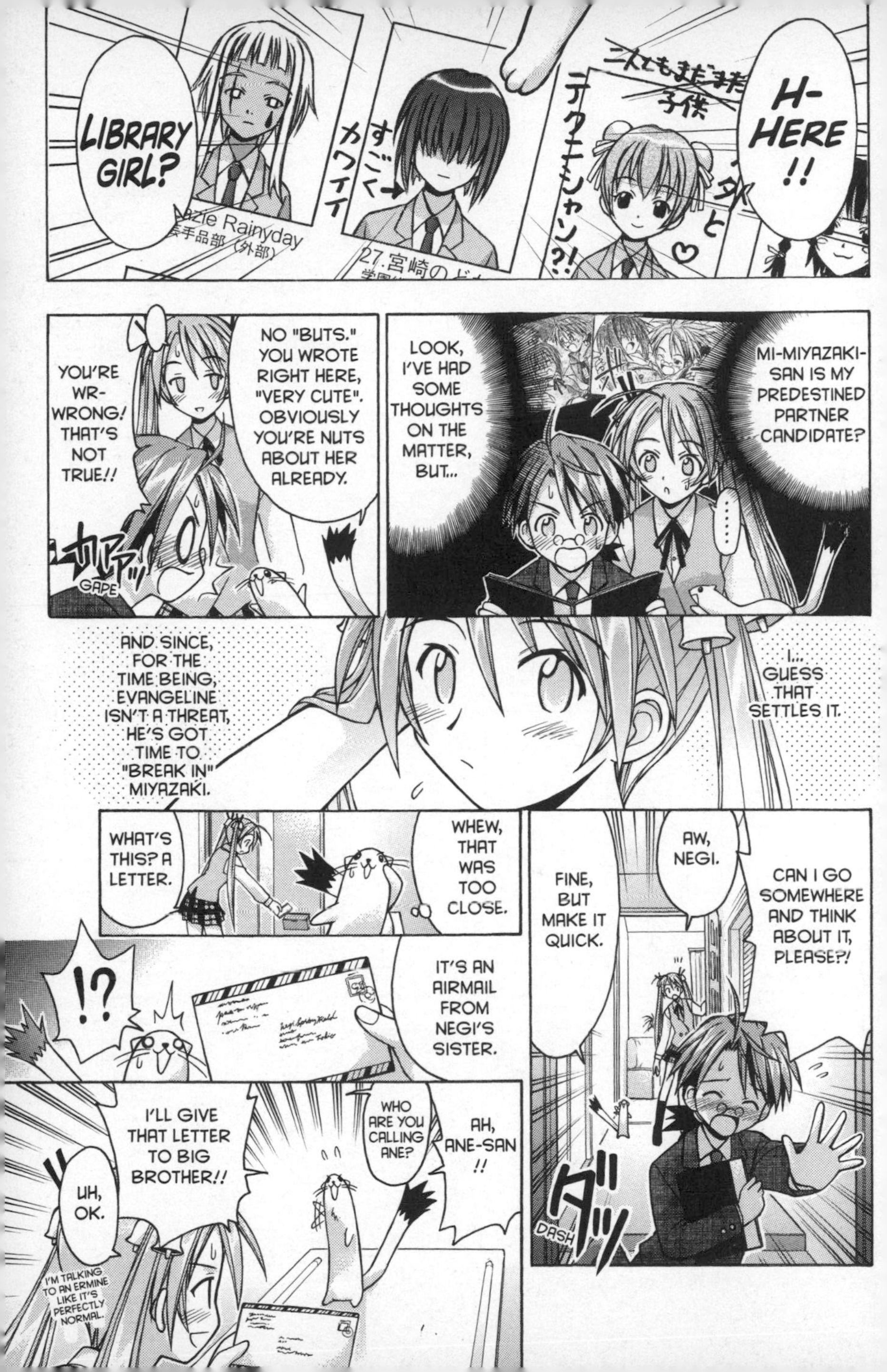
H-HERE!!
テクニシャン?!
すごくカワイイ
LIBRARY GIRL?
MI-MIYAZAKI-SAN IS MY PREDESTINED PARTNER CANDIDATE?
LOOK, I'VE HAD SOME THOUGHTS ON THE MATTER, BUT...
......
NO "BUTS." YOU WROTE RIGHT HERE, "VERY CUTE". OBVIOUSLY YOU'RE NUTS ABOUT HER ALREADY.
YOU'RE WR-WRONG! THAT'S NOT TRUE!!
GAPE
I... GUESS THAT SETTLES IT.
AND SINCE, FOR THE TIME BEING, EVANGELINE ISN'T A THREAT, HE'S GOT TIME TO "BREAK IN" MIYAZAKI.
AW, NEGI.
CAN I GO SOMEWHERE AND THINK ABOUT IT, PLEASE?!
FINE, BUT MAKE IT QUICK.
DASH
WHEW, THAT WAS TOO CLOSE.
WHAT'S THIS? A LETTER.
IT'S AN AIRMAIL FROM NEGI'S SISTER.
!?
AH, ANE-SAN!!
WHO ARE YOU CALLING ANE?
I'LL GIVE THAT LETTER TO BIG BROTHER!!
UH, OK.
I'M TALKING TO AN ERMINE LIKE IT'S PERFECTLY NORMAL.

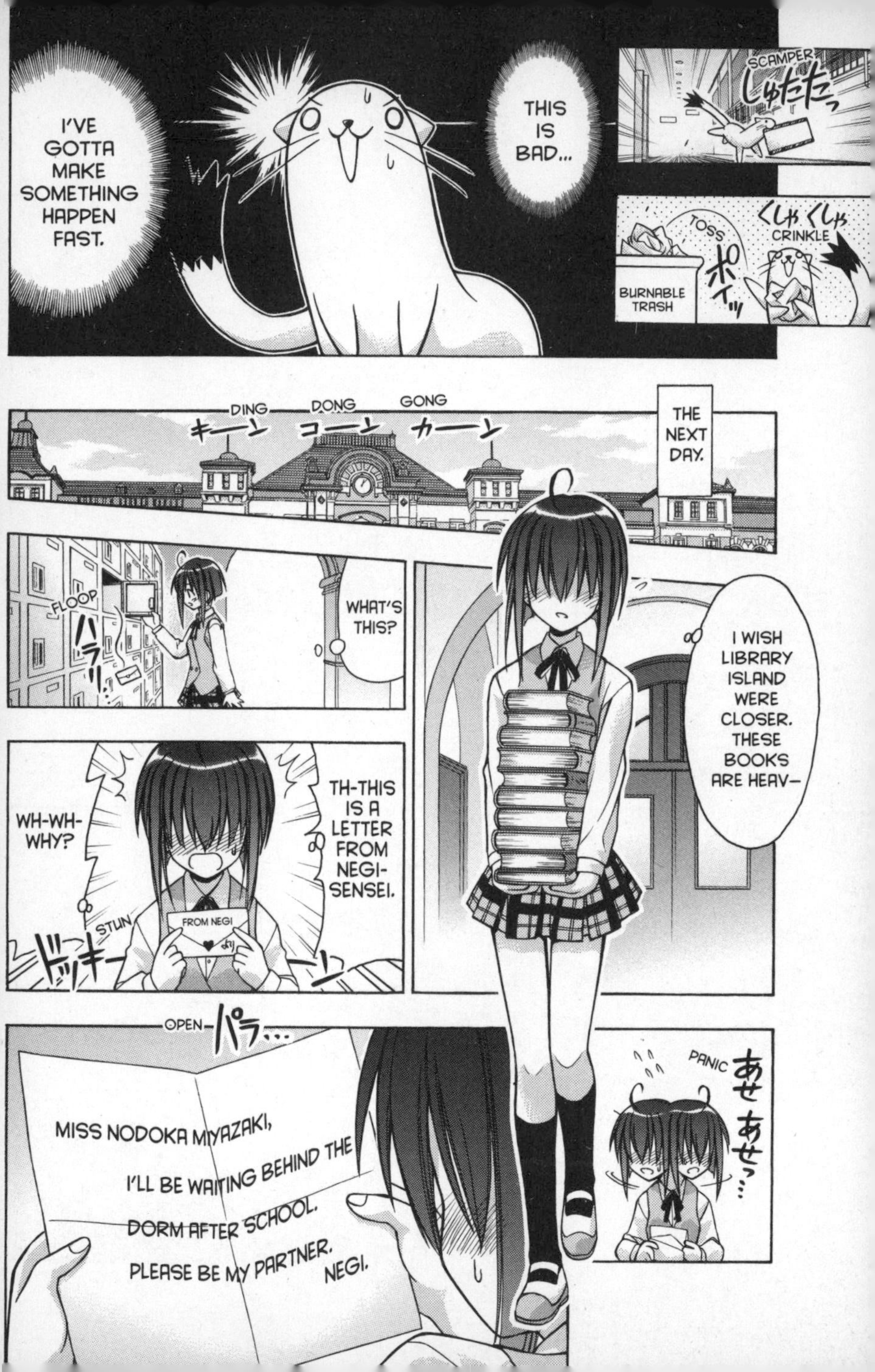
SCAMPER
しゅたたっ
くしゃくしゃ
CRINKLE
TOSS
ポイッ
BURNABLE TRASH
THIS IS BAD...
I'VE GOTTA MAKE SOMETHING HAPPEN FAST.
THE NEXT DAY.
GONG
カーン
DONG
コーン
DING
キーン
I WISH LIBRARY ISLAND WERE CLOSER. THESE BOOKS ARE HEAV—
WHAT'S THIS?
FLOOP
パラリ...
TH-THIS IS A LETTER FROM NEGI-SENSEI.
WH-WH-WHY?
FROM NEGI
STUN
ドッキーン
PANIC
あせあせっ...
OPEN
パラ...
MISS NODOKA MIYAZAKI,
I'LL BE WAITING BEHIND THE DORM AFTER SCHOOL.
PLEASE BE MY PARTNER.
NEGI.

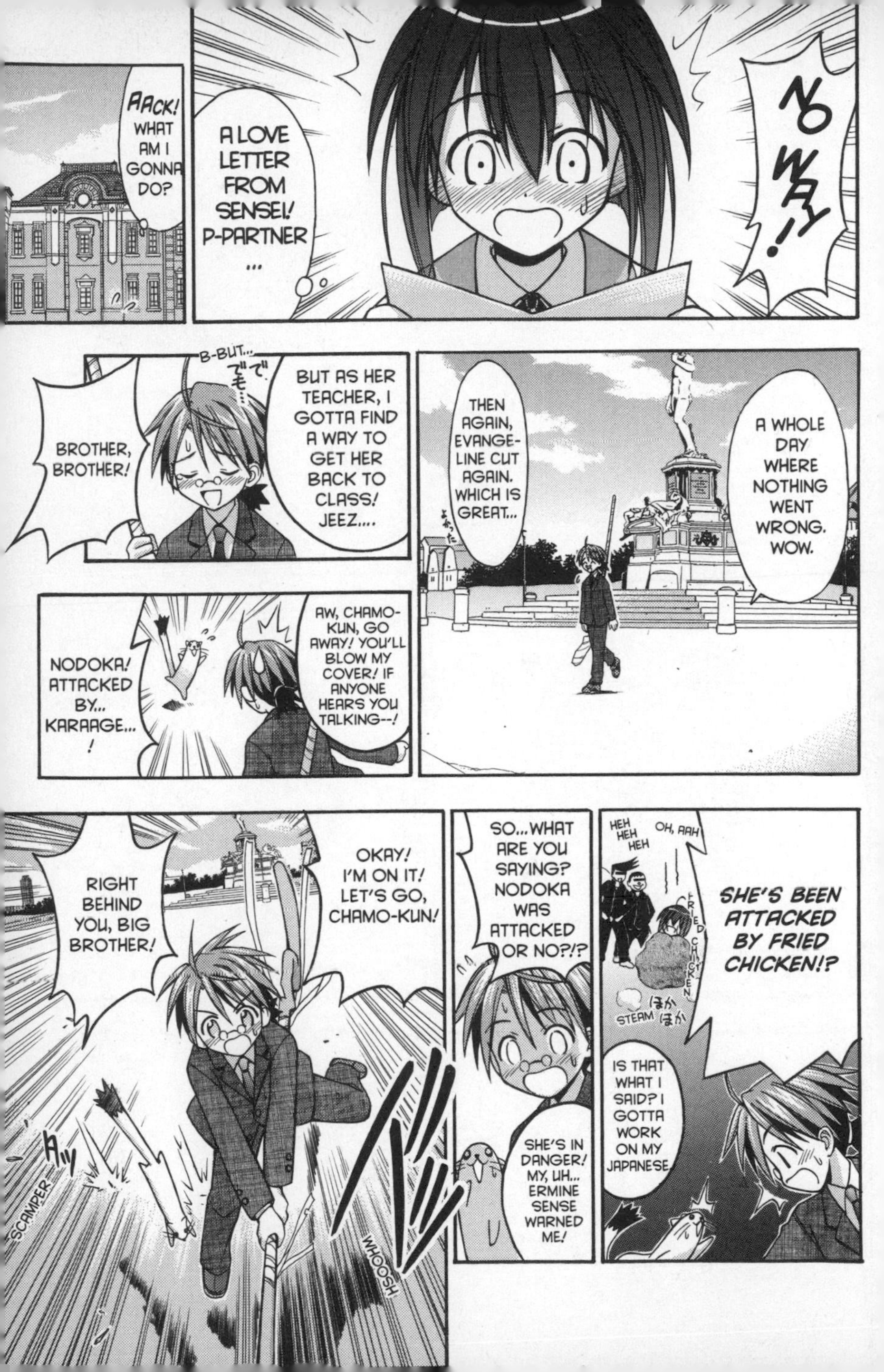
NO WAY!!
A LOVE LETTER FROM SENSEI! P-PARTNER ...
AACK! WHAT AM I GONNA DO?
A WHOLE DAY WHERE NOTHING WENT WRONG. WOW.
THEN AGAIN, EVANGELINE CUT AGAIN. WHICH IS GREAT...
よかった
BUT AS HER TEACHER, I GOTTA FIND A WAY TO GET HER BACK TO CLASS! JEEZ....
B-BUT... でもでも…
BROTHER, BROTHER!
AW, CHAMO-KUN, GO AWAY! YOU'LL BLOW MY COVER! IF ANYONE HEARS YOU TALKING--!
NODOKA! ATTACKED BY... KARAAGE...!
HEH HEH HEH
OH, AAH
SHE'S BEEN ATTACKED BY FRIED CHICKEN!?
FRIED CHICKEN
ほかほか
STEAM
IS THAT WHAT I SAID? I GOTTA WORK ON MY JAPANESE.
SO...WHAT ARE YOU SAYING? NODOKA WAS ATTACKED OR NO?!?
SHE'S IN DANGER! MY, UH... ERMINE SENSE WARNED ME!
OKAY! I'M ON IT! LET'S GO, CHAMO-KUN!
RIGHT BEHIND YOU, BIG BROTHER!
SCAMPER
WHOOSH

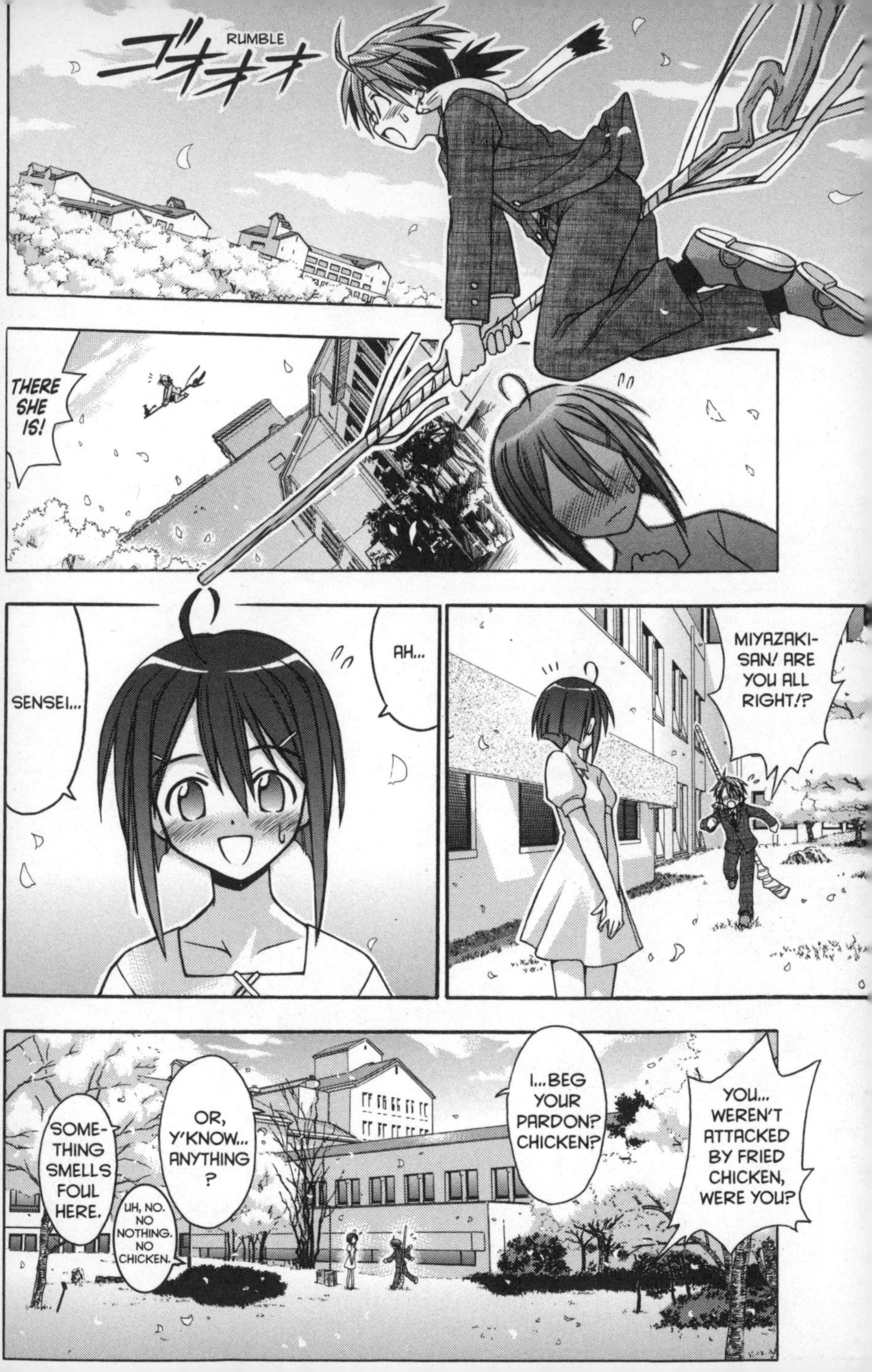
RUMBLE
THERE SHE IS!
MIYAZAKI-SAN! ARE YOU ALL RIGHT!?
AH...
SENSEI...
YOU... WEREN'T ATTACKED BY FRIED CHICKEN, WERE YOU?
I...BEG YOUR PARDON? CHICKEN?
OR, Y'KNOW... ANYTHING?
SOME-THING SMELLS FOUL HERE.
UH, NO. NO NOTHING. NO CHICKEN.

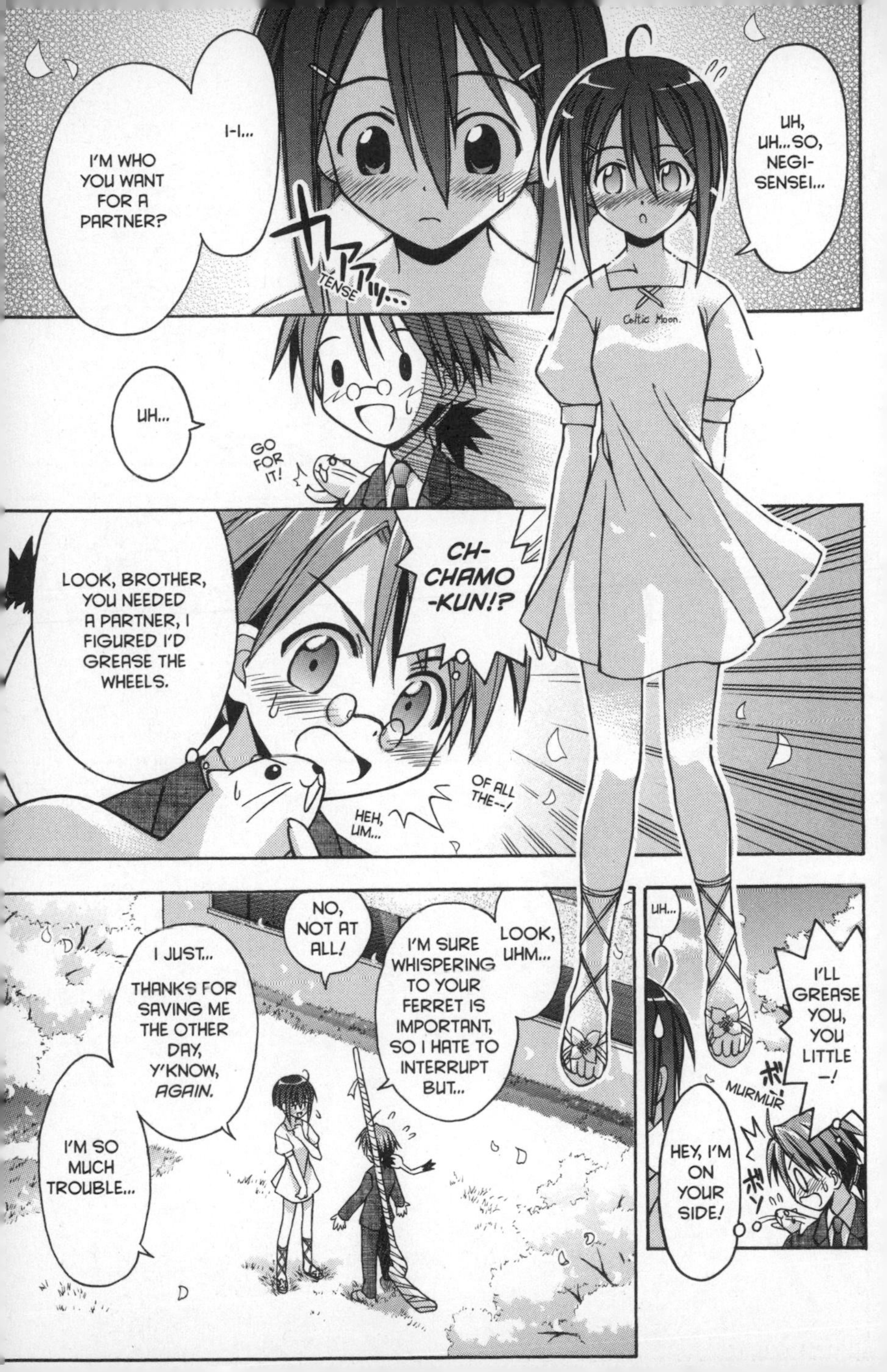
UH, UH...SO, NEGI-SENSEI...
I-I...
I'M WHO YOU WANT FOR A PARTNER?
TENSE
Celtic Moon.
UH...
GO FOR IT!
CH-CHAMO-KUN!?
LOOK, BROTHER, YOU NEEDED A PARTNER, I FIGURED I'D GREASE THE WHEELS.
OF ALL THE--!
HEH, UM...
UH...
I'LL GREASE YOU, YOU LITTLE--!
MURMUR
HEY, I'M ON YOUR SIDE!
LOOK, UHM...
I'M SURE WHISPERING TO YOUR FERRET IS IMPORTANT, SO I HATE TO INTERRUPT BUT...
NO, NOT AT ALL!
I JUST...
THANKS FOR SAVING ME THE OTHER DAY, Y'KNOW, *AGAIN*.
I'M SO MUCH TROUBLE...

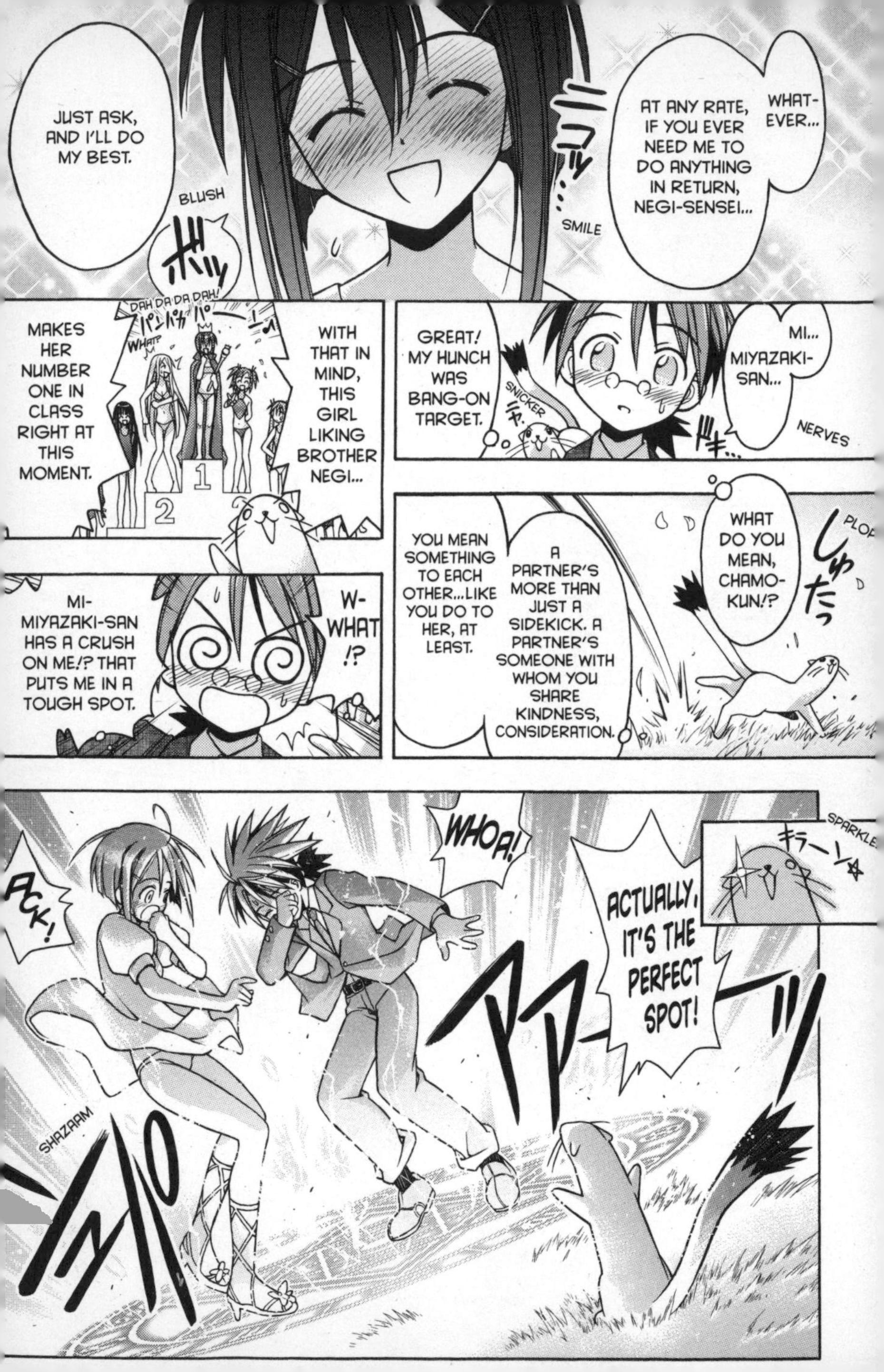
WHAT-EVER...
AT ANY RATE, IF YOU EVER NEED ME TO DO ANYTHING IN RETURN, NEGI-SENSEI...
SMILE
JUST ASK, AND I'LL DO MY BEST.
BLUSH
MI... MIYAZAKI-SAN...
NERVES
GREAT! MY HUNCH WAS BANG-ON TARGET.
SNICKER
WITH THAT IN MIND, THIS GIRL LIKING BROTHER NEGI...
DAH DA DA DAH!
WHAT!?
MAKES HER NUMBER ONE IN CLASS RIGHT AT THIS MOMENT.
PLOP
WHAT DO YOU MEAN, CHAMO-KUN!?
A PARTNER'S MORE THAN JUST A SIDEKICK. A PARTNER'S SOMEONE WITH WHOM YOU SHARE KINDNESS, CONSIDERATION.
YOU MEAN SOMETHING TO EACH OTHER...LIKE YOU DO TO HER, AT LEAST.
W-WHAT!?
MI-MIYAZAKI-SAN HAS A CRUSH ON ME!? THAT PUTS ME IN A TOUGH SPOT.
SPARKLE
ACTUALLY, IT'S THE PERFECT SPOT!
WHOA!
ACK!
SHAZAAM

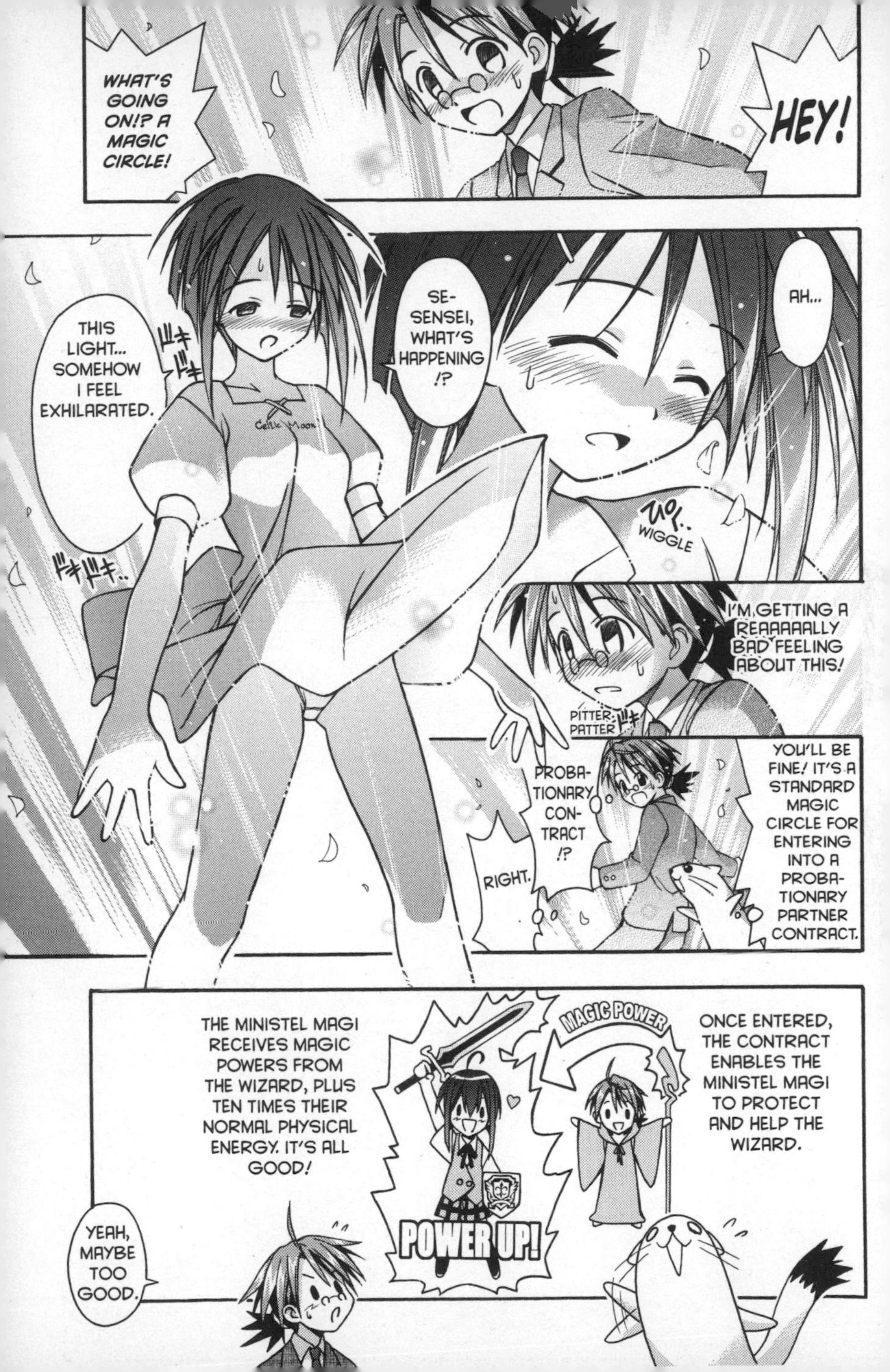
HEY!
WHAT'S GOING ON!? A MAGIC CIRCLE!
AH...
WIGGLE
SE-SENSEI, WHAT'S HAPPENING!?
THIS LIGHT... SOMEHOW I FEEL EXHILARATED.
ドキドキ
ドキドキ..
I'M GETTING A REAAAAALLY BAD FEELING ABOUT THIS!
PITTER-PATTER ドキ
YOU'LL BE FINE! IT'S A STANDARD MAGIC CIRCLE FOR ENTERING INTO A PROBATIONARY PARTNER CONTRACT.
PROBATIONARY CONTRACT!?
RIGHT.
ONCE ENTERED, THE CONTRACT ENABLES THE MINISTEL MAGI TO PROTECT AND HELP THE WIZARD.
MAGIC POWER
THE MINISTEL MAGI RECEIVES MAGIC POWERS FROM THE WIZARD, PLUS TEN TIMES THEIR NORMAL PHYSICAL ENERGY. IT'S ALL GOOD!
POWER UP!
YEAH, MAYBE TOO GOOD.

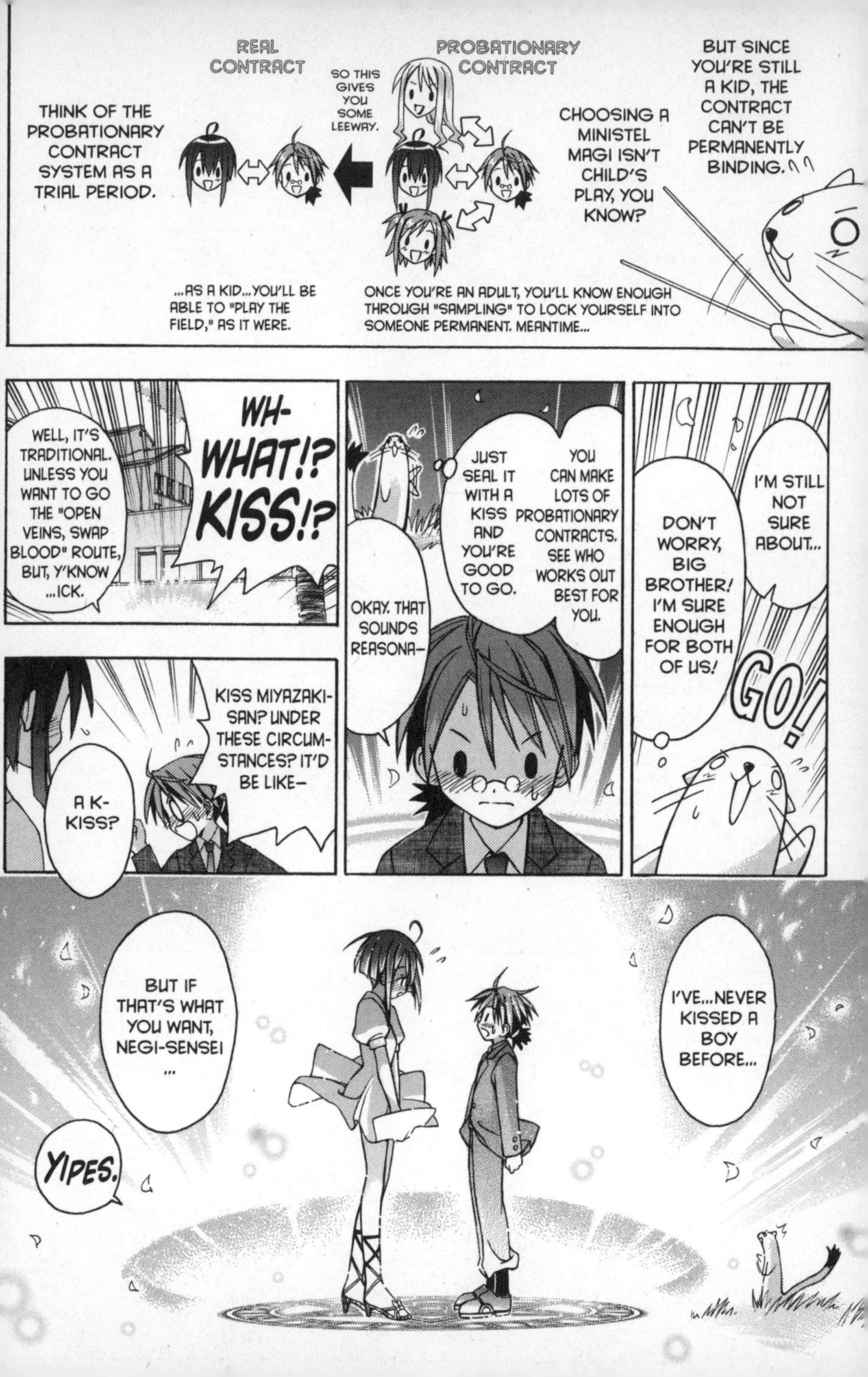
BUT SINCE YOU'RE STILL A KID, THE CONTRACT CAN'T BE PERMANENTLY BINDING.
CHOOSING A MINISTEL MAGI ISN'T CHILD'S PLAY, YOU KNOW?
PROBATIONARY CONTRACT
SO THIS GIVES YOU SOME LEEWAY.
REAL CONTRACT
THINK OF THE PROBATIONARY CONTRACT SYSTEM AS A TRIAL PERIOD.
ONCE YOU'RE AN ADULT, YOU'LL KNOW ENOUGH THROUGH "SAMPLING" TO LOCK YOURSELF INTO SOMEONE PERMANENT. MEANTIME...
...AS A KID...YOU'LL BE ABLE TO "PLAY THE FIELD," AS IT WERE.
I'M STILL NOT SURE ABOUT...
DON'T WORRY, BIG BROTHER! I'M SURE ENOUGH FOR BOTH OF US!
GO!
YOU CAN MAKE LOTS OF PROBATIONARY CONTRACTS. SEE WHO WORKS OUT BEST FOR YOU.
JUST SEAL IT WITH A KISS AND YOU'RE GOOD TO GO.
OKAY. THAT SOUNDS REASONA–
WH-WHAT!? KISS!?
WELL, IT'S TRADITIONAL. UNLESS YOU WANT TO GO THE "OPEN VEINS, SWAP BLOOD" ROUTE, BUT, Y'KNOW ...ICK.
KISS MIYAZAKI-SAN? UNDER THESE CIRCUMSTANCES? IT'D BE LIKE–
A K-KISS?
I'VE...NEVER KISSED A BOY BEFORE...
BUT IF THAT'S WHAT YOU WANT, NEGI-SENSEI ...
YIPES.

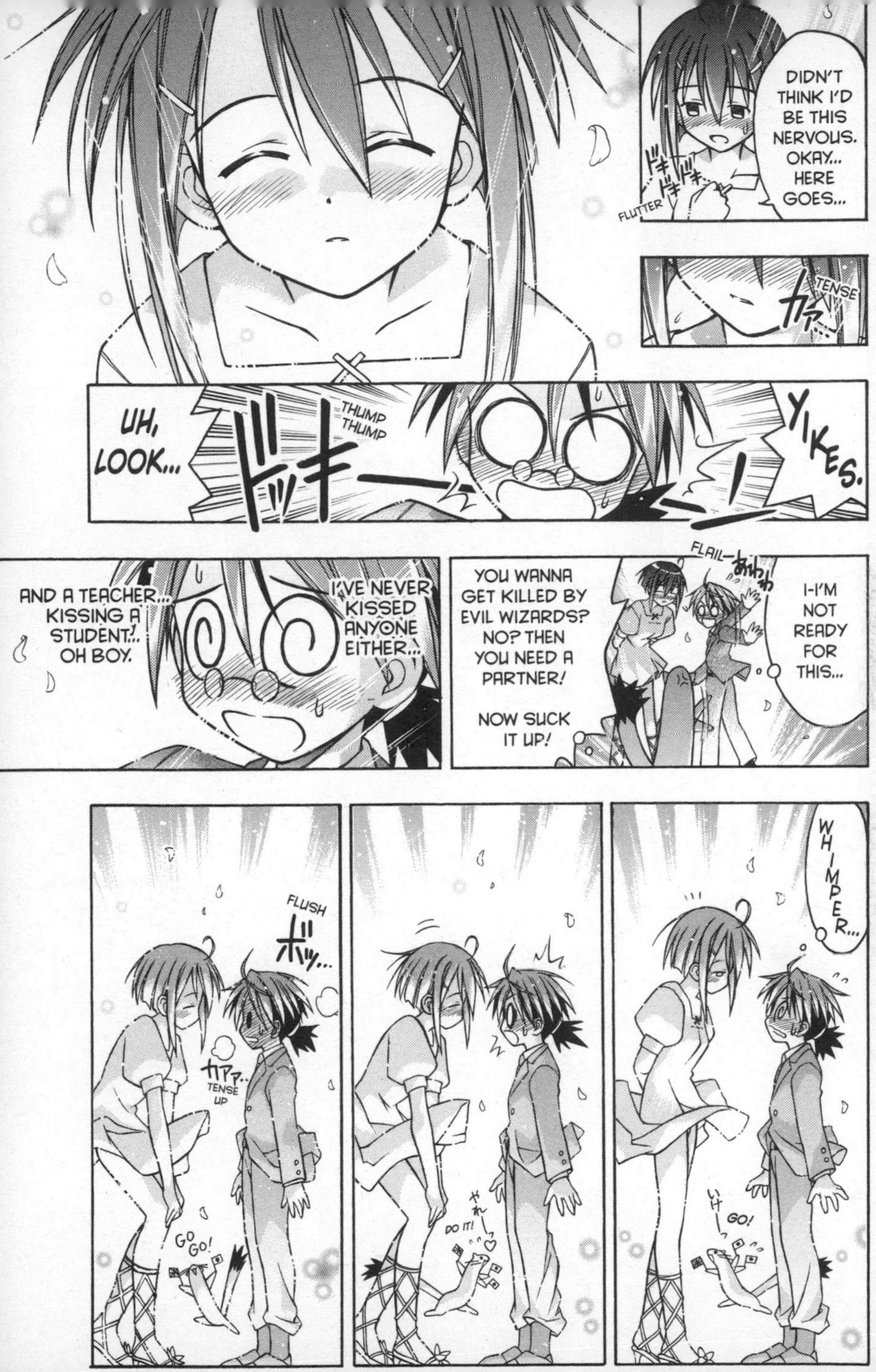

DIDN'T THINK I'D BE THIS NERVOUS. OKAY... HERE GOES...
FLUTTER
TENSE
YIKES.
THUMP THUMP
UH, LOOK...
I-I'M NOT READY FOR THIS...
FLAIL
YOU WANNA GET KILLED BY EVIL WIZARDS? NO? THEN YOU NEED A PARTNER!
NOW SUCK IT UP!
I'VE NEVER KISSED ANYONE EITHER...
AND A TEACHER... KISSING A STUDENT?... OH BOY.
WHIMPER...
GO!
DO IT!
FLUSH
TENSE UP
GO GO!

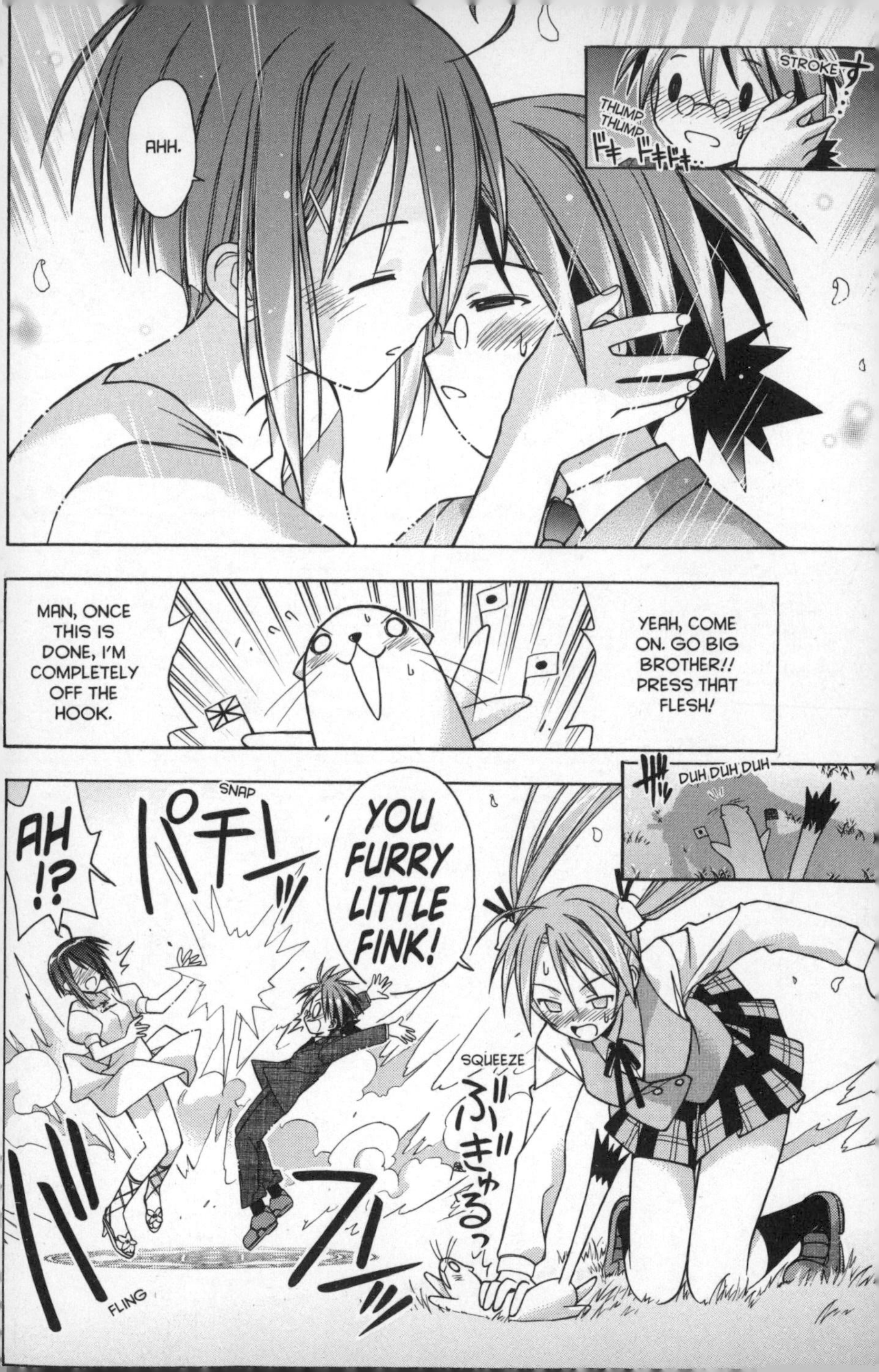
STROKE す
THUMP THUMP ドキ ドキドキ..
AHH.
YEAH, COME ON. GO BIG BROTHER!! PRESS THAT FLESH!
MAN, ONCE THIS IS DONE, I'M COMPLETELY OFF THE HOOK.
DUH DUH DUH
YOU FURRY LITTLE FINK!
SQUEEZE ぶぎゅるっ
SNAP パチーッ
AH !?
FLING ドフッ

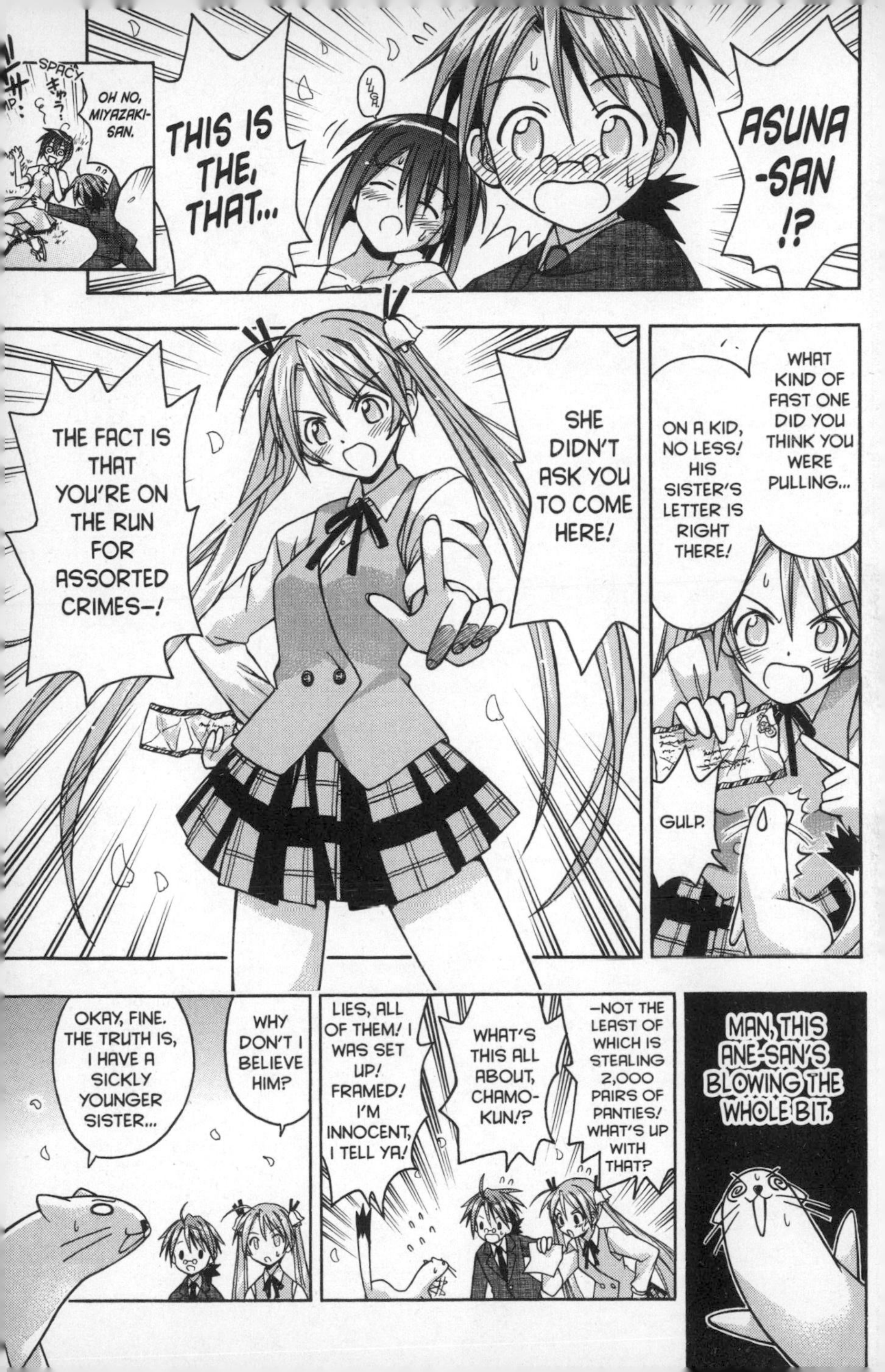
ASUNA-SAN!?
THIS IS THE, THAT...
OH NO, MIYAZAKI-SAN.
SPACY
WHAT KIND OF FAST ONE DID YOU THINK YOU WERE PULLING...
ON A KID, NO LESS! HIS SISTER'S LETTER IS RIGHT THERE!
GULP.
SHE DIDN'T ASK YOU TO COME HERE!
THE FACT IS THAT YOU'RE ON THE RUN FOR ASSORTED CRIMES–!
MAN, THIS ANE-SAN'S BLOWING THE WHOLE BIT.
–NOT THE LEAST OF WHICH IS STEALING 2,000 PAIRS OF PANTIES! WHAT'S UP WITH THAT?
WHAT'S THIS ALL ABOUT, CHAMO-KUN!?
LIES, ALL OF THEM! I WAS SET UP! FRAMED! I'M INNOCENT, I TELL YA!
WHY DON'T I BELIEVE HIM?
OKAY, FINE. THE TRUTH IS, I HAVE A SICKLY YOUNGER SISTER...

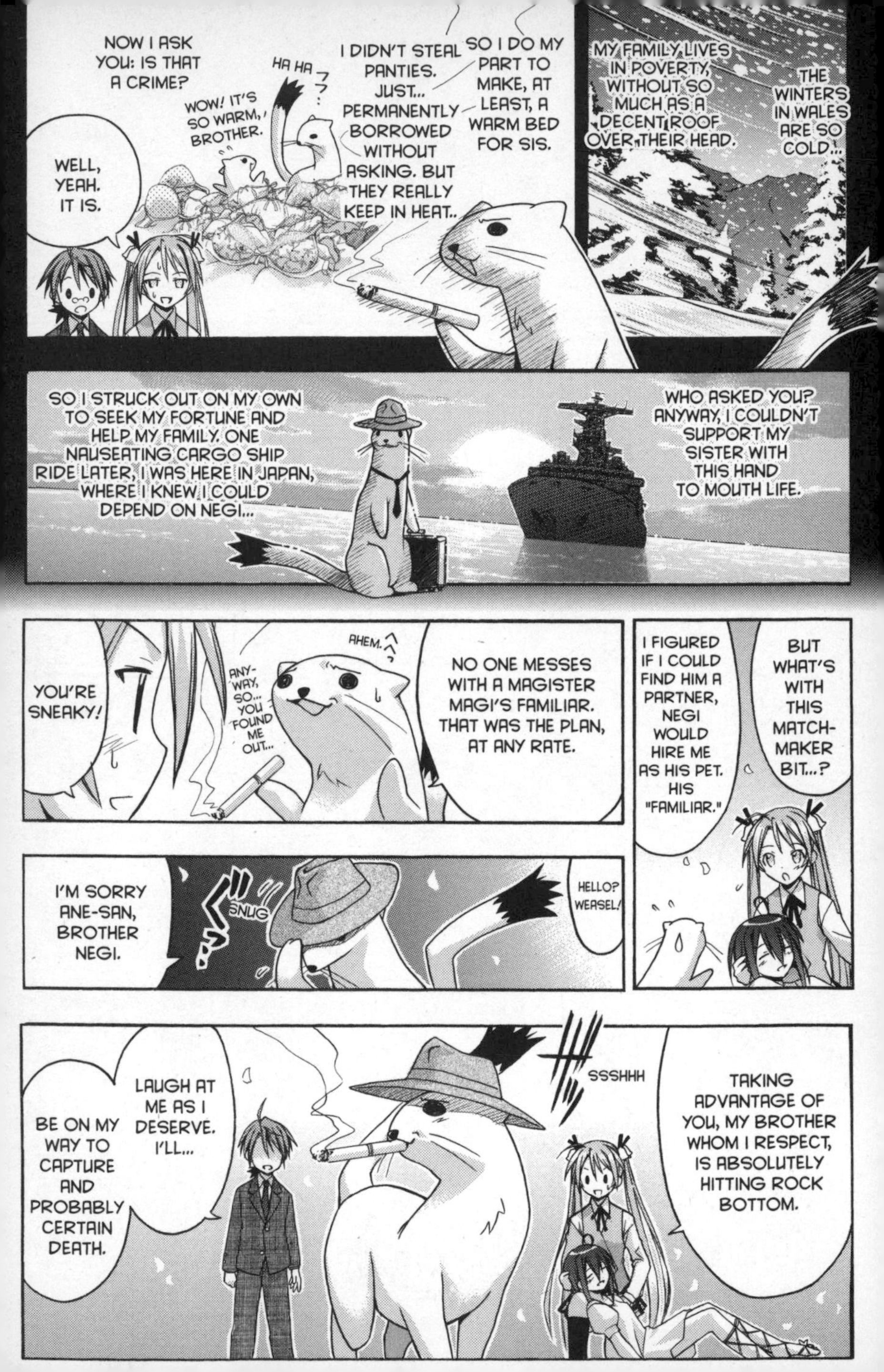
THE WINTERS IN WALES ARE SO COLD...
MY FAMILY LIVES IN POVERTY, WITHOUT SO MUCH AS A DECENT ROOF OVER THEIR HEAD.
SO I DO MY PART TO MAKE, AT LEAST, A WARM BED FOR SIS.
I DIDN'T STEAL PANTIES. JUST... PERMANENTLY BORROWED WITHOUT ASKING. BUT THEY REALLY KEEP IN HEAT..
HA HA
WOW! IT'S SO WARM, BROTHER.
NOW I ASK YOU: IS THAT A CRIME?
WELL, YEAH. IT IS.
WHO ASKED YOU? ANYWAY, I COULDN'T SUPPORT MY SISTER WITH THIS HAND TO MOUTH LIFE.
SO I STRUCK OUT ON MY OWN TO SEEK MY FORTUNE AND HELP MY FAMILY. ONE NAUSEATING CARGO SHIP RIDE LATER, I WAS HERE IN JAPAN, WHERE I KNEW I COULD DEPEND ON NEGI...
BUT WHAT'S WITH THIS MATCH-MAKER BIT...?
I FIGURED IF I COULD FIND HIM A PARTNER, NEGI WOULD HIRE ME AS HIS PET. HIS "FAMILIAR."
NO ONE MESSES WITH A MAGISTER MAGI'S FAMILIAR. THAT WAS THE PLAN, AT ANY RATE.
AHEM.
ANY-WAY, SO... YOU FOUND ME OUT...
YOU'RE SNEAKY!
HELLO? WEASEL!
SNUG
I'M SORRY ANE-SAN, BROTHER NEGI.
TAKING ADVANTAGE OF YOU, MY BROTHER WHOM I RESPECT, IS ABSOLUTELY HITTING ROCK BOTTOM.
SSSHHH
LAUGH AT ME AS I DESERVE. I'LL...
BE ON MY WAY TO CAPTURE AND PROBABLY CERTAIN DEATH.

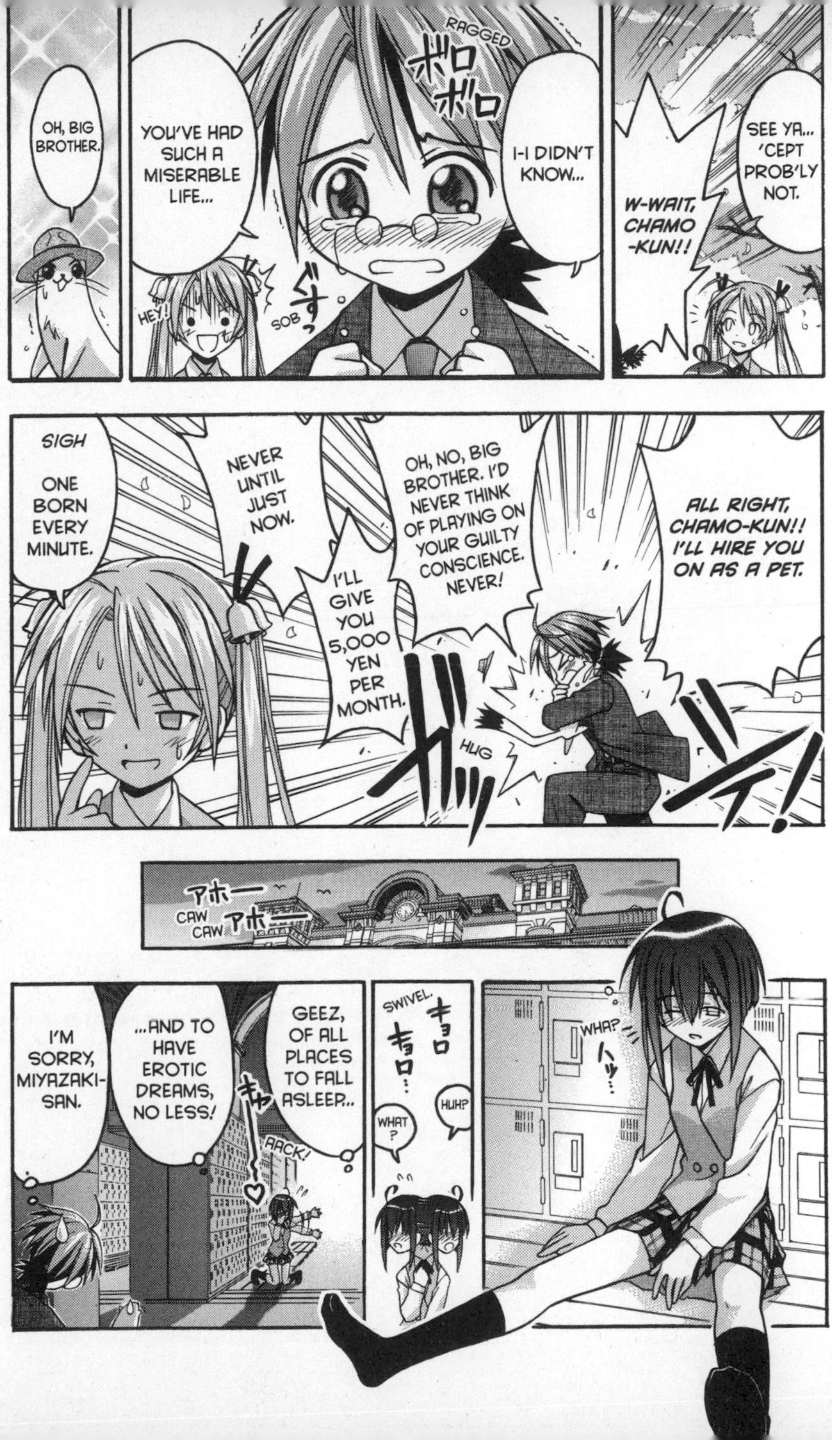
SEE YA... 'CEPT PROB'LY NOT.
W-WAIT, CHAMO-KUN!!
RAGGED
ボロボロ
I-I DIDN'T KNOW...
YOU'VE HAD SUCH A MISERABLE LIFE...
ぐすっ
SOB
HEY!
OH, BIG BROTHER.
ALL RIGHT, CHAMO-KUN!! I'LL HIRE YOU ON AS A PET.
ガバッ
HUG
OH, NO, BIG BROTHER. I'D NEVER THINK OF PLAYING ON YOUR GUILTY CONSCIENCE. NEVER!
I'LL GIVE YOU 5,000 YEN PER MONTH.
NEVER UNTIL JUST NOW.
SIGH
ONE BORN EVERY MINUTE.
アホー
CAW
アホー
CAW
WHA?
ハッ...
SWIVEL.
キョロキョロ...
HUH?
WHAT?
GEEZ, OF ALL PLACES TO FALL ASLEEP...
...AND TO HAVE EROTIC DREAMS, NO LESS!
キャ
AACK!
I'M SORRY, MIYAZAKI-SAN.

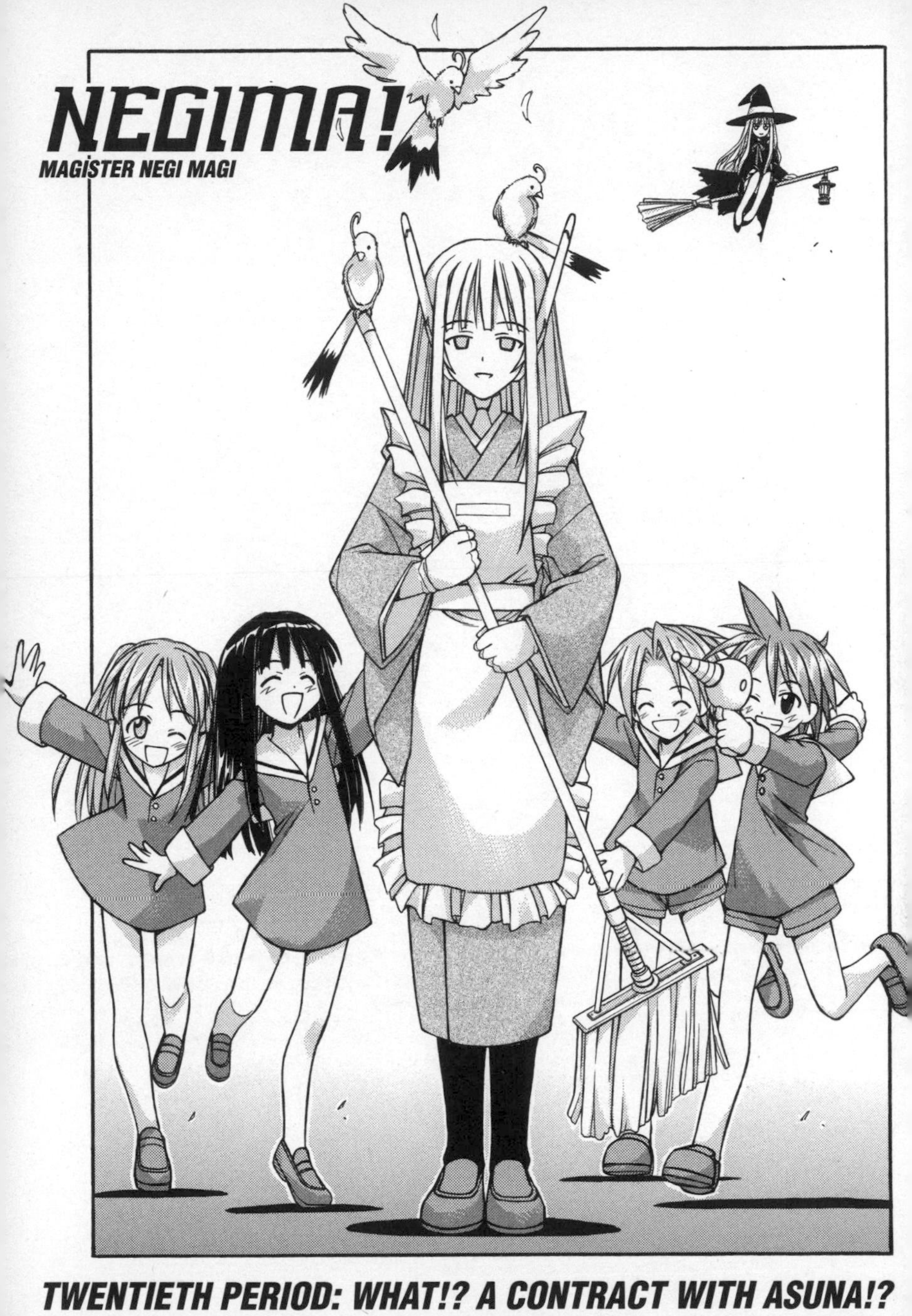
NEGIMA!
MAGISTER NEGI MAGI

TWENTIETH PERIOD: WHAT!? A CONTRACT WITH ASUNA!?

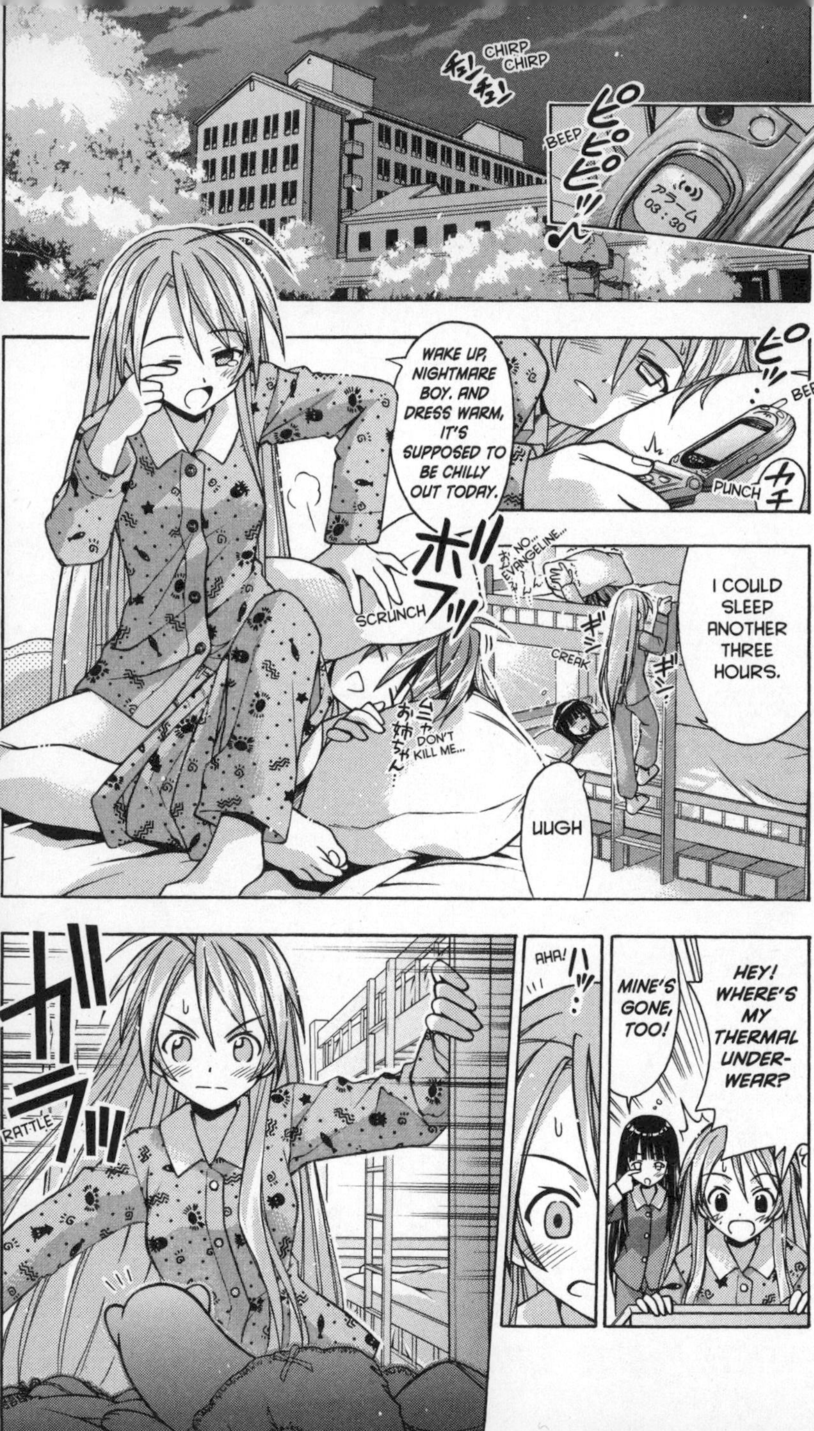
CHIRP CHIRP
BEEP
アラーム
03：30
BEEP
BEEP
PUNCH
WAKE UP, NIGHTMARE BOY. AND DRESS WARM, IT'S SUPPOSED TO BE CHILLY OUT TODAY.
SCRUNCH
I COULD SLEEP ANOTHER THREE HOURS.
NO... EVANGELINE...
CREAK
DON'T KILL ME...
UUGH
HEY! WHERE'S MY THERMAL UNDER-WEAR?
AHA!
MINE'S GONE, TOO!
RATTLE

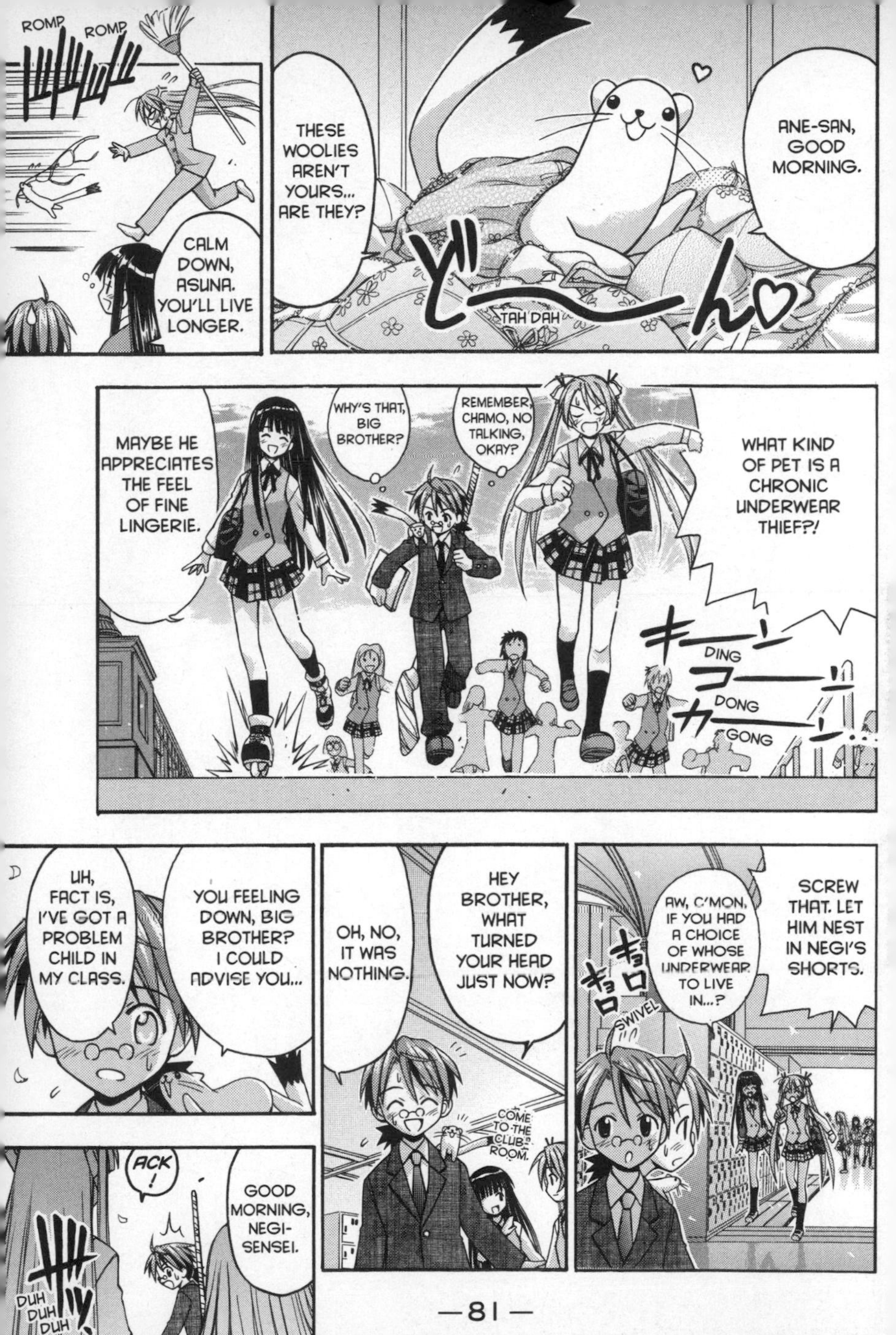
ANE-SAN, GOOD MORNING.
THESE WOOLIES AREN'T YOURS... ARE THEY?
どーん♡
TAH DAH
ROMP ROMP
CALM DOWN, ASUNA. YOU'LL LIVE LONGER.
WHAT KIND OF PET IS A CHRONIC UNDERWEAR THIEF?!
REMEMBER, CHAMO, NO TALKING, OKAY?
WHY'S THAT, BIG BROTHER?
MAYBE HE APPRECIATES THE FEEL OF FINE LINGERIE.
キーン
DING
コーン
DONG
カーン
GONG
SCREW THAT. LET HIM NEST IN NEGI'S SHORTS.
AW, C'MON, IF YOU HAD A CHOICE OF WHOSE UNDERWEAR TO LIVE IN...?
キョロキョロ
SWIVEL
HEY BROTHER, WHAT TURNED YOUR HEAD JUST NOW?
OH, NO, IT WAS NOTHING.
COME TO THE CLUB ROOM.
YOU FEELING DOWN, BIG BROTHER? I COULD ADVISE YOU...
UH, FACT IS, I'VE GOT A PROBLEM CHILD IN MY CLASS.
GOOD MORNING, NEGI-SENSEI.
ACK!
DUH DUH DUH

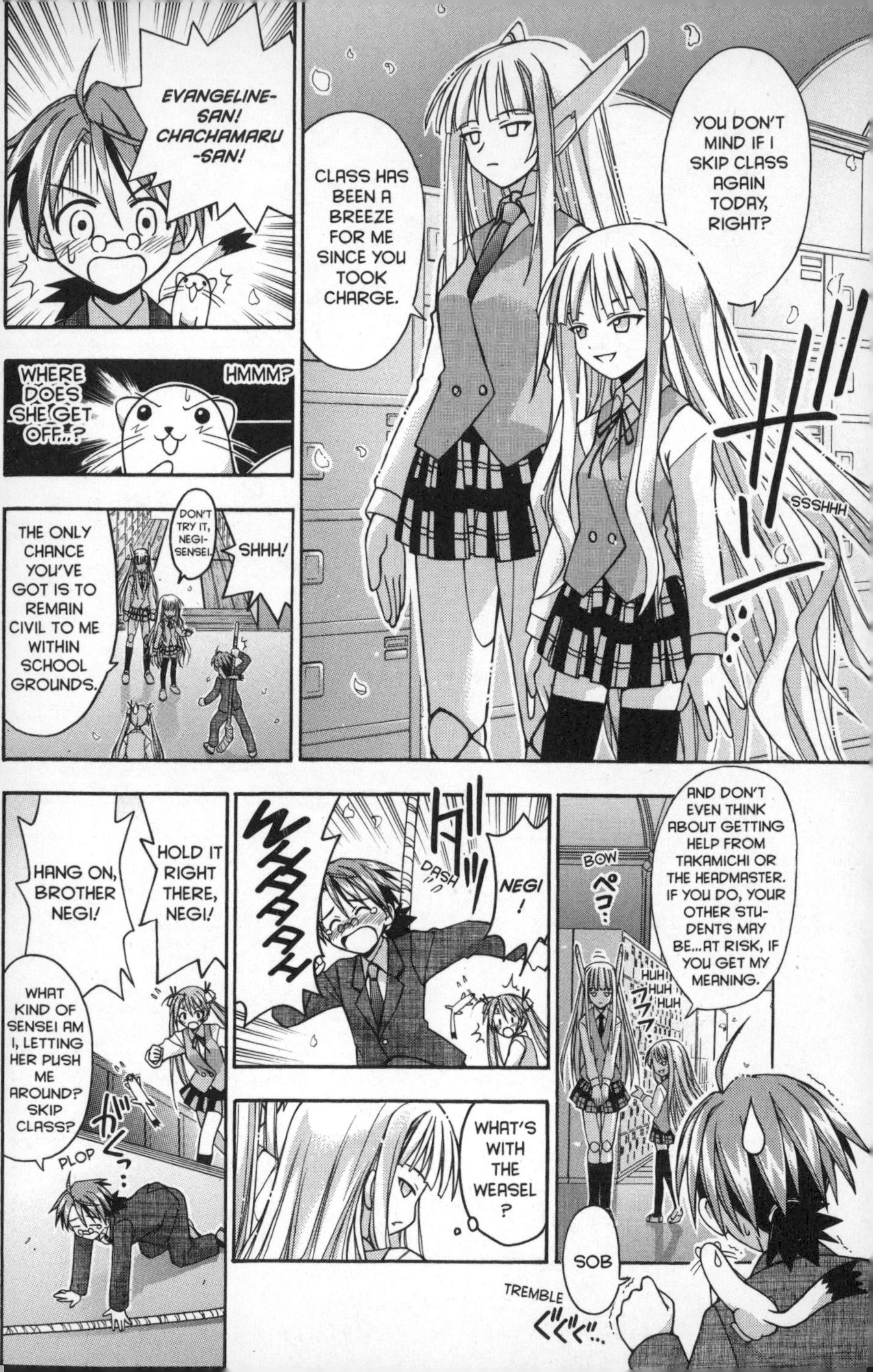
YOU DON'T MIND IF I SKIP CLASS AGAIN TODAY, RIGHT?
CLASS HAS BEEN A BREEZE FOR ME SINCE YOU TOOK CHARGE.
SSSHHH
EVANGELINE-SAN! CHACHAMARU-SAN!
HMMM?
WHERE DOES SHE GET OFF...?
SHHH!
DON'T TRY IT, NEGI-SENSEI.
THE ONLY CHANCE YOU'VE GOT IS TO REMAIN CIVIL TO ME WITHIN SCHOOL GROUNDS.
AND DON'T EVEN THINK ABOUT GETTING HELP FROM TAKAMICHI OR THE HEADMASTER. IF YOU DO, YOUR OTHER STUDENTS MAY BE...AT RISK, IF YOU GET MY MEANING.
BOW
HUH HUH HUH
SOB
TREMBLE
NEGI!
DASH
WHAAAAH
WHAT'S WITH THE WEASEL?
HOLD IT RIGHT THERE, NEGI!
HANG ON, BROTHER NEGI!
WHAT KIND OF SENSEI AM I, LETTING HER PUSH ME AROUND? SKIP CLASS?
PLOP

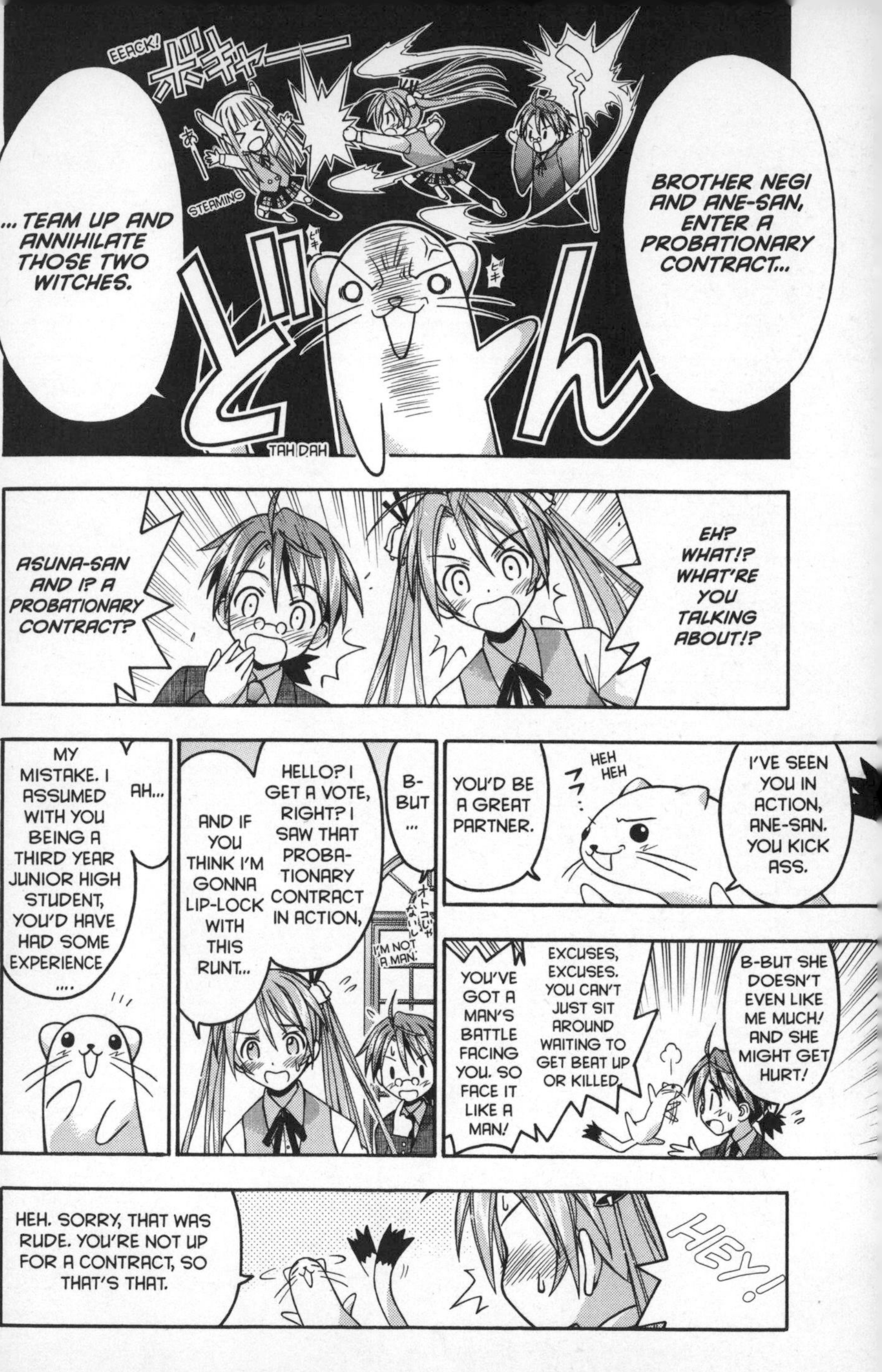
BROTHER NEGI AND ANE-SAN, ENTER A PROBATIONARY CONTRACT...
EEACK!
STEAMING
...TEAM UP AND ANNIHILATE THOSE TWO WITCHES.
TAH DAH
EH? WHAT!? WHAT'RE YOU TALKING ABOUT!?
ASUNA-SAN AND I!? A PROBATIONARY CONTRACT?
I'VE SEEN YOU IN ACTION, ANE-SAN. YOU KICK ASS.
HEH HEH
YOU'D BE A GREAT PARTNER.
B-BUT SHE DOESN'T EVEN LIKE ME MUCH! AND SHE MIGHT GET HURT!
EXCUSES, EXCUSES. YOU CAN'T JUST SIT AROUND WAITING TO GET BEAT UP OR KILLED.
YOU'VE GOT A MAN'S BATTLE FACING YOU. SO FACE IT LIKE A MAN!
B-BUT ...
HELLO!? I GET A VOTE, RIGHT!? I SAW THAT PROBATIONARY CONTRACT IN ACTION,
AND IF YOU THINK I'M GONNA LIP-LOCK WITH THIS RUNT...
I'M NOT A MAN.
AH...
MY MISTAKE. I ASSUMED WITH YOU BEING A THIRD YEAR JUNIOR HIGH STUDENT, YOU'D HAVE HAD SOME EXPERIENCE ....
HEY!
HEH. SORRY, THAT WAS RUDE. YOU'RE NOT UP FOR A CONTRACT, SO THAT'S THAT.

WONDER WEASEL! LISTEN TO WHAT I'M SAYING!

AND SINCE YOU LOVE EXCITEMENT, IT'S A GO! TERRIFIC!

SO, BROTHER HOW ABOUT YOU? YOU UP FOR IT?

THERE'S NO DANGER.

NOT... IMME-DIATE...

IT'S JUST, THE WHOLE MAGIC PARTNER THING... IT'S LIKE GOING STEADY WITH A HAND GRENADE!

BACK UP! I'VE GOT EXPERIENCE! LOADS! EXPERIENCE OUT MY EARS!

AND IF SHE KEEPS CUTTING, I'LL LOSE MY TEACHING POST ANYWAY.

FLUSTER

BUT I...I GUESS IT'S BETTER TO CHALLENGE THEM ON MY SCHEDULE THAN THEIRS, RIGHT?

IT'S ONLY TEMPORARY, AND JUST THIS ONCE!

UH!

I-I BEG YOU, ASUNA-SAN.

TERRIFIC! DONE DEAL!

OKAY, THEN! I'LL DO IT!

I DIDN'T DO ANY DEAL! YOU'RE DOING ALL THE DEALING!

IF IT'S JUST THIS ONCE....

WELL...

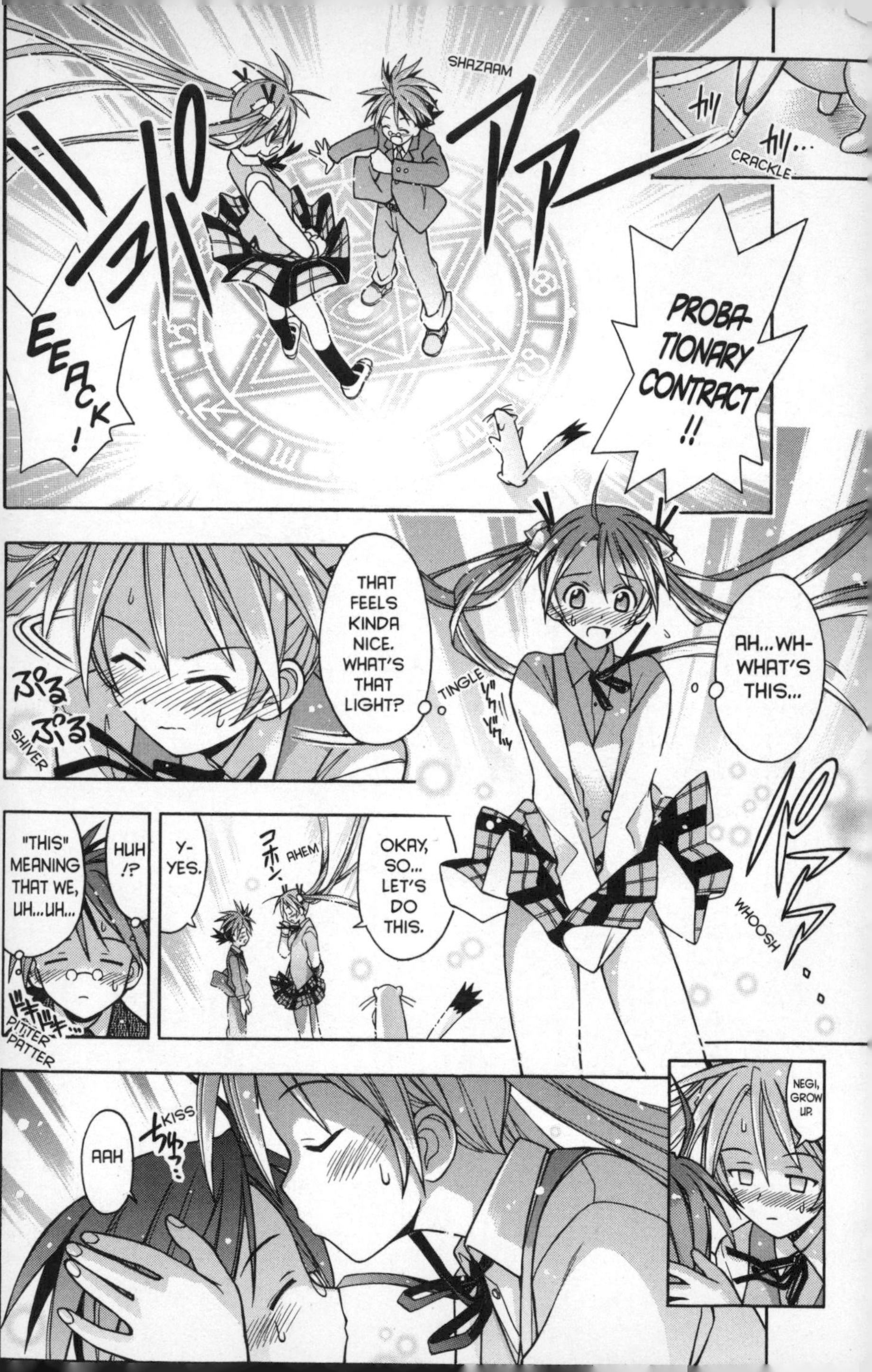
CRACKLE
SHAZAAM
PROBATIONARY CONTRACT!!
EEEACK!
AH...WH-WHAT'S THIS...
TINGLE
WHOOSH
THAT FEELS KINDA NICE. WHAT'S THAT LIGHT?
SHIVER
OKAY, SO... LET'S DO THIS.
AHEM
Y-YES.
HUH!?
"THIS" MEANING THAT WE, UH...UH...
PITTER PATTER
NEGI, GROW UP.
KISS
AAH

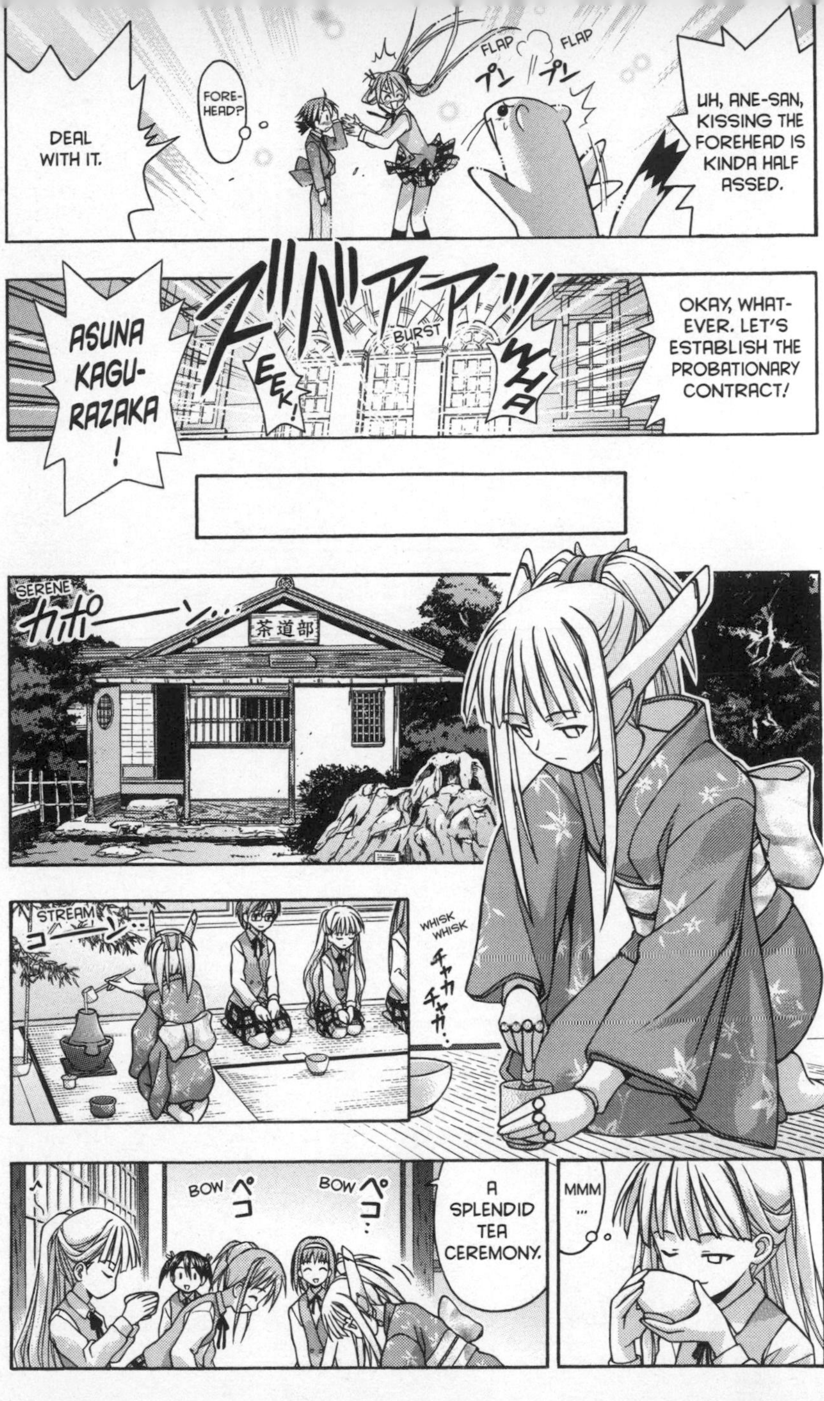
UH, ANE-SAN, KISSING THE FOREHEAD IS KINDA HALF ASSED.
FLAP プン
FLAP プン
FORE-HEAD?
DEAL WITH IT.
OKAY, WHATEVER. LET'S ESTABLISH THE PROBATIONARY CONTRACT!
WHA
BURST
ズバアアッ
EEK!
ASUNA KAGU-RAZAKA!
WHISK WHISK
チャカチャカ...
SERENE
カポーン...
茶道部
STREAM
コーー...
MMM...
A SPLENDID TEA CEREMONY.
BOW ペコ
BOW ペコ

YES, MISTRESS.

HMMM

PERHAPS WE NEED TO SPEAK TO NEGI'S "ADVISOR."

MEANTIME, STAY AT MY SIDE.

OH, IT'S TAKA-MICHI.

HI THERE, EVA.

THE HEADMASTER WANTS YOU. HE SAID TO COME ALONE.

BOW

へ...

WE'RE DOING A JOB YOU KNOW.

WHAT ARE YOU DOING HERE?

MIS-TRESS.

BE CAREFUL.

....

NOTHING YOU NEED WORRY ABOUT.

"AMBUSH"? EXCUSE ME, BUT...IS SOMETHING WRONG?

CHACHAMARU, I'LL BE BACK SOON. STAY OUT IN THE OPEN TO AVOID AMBUSH.

ALL RIGHT. TELL HIM I'LL BE RIGHT THERE.

コク...
NOD

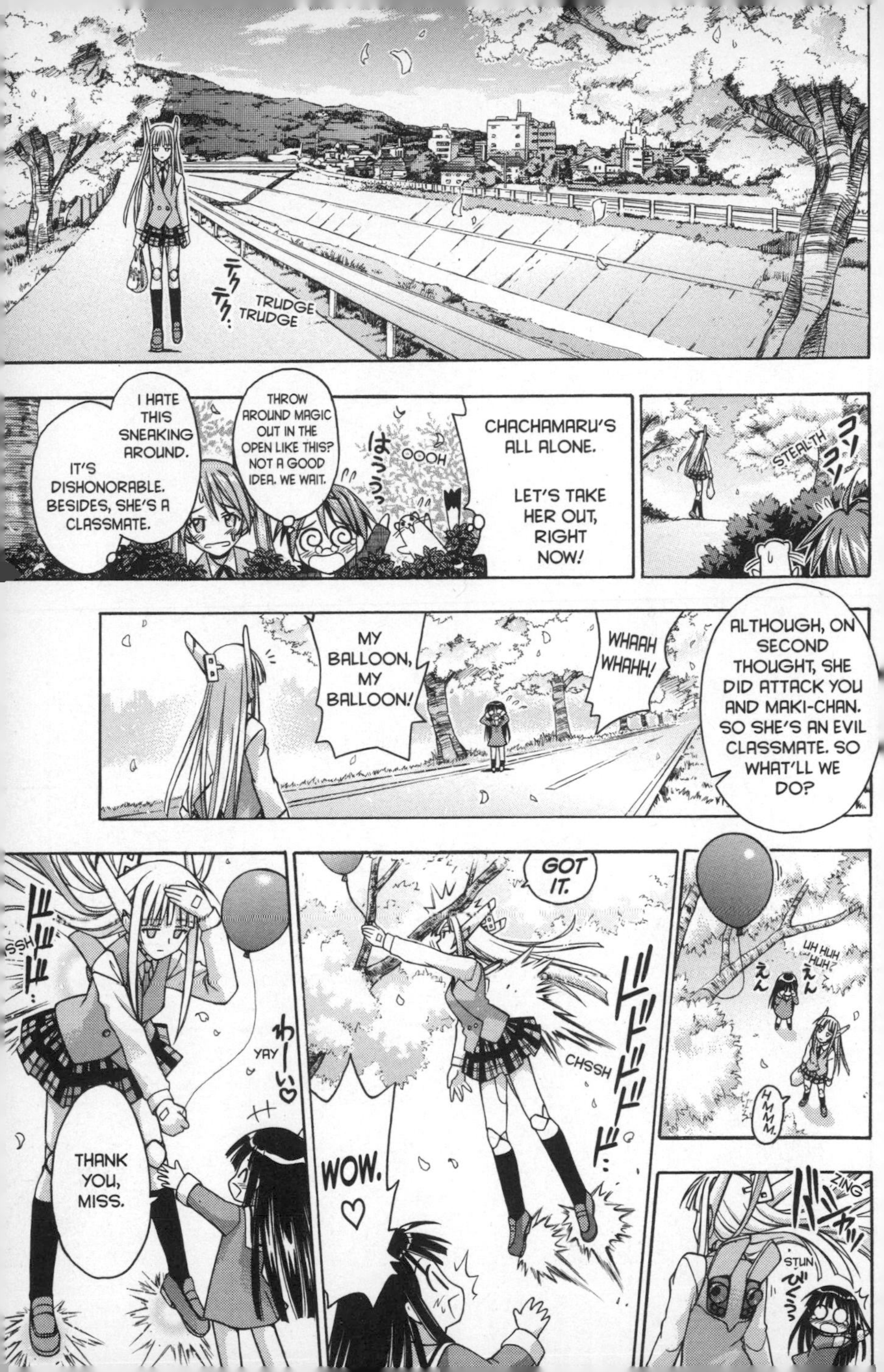
テクテク
TRUDGE TRUDGE
コソコソ
STEALTH
CHACHAMARU'S ALL ALONE.
LET'S TAKE HER OUT, RIGHT NOW!
はうう
OOOH
THROW AROUND MAGIC OUT IN THE OPEN LIKE THIS? NOT A GOOD IDEA. WE WAIT.
I HATE THIS SNEAKING AROUND.
IT'S DISHONORABLE. BESIDES, SHE'S A CLASSMATE.
ALTHOUGH, ON SECOND THOUGHT, SHE DID ATTACK YOU AND MAKI-CHAN. SO SHE'S AN EVIL CLASSMATE. SO WHAT'LL WE DO?
WHAAH WHAHH!
MY BALLOON, MY BALLOON!
えんえん
UH HUH HUH?
HMMM.
ZING
STUN
GOT IT.
CHSSH
WOW.
♡
SSH
YAY
わーい♡
THANK YOU, MISS.

ザァ GGSSHHH

アァア...

おぉ WHOA

GRIND

ザボ WOMP WOMP

HEY, WATCH IT! STAY PUT! SHE CAN'T KNOW WE'RE TAILING HER!

THAT KITTEN! HOW AWFUL!

SPRING

MEW MEW

ザッ TRUDGE TRUDGE

ザッ

オォ WHOA

CLAP CLAP パチパチパチ

パチ パチ

TYPICAL CHACHAMARU

THAT FIGURES...

CHACHAMARU AGAIN

MEW

WHERE IS SHE GOING?

WELL THEN...

THAT'S GREAT, ISN'T IT?

CARING, POPULAR AROUND TOWN. SHE'S A NICE PERSON.

NO! IT'LL JUST PUT YOU OFF GUARD!

リンゴーン GONG GONG リンゴーン

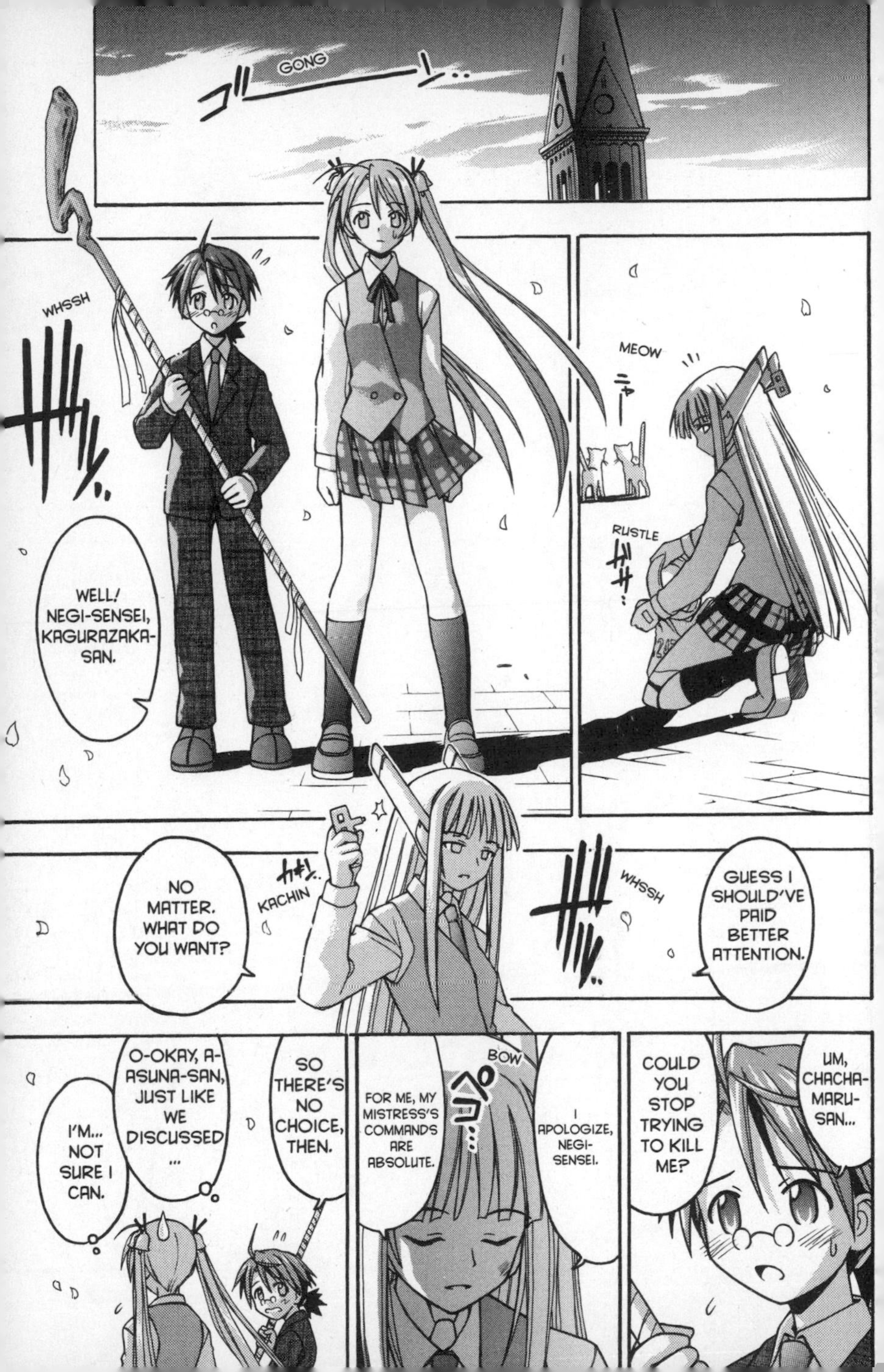
GONG
MEOW
RUSTLE
WHSSH
WELL! NEGI-SENSEI, KAGURAZAKA-SAN.
GUESS I SHOULD'VE PAID BETTER ATTENTION.
WHSSH
KACHIN
NO MATTER. WHAT DO YOU WANT?
UM, CHACHA-MARU-SAN...
COULD YOU STOP TRYING TO KILL ME?
I APOLOGIZE, NEGI-SENSEI.
BOW
FOR ME, MY MISTRESS'S COMMANDS ARE ABSOLUTE.
SO THERE'S NO CHOICE, THEN.
O-OKAY, A-ASUNA-SAN, JUST LIKE WE DISCUSSED...
I'M... NOT SURE I CAN.

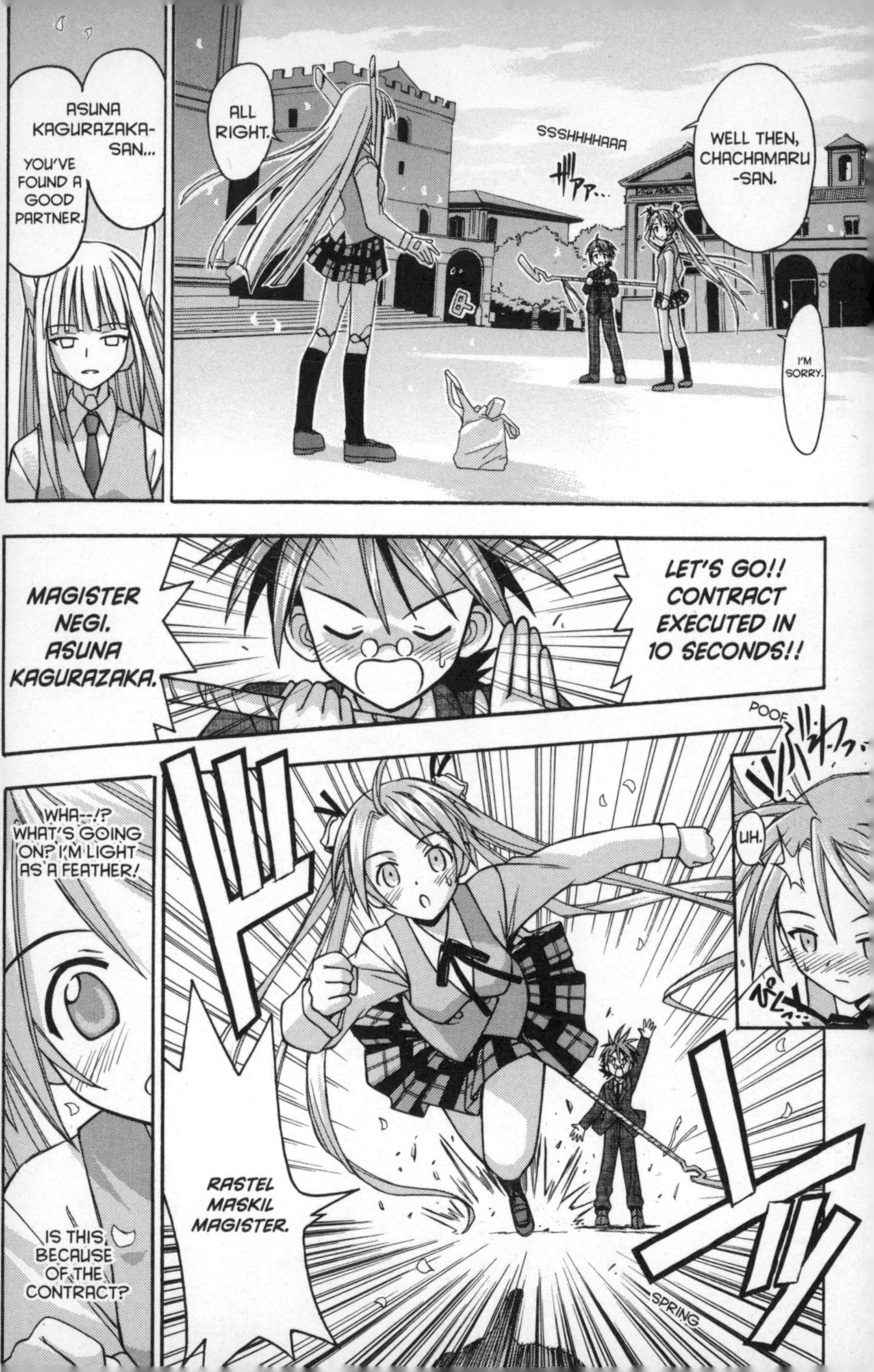
WELL THEN, CHACHAMARU-SAN.
SSSHHHHAAA
ALL RIGHT.
I'M SORRY.
ASUNA KAGURAZAKA-SAN...
YOU'VE FOUND A GOOD PARTNER.
LET'S GO!! CONTRACT EXECUTED IN 10 SECONDS!!
MAGISTER NEGI. ASUNA KAGURAZAKA.
POOF
UH.
RASTEL MASKIL MAGISTER.
SPRING
WHA--!? WHAT'S GOING ON? I'M LIGHT AS A FEATHER!
IS THIS BECAUSE OF THE CONTRACT?

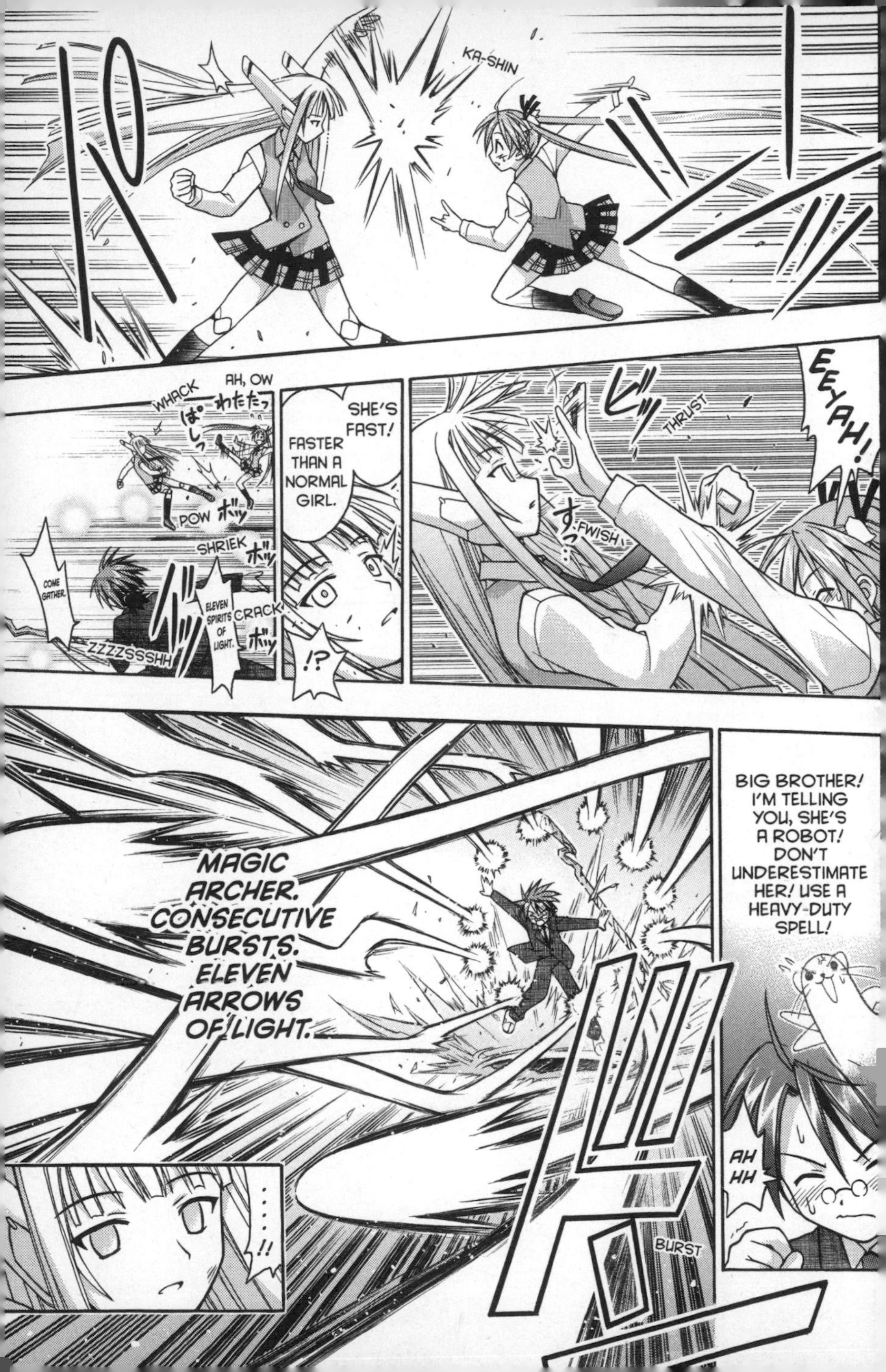
KA-SHIN
EEYAH!
ビッ
THRUST
すっ
FWISH
SHE'S FAST!
FASTER THAN A NORMAL GIRL.
!?
AH, OW
わたたっ
WHACK
ぱしっ
POW
ボッ
SHRIEK
ボッ
COME GATHER.
ELEVEN SPIRITS OF LIGHT.
CRACK
ボッ
ZZZZSSSHH
BIG BROTHER! I'M TELLING YOU, SHE'S A ROBOT! DON'T UNDERESTIMATE HER! USE A HEAVY-DUTY SPELL!
AH HH
MAGIC ARCHER. CONSECUTIVE BURSTS. ELEVEN ARROWS OF LIGHT.
BURST
......!!

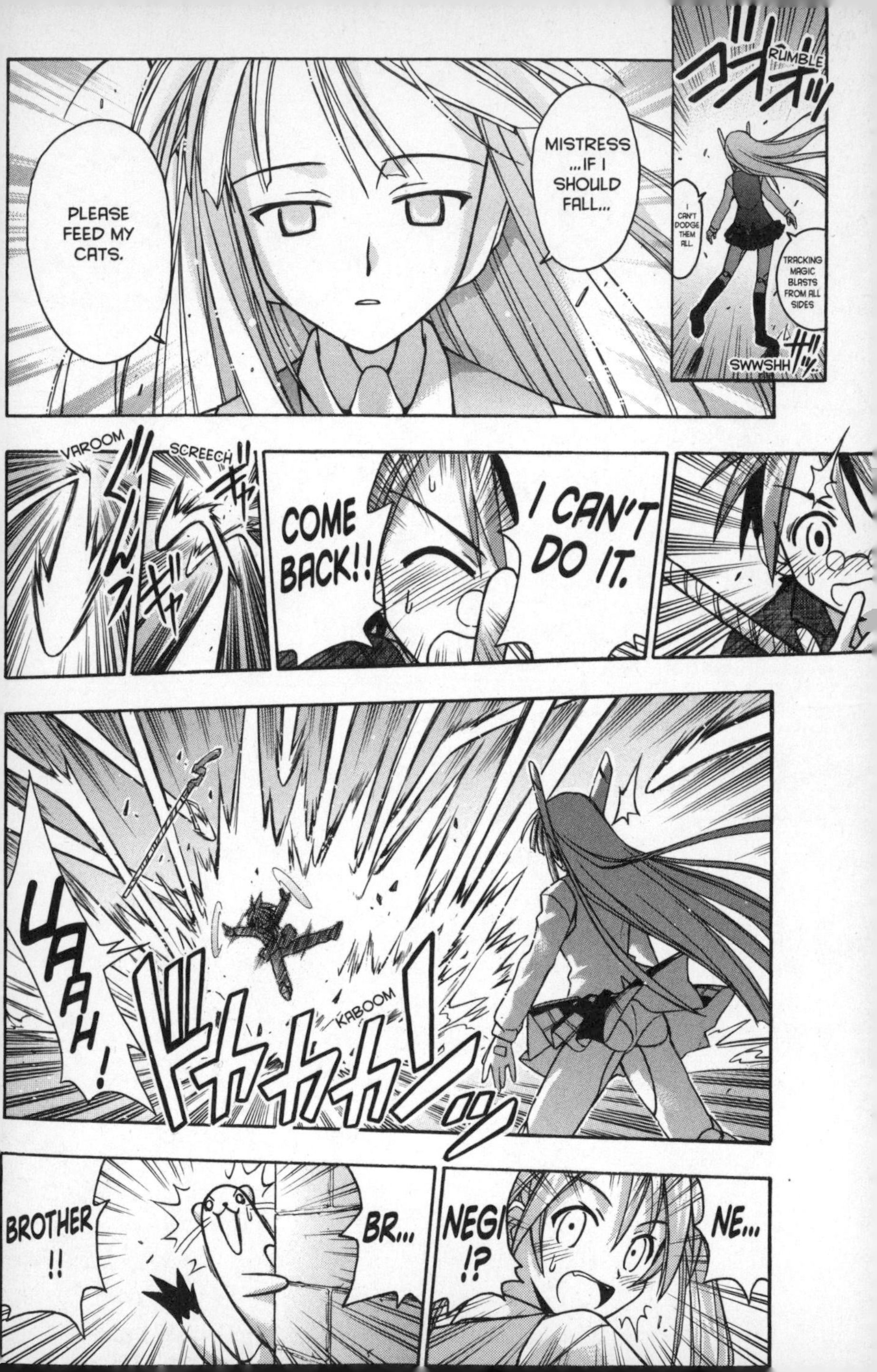
RUMBLE
TRACKING MAGIC BLASTS FROM ALL SIDES
I CAN'T DODGE THEM ALL.
SWWSHH
MISTRESS ...IF I SHOULD FALL...
PLEASE FEED MY CATS.
I CAN'T DO IT.
COME BACK!!
SCREECH
VAROOM
KABOOM
UAAH!
NE...
NEGI !?
BR...
BROTHER !!

WHOOSH

ACK.

OH OOOO

·····

RUMBLE
DIZZY

B-BIG BROTHER. WHY DID YOU CALL BACK THE ARROWS!?

EEYAH!

NEGI, ARE YOU ALL RIGHT!?

YOU'RE A FOOL! LET'S GET YOU TO THE NURSE!

BOTTOM LINE, CHACHA-MARU IS MY STUDENT, AND I CAN'T HURT HER.

THE ARROWS HAD MORE KICK THAN I EXPECTED.

OOHH

RUMBLE

YOU HAD HER ON THE ROPES! THAT WAS JUST... JUST FOOLISH!

AAAH! SHE'S GETTING AWAY!

NEGI SPRINGFIELD.

NEGI SENSEI.

TAP

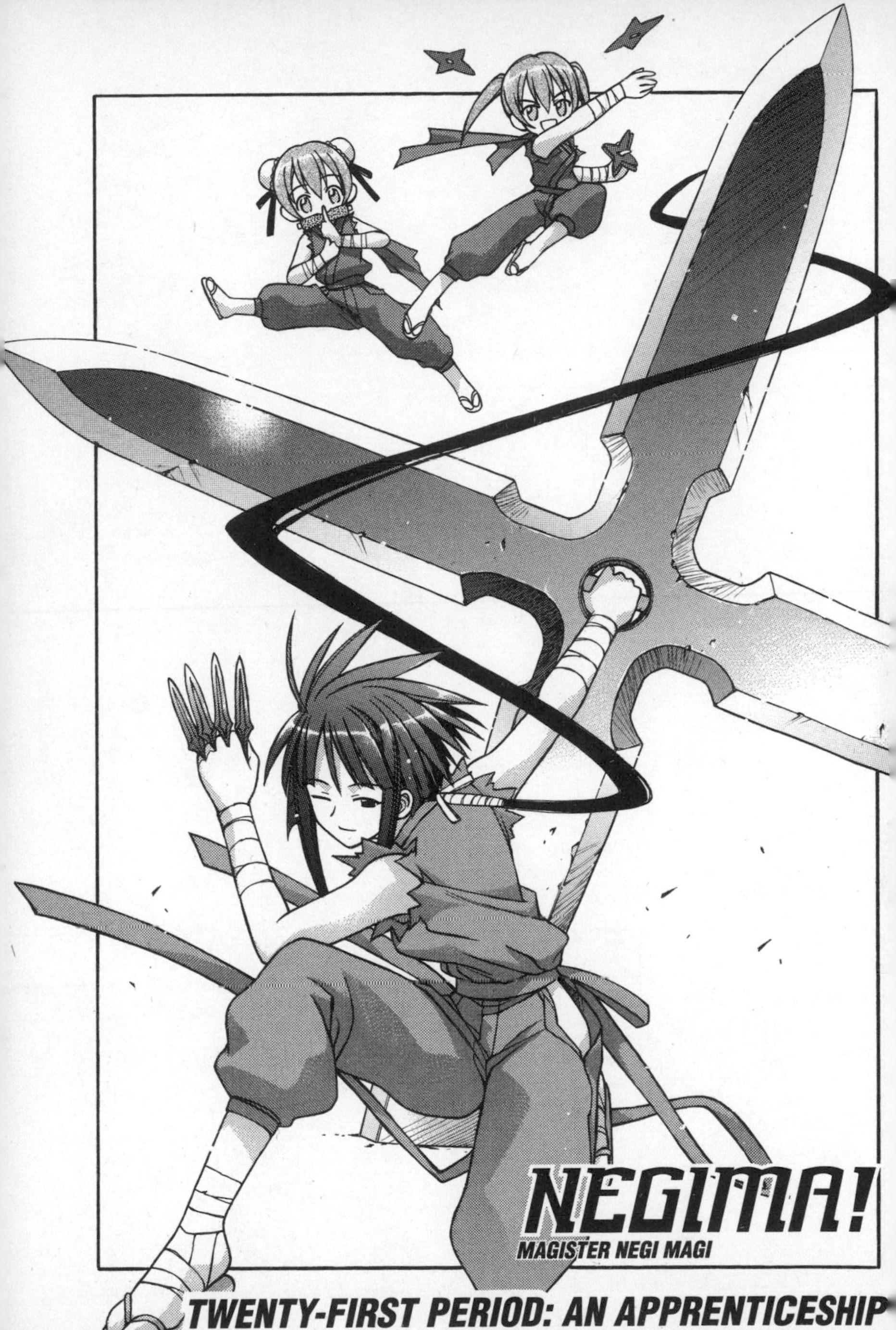
NEGIMA!
MAGISTER NEGI MAGI
TWENTY-FIRST PERIOD: AN APPRENTICESHIP

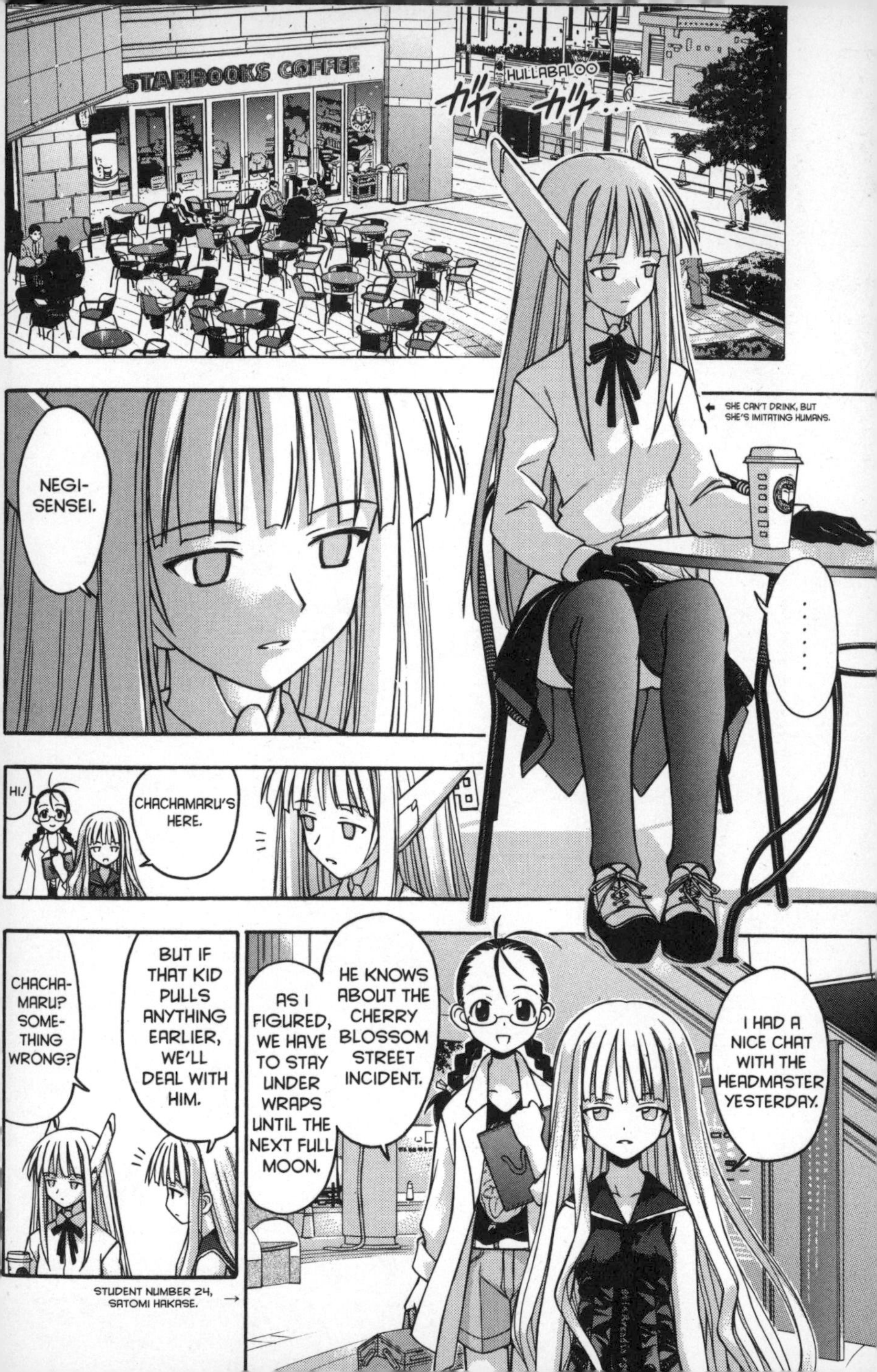
STARBOOKS COFFEE
HULLABALOO
ガヤ ガヤ…
SHE CAN'T DRINK, BUT SHE'S IMITATING HUMANS.
……
NEGI-SENSEI.
CHACHAMARU'S HERE.
HI!
I HAD A NICE CHAT WITH THE HEADMASTER YESTERDAY.
HE KNOWS ABOUT THE CHERRY BLOSSOM STREET INCIDENT.
AS I FIGURED, WE HAVE TO STAY UNDER WRAPS UNTIL THE NEXT FULL MOON.
STUDENT NUMBER 24, SATOMI HAKASE.
BUT IF THAT KID PULLS ANYTHING EARLIER, WE'LL DEAL WITH HIM.
CHACHA-MARU? SOME-THING WRONG?

UH...

. . . . .

DID SOMETHING HAPPEN YESTERDAY? YOU'VE BEEN ACTING STRANGE.

DRILL

SIP

IS THAT SO? I HOPE THAT'S THE CASE.

I'M TAKING YOUR COFFEE.

NO, NOTHING HAPPENED.

BETTER BE CAREFUL, CHACHAMARU.

OOOOKAY. HUNH. THIS TASTES LIKE BUILT-UP SLUDGE.

SOMETHING THAT HAS NOTHING TO DO WITH YOU, HAKASE.

WHAT ARE YOU TWO TALKING ABOUT?

INSTEAD YOU SNATCHED DEFEAT FROM THE JAWS OF VICTORY BY TAKING PITY ON HER!

WE'RE IN DANGER, BROTHER! IF YOU'D NAILED THAT ROBOT CHACHAMARU YESTERDAY, THEY'D BOTH BE ON THE ROPES.

IF SHE TELLS EVA YOU HAVE A PARTNER, THEY'LL PROBABLY LAUNCH A PREEMPTIVE STRIKE OF SOME KIND.

NOW, NOT ONLY IS SHE STILL FREE TO ATTACK, BUT THEY'LL BE CAUTIOUS, WHEREAS YESTERDAY THEY HAD THEIR GUARDS DOWN.

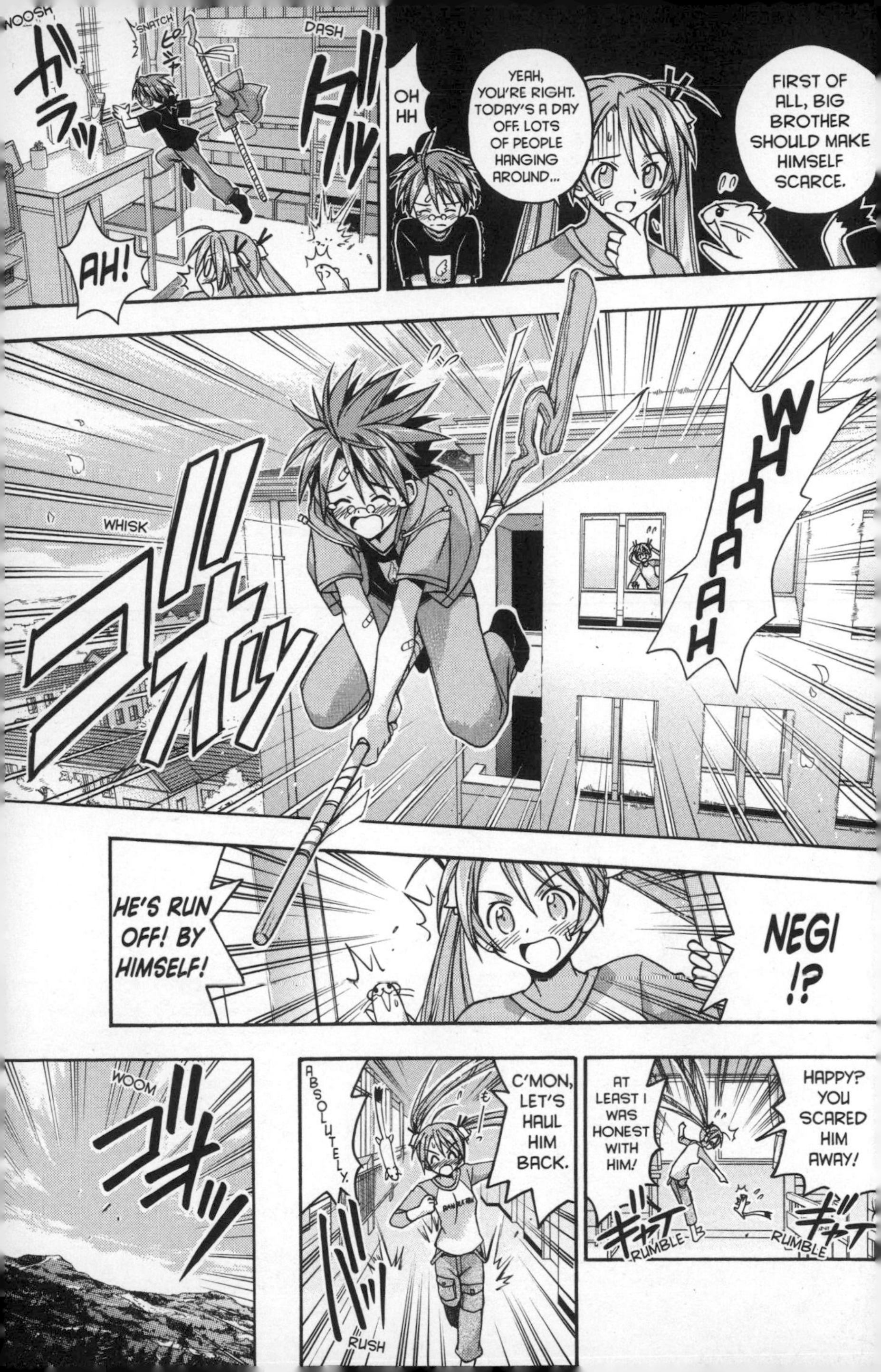
FIRST OF ALL, BIG BROTHER SHOULD MAKE HIMSELF SCARCE.
YEAH, YOU'RE RIGHT. TODAY'S A DAY OFF. LOTS OF PEOPLE HANGING AROUND...
OH HH
DASH
SNATCH
WOOSH
AH!
WHAAAAAH
WHISK
NEGI !?
HE'S RUN OFF! BY HIMSELF!
HAPPY? YOU SCARED HIM AWAY!
AT LEAST I WAS HONEST WITH HIM!
RUMBLE
RUMBLE
C'MON, LET'S HAUL HIM BACK.
ABSOLUTELY.
RUSH
WOOM

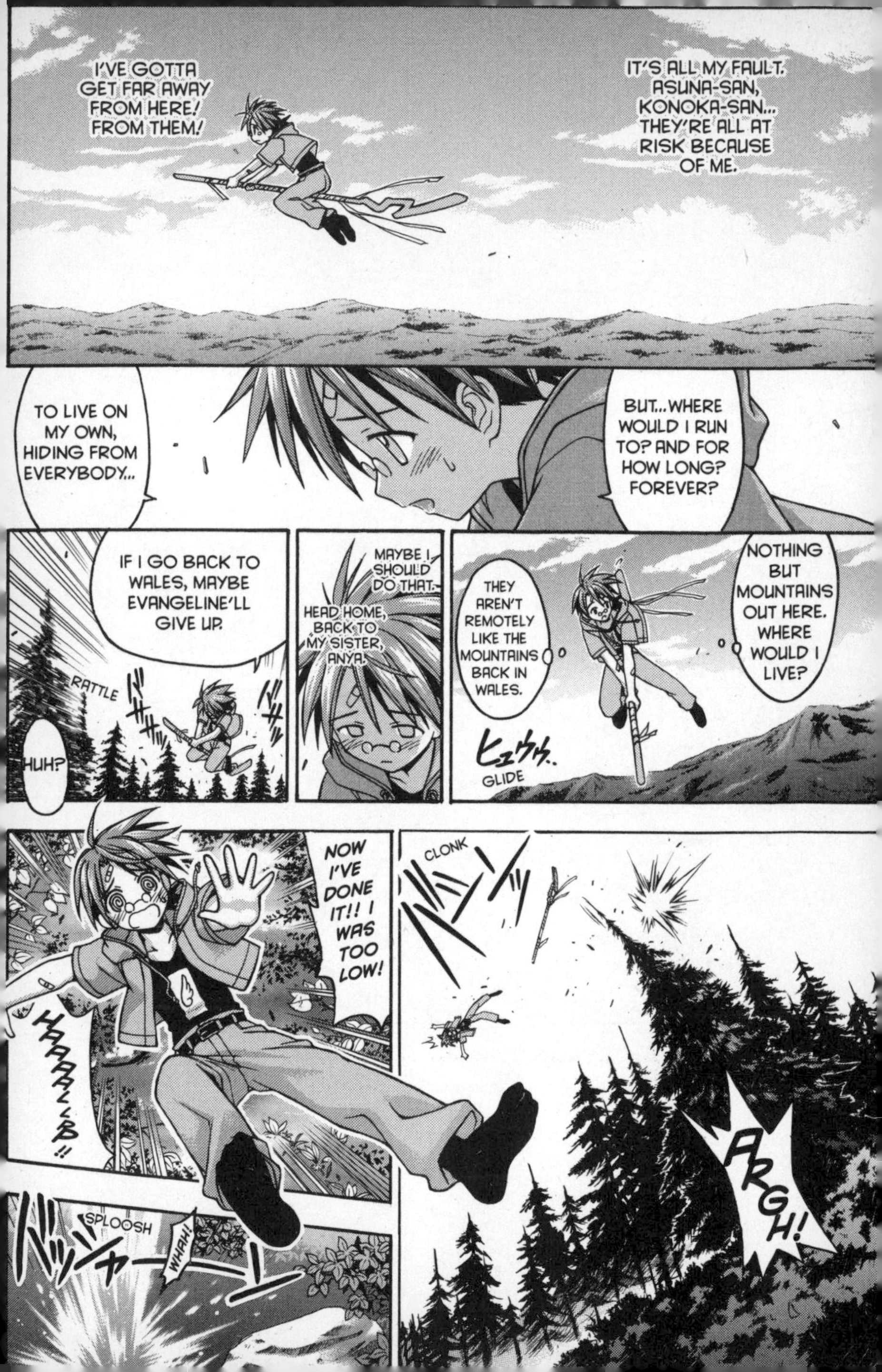
IT'S ALL MY FAULT. ASUNA-SAN, KONOKA-SAN... THEY'RE ALL AT RISK BECAUSE OF ME.
I'VE GOTTA GET FAR AWAY FROM HERE! FROM THEM!
BUT...WHERE WOULD I RUN TO? AND FOR HOW LONG? FOREVER?
TO LIVE ON MY OWN, HIDING FROM EVERYBODY...
NOTHING BUT MOUNTAINS OUT HERE. WHERE WOULD I LIVE?
THEY AREN'T REMOTELY LIKE THE MOUNTAINS BACK IN WALES.
GLIDE
MAYBE I SHOULD DO THAT.
HEAD HOME, BACK TO MY SISTER, ANYA.
IF I GO BACK TO WALES, MAYBE EVANGELINE'LL GIVE UP.
RATTLE
HUH?
CLONK
ARGH!
NOW I'VE DONE IT!! I WAS TOO LOW!
SPLOOSH
WHAH!

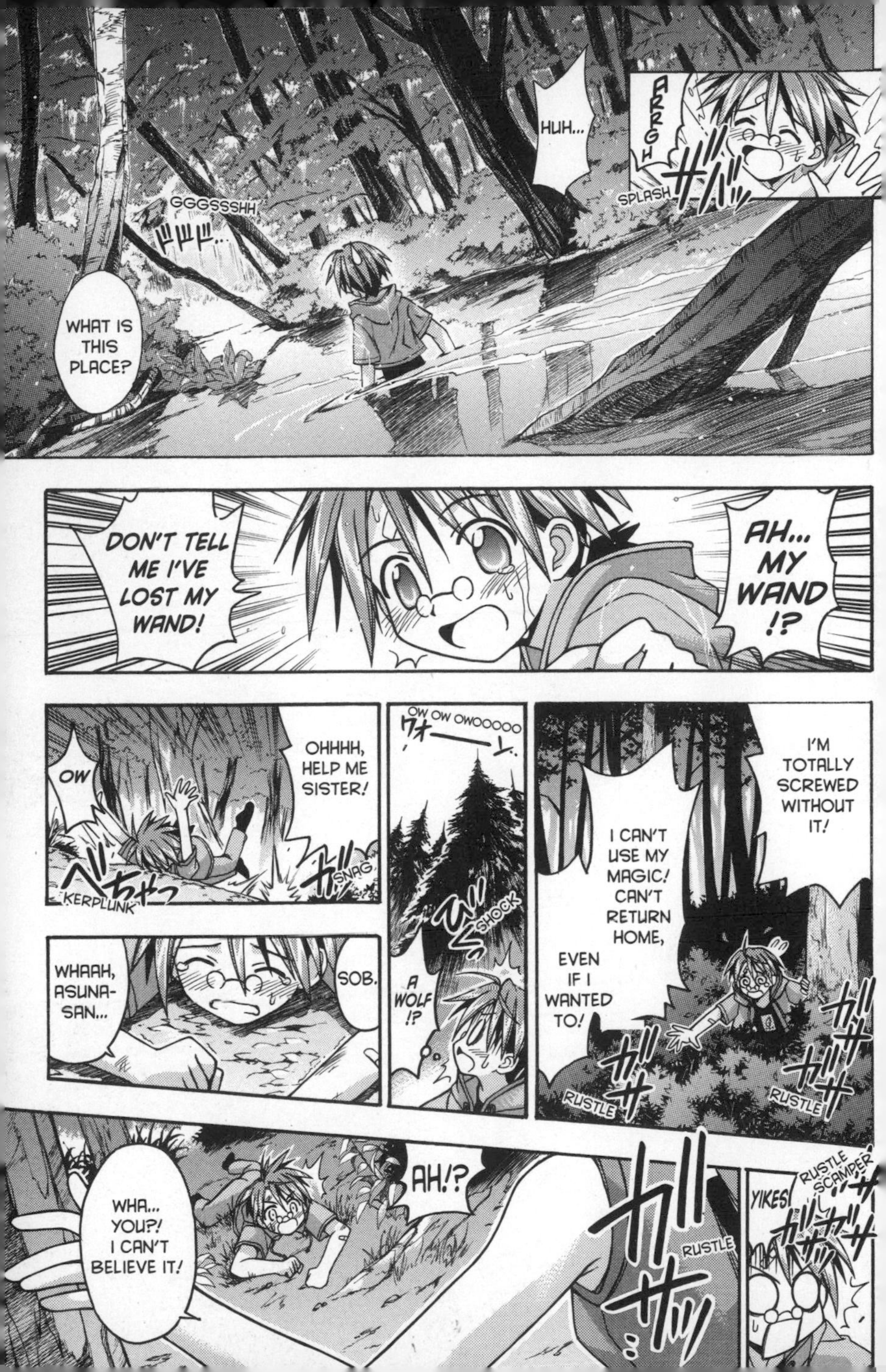
ARRGH
SPLASH
HUH...
GGGSSSHH
WHAT IS THIS PLACE?
AH... MY WAND !?
DON'T TELL ME I'VE LOST MY WAND!
I'M TOTALLY SCREWED WITHOUT IT!
I CAN'T USE MY MAGIC! CAN'T RETURN HOME,
EVEN IF I WANTED TO!
RUSTLE
RUSTLE
OW OW OWOOOOO
SHOCK
A WOLF !?
OHHHH, HELP ME SISTER!
OW
SNAG
KERPLUNK
SOB.
WHAAH, ASUNA-SAN...
RUSTLE SCAMPER
YIKES!
RUSTLE
AH!?
WHA... YOU?! I CAN'T BELIEVE IT!

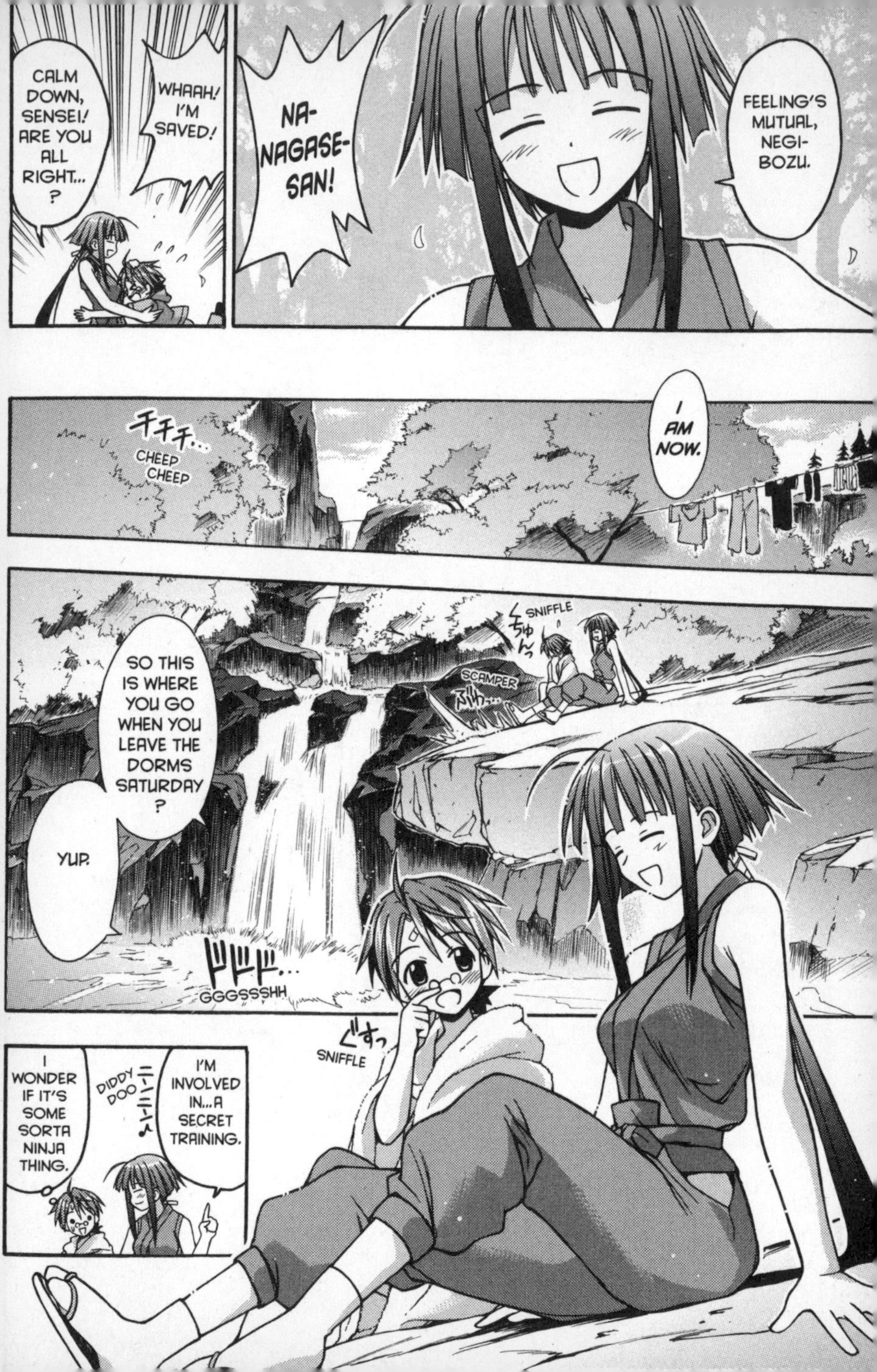
FEELING'S MUTUAL, NEGI-BOZU.
NA-NAGASE-SAN!
WHAAH! I'M SAVED!
CALM DOWN, SENSEI! ARE YOU ALL RIGHT...?
I AM NOW.
チチチ... CHEEP CHEEP
くちゅんっ SNIFFLE
SCAMPER
SO THIS IS WHERE YOU GO WHEN YOU LEAVE THE DORMS SATURDAY?
YUP.
ドドド... GGGSSSHH
ぐすっ SNIFFLE
I'M INVOLVED IN...A SECRET TRAINING.
DIDDY DOO
I WONDER IF IT'S SOME SORTA NINJA THING.

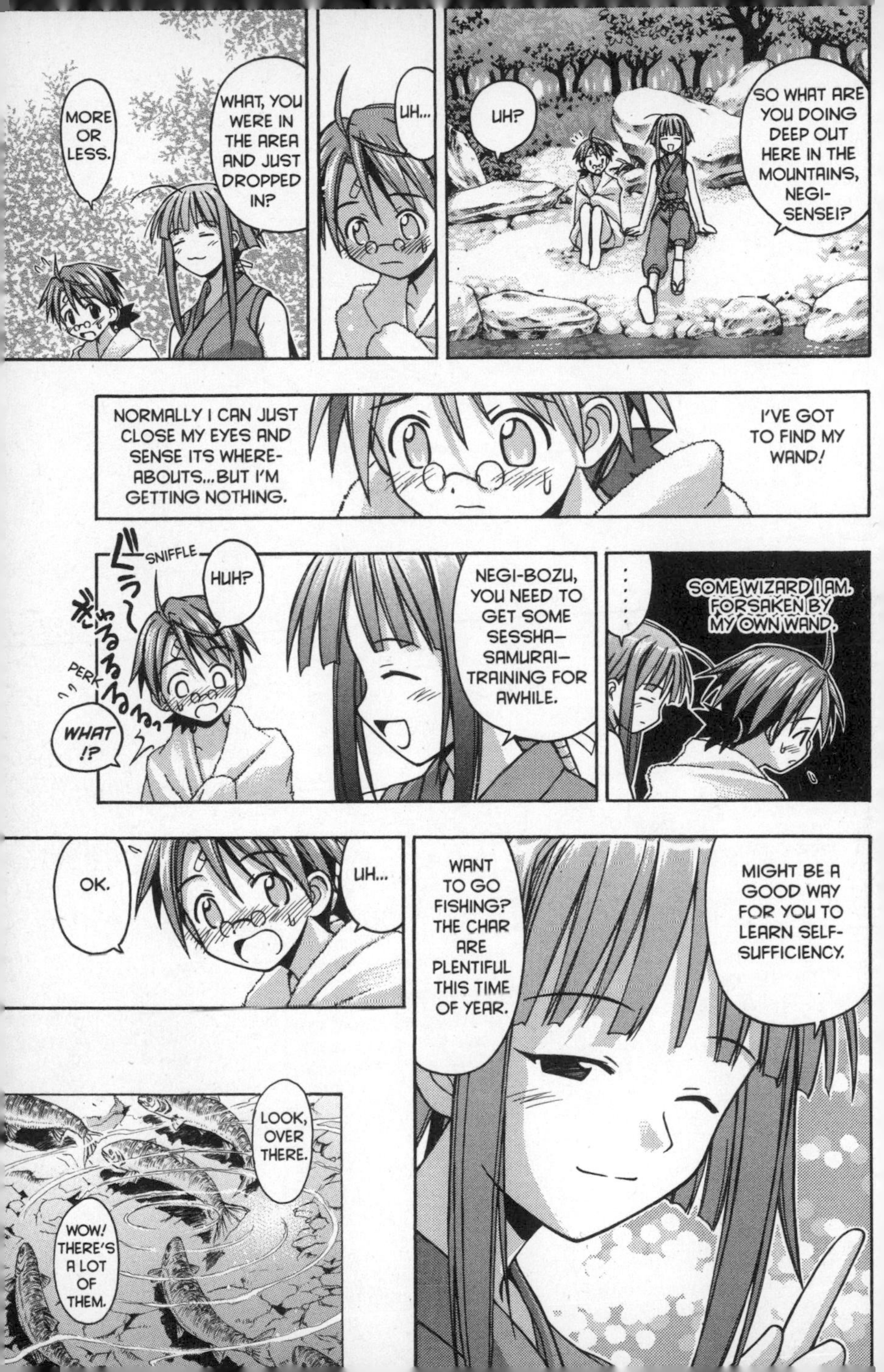
SO WHAT ARE YOU DOING DEEP OUT HERE IN THE MOUNTAINS, NEGI-SENSEI?
UH?
UH...
WHAT, YOU WERE IN THE AREA AND JUST DROPPED IN?
MORE OR LESS.
I'VE GOT TO FIND MY WAND!
NORMALLY I CAN JUST CLOSE MY EYES AND SENSE ITS WHERE-ABOUTS...BUT I'M GETTING NOTHING.
SOME WIZARD I AM. FORSAKEN BY MY OWN WAND.
......
NEGI-BOZU, YOU NEED TO GET SOME SESSHA—SAMURAI—TRAINING FOR AWHILE.
SNIFFLE
HUH?
PERK
WHAT !?
MIGHT BE A GOOD WAY FOR YOU TO LEARN SELF-SUFFICIENCY.
WANT TO GO FISHING? THE CHAR ARE PLENTIFUL THIS TIME OF YEAR.
UH...
OK.
LOOK, OVER THERE.
WOW! THERE'S A LOT OF THEM.

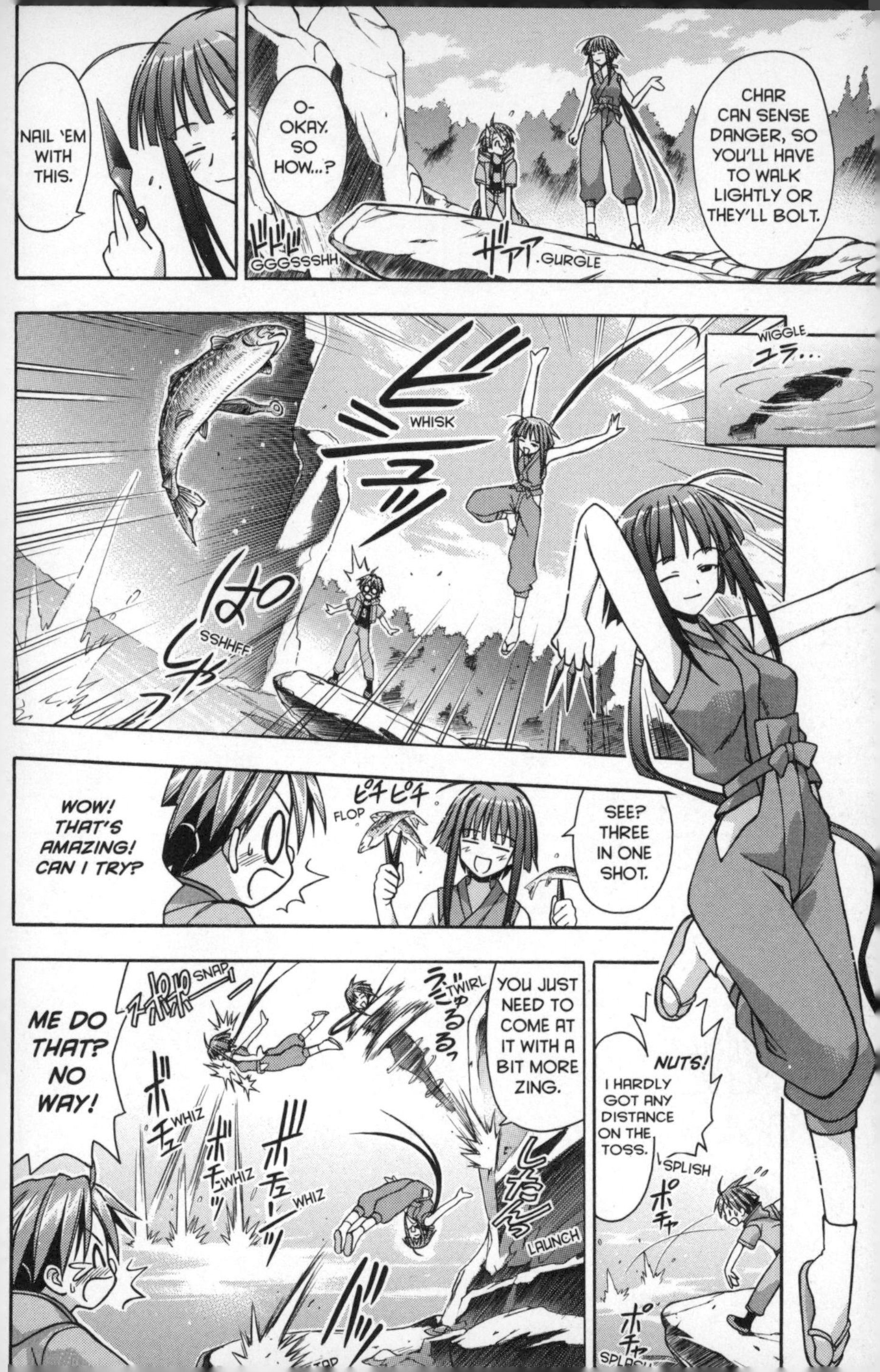
CHAR CAN SENSE DANGER, SO YOU'LL HAVE TO WALK LIGHTLY OR THEY'LL BOLT.
O-OKAY. SO HOW...?
GURGLE
GGGSSSHH
NAIL 'EM WITH THIS.
WIGGLE
WHISK
SSHHFF
SEE? THREE IN ONE SHOT.
FLOP
WOW! THAT'S AMAZING! CAN I TRY?
NUTS!
I HARDLY GOT ANY DISTANCE ON THE TOSS.
SPLISH
YOU JUST NEED TO COME AT IT WITH A BIT MORE ZING.
TWIRL
SNAP
LAUNCH
WHIZ
WHIZ
WHIZ
ME DO THAT? NO WAY!

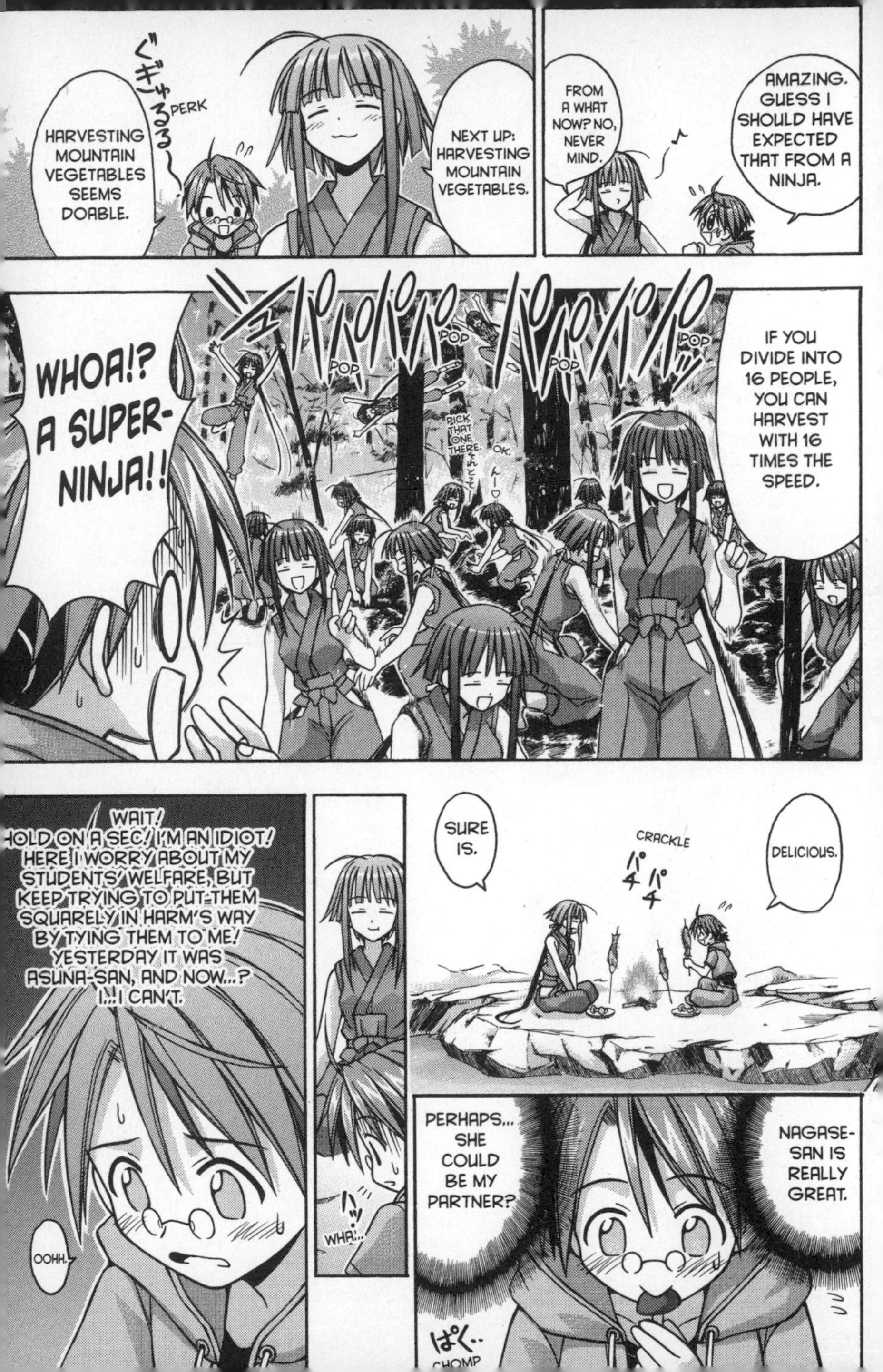
AMAZING. GUESS I SHOULD HAVE EXPECTED THAT FROM A NINJA.
FROM A WHAT NOW? NO, NEVER MIND.
NEXT UP: HARVESTING MOUNTAIN VEGETABLES.
ぐぎゅるる~
PERK
HARVESTING MOUNTAIN VEGETABLES SEEMS DOABLE.
IF YOU DIVIDE INTO 16 PEOPLE, YOU CAN HARVEST WITH 16 TIMES THE SPEED.
POP
POP
POP
POP
OK.
PICK THAT ONE THERE.
WHOA!? A SUPER-NINJA!!
DELICIOUS.
CRACKLE
SURE IS.
NAGASE-SAN IS REALLY GREAT.
PERHAPS... SHE COULD BE MY PARTNER?
ぱく..
CHOMP
WHA...!
WAIT! HOLD ON A SEC! I'M AN IDIOT! HERE I WORRY ABOUT MY STUDENTS' WELFARE, BUT KEEP TRYING TO PUT THEM SQUARELY IN HARM'S WAY BY TYING THEM TO ME! YESTERDAY IT WAS ASUNA-SAN, AND NOW...? I...I CAN'T.
OOHH.

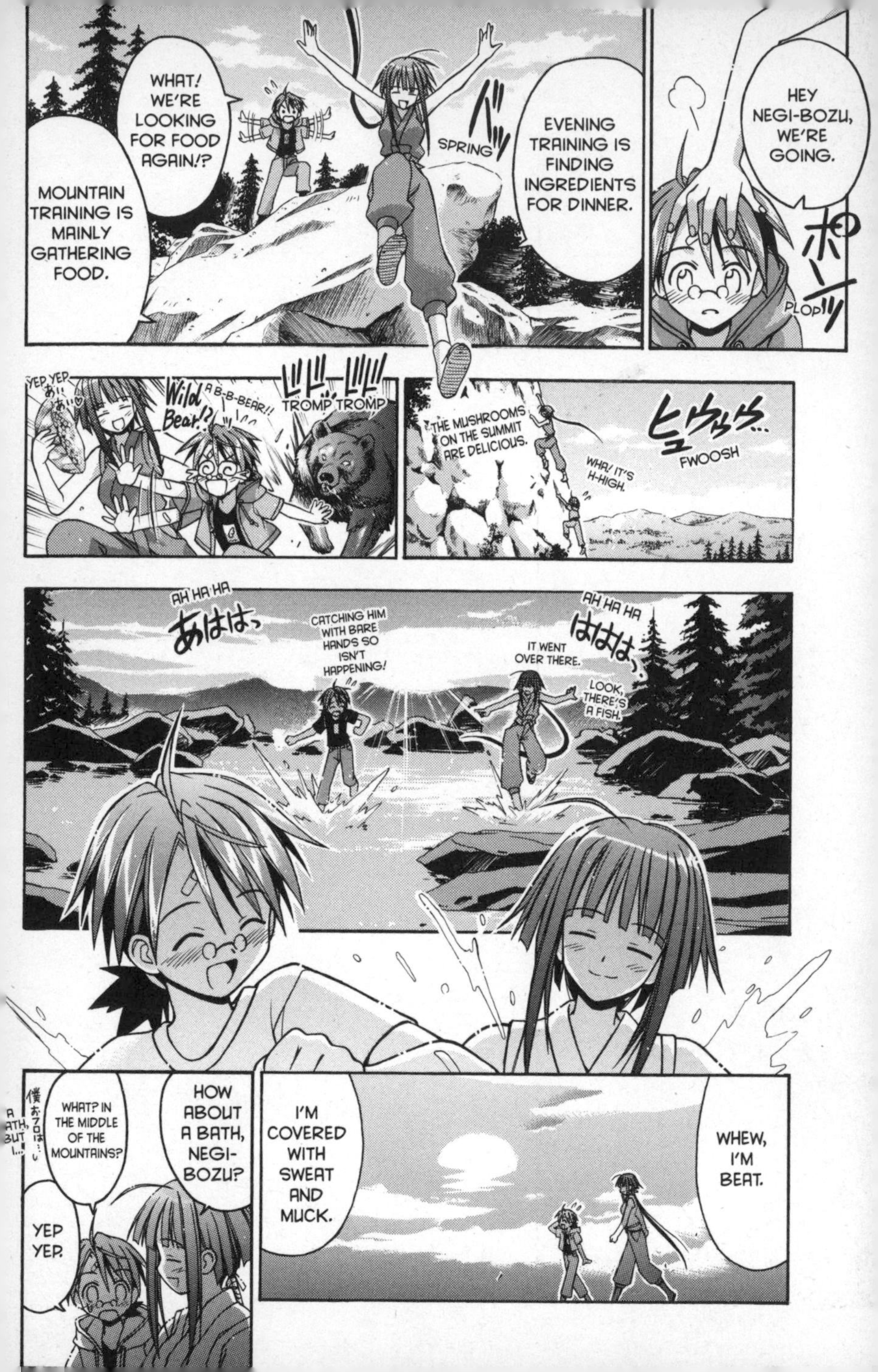
HEY NEGI-BOZU, WE'RE GOING.
PLOP
EVENING TRAINING IS FINDING INGREDIENTS FOR DINNER.
SPRING
WHAT! WE'RE LOOKING FOR FOOD AGAIN!?
MOUNTAIN TRAINING IS MAINLY GATHERING FOOD.
THE MUSHROOMS ON THE SUMMIT ARE DELICIOUS.
WHA! IT'S H-HIGH.
FWOOSH
TROMP TROMP
A B-B-BEAR!!
Wild Bear!?
YEP YEP
AH HA HA
ははは
IT WENT OVER THERE.
LOOK, THERE'S A FISH.
CATCHING HIM WITH BARE HANDS SO ISN'T HAPPENING!
AH HA HA
あはは
WHEW, I'M BEAT.
I'M COVERED WITH SWEAT AND MUCK.
HOW ABOUT A BATH, NEGI-BOZU?
WHAT? IN THE MIDDLE OF THE MOUNTAINS?
A BATH, BUT I...!
YEP YEP.

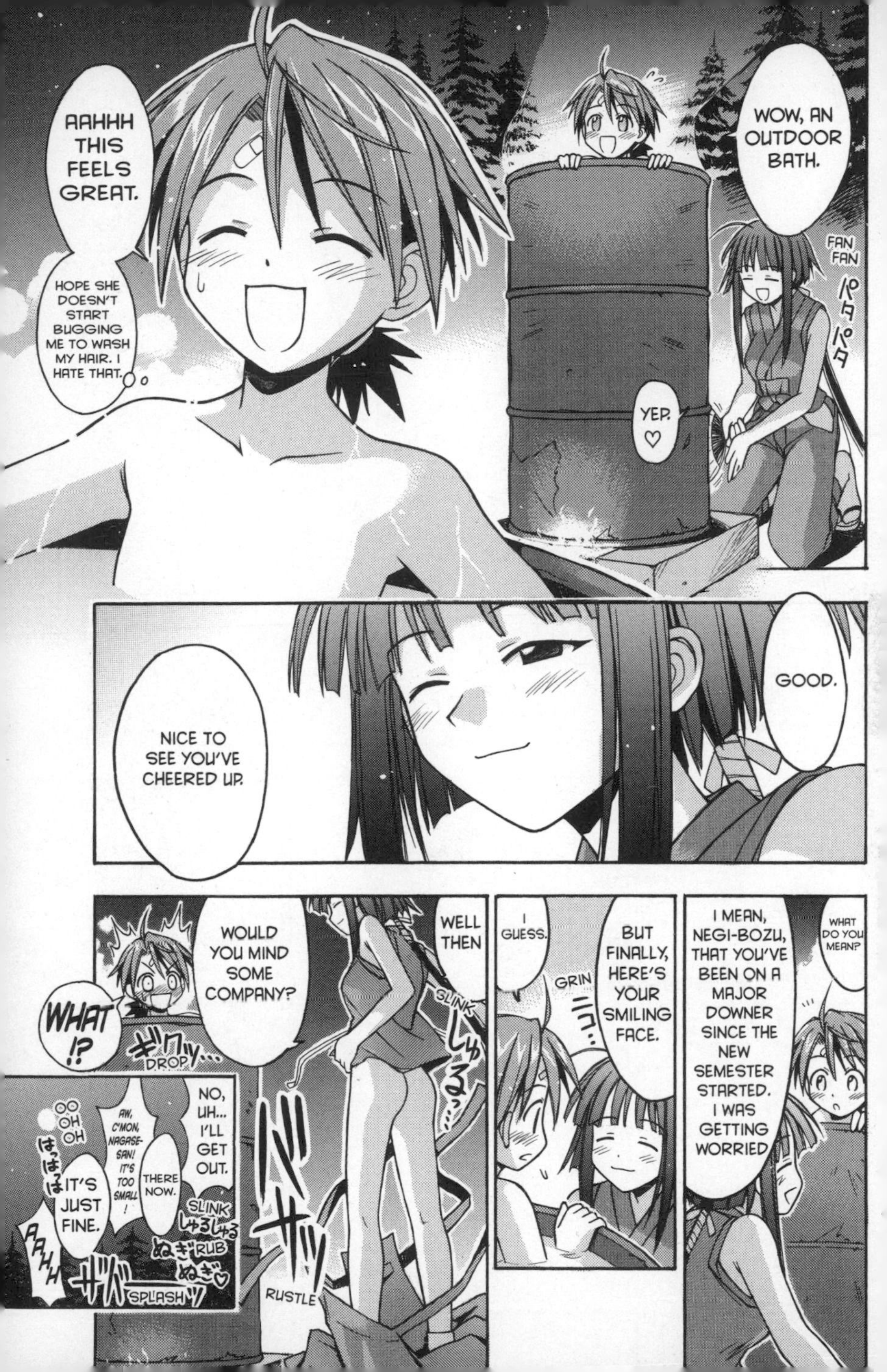
WOW, AN OUTDOOR BATH.
FAN FAN
パタパタ
YEP. ♡
AAHHH THIS FEELS GREAT.
HOPE SHE DOESN'T START BUGGING ME TO WASH MY HAIR. I HATE THAT.
GOOD.
NICE TO SEE YOU'VE CHEERED UP.
WHAT DO YOU MEAN?
I MEAN, NEGI-BOZU, THAT YOU'VE BEEN ON A MAJOR DOWNER SINCE THE NEW SEMESTER STARTED. I WAS GETTING WORRIED
BUT FINALLY, HERE'S YOUR SMILING FACE.
GRIN
ニコ…
I GUESS.
WELL THEN
WOULD YOU MIND SOME COMPANY?
SLINK
しゅるっ…
WHAT!?
ギクッ… DROP
バサッ
RUSTLE
NO, UH... I'LL GET OUT.
AW, C'MON, NAGASE-SAN! IT'S TOO SMALL!
THERE NOW.
SLINK
しゅるしゅる
ぬぎ RUB ぬぎ♡
OH OH
はっはっは
IT'S JUST FINE.
AAHH
ザバー
SPLASH

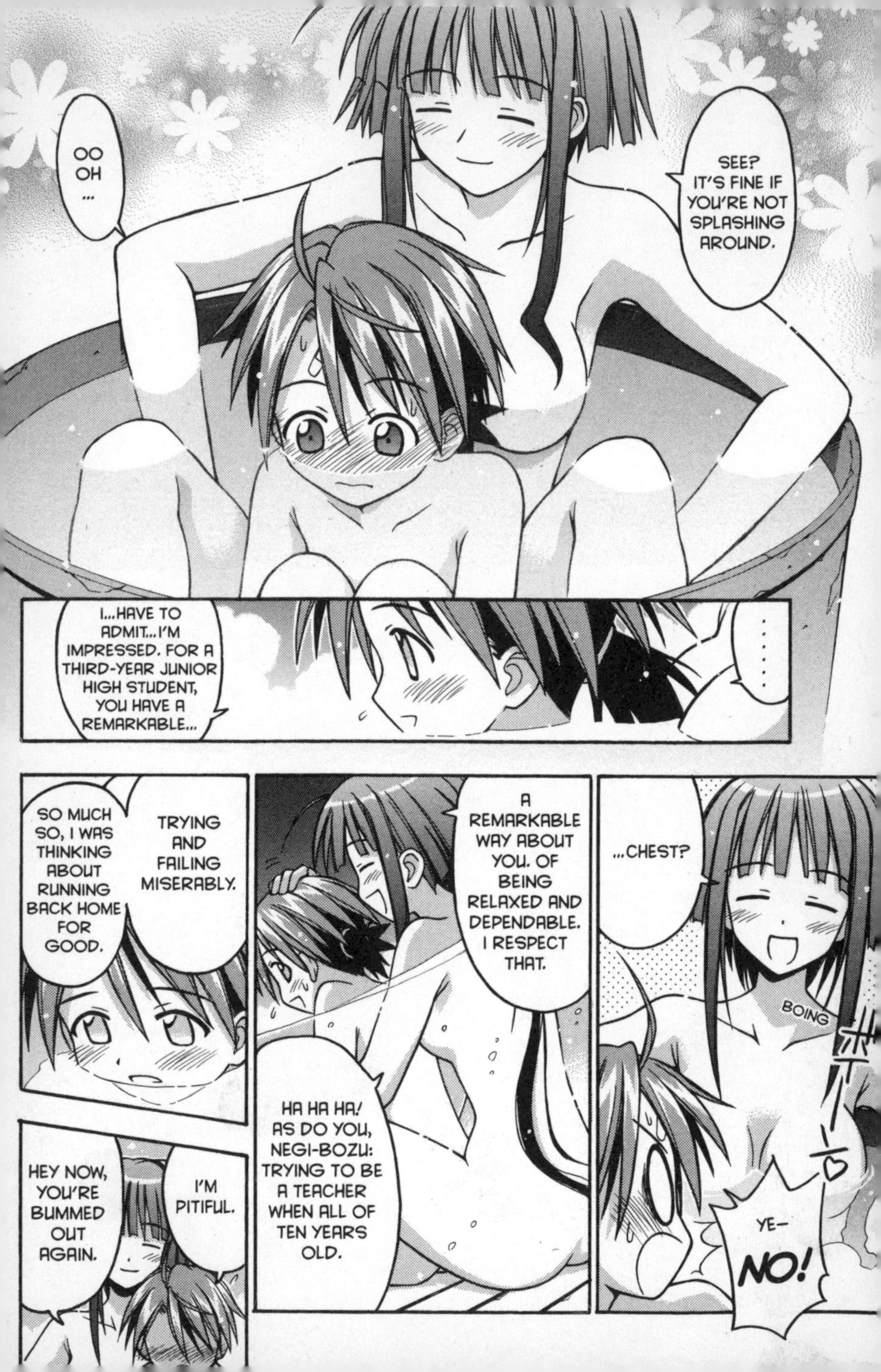
SEE? IT'S FINE IF YOU'RE NOT SPLASHING AROUND.
OO OH ...
......
I...HAVE TO ADMIT...I'M IMPRESSED. FOR A THIRD-YEAR JUNIOR HIGH STUDENT, YOU HAVE A REMARKABLE...
...CHEST?
BOING
YE—
NO!
A REMARKABLE WAY ABOUT YOU. OF BEING RELAXED AND DEPENDABLE. I RESPECT THAT.
HA HA HA! AS DO YOU, NEGI-BOZU: TRYING TO BE A TEACHER WHEN ALL OF TEN YEARS OLD.
TRYING AND FAILING MISERABLY.
SO MUCH SO, I WAS THINKING ABOUT RUNNING BACK HOME FOR GOOD.
I'M PITIFUL.
HEY NOW, YOU'RE BUMMED OUT AGAIN.

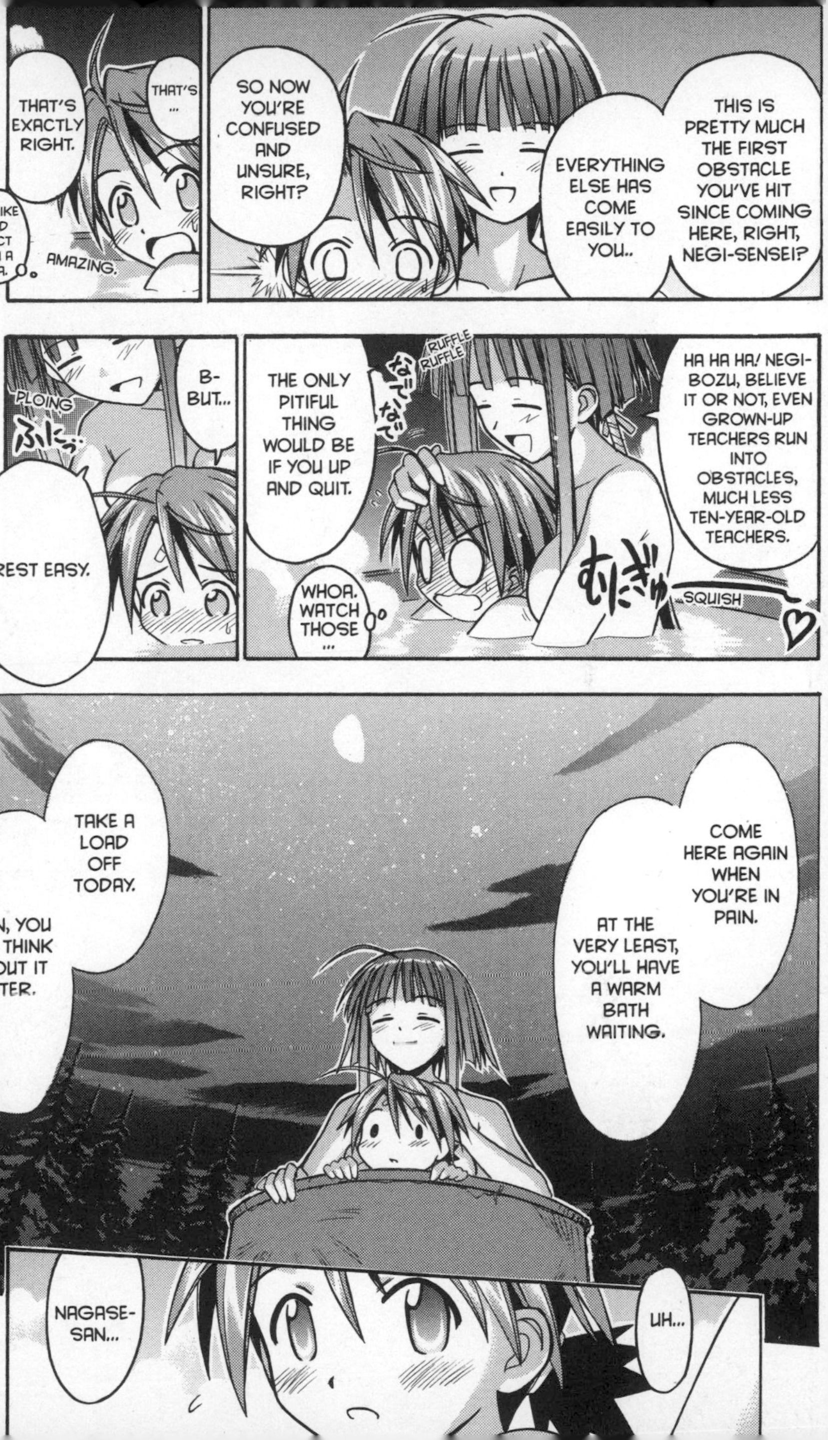
THIS IS PRETTY MUCH THE FIRST OBSTACLE YOU'VE HIT SINCE COMING HERE, RIGHT, NEGI-SENSEI?
EVERYTHING ELSE HAS COME EASILY TO YOU..
SO NOW YOU'RE CONFUSED AND UNSURE, RIGHT?
THAT'S ...
THAT'S EXACTLY RIGHT.
AMAZING.
JUST LIKE YOU'D EXPECT FROM A NINJA.
HA HA HA! NEGI-BOZU, BELIEVE IT OR NOT, EVEN GROWN-UP TEACHERS RUN INTO OBSTACLES, MUCH LESS TEN-YEAR-OLD TEACHERS.
なでなで
RUFFLE RUFFLE
THE ONLY PITIFUL THING WOULD BE IF YOU UP AND QUIT.
むにぎゅ
SQUISH
WHOA. WATCH THOSE ...
B-BUT...
ふにっ
PLOING
REST EASY.
COME HERE AGAIN WHEN YOU'RE IN PAIN.
AT THE VERY LEAST, YOU'LL HAVE A WARM BATH WAITING.
TAKE A LOAD OFF TODAY.
THEN, YOU CAN THINK ABOUT IT LATER.
UH...
NAGASE-SAN...

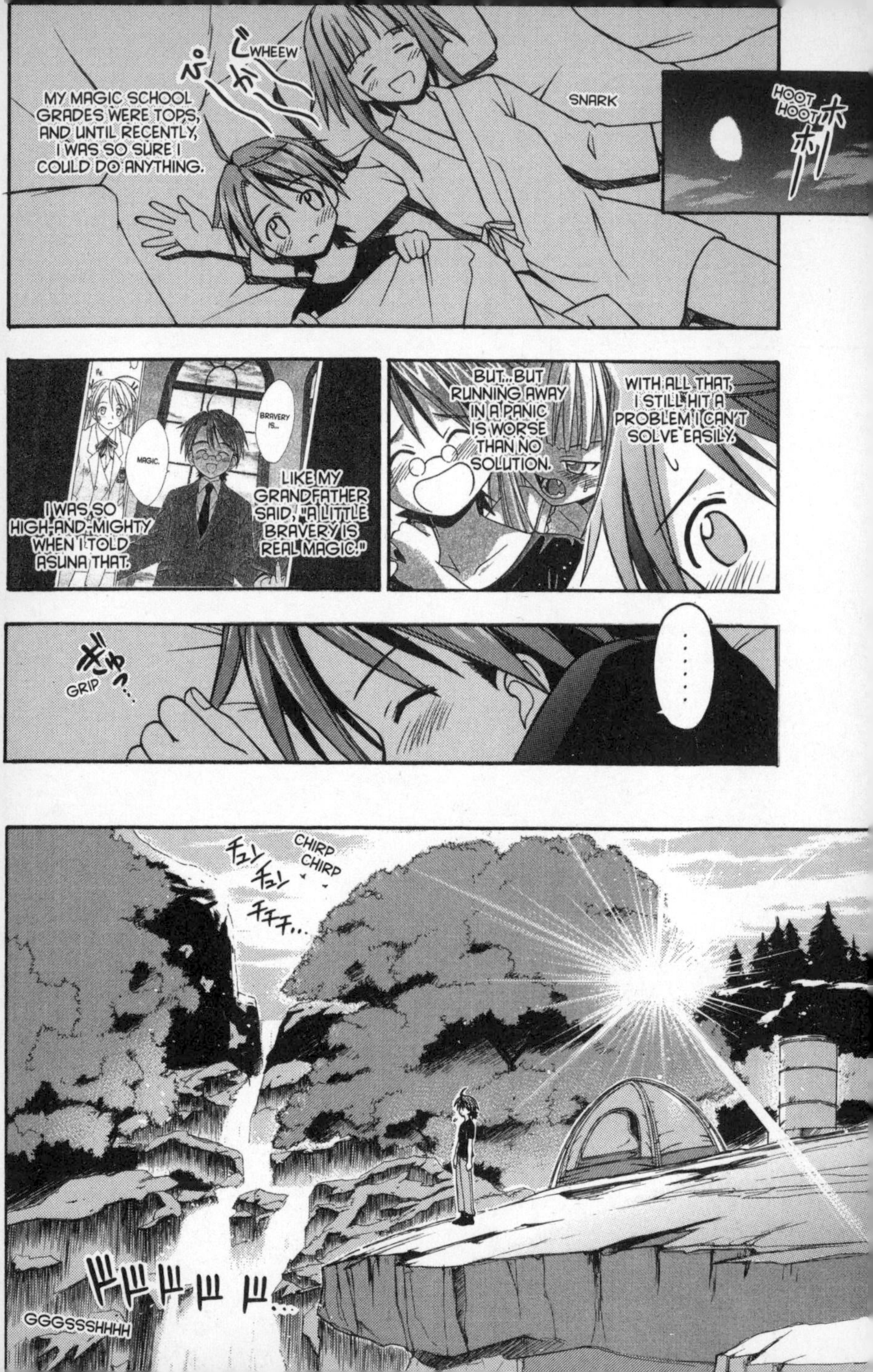
HOOT HOOT
SNARK
WHEEW
MY MAGIC SCHOOL GRADES WERE TOPS, AND UNTIL RECENTLY, I WAS SO SURE I COULD DO ANYTHING.
WITH ALL THAT, I STILL HIT A PROBLEM I CAN'T SOLVE EASILY.
BUT...BUT RUNNING AWAY IN A PANIC IS WORSE THAN NO SOLUTION.
LIKE MY GRANDFATHER SAID, "A LITTLE BRAVERY IS REAL MAGIC."
BRAVERY IS...
MAGIC.
I WAS SO HIGH-AND-MIGHTY WHEN I TOLD ASUNA THAT.
......
GRIP
CHIRP CHIRP
GGGSSSHHHH

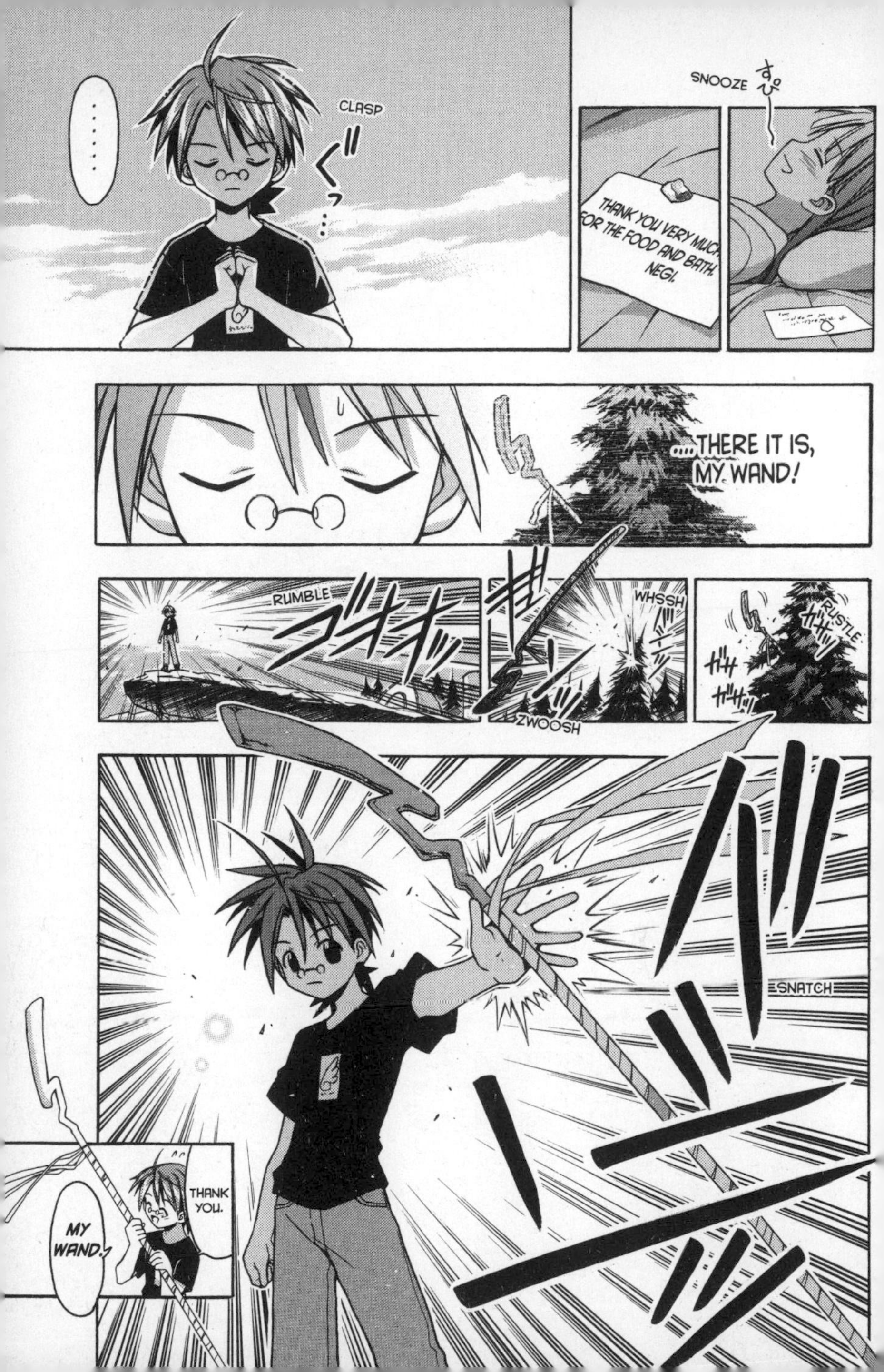
SNOOZE
THANK YOU VERY MUCH FOR THE FOOD AND BATH. NEGI.
......
CLASP
....THERE IT IS, MY WAND!
RUSTLE
WHSSH
ZWOOSH
RUMBLE
SNATCH
THANK YOU.
MY WAND.

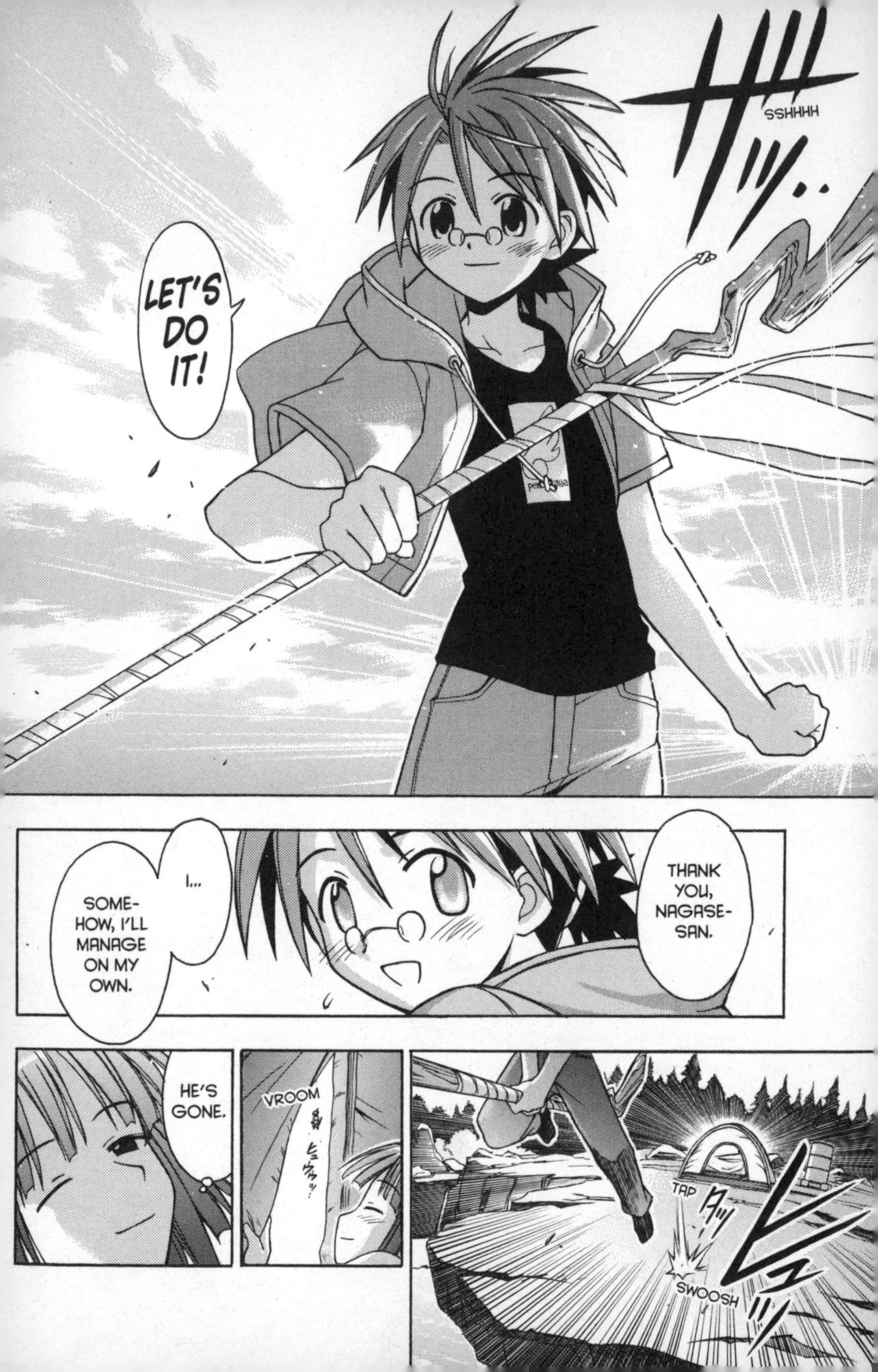
SSHHHH
LET'S DO IT!
THANK YOU, NAGASE-SAN.
I... SOME-HOW, I'LL MANAGE ON MY OWN.
TAP
SWOOSH
VROOM
HE'S GONE.

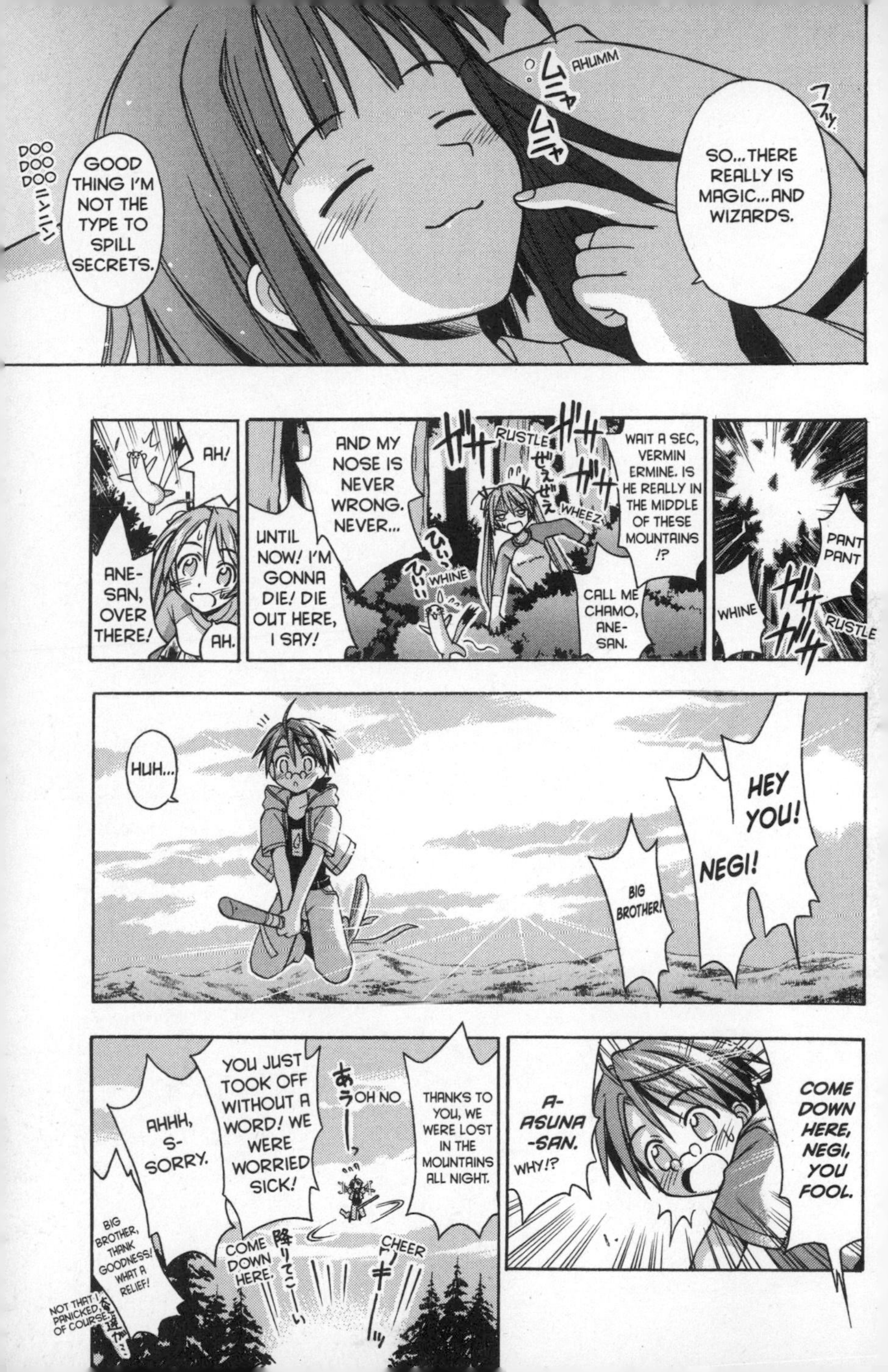
SO... THERE REALLY IS MAGIC... AND WIZARDS.
AHUMM
GOOD THING I'M NOT THE TYPE TO SPILL SECRETS.
DOO DOO DOO
PANT PANT
WHINE
RUSTLE
WAIT A SEC, VERMIN ERMINE. IS HE REALLY IN THE MIDDLE OF THESE MOUNTAINS !?
CALL ME CHAMO, ANE-SAN.
RUSTLE
WHEEZ
AND MY NOSE IS NEVER WRONG. NEVER...
UNTIL NOW! I'M GONNA DIE! DIE OUT HERE, I SAY!
WHINE
AH!
ANE-SAN, OVER THERE!
AH.
HEY YOU!
NEGI!
BIG BROTHER!
HUH...
COME DOWN HERE, NEGI, YOU FOOL.
A-ASUNA-SAN.
WHY!?
THANKS TO YOU, WE WERE LOST IN THE MOUNTAINS ALL NIGHT.
OH NO
CHEER
YOU JUST TOOK OFF WITHOUT A WORD! WE WERE WORRIED SICK!
AHHH, S-SORRY.
COME DOWN HERE.
BIG BROTHER, THANK GOODNESS! WHAT A RELIEF!
NOT THAT I PANICKED, OF COURSE.

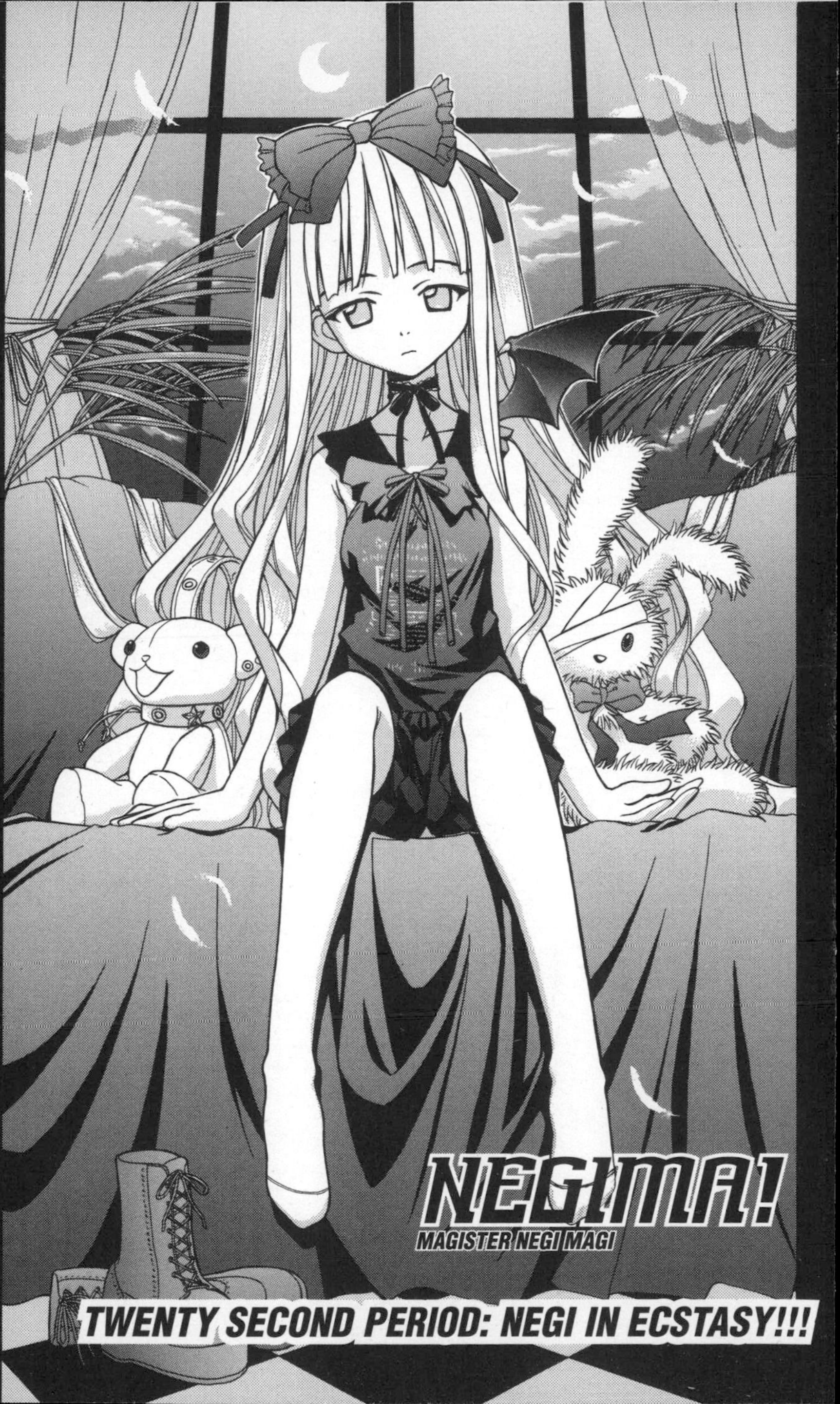
NEGIMA!
MAGISTER NEGI MAGI
TWENTY SECOND PERIOD: NEGI IN ECSTASY!!!

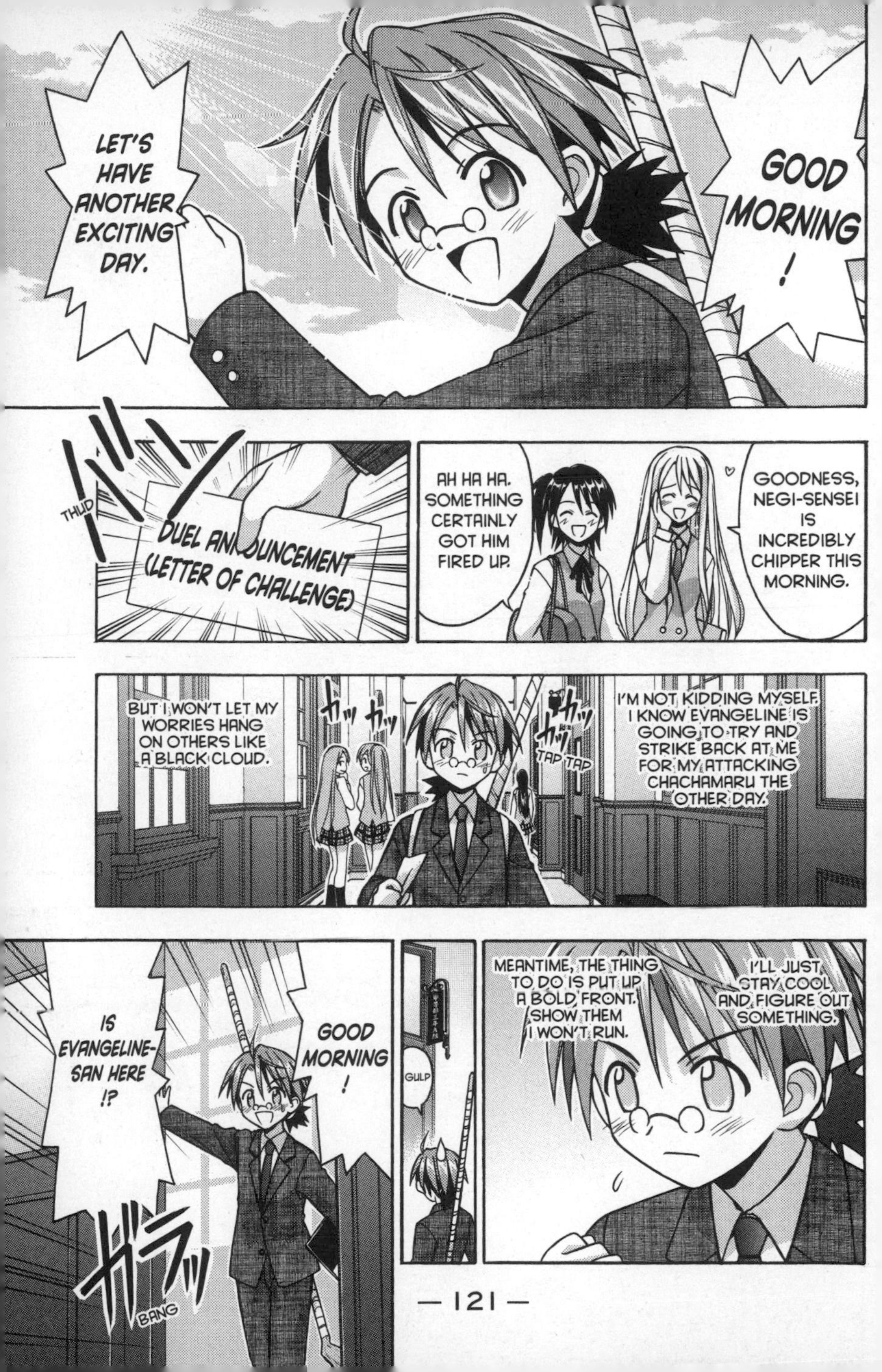
GOOD MORNING!
LET'S HAVE ANOTHER EXCITING DAY.
GOODNESS, NEGI-SENSEI IS INCREDIBLY CHIPPER THIS MORNING.
AH HA HA. SOMETHING CERTAINLY GOT HIM FIRED UP.
THUD
DUEL ANNOUNCEMENT (LETTER OF CHALLENGE)
I'M NOT KIDDING MYSELF. I KNOW EVANGELINE IS GOING TO TRY AND STRIKE BACK AT ME FOR MY ATTACKING CHACHAMARU THE OTHER DAY.
TAP TAP
BUT I WON'T LET MY WORRIES HANG ON OTHERS LIKE A BLACK CLOUD.
I'LL JUST STAY COOL AND FIGURE OUT SOMETHING.
MEANTIME, THE THING TO DO IS PUT UP A BOLD FRONT. SHOW THEM I WON'T RUN.
GULP
GOOD MORNING!
IS EVANGELINE-SAN HERE!?
BANG

THERE'S A MESSAGE THAT SHE'S SICK AND TAKING THE DAY OFF.

UH...HUH ...IS THAT RIGHT.

EVANGELINE HASN'T COME YET.

CHATTER

G-GOOD MORNING.

OH, GOOD MORNING, NEGI-KUN.

GOOD MORNING

MORNIN'

AH! NEGI, WHERE'RE YOU GOING?

SEE YA!!

DASH

PANT PANT. AM I LATE? AM I--

YOU'RE FINE.

SHE'S DITCHING AGAIN... HUNH. MAYBE SHE'S AS AFRAID TO FACE ME AS I WAS TO FACE HER.

OH, RIGHT. LIKE A WIZARD VAMPIRE GETS LAID LOW WITH THE SNIFFLES.

WHAT A DIFFERENCE A WEEKEND MAKES.

HAVE YOU NOTICED BIG BROTHER'S ATTITUDE CHANGE SINCE YESTERDAY? SOMETHING MUST'VE TURNED HIM AROUND. BUT WHAT?

WHISPER

WHAT'S GOTTEN INTO HIM? HE'S SO FULL OF ENERGY. IT MUST HAVE SOMETHING TO DO WITH EVANGELINE.

ACADEMY CITY, NUMBER 29, SAKURA-GAOKA-4 CHOME. IS THIS IT?

ACCORDING TO THE CLASS LIST, EVANGELINE-SAN LIVES OFF CAMPUS.

UH...

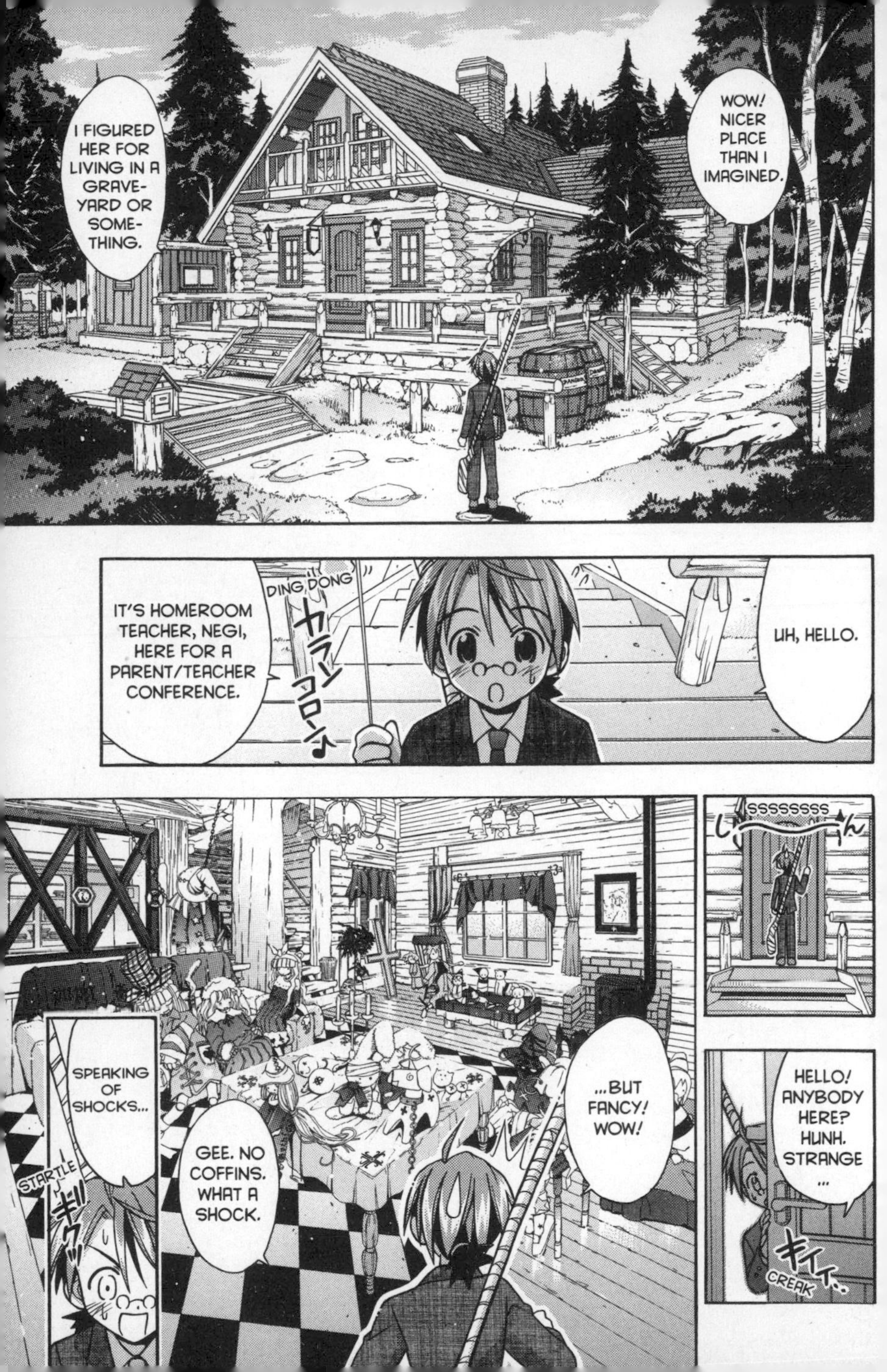
WOW! NICER PLACE THAN I IMAGINED.
I FIGURED HER FOR LIVING IN A GRAVEYARD OR SOMETHING.
UH, HELLO.
DING DONG
カラン コローン♪
IT'S HOMEROOM TEACHER, NEGI, HERE FOR A PARENT/TEACHER CONFERENCE.
SSSSSSSS
しーん
HELLO! ANYBODY HERE? HUNH. STRANGE ...
キイイ..
CREAK
...BUT FANCY! WOW!
GEE. NO COFFINS. WHAT A SHOCK.
SPEAKING OF SHOCKS...
STARTLE
ギクッ

SHE'S BURNING UP!

HOLY--! SHE REALLY IS SICK!

WHOA!? WHAT'S GOING ON!?

PLUNK
ぽてっ…

SMIRK

UGH.

CRACK

"HAY FEVER"? WHAT KINDA VAMPIRE IS SHE?

YES. SHE HAS EVERY FEVER FROM REGULAR TO HAY. I'M PUTTING HER TO BED.

BONG BONG

CLICK

CLANK

DOESN'T SOUND SO HOT, EITHER.

WHEEZ WHEEZ

SHE REALLY DOESN'T LOOK WELL.

WHAT!? M-ME!?

I HAVE SOME CONNECTIONS AT UNIVERSITY HOSPITAL WHO CAN SLIP ME THE ANTIBIOTICS SHE REALLY NEEDS...NO QUESTIONS ASKED, YOU KNOW? CAN YOU WATCH HER WHILE I'M OUT?

THAT IS TO SAY, A NON-MAGICAL, NON-WIZARDING TEN-YEAR-OLD, OF COURSE.

AT THE MOMENT, SHE'S SO WEAK, SHE'S ABOUT AS DANGEROUS AS A TEN-YEAR-OLD.

NEGI-SENSEI.

OH. OF COURSE.

O...OKAY. BUT HURRY BACK. I HAVE CLASS TO TEACH.

SHE TRUSTS ME TO GUARD MY HELPLESS ENEMY? WHAT IS SHE THINKING?

I NEED SOMEONE DEPEND-ABLE, SENSEI. YOU'RE IT.

YES.

...LIKE SANDPAPER. THIRSTY... SO...

HUNH HUNH THROAT FEELS LIKE...

GEEZ... YOU'RE REALLY SUFFER-ING, AREN'T YOU, EVANGE-LINE?

I WONDER IF...? MY HEALING SPELL MIGHT BE EFFECTIVE ON THAT RASPY THROAT.

COUGH COUGH

UGH, HACK HACK.

NOT DRINKING, HUH. WHAT DO YOU NEED? TEA? COLA? THERE MUST BE SOME-THING YOU--? OH. OH, UCK, I KNOW. BLOOD, RIGHT?

HACK COUGH

UGHH

SURE. HERE'S... HERE'S SOME WATER...

"IT"? WHAT—AHHH. THE SUNLIGHT. GOT'CHA.

BURNING UP...MAKE IT...GO AWAY...

ACCKK! HERE, HAVE JUST A LITTLE SIP.

SUCK SUCK

GULP GULP

GREAT. SHE'S NOT WEARING UNDERWEAR. FIGURES.

SHE'LL GET CHILLS IF I DON'T CHANGE HER.

HER PAJAMAS ARE SOAKED THROUGH WITH SWEAT.

SHIVER

PANT PANT, SO COLD...

NOT LOOKING AT ALL, NOPE.

SQUIRM

I'M NOT LOOKING, I'M NOT LOOKING... I'M HER TEACHER, LA LA LA...

OKAY...AT LEAST SHE STOPPED THRASHING AROUND AND MOANING.

WHISK

COME FOR THE FIGHT, STAY FOR THE NURSING.

BOY, THIS HAS TURNED INTO ONE WEIRD MORNING.

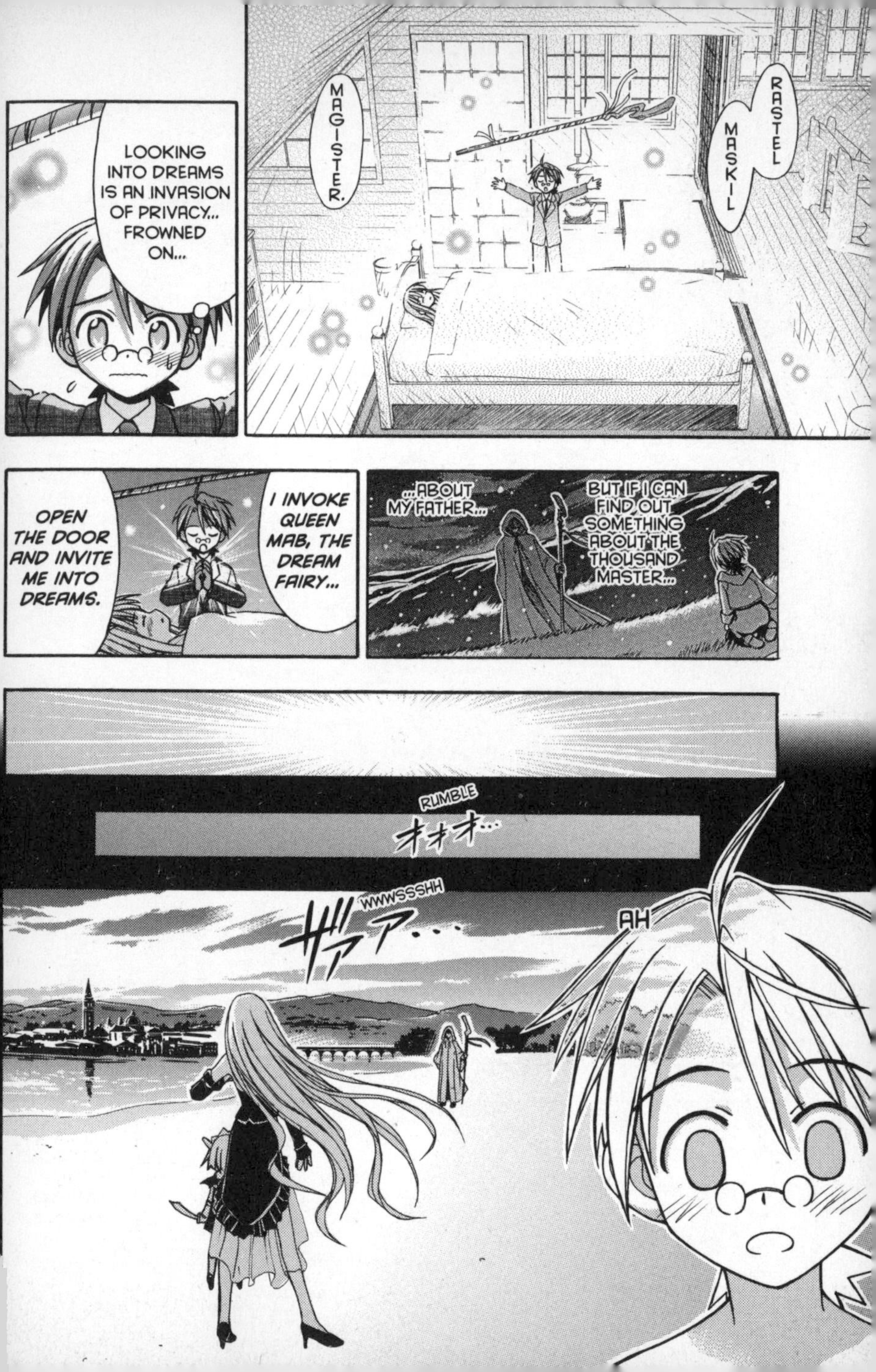
RASTEL MASKIL
MAGISTER.
LOOKING INTO DREAMS IS AN INVASION OF PRIVACY... FROWNED ON...
BUT IF I CAN FIND OUT SOMETHING ABOUT THE THOUSAND MASTER...
...ABOUT MY FATHER...
I INVOKE QUEEN MAB, THE DREAM FAIRY...
OPEN THE DOOR AND INVITE ME INTO DREAMS.
RUMBLE
オォォ…
AH
WWWSSSHH
ザァア…

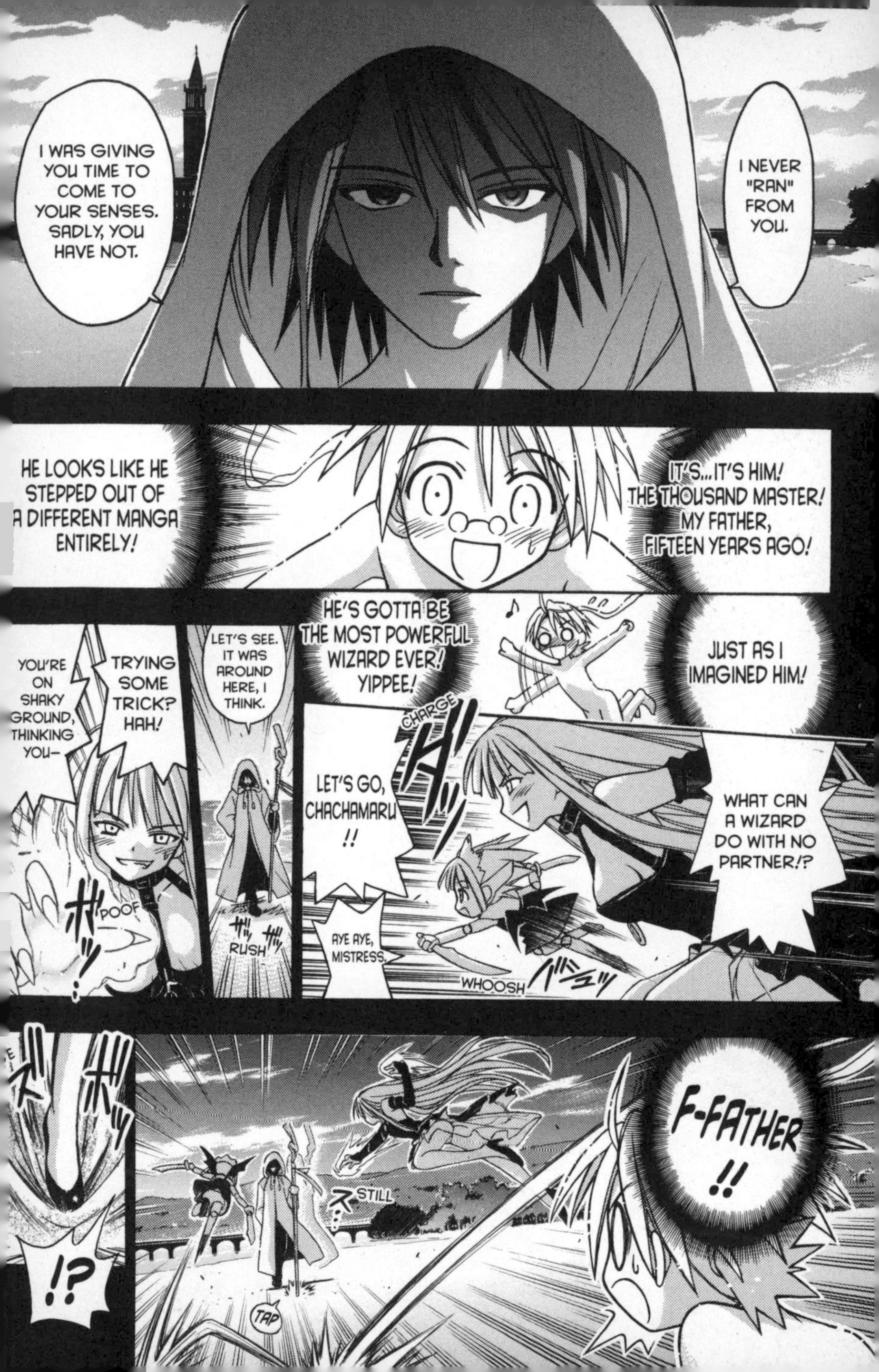
I NEVER "RAN" FROM YOU.
I WAS GIVING YOU TIME TO COME TO YOUR SENSES. SADLY, YOU HAVE NOT.
IT'S...IT'S HIM! THE THOUSAND MASTER! MY FATHER, FIFTEEN YEARS AGO!
HE LOOKS LIKE HE STEPPED OUT OF A DIFFERENT MANGA ENTIRELY!
JUST AS I IMAGINED HIM!
HE'S GOTTA BE THE MOST POWERFUL WIZARD EVER! YIPPEE!
WHAT CAN A WIZARD DO WITH NO PARTNER!?
CHARGE
LET'S GO, CHACHAMARU!!
AYE AYE, MISTRESS.
WHOOSH
LET'S SEE. IT WAS AROUND HERE, I THINK.
RUSH
TRYING SOME TRICK? HAH!
YOU'RE ON SHAKY GROUND, THINKING YOU—
POOF
F-FATHER!!
STILL
TAP
!?

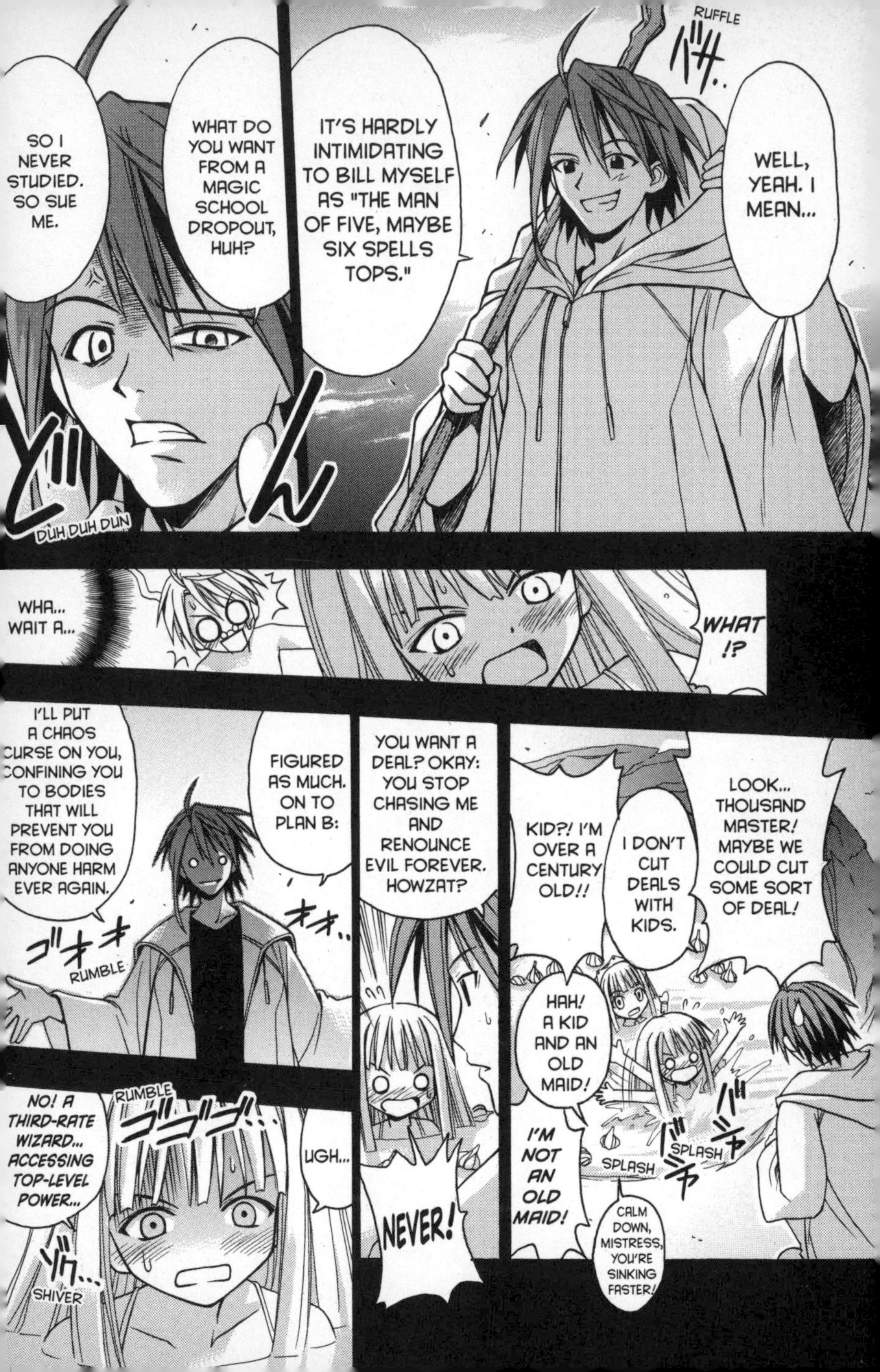
RUFFLE
WELL, YEAH. I MEAN...
IT'S HARDLY INTIMIDATING TO BILL MYSELF AS "THE MAN OF FIVE, MAYBE SIX SPELLS TOPS."
WHAT DO YOU WANT FROM A MAGIC SCHOOL DROPOUT, HUH?
SO I NEVER STUDIED. SO SUE ME.
DUH DUH DUN
WHAT !?
WHA... WAIT A...
LOOK... THOUSAND MASTER! MAYBE WE COULD CUT SOME SORT OF DEAL!
I DON'T CUT DEALS WITH KIDS.
KID?! I'M OVER A CENTURY OLD!!
HAH! A KID AND AN OLD MAID!
SPLASH
SPLASH
I'M NOT AN OLD MAID!
CALM DOWN, MISTRESS, YOU'RE SINKING FASTER!
YOU WANT A DEAL? OKAY: YOU STOP CHASING ME AND RENOUNCE EVIL FOREVER. HOWZAT?
NEVER!
FIGURED AS MUCH. ON TO PLAN B:
I'LL PUT A CHAOS CURSE ON YOU, CONFINING YOU TO BODIES THAT WILL PREVENT YOU FROM DOING ANYONE HARM EVER AGAIN.
RUMBLE
UGH...
RUMBLE
NO! A THIRD-RATE WIZARD... ACCESSING TOP-LEVEL POWER...
SHIVER

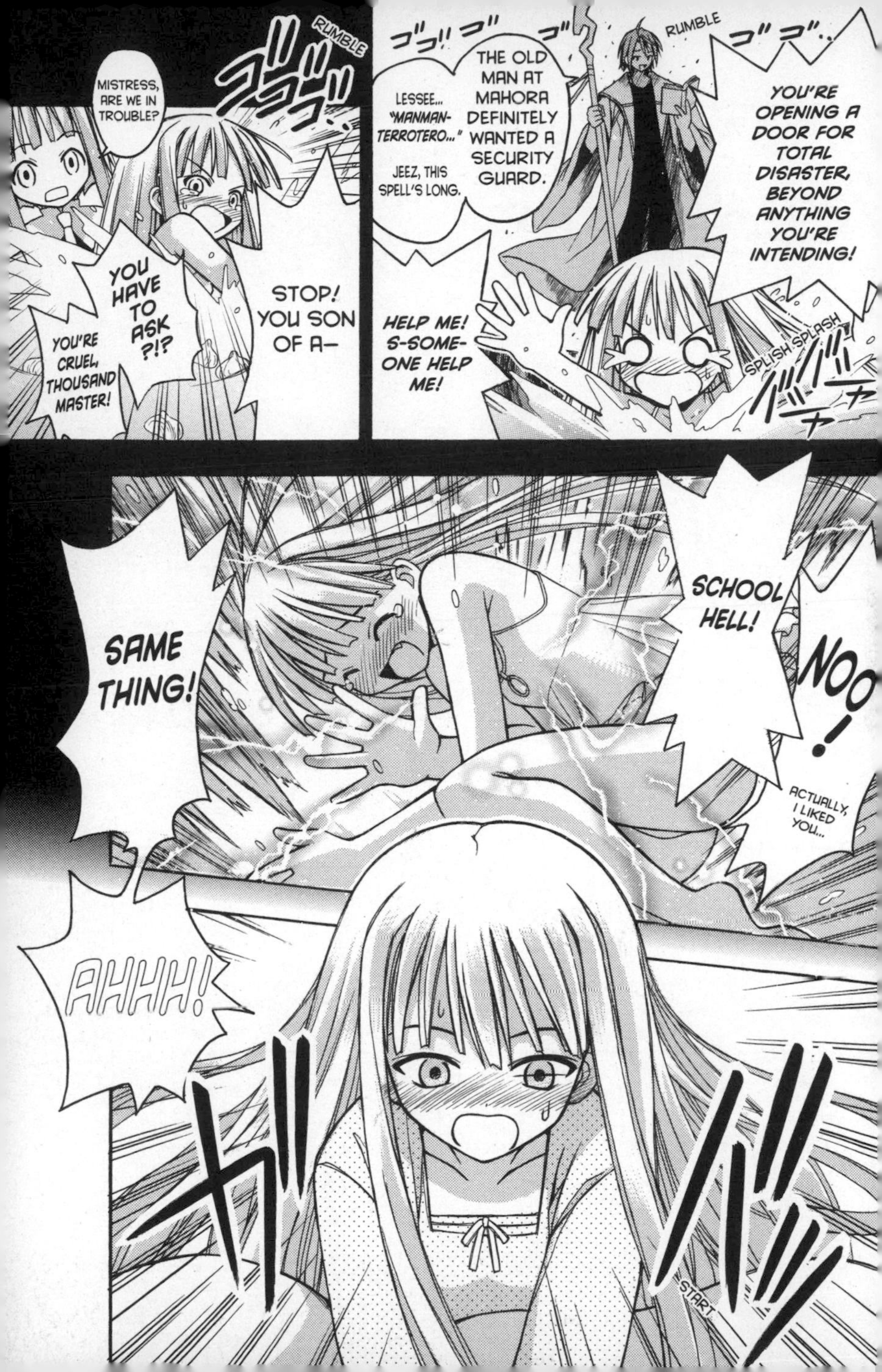
RUMBLE
YOU'RE OPENING A DOOR FOR TOTAL DISASTER, BEYOND ANYTHING YOU'RE INTENDING!
THE OLD MAN AT MAHORA DEFINITELY WANTED A SECURITY GUARD.
LESSEE... "MANMAN-TERROTERO..." JEEZ, THIS SPELL'S LONG.
HELP ME! S-SOMEONE HELP ME!
SPLISH SPLASH
RUMBLE
MISTRESS, ARE WE IN TROUBLE?
STOP! YOU SON OF A–
YOU HAVE TO ASK ?!?
YOU'RE CRUEL, THOUSAND MASTER!
SCHOOL HELL!
NOO!
ACTUALLY, I LIKED YOU...
SAME THING!
AHHH!
START

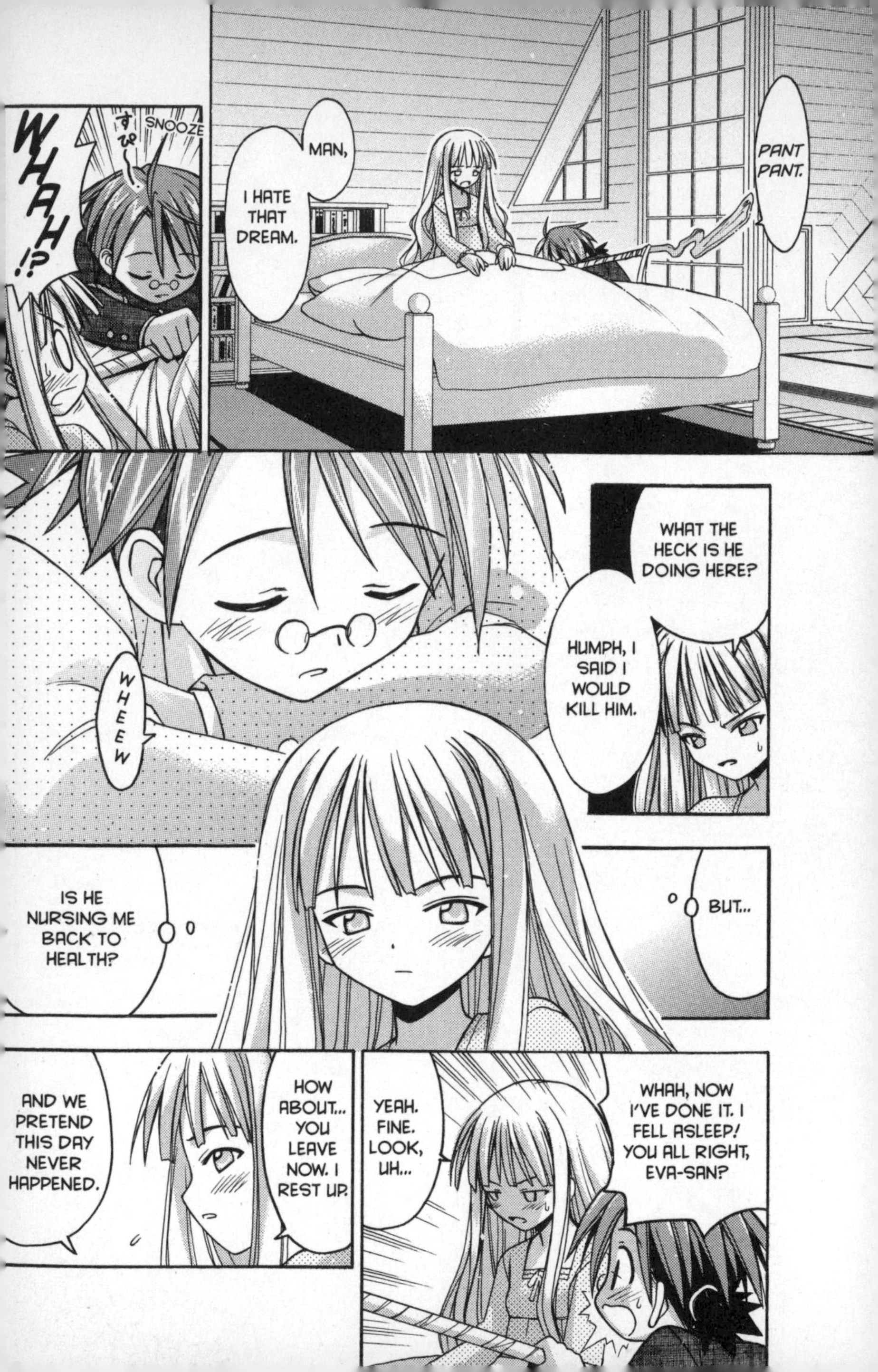
PANT PANT.
MAN, I HATE THAT DREAM.
WHAH!?
すぴ～
SNOOZE
WHAT THE HECK IS HE DOING HERE?
HUMPH, I SAID I WOULD KILL HIM.
WHEEEW
BUT...
IS HE NURSING ME BACK TO HEALTH?
WHAH, NOW I'VE DONE IT. I FELL ASLEEP! YOU ALL RIGHT, EVA-SAN?
YEAH. FINE. LOOK, UH...
HOW ABOUT... YOU LEAVE NOW. I REST UP.
AND WE PRETEND THIS DAY NEVER HAPPENED.

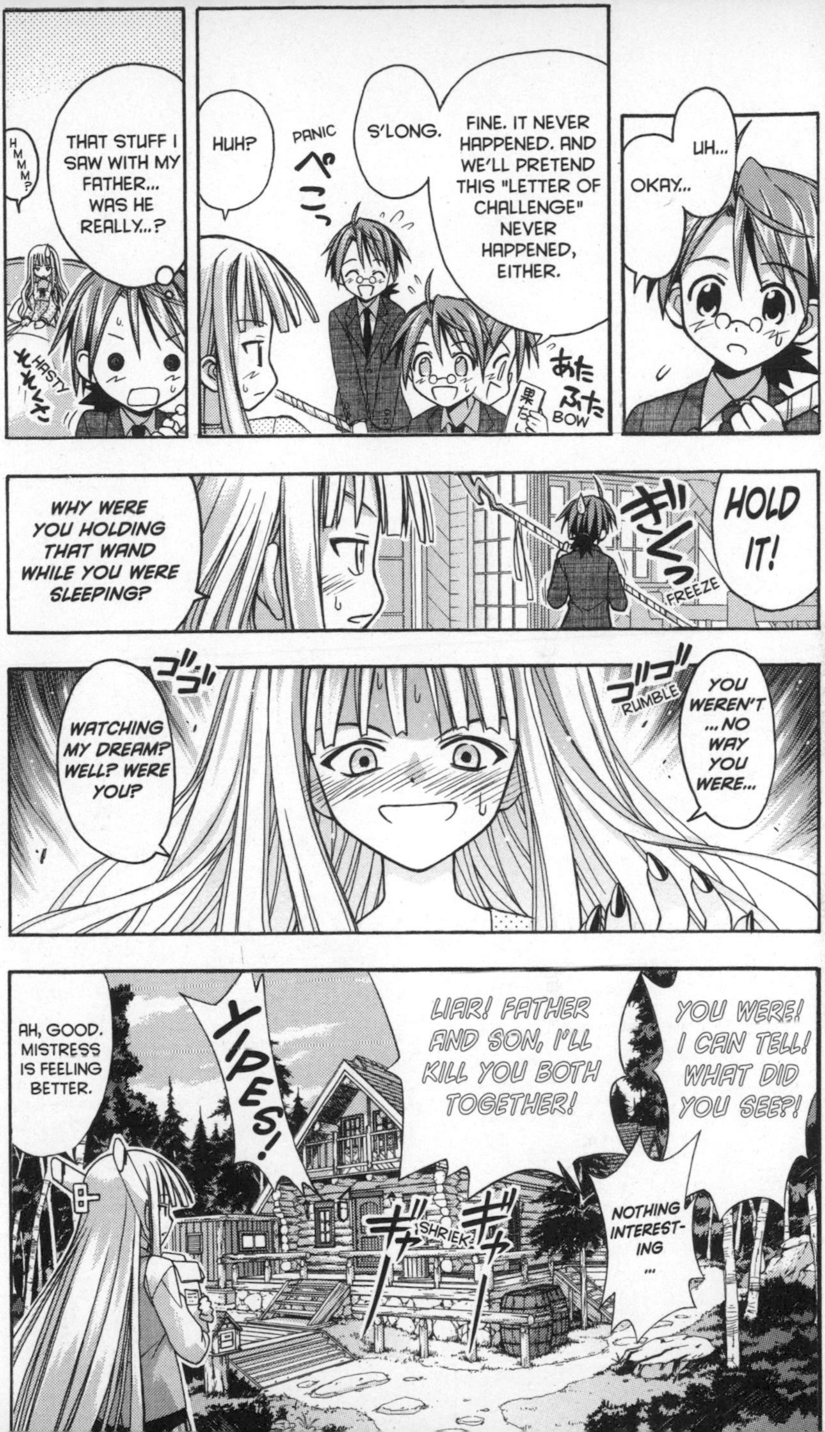
UH...
OKAY...
FINE. IT NEVER HAPPENED. AND WE'LL PRETEND THIS "LETTER OF CHALLENGE" NEVER HAPPENED, EITHER.
あたふた BOW
S'LONG.
PANIC ぺこっ
HUH?
HMMM?
THAT STUFF I SAW WITH MY FATHER... WAS HE REALLY...?
HASTY そそくさ
HOLD IT!
ぎくっ FREEZE
WHY WERE YOU HOLDING THAT WAND WHILE YOU WERE SLEEPING?
YOU WEREN'T ...NO WAY YOU WERE...
ゴゴゴ RUMBLE
ゴゴ
WATCHING MY DREAM? WELL? WERE YOU?
YOU WERE! I CAN TELL! WHAT DID YOU SEE?!
LIAR! FATHER AND SON, I'LL KILL YOU BOTH TOGETHER!
NOTHING INTEREST-ING ...
ギャー SHRIEK ギャー
YIPES!
AH, GOOD. MISTRESS IS FEELING BETTER.

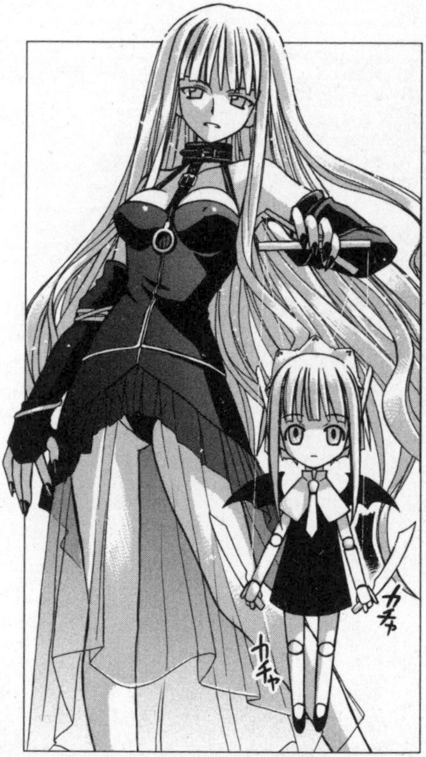
カチャ
カチャ

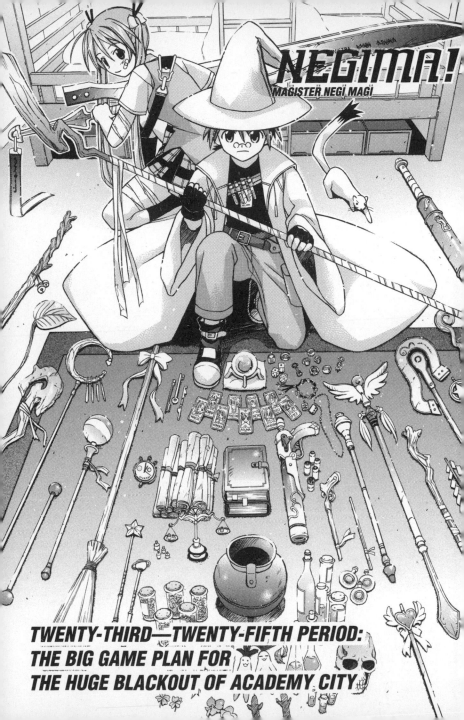

NEGIMA!
MAGISTER NEGI MAGI

TWENTY-THIRD—TWENTY-FIFTH PERIOD: THE BIG GAME PLAN FOR THE HUGE BLACKOUT OF ACADEMY CITY

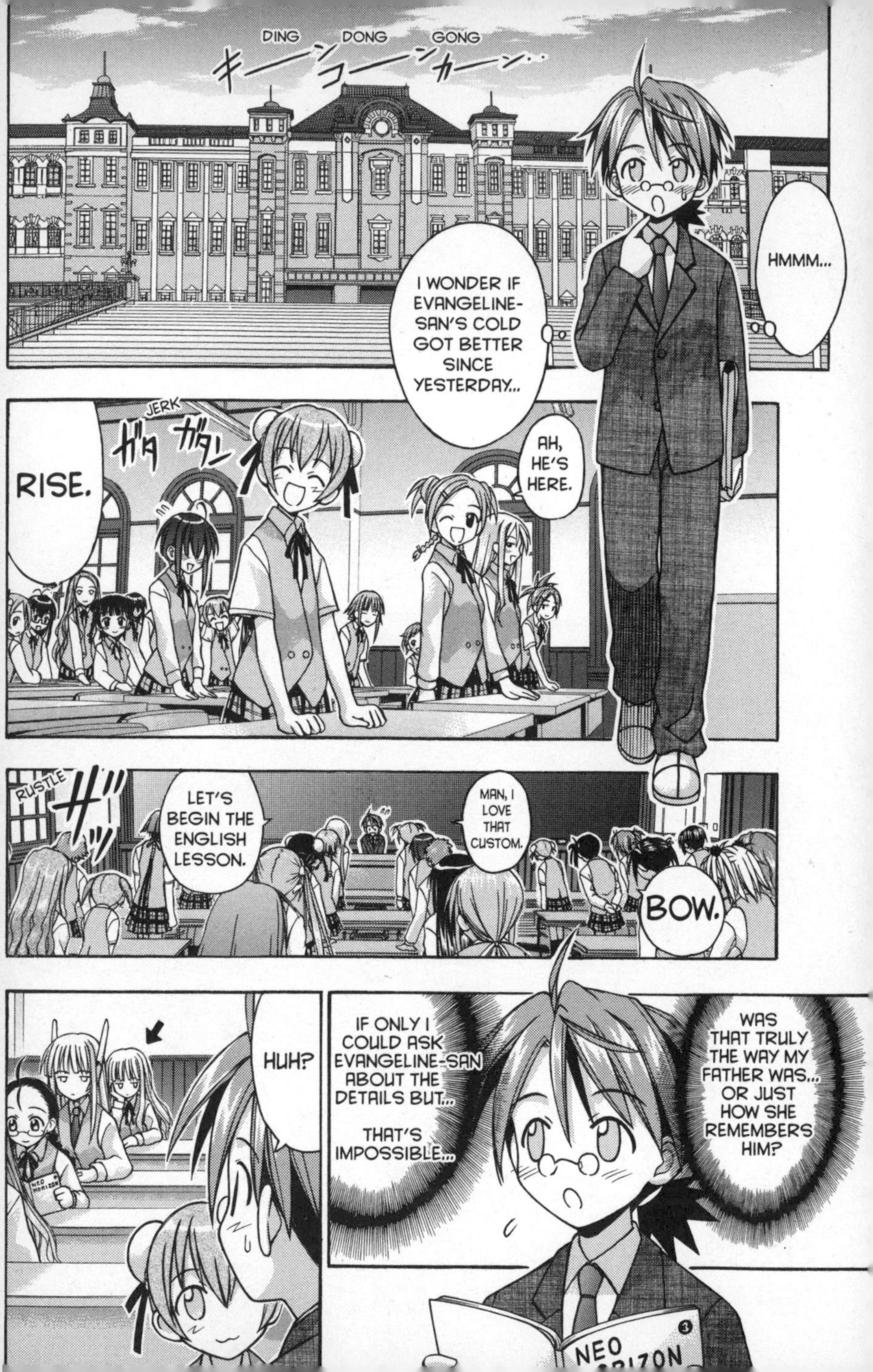
DING DONG GONG
キーンコーンカーン・・
HMMM...
I WONDER IF EVANGELINE-SAN'S COLD GOT BETTER SINCE YESTERDAY...
AH, HE'S HERE.
JERK
ガタ ガタン
RISE.
BOW.
MAN, I LOVE THAT CUSTOM.
LET'S BEGIN THE ENGLISH LESSON.
RUSTLE
ザッ
WAS THAT TRULY THE WAY MY FATHER WAS... OR JUST HOW SHE REMEMBERS HIM?
IF ONLY I COULD ASK EVANGELINE-SAN ABOUT THE DETAILS BUT...
THAT'S IMPOSSIBLE...
NEO HORIZON
HUH?

STUN

WHAH--!

EVANGE-LINE-SAN!?

HMPH.

DUH DUN

FLAP

FLUTTER

WHY... SHOULDN'T EVANGELINE-SAN BE HERE?

N-NEGI-SENSEI, WHAT'S WRONG?

YOU THROWING DOWN ANOTHER CHALLENGE, EVANGELINE-SAN? HUH? THAT WHY YOU'RE HERE!?! BECAUSE IF YOU THINK--!

AH! IS THAT RIGHT?

WHAT!

I FIGURED I WAS OBLIGATED AFTER, Y'KNOW, YOU LOOKED AFTER ME.

RIGHT. WHY SHOULDN'T I BE. IF YOU GOTTA KNOW...

UH, YEAH.

GUILTY

Y-YOUR COLD IS ALL RIGHT!?

GOOD TO SEE YOU.

OKAY, WELL... REALLY. THANK YOU VERY MUCH.

HE LOOKED AFTER HER?

OKAY, THIS IS NEWS!

"IT IS NO USE CRYING OVER SPILT MILK."

NEGI-KUN'S IN A GREAT MOOD HUH.

LET'S DISCUSS THE PHRASE,

ALL RIGHT THEN, LET'S BEGIN FROM PAGE 31 IN THE TEXT.

AK HA HA

YEEAH

AND IT'S ALWAYS GOOD TO FACE CHALLENGES WITH BRAVERY.

WELL...GLAD YOU HAD A CHANGE OF HEART.

SOMETHING FISHY'S GOING ON.

THINK SO?

SHE'S A MURDEROUS, WANTED VAMPIRE. REFORMING HER CAN'T BE THAT EASY.

YEAH, BUT I'M DARNED CUTE. ASK ANYONE!

OOO, HE'S SO CUTE!

STAY OFF MY SHOULDER. YOU'RE NEGI'S PET, NOT MINE.

I CAN'T BELIEVE HE GOT EVANGELINE TO GO TO CLASS.

I DON'T KNOW WHAT HAPPENED BUT...

HUMPH.

HOW ARE WE DOING?

TAPEDY TAP

PLINK

DZZZZ

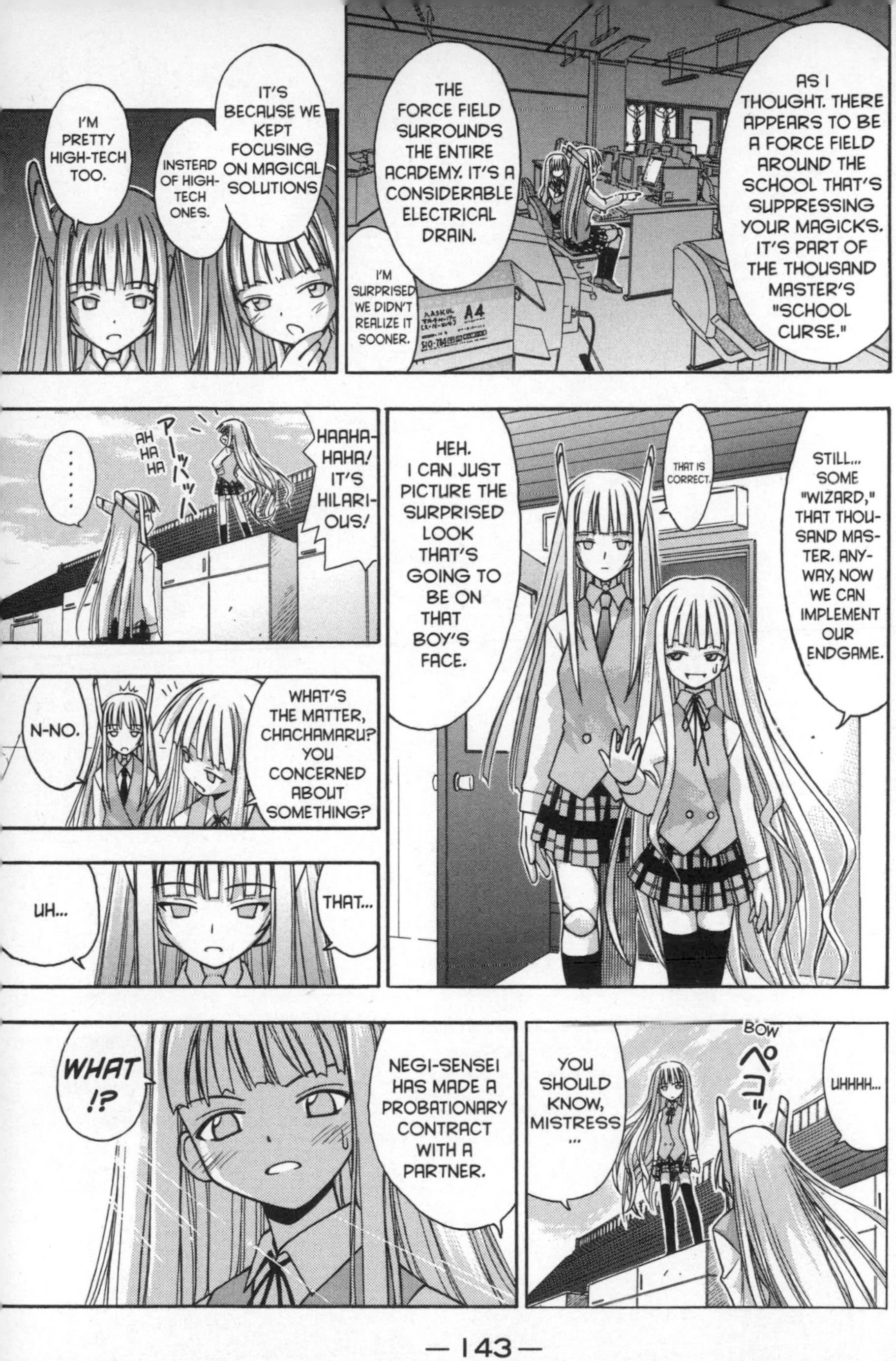
AS I THOUGHT. THERE APPEARS TO BE A FORCE FIELD AROUND THE SCHOOL THAT'S SUPPRESSING YOUR MAGICKS. IT'S PART OF THE THOUSAND MASTER'S "SCHOOL CURSE."
THE FORCE FIELD SURROUNDS THE ENTIRE ACADEMY. IT'S A CONSIDERABLE ELECTRICAL DRAIN.
I'M SURPRISED WE DIDN'T REALIZE IT SOONER.
IT'S BECAUSE WE KEPT FOCUSING ON MAGICAL SOLUTIONS
INSTEAD OF HIGH-TECH ONES.
I'M PRETTY HIGH-TECH TOO.
STILL... SOME "WIZARD," THAT THOUSAND MASTER. ANYWAY, NOW WE CAN IMPLEMENT OUR ENDGAME.
THAT IS CORRECT.
HEH. I CAN JUST PICTURE THE SURPRISED LOOK THAT'S GOING TO BE ON THAT BOY'S FACE.
HAAHAHAHA! IT'S HILARIOUS!
AH HA HA
......
WHAT'S THE MATTER, CHACHAMARU? YOU CONCERNED ABOUT SOMETHING?
N-NO.
THAT...
UH...
BOW
ペコッ
UHHHH...
YOU SHOULD KNOW, MISTRESS...
NEGI-SENSEI HAS MADE A PROBATIONARY CONTRACT WITH A PARTNER.
WHAT!?

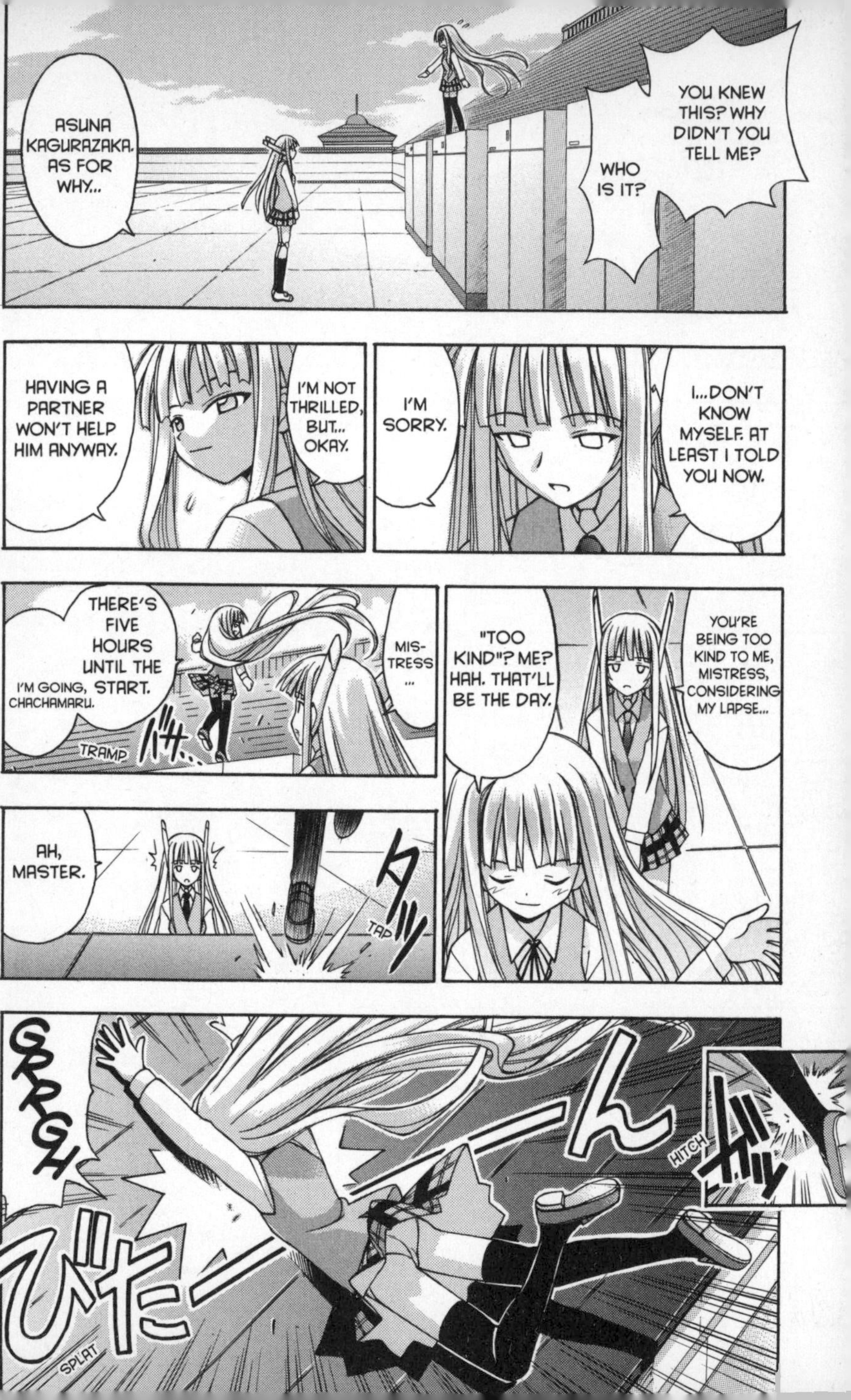
YOU KNEW THIS? WHY DIDN'T YOU TELL ME?
WHO IS IT?
ASUNA KAGURAZAKA. AS FOR WHY...
I...DON'T KNOW MYSELF. AT LEAST I TOLD YOU NOW.
I'M SORRY.
I'M NOT THRILLED, BUT... OKAY.
HAVING A PARTNER WON'T HELP HIM ANYWAY.
YOU'RE BEING TOO KIND TO ME, MISTRESS, CONSIDERING MY LAPSE...
"TOO KIND"? ME? HAH. THAT'LL BE THE DAY.
MIS-TRESS...
THERE'S FIVE HOURS UNTIL THE START.
I'M GOING, CHACHAMARU.
TRAMP
TAP
AH, MASTER.
HITCH
GRRGH
SPLAT

BUT HIS GUARD'LL BE DOWN SINCE THERE'S NO FULL MOON TONIGHT, SO THAT MEANS WE'LL BE ABLE TO KICK THE CRAP OUT OF HIM AND WHOEVER'S HELPING HIM!

AND IT'S THE FAULT OF NEGI SPRINGFIELD'S FAMILY!

MISTRESS, YOUR NOSE IS BLEEDING.

OONAH!

I FORGOT I CAN'T FLY! I HATE THIS STUPID HUMAN WEAKNESS.

AND "DARK EVANGEL," THE FEARED QUEEN, OF THE NIGHT WILL MAKE HER RETURN!!

TONIGHT, HIS LIFE'S BLOOD WILL UNDO THE CURSE...

GREAT, MISTRESS, NOW LET ME STICK THIS TISSUE UP YOUR NOSE...

RUCKUS

UH, NOTHING. HER NAME JUST SLIPPED OUT.

HUH, WHAT DID KAEDE DO?

ALL THANKS TO YOU, ASUNA-SAN, AND CHAMO-KUN, AND NAGASE-SAN.

ISN'T IT GREAT! EVANGELINE-SAN RETURNED TO THE CLASSROOM.

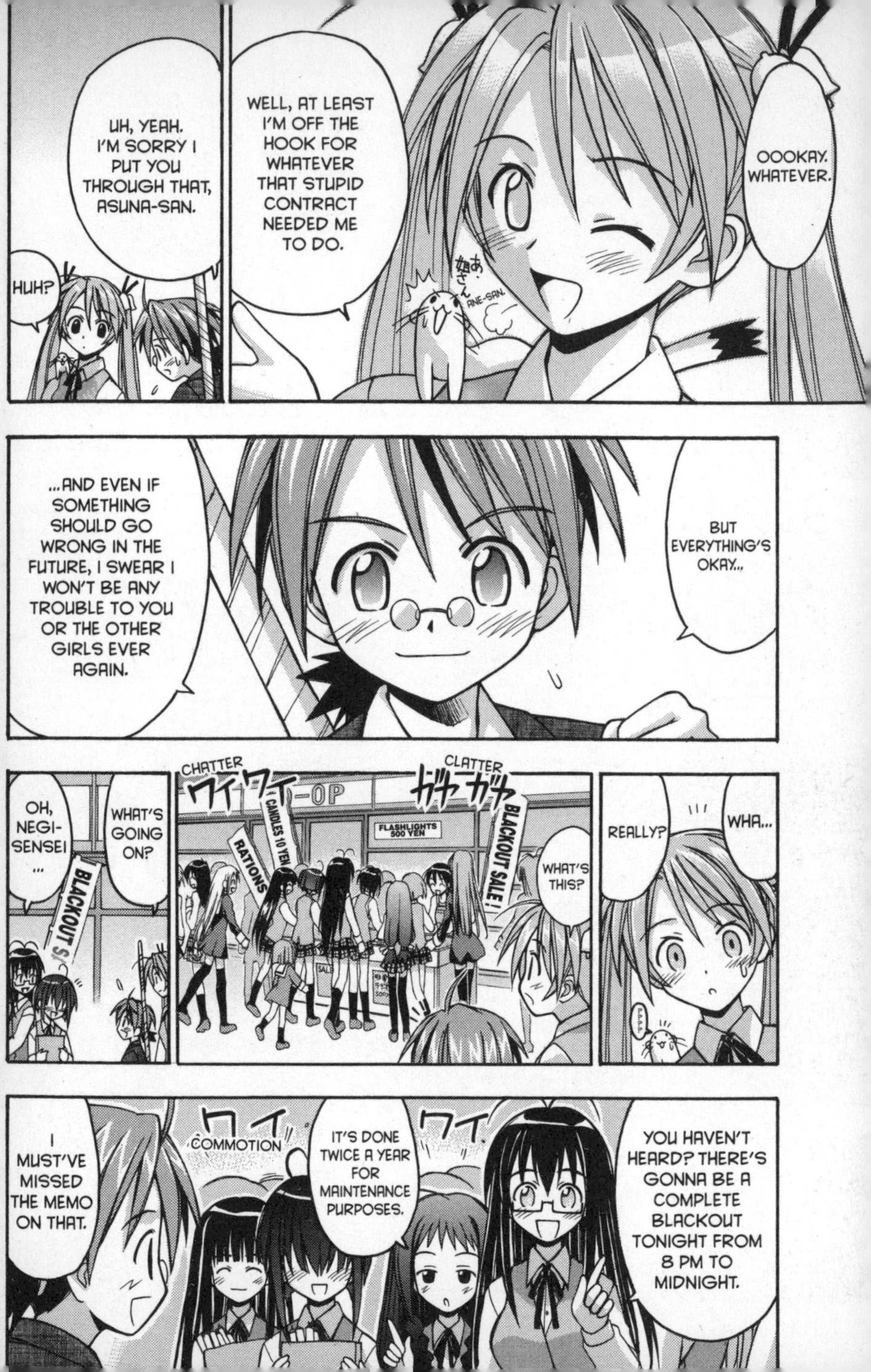

OOOKAY. WHATEVER.
WELL, AT LEAST I'M OFF THE HOOK FOR WHATEVER THAT STUPID CONTRACT NEEDED ME TO DO.
あ、姉さん
ANE-SAN.
UH, YEAH. I'M SORRY I PUT YOU THROUGH THAT, ASUNA-SAN.
HUH?
BUT EVERYTHING'S OKAY...
...AND EVEN IF SOMETHING SHOULD GO WRONG IN THE FUTURE, I SWEAR I WON'T BE ANY TROUBLE TO YOU OR THE OTHER GIRLS EVER AGAIN.
WHA...
REALLY?
CLATTER
ガヤガヤ
CHATTER
ワイワイ
-OP
BLACKOUT SALE!
FLASHLIGHTS 500 YEN
CANDLES 10 YEN
RATIONS
WHAT'S THIS?
WHAT'S GOING ON?
OH, NEGI-SENSEI ...
YOU HAVEN'T HEARD? THERE'S GONNA BE A COMPLETE BLACKOUT TONIGHT FROM 8 PM TO MIDNIGHT.
ワイ
IT'S DONE TWICE A YEAR FOR MAINTENANCE PURPOSES.
ワイ
COMMOTION
I MUST'VE MISSED THE MEMO ON THAT.

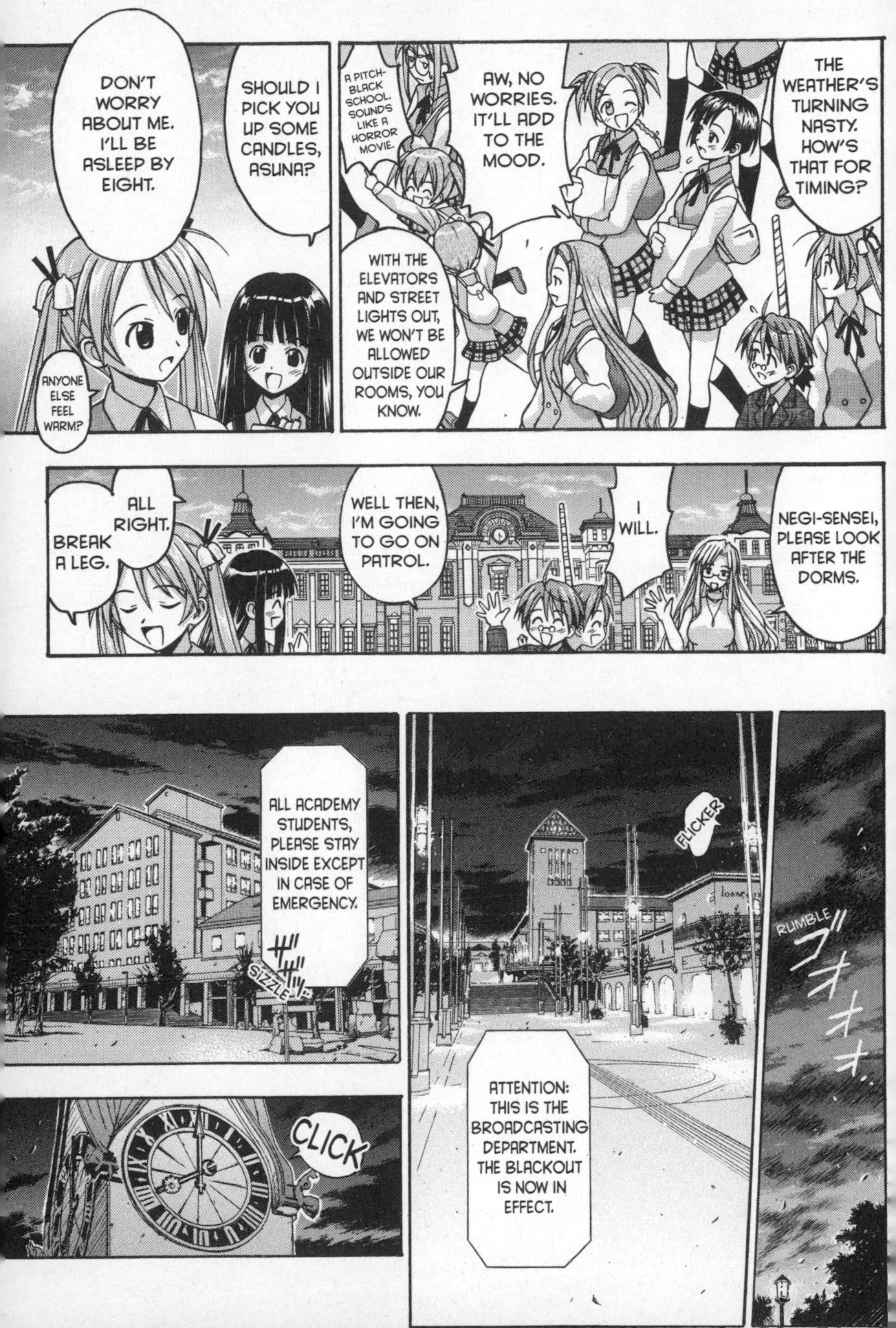
THE WEATHER'S TURNING NASTY. HOW'S THAT FOR TIMING?
AW, NO WORRIES. IT'LL ADD TO THE MOOD.
A PITCH-BLACK SCHOOL. SOUNDS LIKE A HORROR MOVIE.
WITH THE ELEVATORS AND STREET LIGHTS OUT, WE WON'T BE ALLOWED OUTSIDE OUR ROOMS, YOU KNOW.
SHOULD I PICK YOU UP SOME CANDLES, ASUNA?
DON'T WORRY ABOUT ME. I'LL BE ASLEEP BY EIGHT.
ANYONE ELSE FEEL WARM?
NEGI-SENSEI, PLEASE LOOK AFTER THE DORMS.
I WILL.
WELL THEN, I'M GOING TO GO ON PATROL.
ALL RIGHT.
BREAK A LEG.
RUMBLE
FLICKER
ATTENTION: THIS IS THE BROADCASTING DEPARTMENT. THE BLACKOUT IS NOW IN EFFECT.
ALL ACADEMY STUDENTS, PLEASE STAY INSIDE EXCEPT IN CASE OF EMERGENCY.
SIZZLE
CLICK

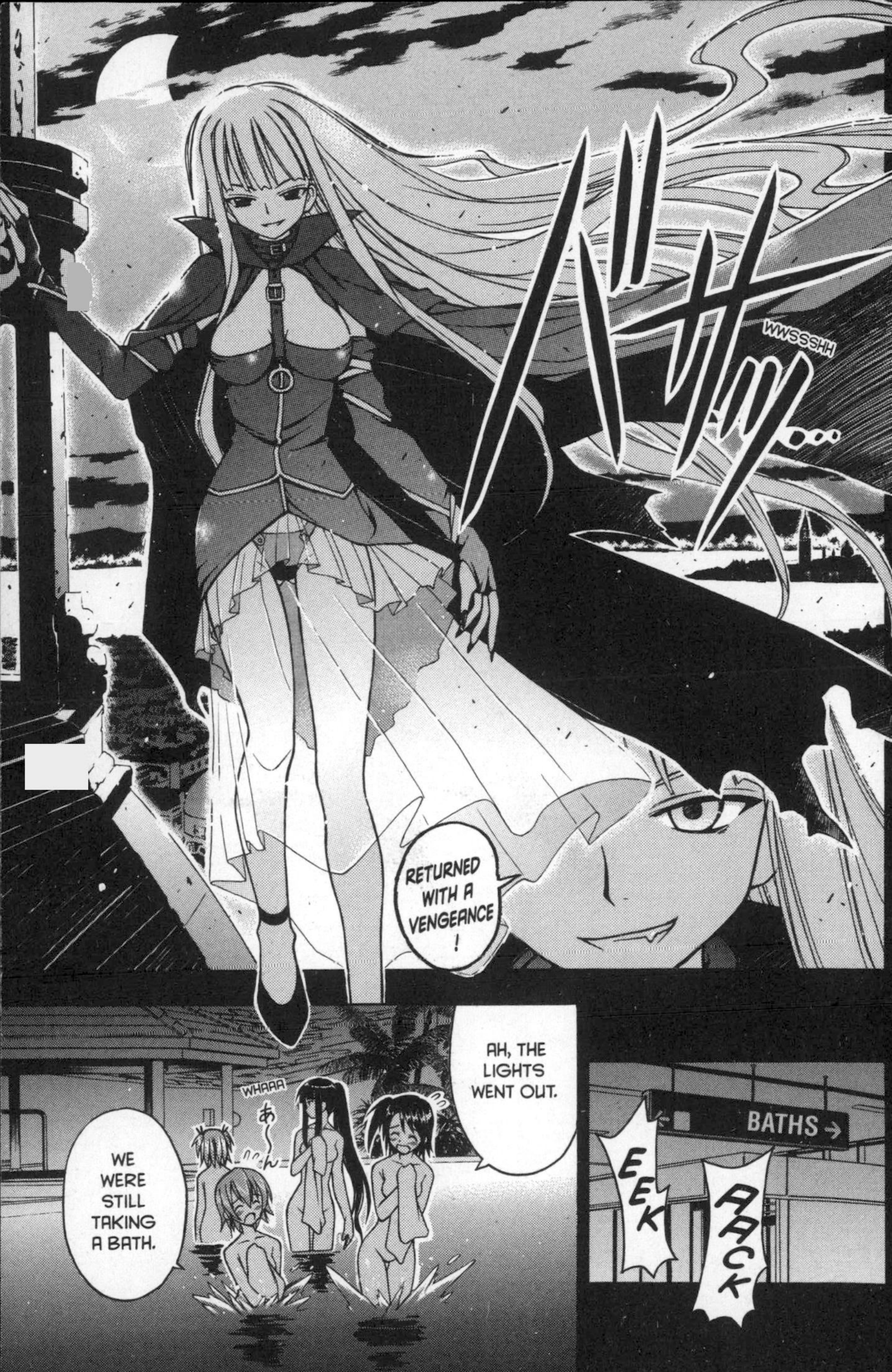
WWSSSHH
RETURNED WITH A VENGEANCE!
BATHS →
EEK
AACK
AH, THE LIGHTS WENT OUT.
WHAAA
WE WERE STILL TAKING A BATH.

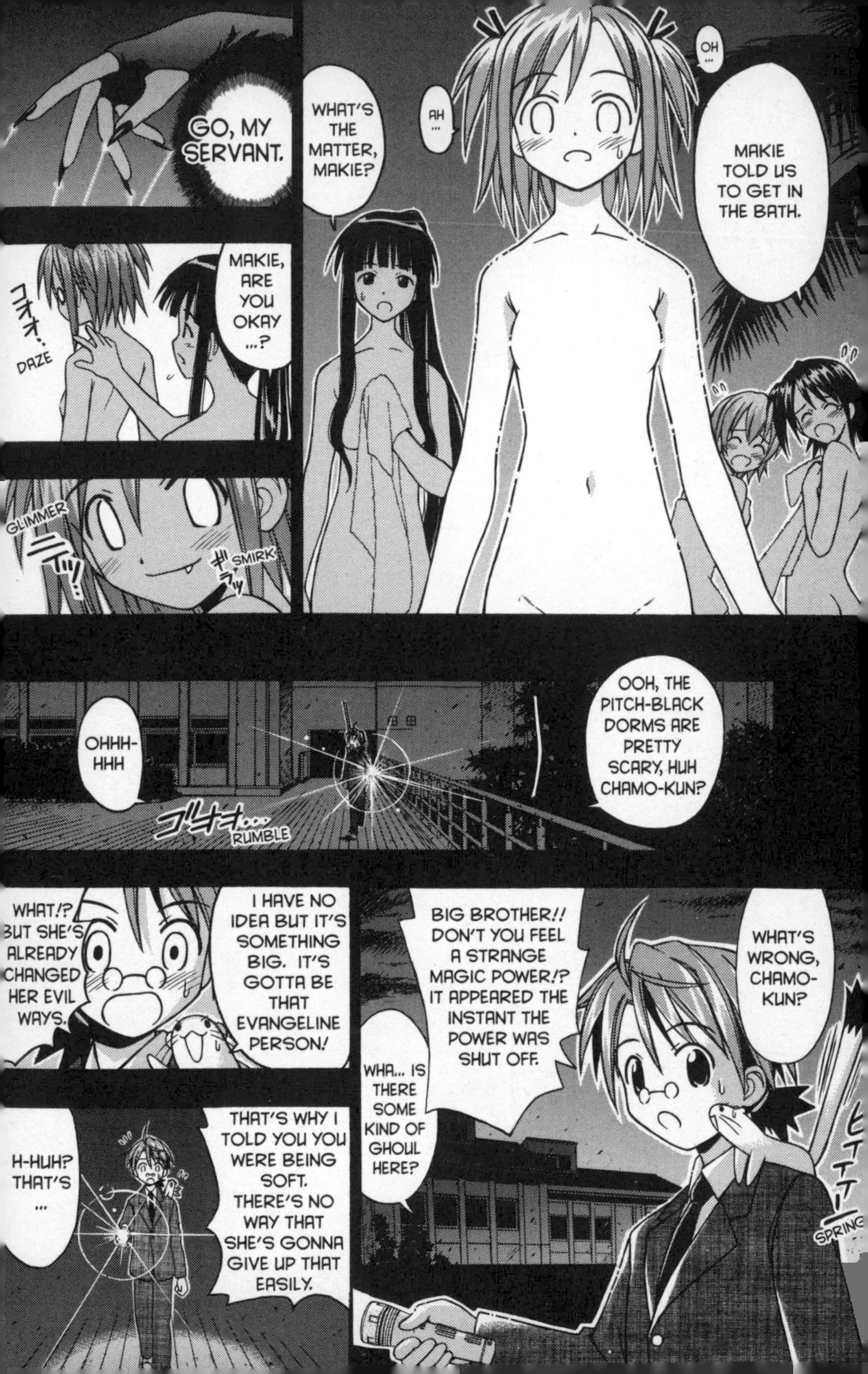
OH ...
MAKIE TOLD US TO GET IN THE BATH.
AH ...
WHAT'S THE MATTER, MAKIE?
GO, MY SERVANT.
MAKIE, ARE YOU OKAY ...?
DAZE
GLIMMER
SMIRK
OOH, THE PITCH-BLACK DORMS ARE PRETTY SCARY, HUH CHAMO-KUN?
OHHH-HHH
RUMBLE
WHAT'S WRONG, CHAMO-KUN?
SPRING
BIG BROTHER!! DON'T YOU FEEL A STRANGE MAGIC POWER!? IT APPEARED THE INSTANT THE POWER WAS SHUT OFF.
WHA... IS THERE SOME KIND OF GHOUL HERE?
I HAVE NO IDEA BUT IT'S SOMETHING BIG. IT'S GOTTA BE THAT EVANGELINE PERSON!
WHAT!? BUT SHE'S ALREADY CHANGED HER EVIL WAYS.
THAT'S WHY I TOLD YOU YOU WERE BEING SOFT. THERE'S NO WAY THAT SHE'S GONNA GIVE UP THAT EASILY.
H-HUH? THAT'S ...

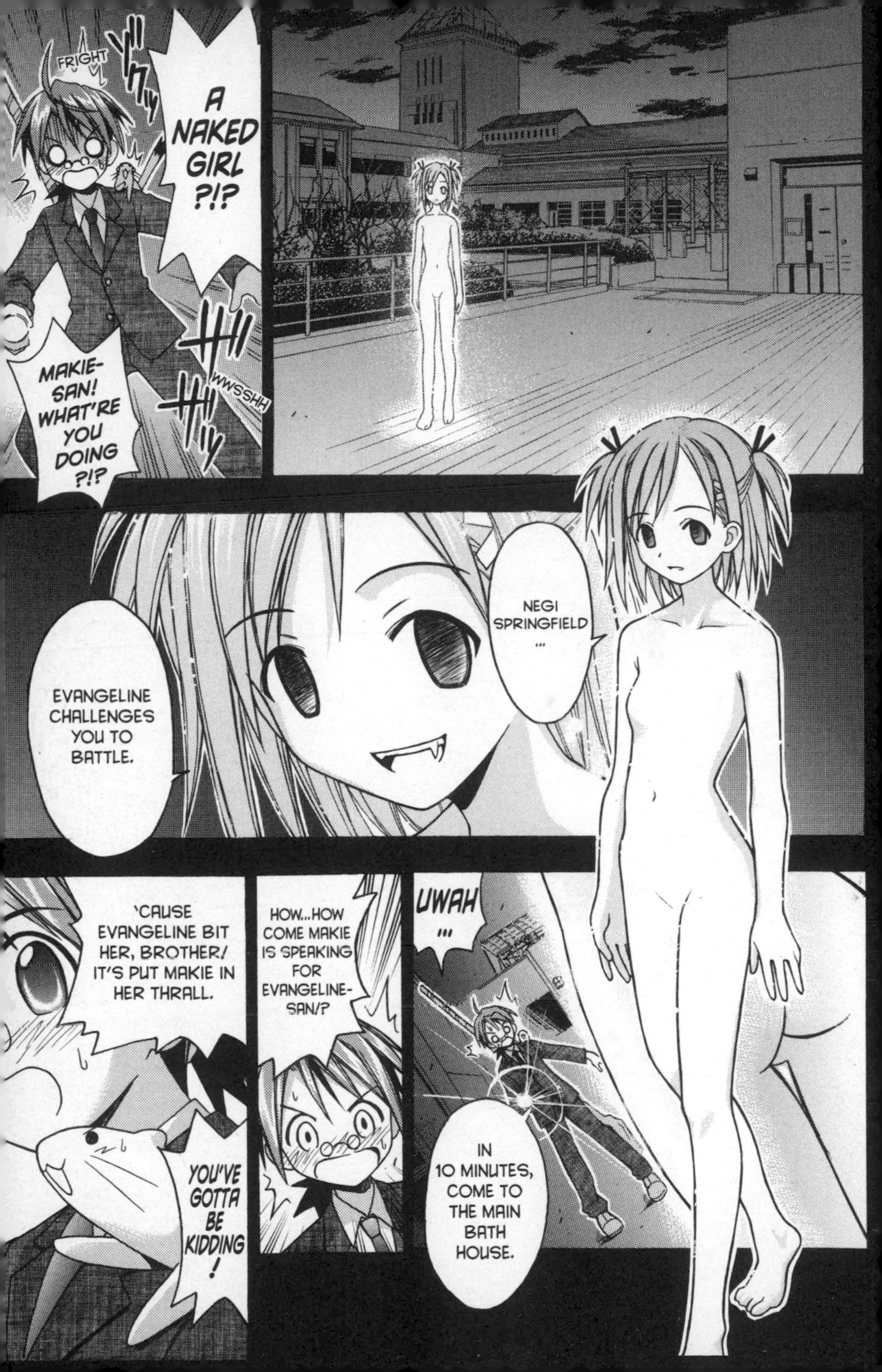
A NAKED GIRL ?!?
FRIGHT
WWSSHH
MAKIE-SAN! WHAT'RE YOU DOING ?!?
NEGI SPRINGFIELD ...
EVANGELINE CHALLENGES YOU TO BATTLE.
UWAH ...
IN 10 MINUTES, COME TO THE MAIN BATH HOUSE.
HOW...HOW COME MAKIE IS SPEAKING FOR EVANGELINE-SAN/?
YOU'VE GOTTA BE KIDDING !
'CAUSE EVANGELINE BIT HER, BROTHER! IT'S PUT MAKIE IN HER THRALL.

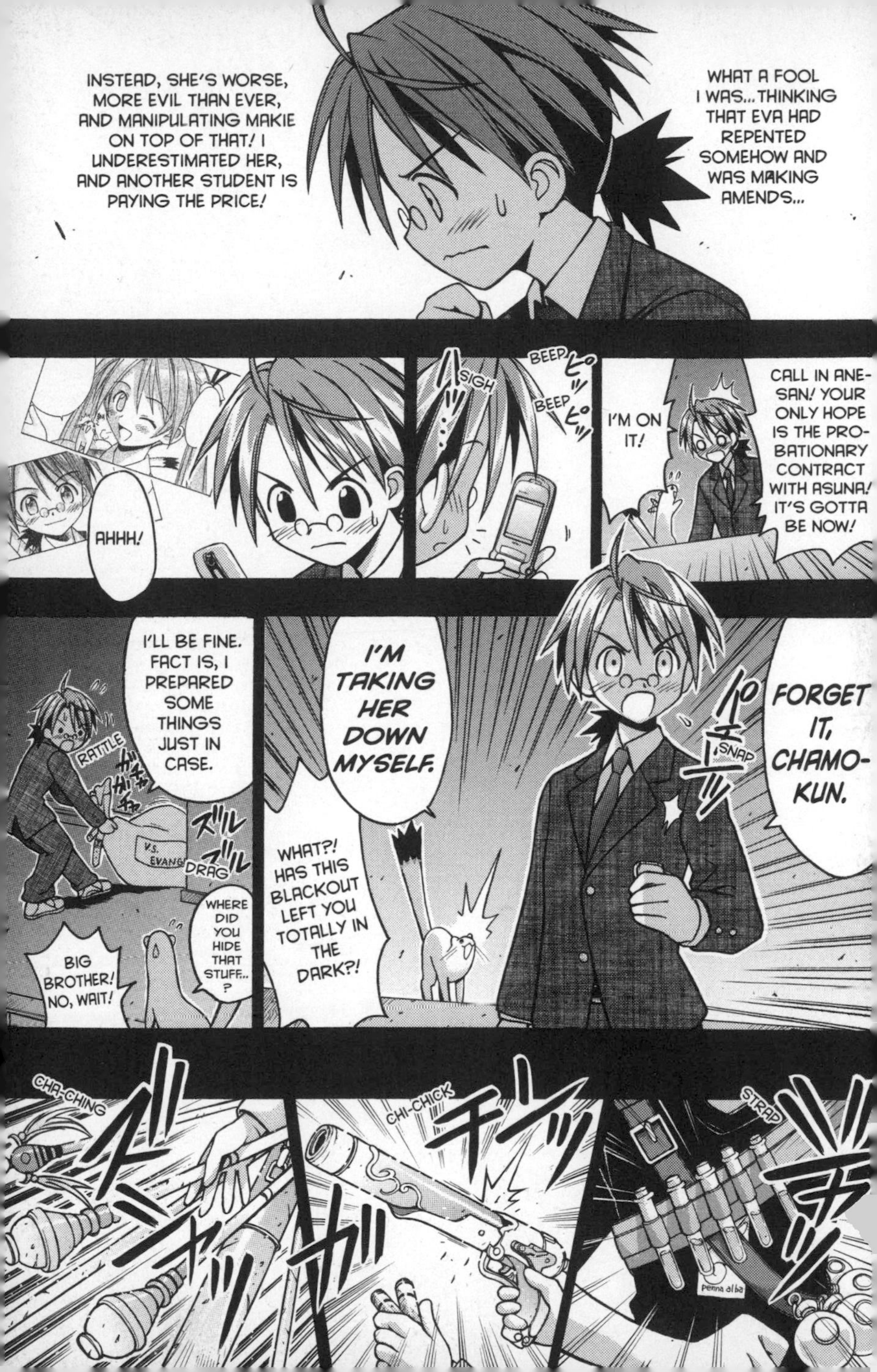
WHAT A FOOL I WAS... THINKING THAT EVA HAD REPENTED SOMEHOW AND WAS MAKING AMENDS...
INSTEAD, SHE'S WORSE, MORE EVIL THAN EVER, AND MANIPULATING MAKIE ON TOP OF THAT! I UNDERESTIMATED HER, AND ANOTHER STUDENT IS PAYING THE PRICE!
CALL IN ANE-SAN! YOUR ONLY HOPE IS THE PROBATIONARY CONTRACT WITH ASUNA! IT'S GOTTA BE NOW!
I'M ON IT!
BEEP
BEEP
SIGH
AHHH!
FORGET IT, CHAMO-KUN.
SNAP
I'M TAKING HER DOWN MYSELF.
WHAT?! HAS THIS BLACKOUT LEFT YOU TOTALLY IN THE DARK?!
I'LL BE FINE. FACT IS, I PREPARED SOME THINGS JUST IN CASE.
RATTLE
V.S. EVANG
DRAG
WHERE DID YOU HIDE THAT STUFF...?
BIG BROTHER! NO, WAIT!
STRAP
penna alba
CHI-CHICK
CHA-CHING

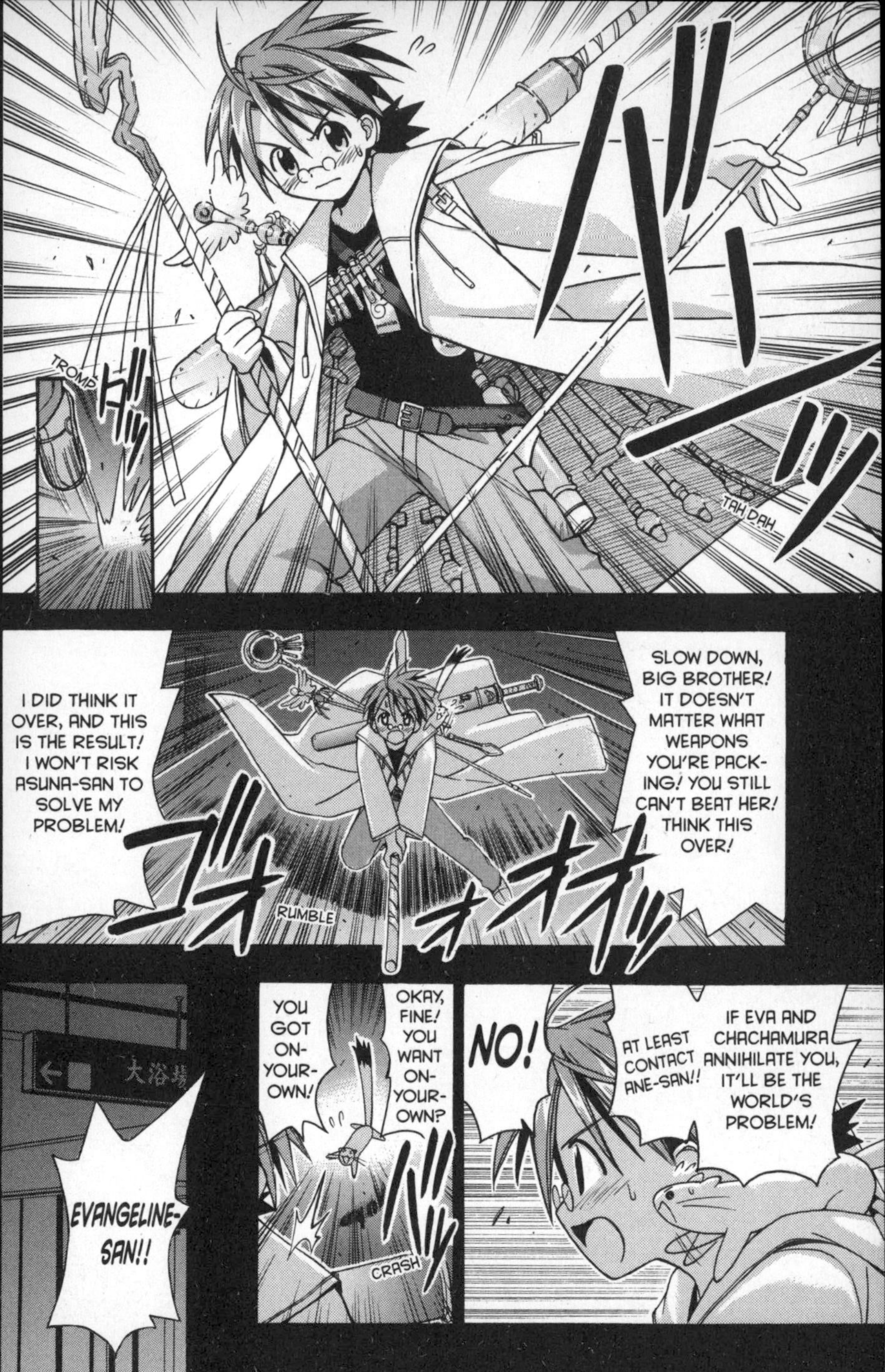
TROMP
TAH DAH
SLOW DOWN, BIG BROTHER! IT DOESN'T MATTER WHAT WEAPONS YOU'RE PACKING! YOU STILL CAN'T BEAT HER! THINK THIS OVER!
I DID THINK IT OVER, AND THIS IS THE RESULT! I WON'T RISK ASUNA-SAN TO SOLVE MY PROBLEM!
RUMBLE
IF EVA AND CHACHAMURA ANNIHILATE YOU, IT'LL BE THE WORLD'S PROBLEM!
AT LEAST CONTACT ANE-SAN!!
NO!
OKAY, FINE! YOU WANT ON-YOUR-OWN?
YOU GOT ON-YOUR-OWN!
CRASH
大浴場
EVANGELINE-SAN!!

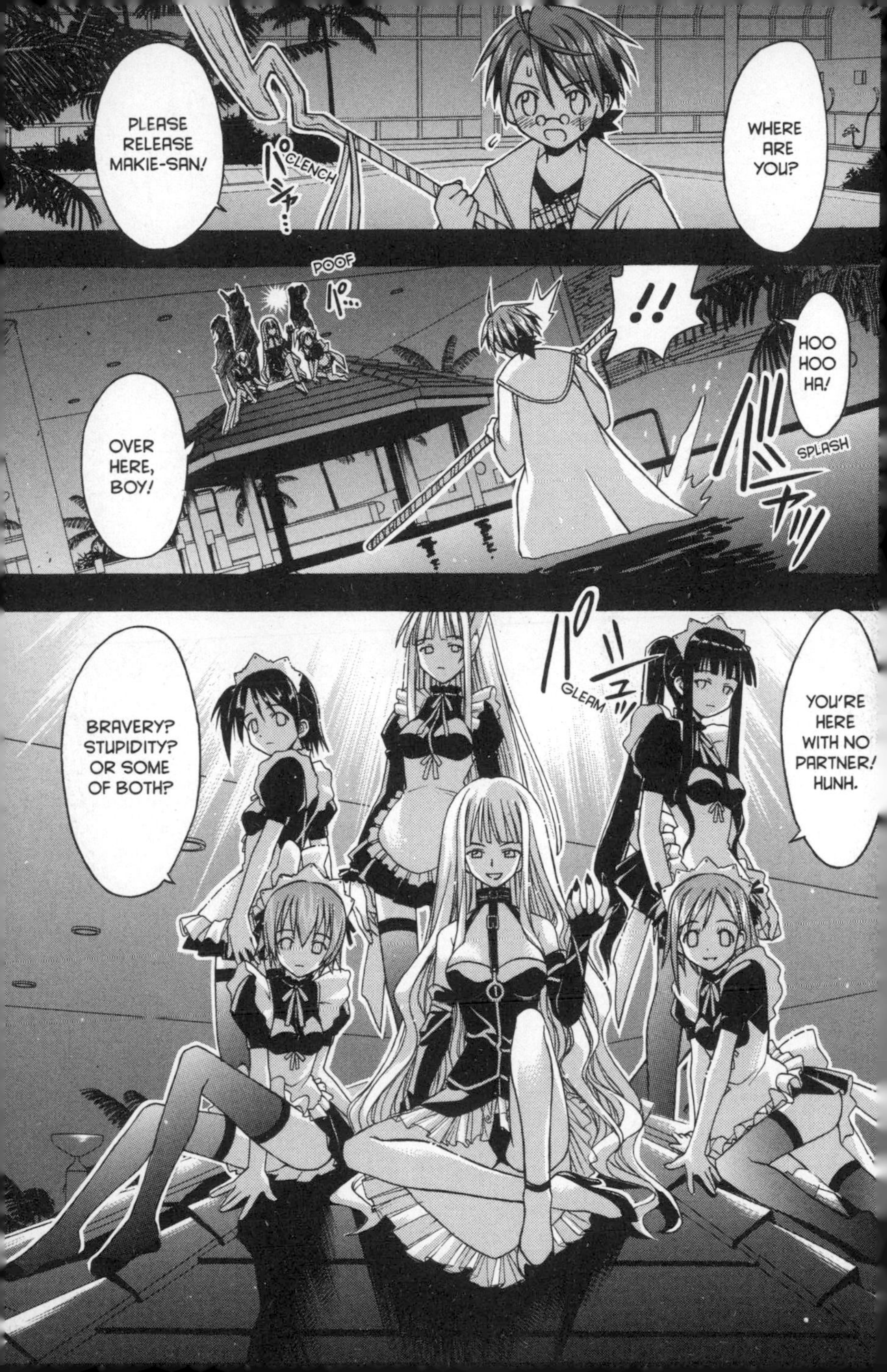
WHERE ARE YOU?
CLENCH
PLEASE RELEASE MAKIE-SAN!
!!
HOO HOO HA!
SPLASH
POOF
OVER HERE, BOY!
YOU'RE HERE WITH NO PARTNER! HUNH.
GLEAM
BRAVERY? STUPIDITY? OR SOME OF BOTH?

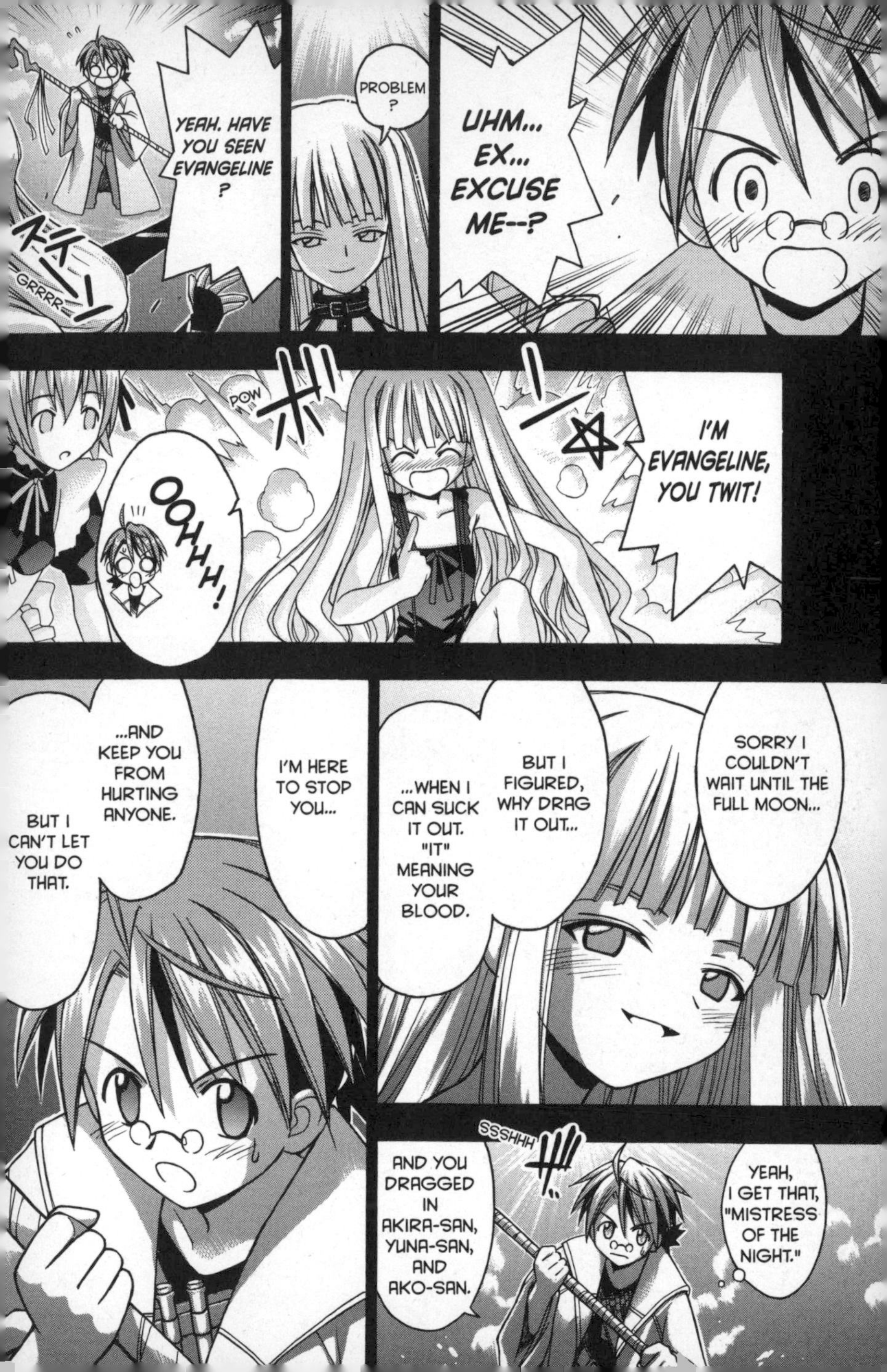
UHM... EX... EXCUSE ME--?
PROBLEM?
YEAH. HAVE YOU SEEN EVANGELINE?
GRRRR
I'M EVANGELINE, YOU TWIT!
POW
OOHHHH!
SORRY I COULDN'T WAIT UNTIL THE FULL MOON...
BUT I FIGURED, WHY DRAG IT OUT...
...WHEN I CAN SUCK IT OUT. "IT" MEANING YOUR BLOOD.
YEAH, I GET THAT, "MISTRESS OF THE NIGHT."
SSSHHH
AND YOU DRAGGED IN AKIRA-SAN, YUNA-SAN, AND AKO-SAN.
I'M HERE TO STOP YOU...
...AND KEEP YOU FROM HURTING ANYONE.
BUT I CAN'T LET YOU DO THAT.

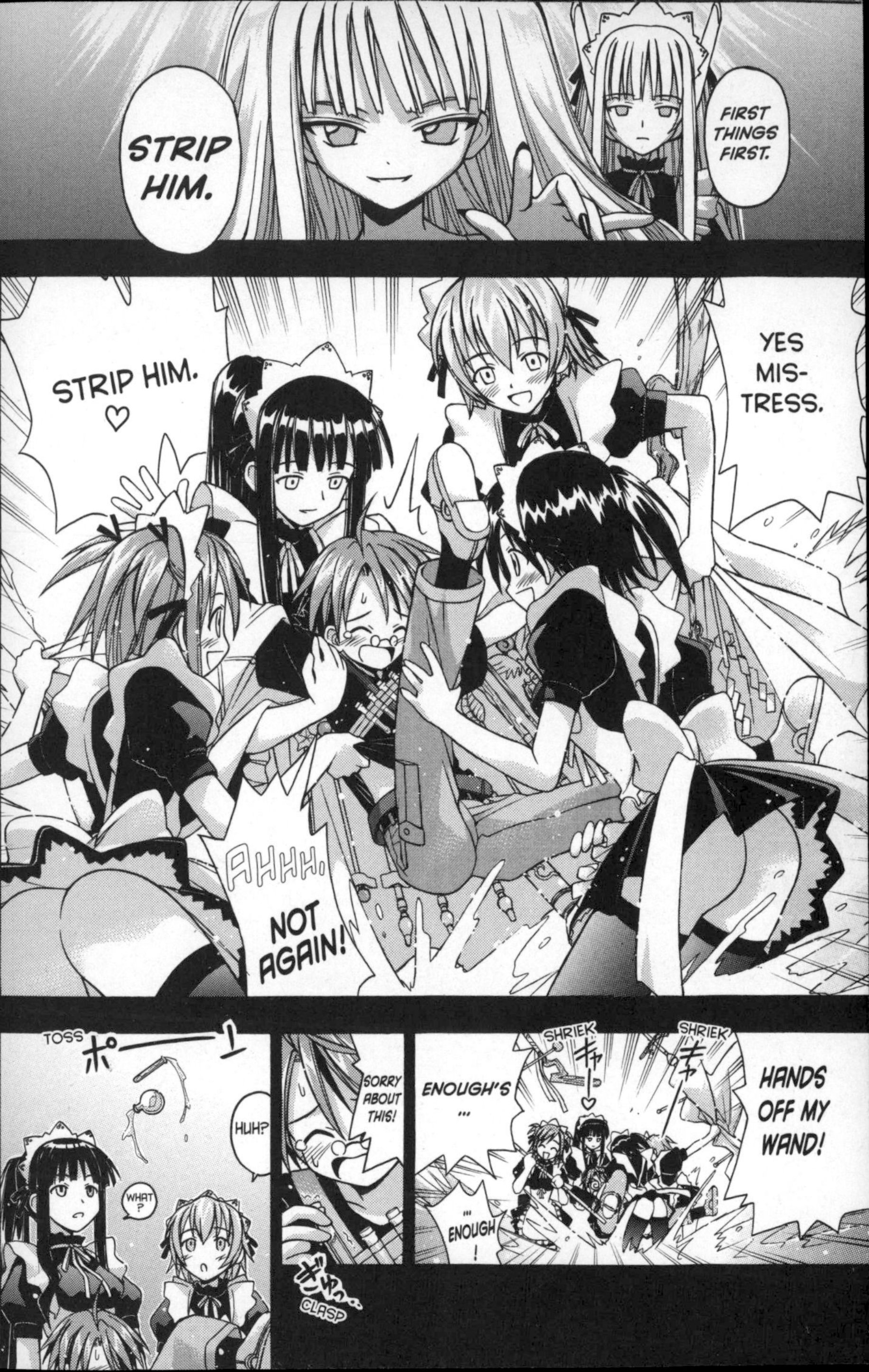
FIRST THINGS FIRST.
STRIP HIM.
YES MIS-TRESS.
STRIP HIM. ♡
AHHH,
NOT AGAIN!
SHRIEK
SHRIEK
HANDS OFF MY WAND!
ENOUGH'S ...
... ENOUGH !
SORRY ABOUT THIS!
CLASP
TOSS
HUH?
WHAT ?

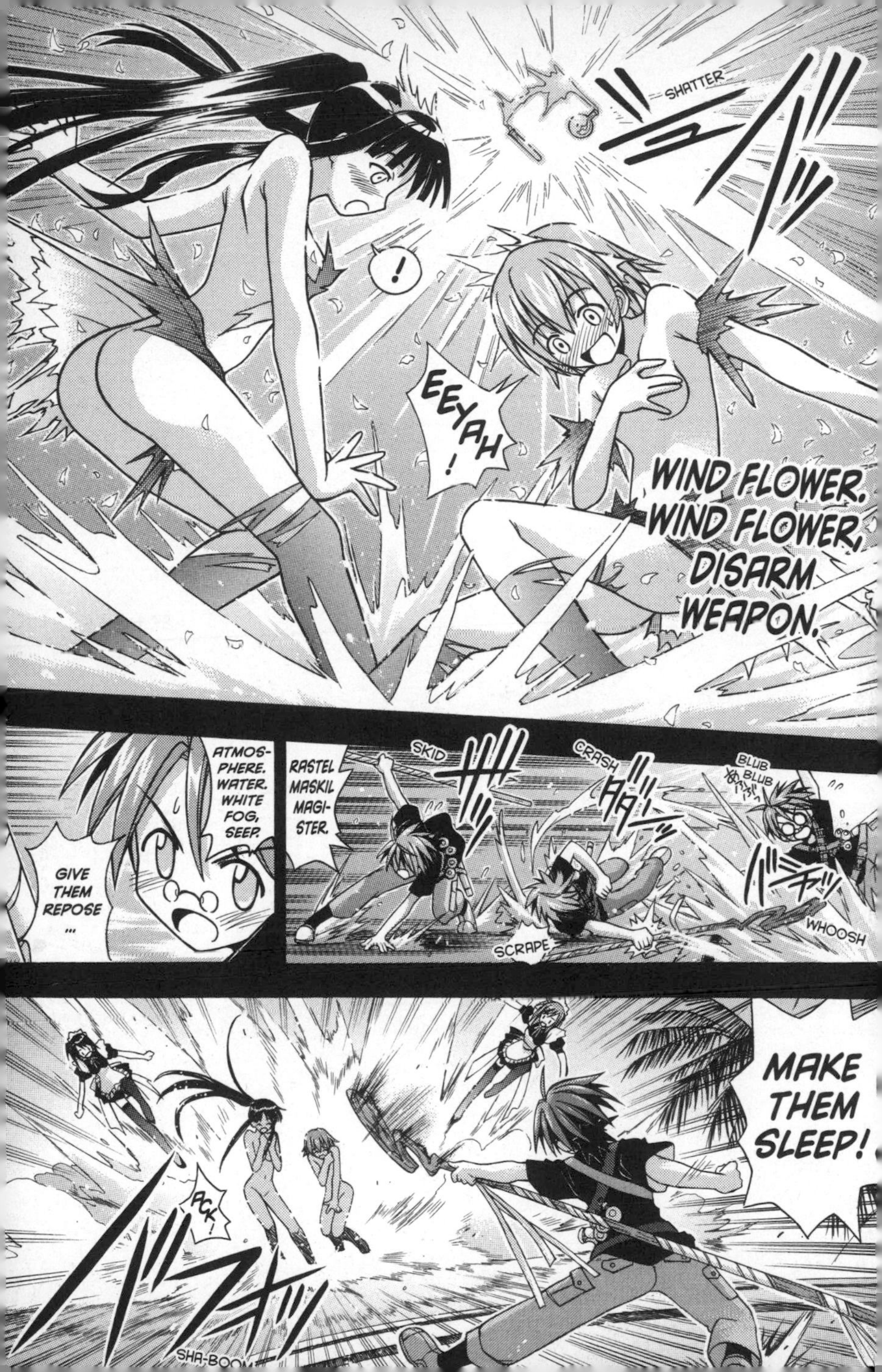
SHATTER
!
EEYAH!
WIND FLOWER. WIND FLOWER, DISARM WEAPON.
BLUB BLUB
WHOOSH
CRASH
SKID
RASTEL MASKIL MAGISTER.
SCRAPE
ATMOSPHERE. WATER. WHITE FOG, SEEP.
GIVE THEM REPOSE ...
MAKE THEM SLEEP!
ACK!
SHA-BOOM

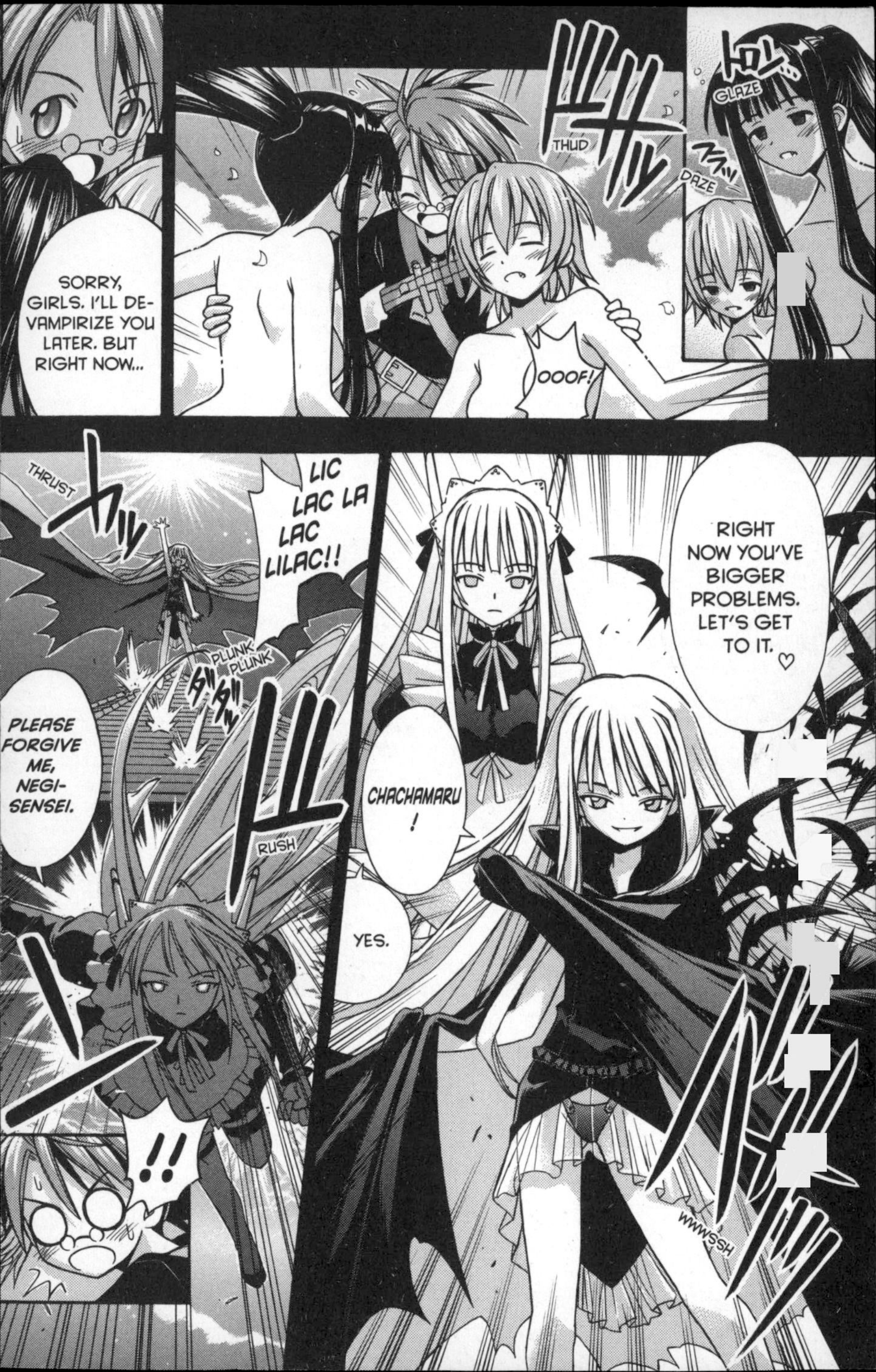
GLAZE
DAZE
THUD
OOOF!
SORRY, GIRLS. I'LL DE-VAMPIRIZE YOU LATER. BUT RIGHT NOW...
RIGHT NOW YOU'VE BIGGER PROBLEMS. LET'S GET TO IT. ♡
CHACHAMARU!
YES.
WWWSSH
THRUST
LIC LAC LA LAC LILAC!!
PLUNK PLUNK
RUSH
PLEASE FORGIVE ME, NEGI-SENSEI.
!!

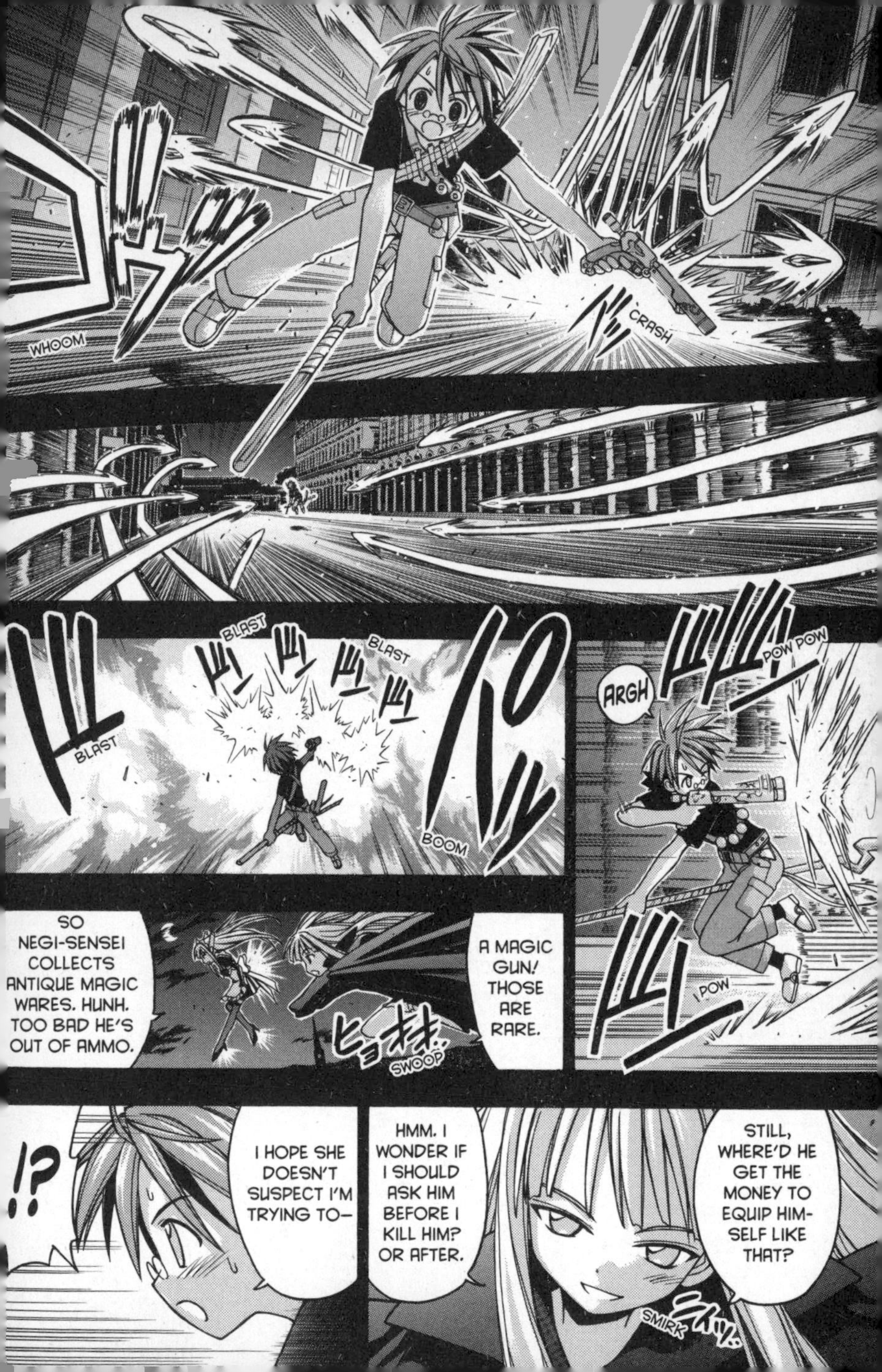
CRASH
WHOOM
ARGH
POW POW
POW
BLAST
BLAST
BLAST
BOOM
A MAGIC GUN! THOSE ARE RARE.
SO NEGI-SENSEI COLLECTS ANTIQUE MAGIC WARES. HUNH. TOO BAD HE'S OUT OF AMMO.
SWOOP
STILL, WHERE'D HE GET THE MONEY TO EQUIP HIM-SELF LIKE THAT?
HMM. I WONDER IF I SHOULD ASK HIM BEFORE I KILL HIM? OR AFTER.
SMIRK
I HOPE SHE DOESN'T SUSPECT I'M TRYING TO—
!?

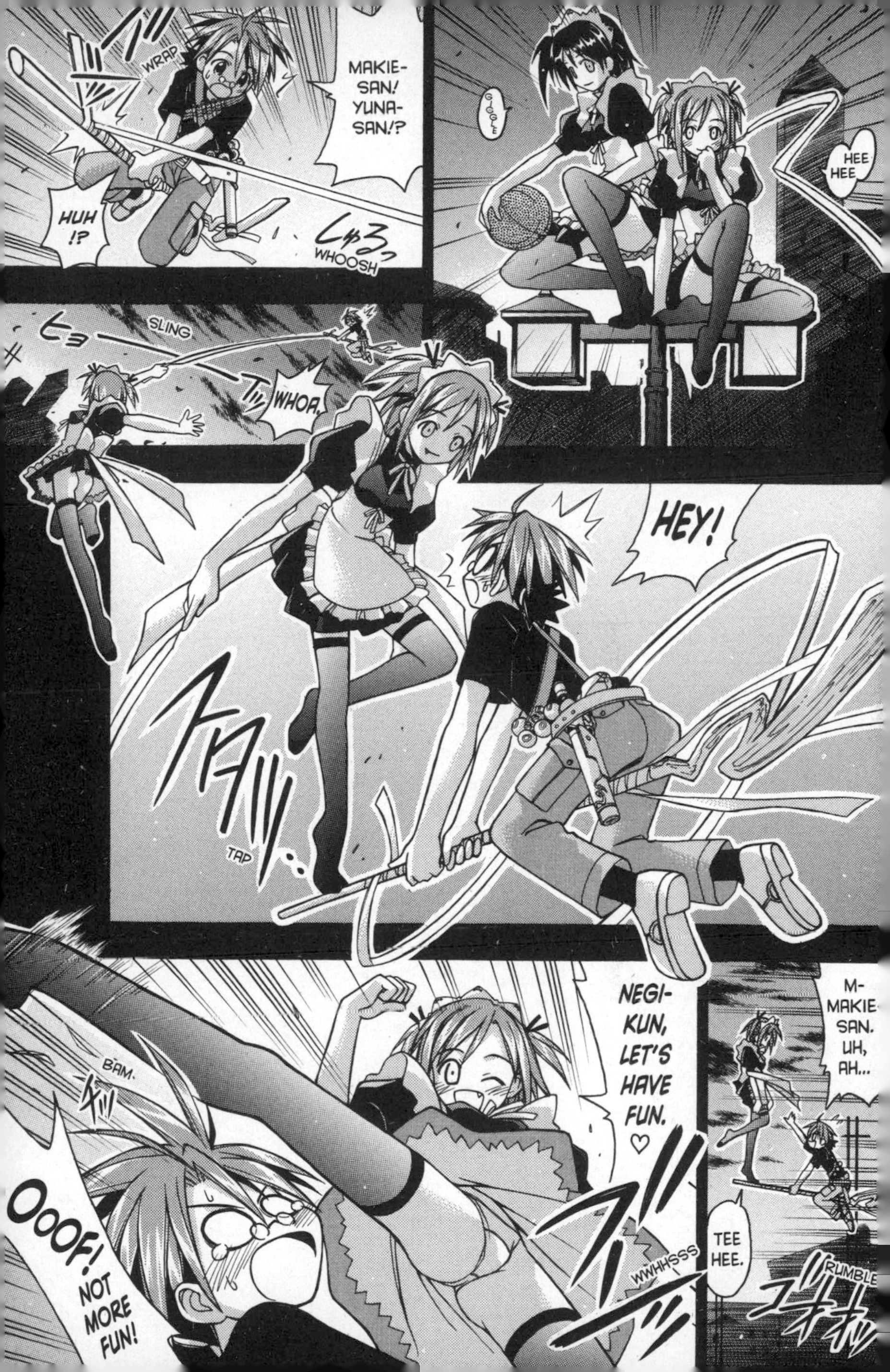
GIGGLE
HEE HEE
WRAP
MAKIE-SAN! YUNA-SAN!?
HUH !?
WHOOSH
SLING
WHOA.
HEY!
TAP
M-MAKIE-SAN. UH, AH...
TEE HEE.
RUMBLE
NEGI-KUN, LET'S HAVE FUN. ♡
WWHHSSS
BAM
OOOF! NOT MORE FUN!

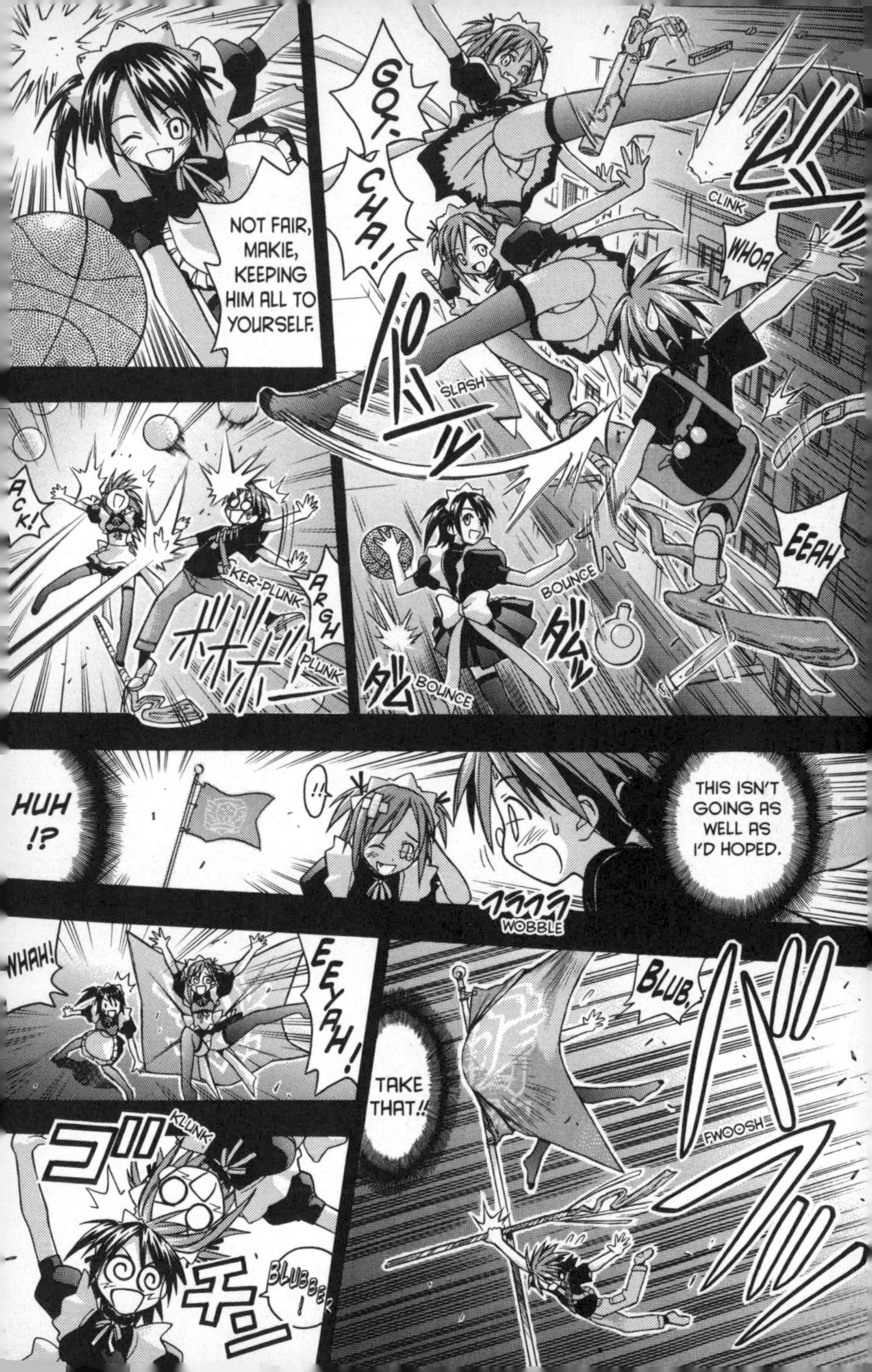
GOT-CHA!
CLINK
WHOA
SLASH
EEAH
NOT FAIR, MAKIE, KEEPING HIM ALL TO YOURSELF.
BOUNCE
BOUNCE
ACK!
KER-PLUNK
ARGH
PLUNK
THIS ISN'T GOING AS WELL AS I'D HOPED.
!!
WOBBLE
HUH!?
BLUB.
TAKE THAT!!
FWOOSH
EEYAH!
WHAH!
KLUNK
BLUBBER!

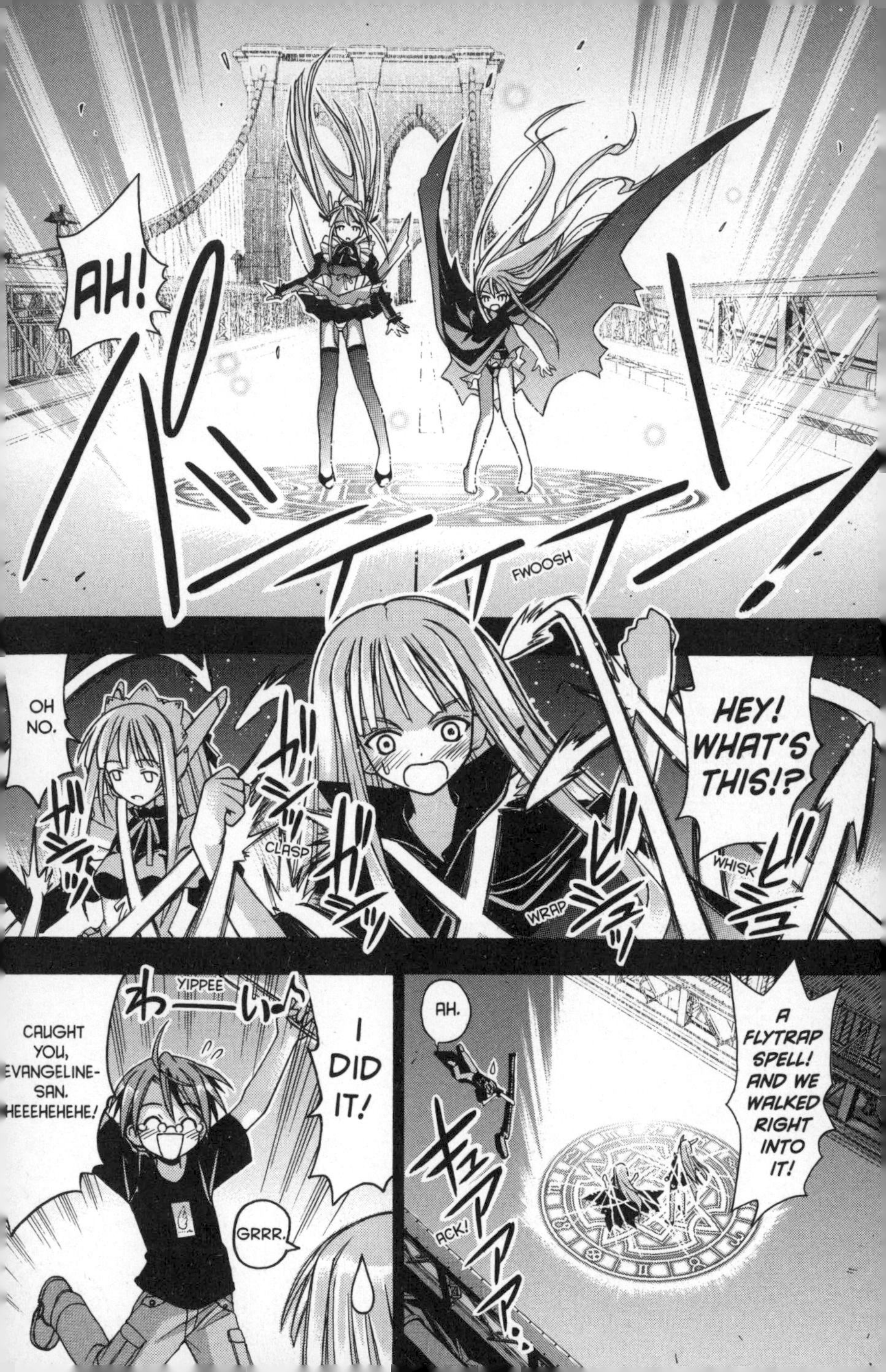

AH!
FWOOSH
HEY! WHAT'S THIS!?
WHISK
WRAP
CLASP
OH NO.
A FLYTRAP SPELL! AND WE WALKED RIGHT INTO IT!
AH.
ACK!
I DID IT!
YIPPEE
CAUGHT YOU, EVANGELINE-SAN. HEEEHEHEHE!
GRRR.

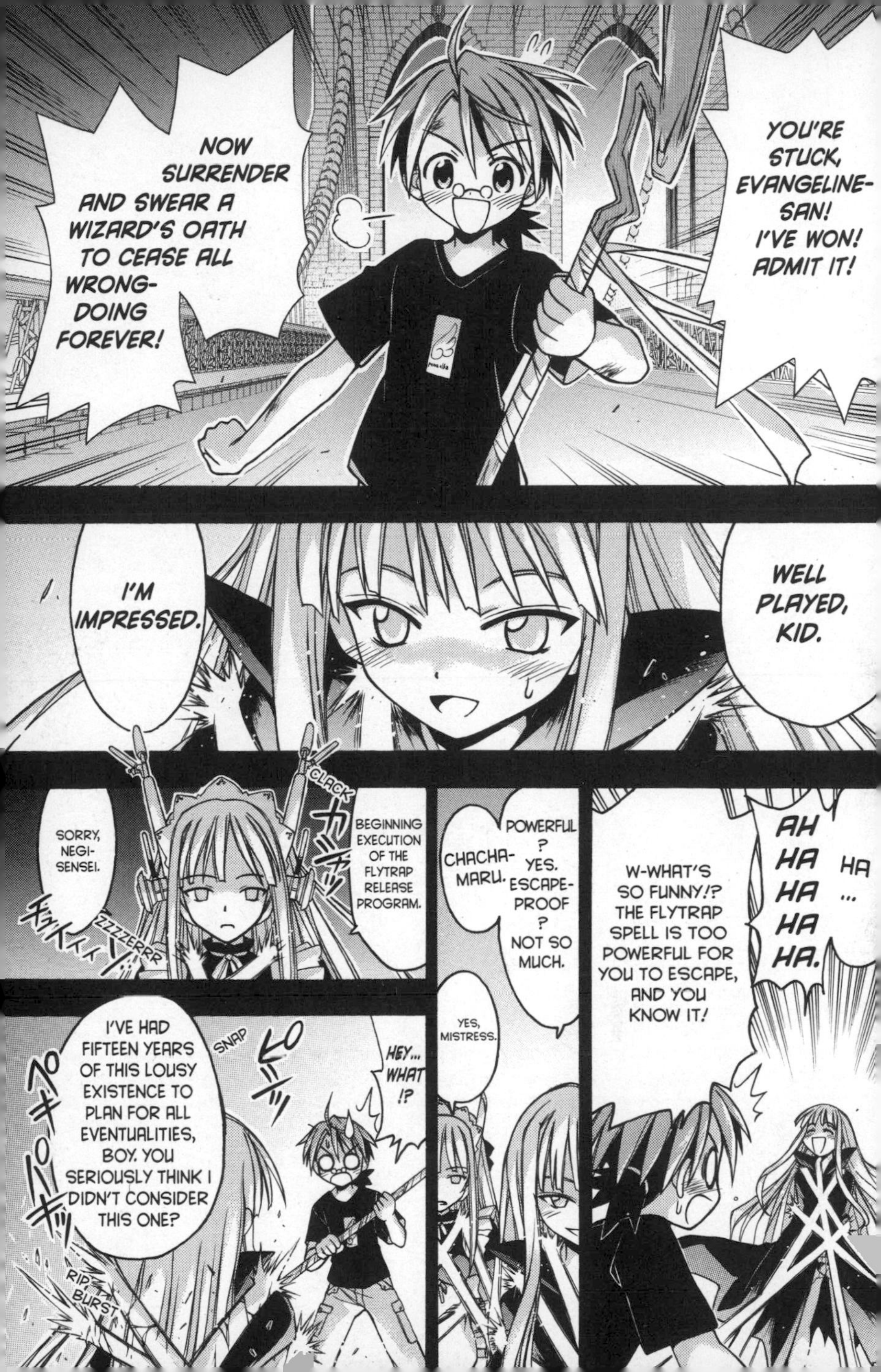
YOU'RE STUCK, EVANGELINE-SAN! I'VE WON! ADMIT IT!
NOW SURRENDER AND SWEAR A WIZARD'S OATH TO CEASE ALL WRONG-DOING FOREVER!
WELL PLAYED, KID.
I'M IMPRESSED.
AH HA HA HA HA
HA ...
HA.
W-WHAT'S SO FUNNY!? THE FLYTRAP SPELL IS TOO POWERFUL FOR YOU TO ESCAPE, AND YOU KNOW IT!
POWERFUL? YES. ESCAPE-PROOF? NOT SO MUCH.
CHACHA-MARU.
YES, MISTRESS.
BEGINNING EXECUTION OF THE FLYTRAP RELEASE PROGRAM.
CLACK
SORRY, NEGI-SENSEI.
ZZZZZERRR
HEY... WHAT!?
SNAP
I'VE HAD FIFTEEN YEARS OF THIS LOUSY EXISTENCE TO PLAN FOR ALL EVENTUALITIES, BOY. YOU SERIOUSLY THINK I DIDN'T CONSIDER THIS ONE?
RIP
BURST

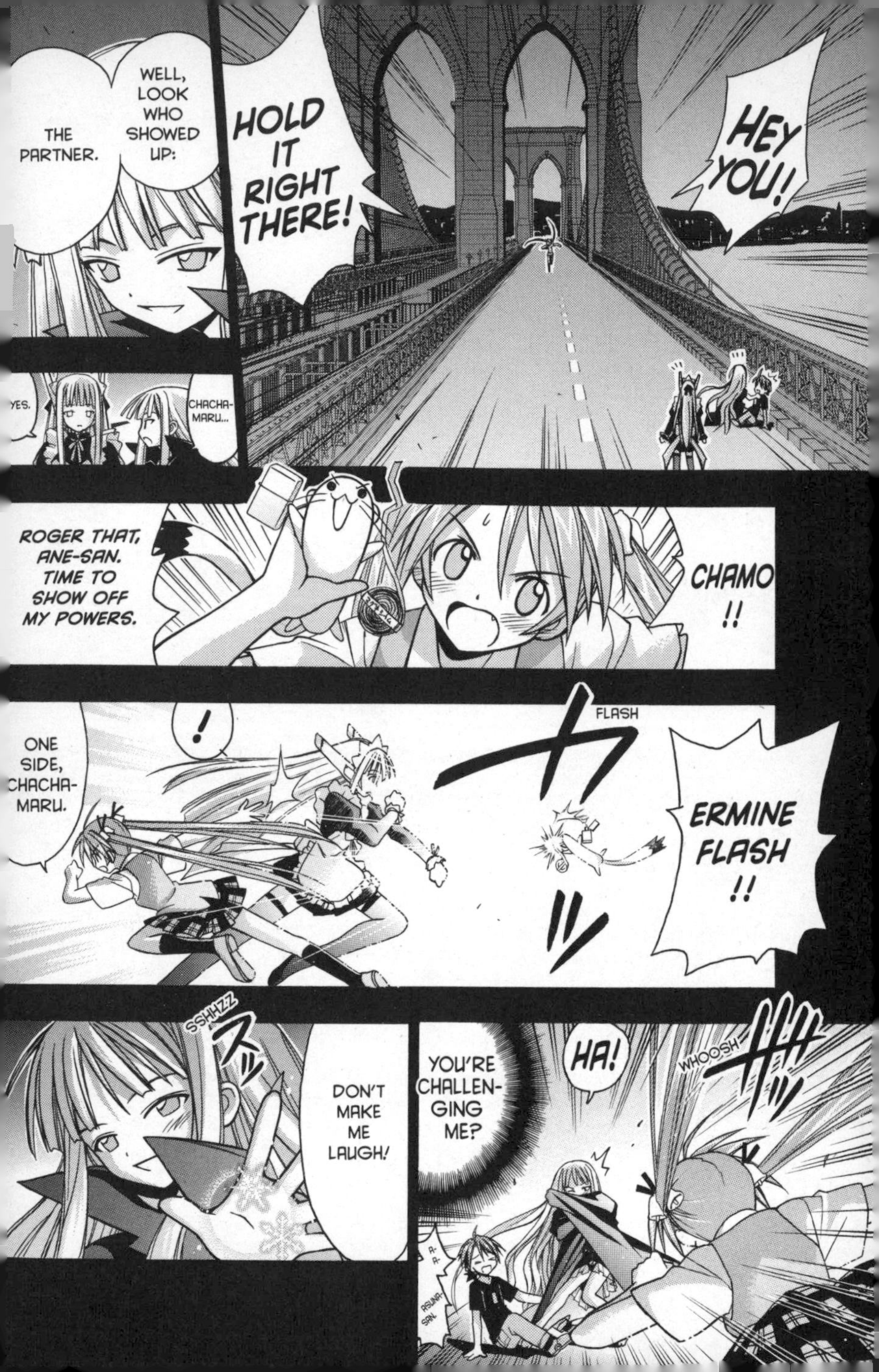
HEY YOU!!
HOLD IT RIGHT THERE!
WELL, LOOK WHO SHOWED UP:
THE PARTNER.
CHACHA-MARU...
YES.
CHAMO!!
ROGER THAT, ANE-SAN. TIME TO SHOW OFF MY POWERS.
ERMINE FLASH!!
FLASH
!
ONE SIDE, CHACHA-MARU.
WHOOSH
HA!
YOU'RE CHALLENGING ME?
A-A-ASUNA-SAN.
SSHHZZZ
DON'T MAKE ME LAUGH!

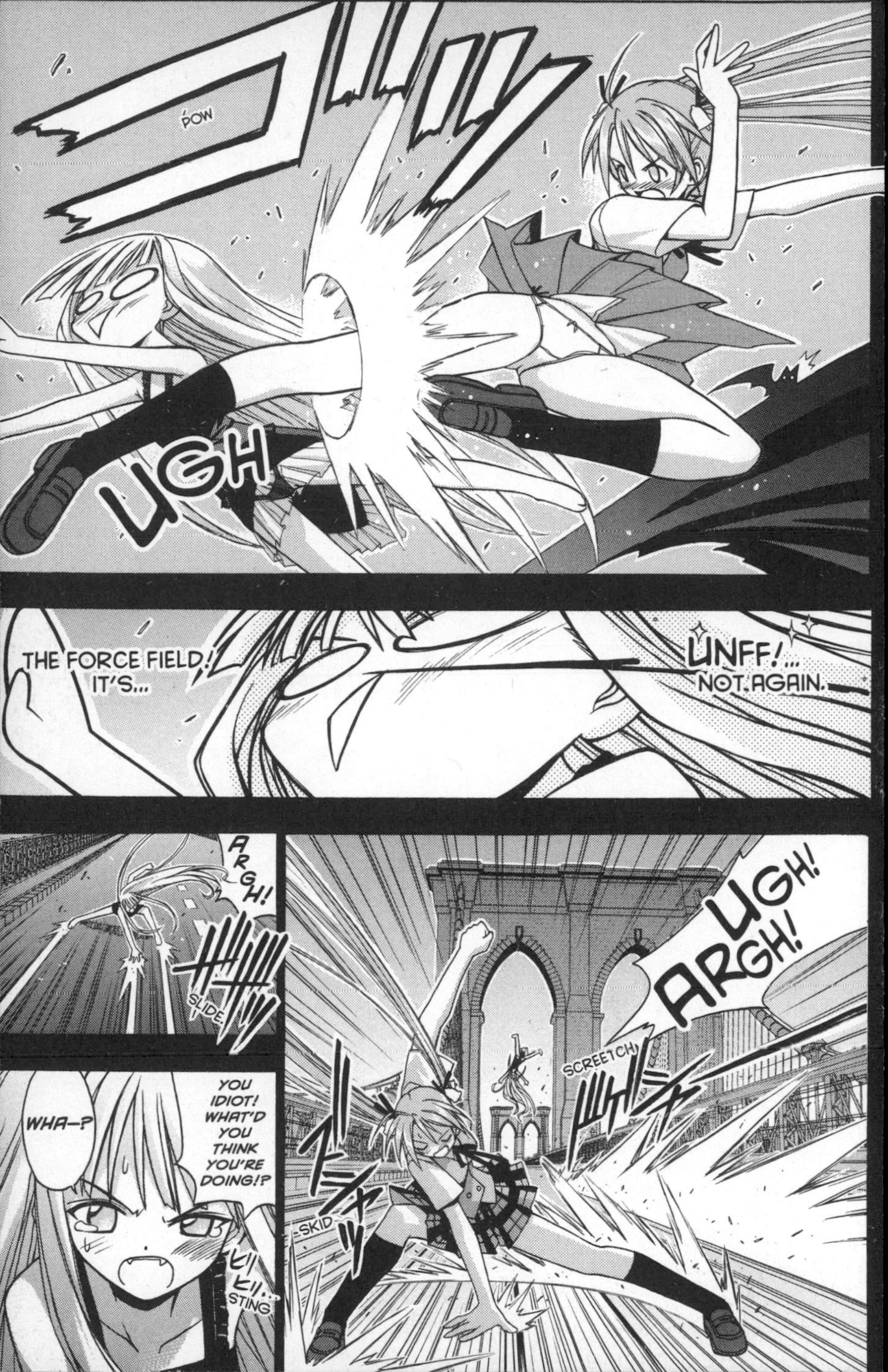
POW
UGH
UNFF!... NOT AGAIN.
THE FORCE FIELD! IT'S...
UGH! ARGH!
SCREETCH
SKID
ARGH!
SLIDE
YOU IDIOT! WHAT'D YOU THINK YOU'RE DOING!?
WHA-?
STING

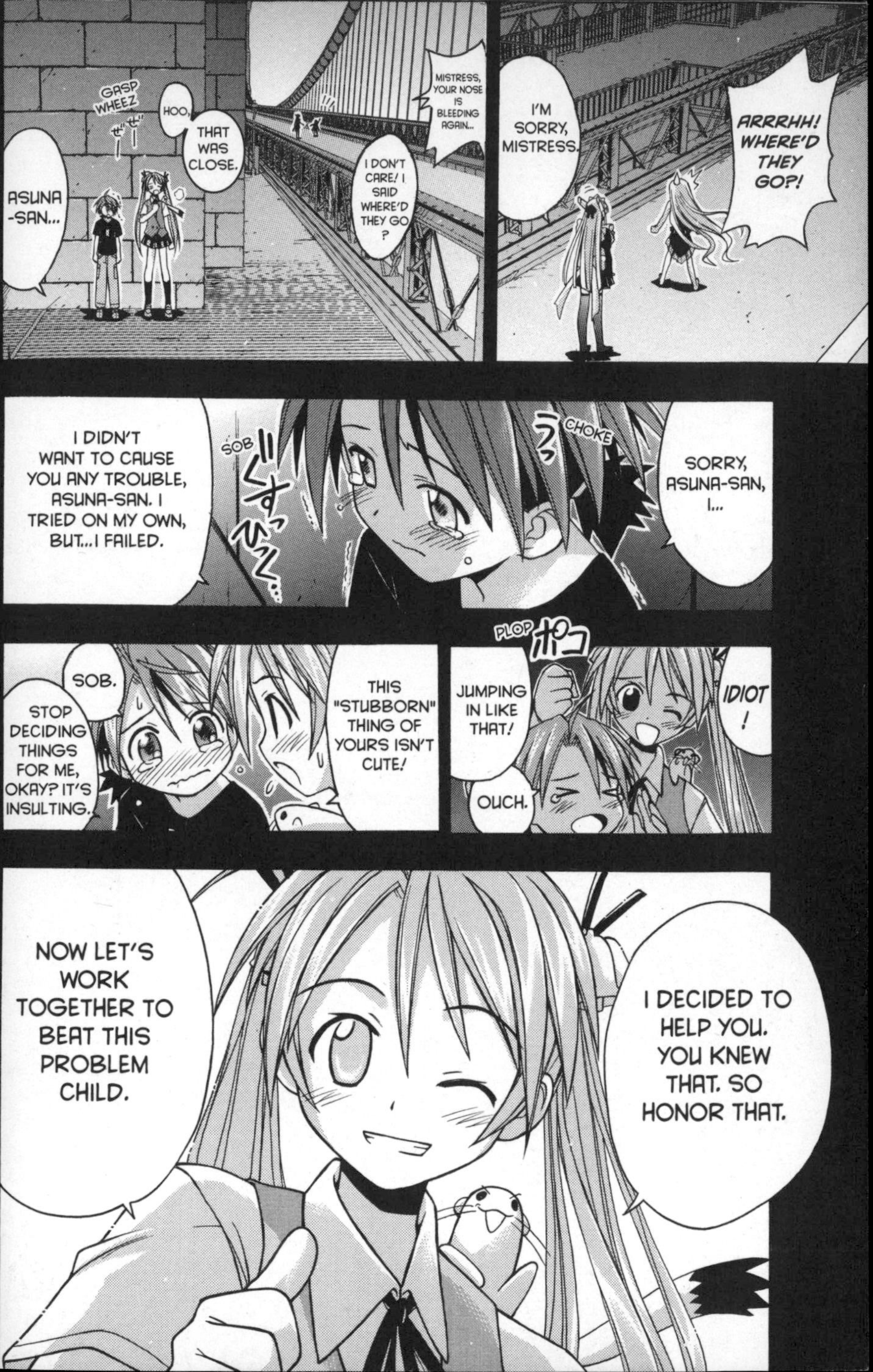
ARRRHH! WHERE'D THEY GO?!
I'M SORRY, MISTRESS.
MISTRESS, YOUR NOSE IS BLEEDING AGAIN...
I DON'T CARE! I SAID WHERE'D THEY GO?
HOO, THAT WAS CLOSE.
GASP WHEEZ
ASUNA-SAN...
SORRY, ASUNA-SAN, I...
CHOKE
SOB
I DIDN'T WANT TO CAUSE YOU ANY TROUBLE, ASUNA-SAN. I TRIED ON MY OWN, BUT...I FAILED.
IDIOT!
PLOP ポコ
JUMPING IN LIKE THAT!
OUCH.
THIS "STUBBORN" THING OF YOURS ISN'T CUTE!
SOB.
STOP DECIDING THINGS FOR ME, OKAY? IT'S INSULTING.
I DECIDED TO HELP YOU. YOU KNEW THAT. SO HONOR THAT.
NOW LET'S WORK TOGETHER TO BEAT THIS PROBLEM CHILD.

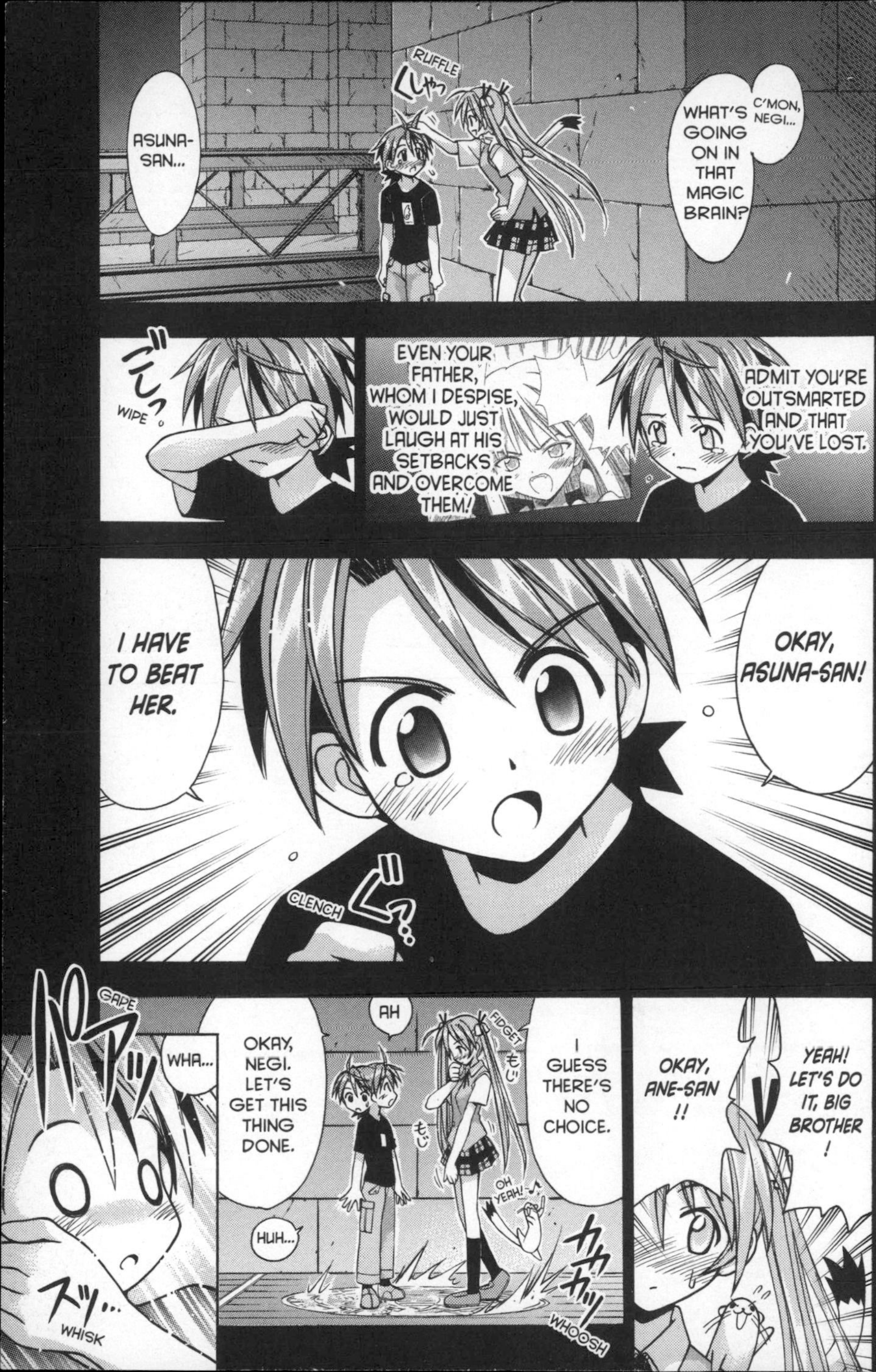
C'MON, NEGI...
WHAT'S GOING ON IN THAT MAGIC BRAIN?
RUFFLE
くしゃっ
ASUNA-SAN...
ADMIT YOU'RE OUTSMARTED AND THAT YOU'VE LOST.
EVEN YOUR FATHER, WHOM I DESPISE, WOULD JUST LAUGH AT HIS SETBACKS AND OVERCOME THEM!
WIPE
OKAY, ASUNA-SAN!
I HAVE TO BEAT HER.
CLENCH
YEAH! LET'S DO IT, BIG BROTHER!
OKAY, ANE-SAN!!
I GUESS THERE'S NO CHOICE.
FIDGET
もじ
もじ
AH
OKAY, NEGI. LET'S GET THIS THING DONE.
OH YEAH!♪
HUH...
WHOOSH
GAPE
WHA...
ズッ...
WHISK

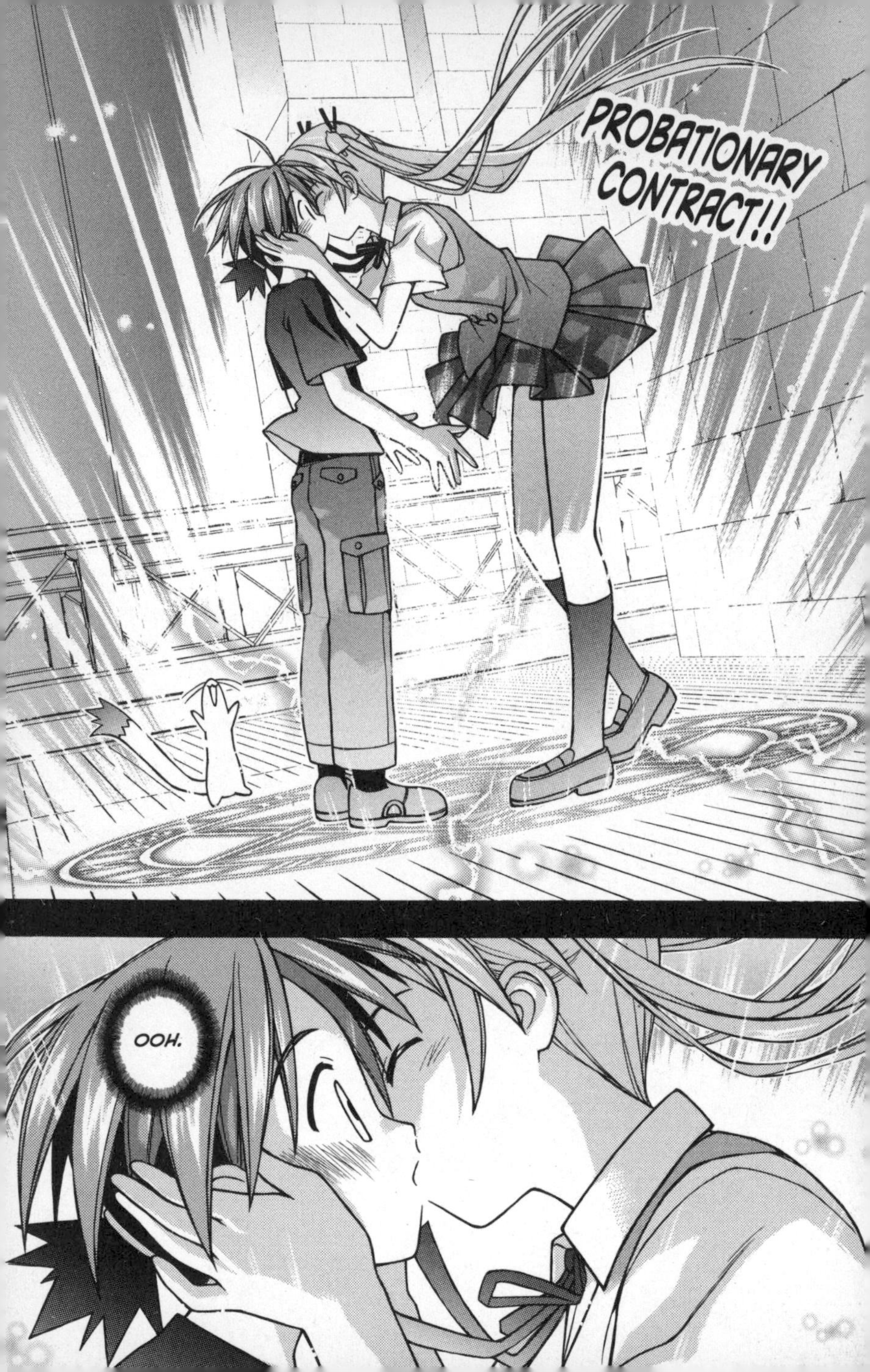
PROBATIONARY CONTRACT!!
OOH.

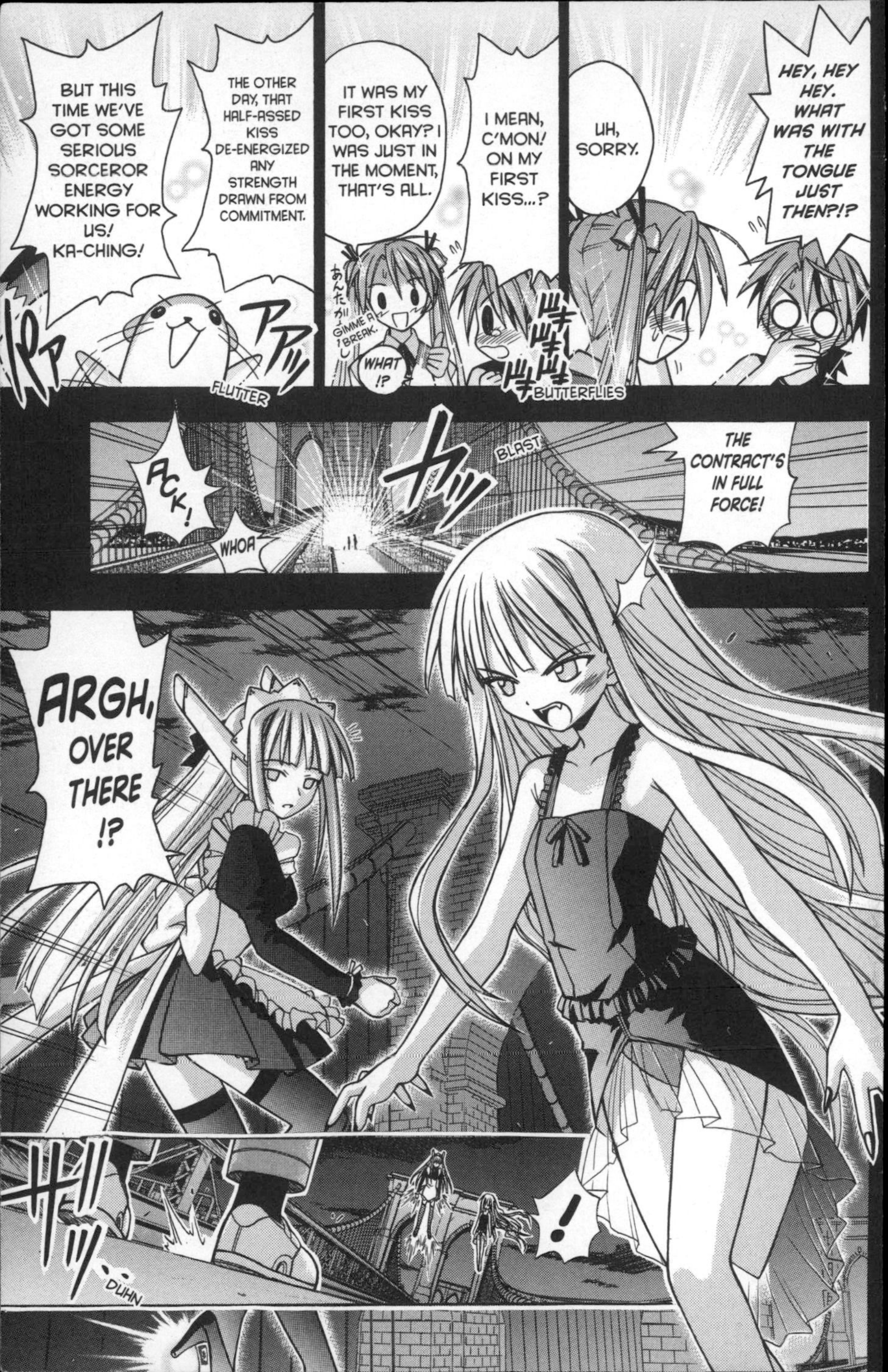
HEY, HEY HEY. WHAT WAS WITH THE TONGUE JUST THEN?!?
UH, SORRY.
I MEAN, C'MON! ON MY FIRST KISS...?
IT WAS MY FIRST KISS TOO, OKAY? I WAS JUST IN THE MOMENT, THAT'S ALL.
BUTTERFLIES
GIMME A BREAK.
WHAT !?
THE OTHER DAY, THAT HALF-ASSED KISS DE-ENERGIZED ANY STRENGTH DRAWN FROM COMMITMENT.
BUT THIS TIME WE'VE GOT SOME SERIOUS SORCEROR ENERGY WORKING FOR US! KA-CHING!
FLUTTER
THE CONTRACT'S IN FULL FORCE!
BLAST
ACK!
WHOA
ARGH, OVER THERE !?
!
DUHN

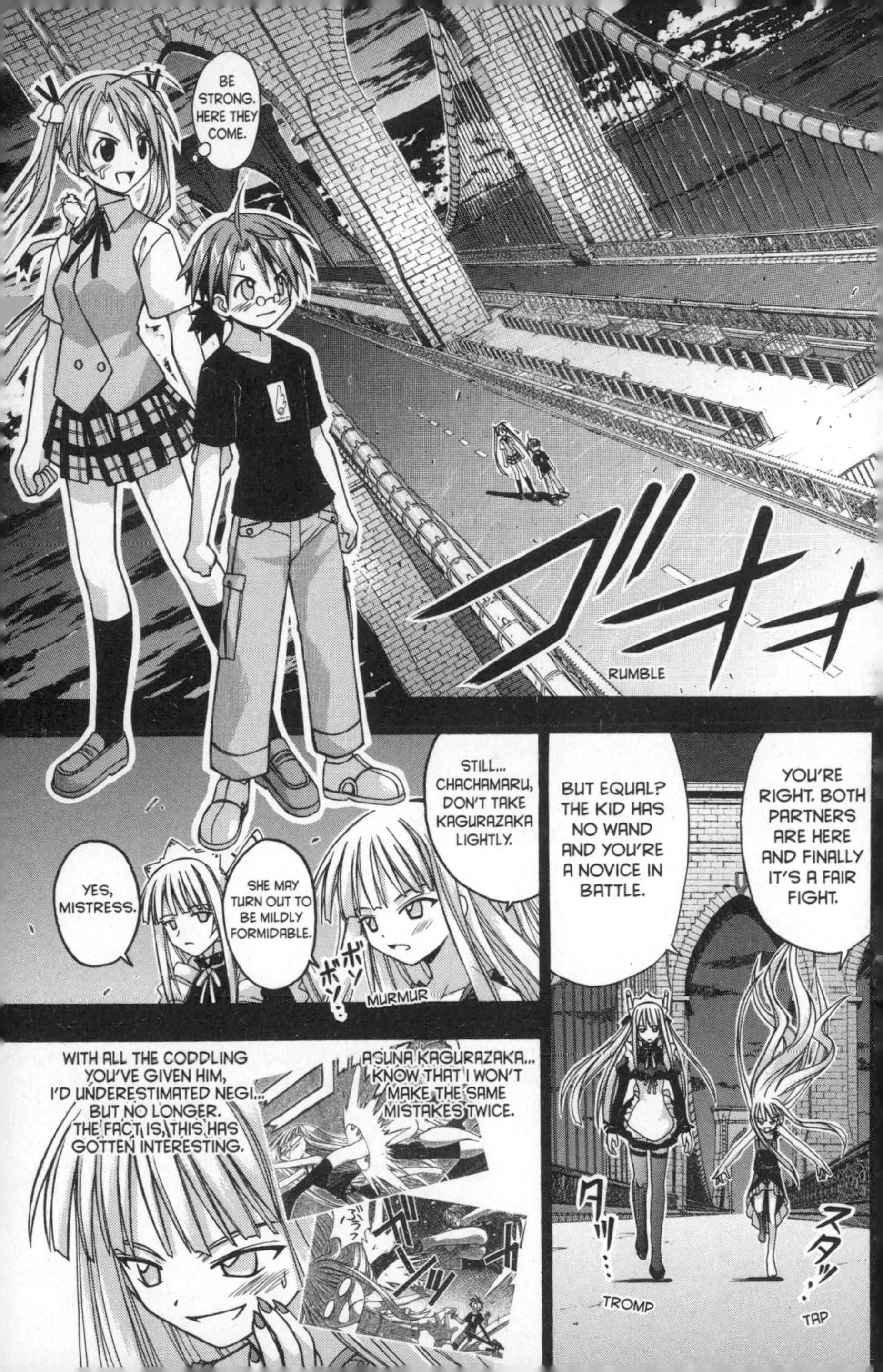
BE STRONG. HERE THEY COME.
RUMBLE
YOU'RE RIGHT. BOTH PARTNERS ARE HERE AND FINALLY IT'S A FAIR FIGHT.
BUT EQUAL? THE KID HAS NO WAND AND YOU'RE A NOVICE IN BATTLE.
TROMP
TAP
STILL... CHACHAMARU, DON'T TAKE KAGURAZAKA LIGHTLY.
SHE MAY TURN OUT TO BE MILDLY FORMIDABLE.
MURMUR
YES, MISTRESS.
ASUNA KAGURAZAKA... KNOW THAT I WON'T MAKE THE SAME MISTAKES TWICE.
WITH ALL THE CODDLING YOU'VE GIVEN HIM, I'D UNDERESTIMATED NEGI... BUT NO LONGER. THE FACT IS, THIS HAS GOTTEN INTERESTING.

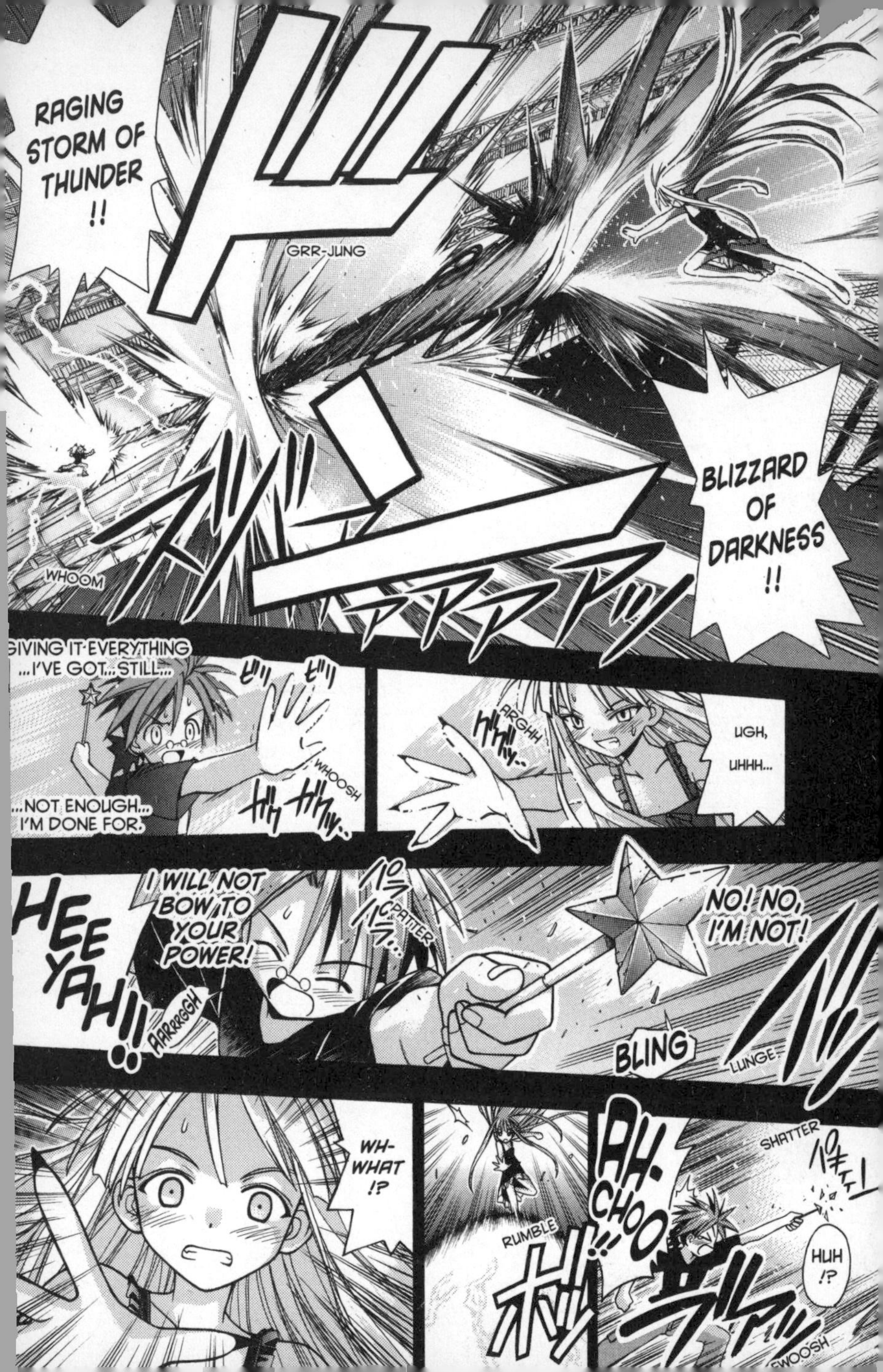
BLIZZARD OF DARKNESS !!
RAGING STORM OF THUNDER !!
GRR-JUNG
WHOOM
UGH, UHHH...
ARGHH
GIVING IT EVERYTHING ...I'VE GOT... STILL...
WHOOSH
...NOT ENOUGH... I'M DONE FOR.
NO! NO, I'M NOT!
LUNGE
BLING
PATTER
I WILL NOT BOW TO YOUR POWER!
HEE YAH!!
AARRRGGH
SHATTER
HUH !?
AH-CHOO!!
RUMBLE
FWOOSH
WH- WHAT !?

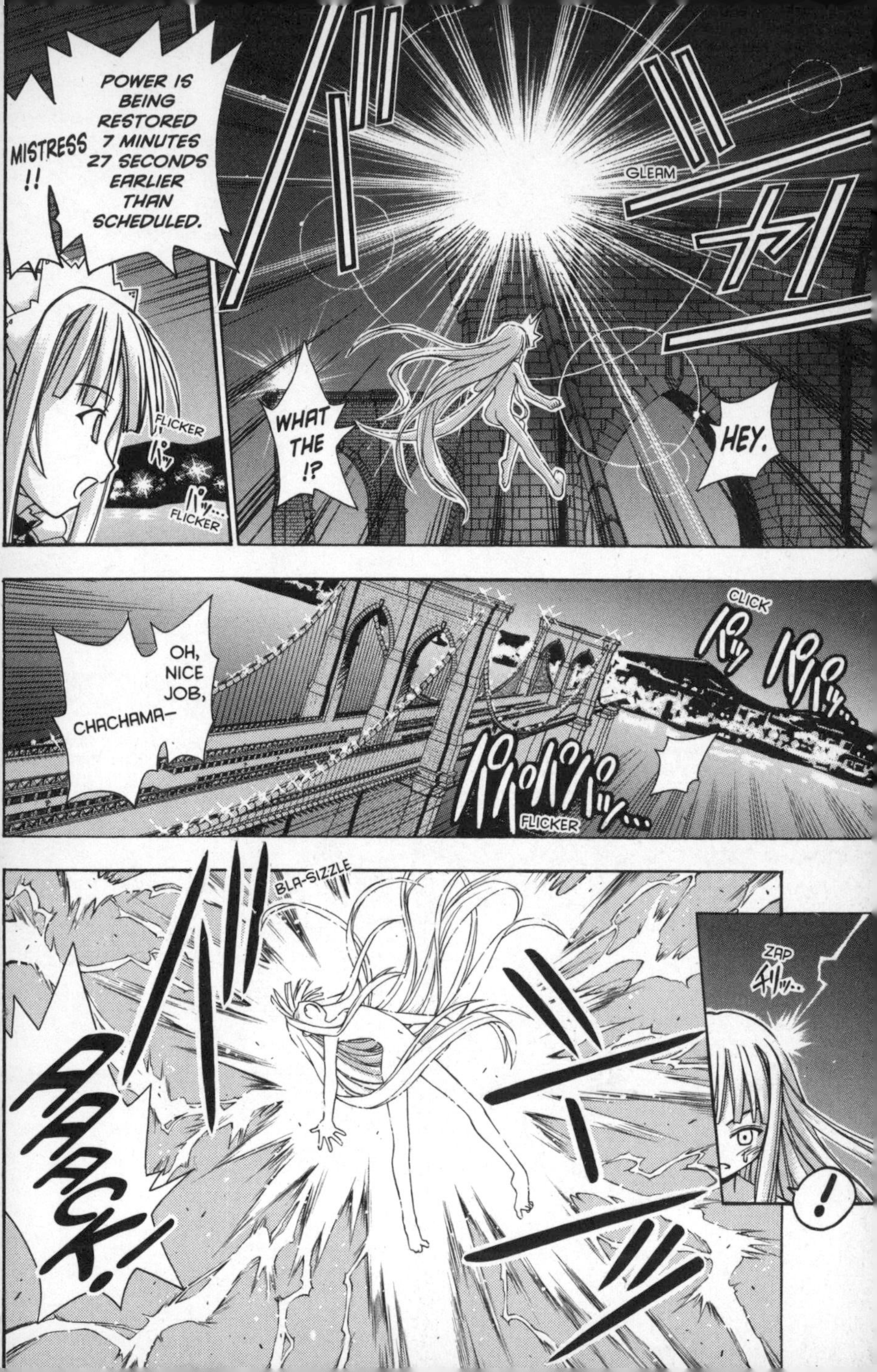
GLEAM
HEY.
WHAT THE !?
POWER IS BEING RESTORED 7 MINUTES 27 SECONDS EARLIER THAN SCHEDULED.
MISTRESS !!
FLICKER
FLICKER
CLICK
OH, NICE JOB, CHACHAMA—
FLICKER
ZAP
!
BLA-SIZZLE
AAACK!

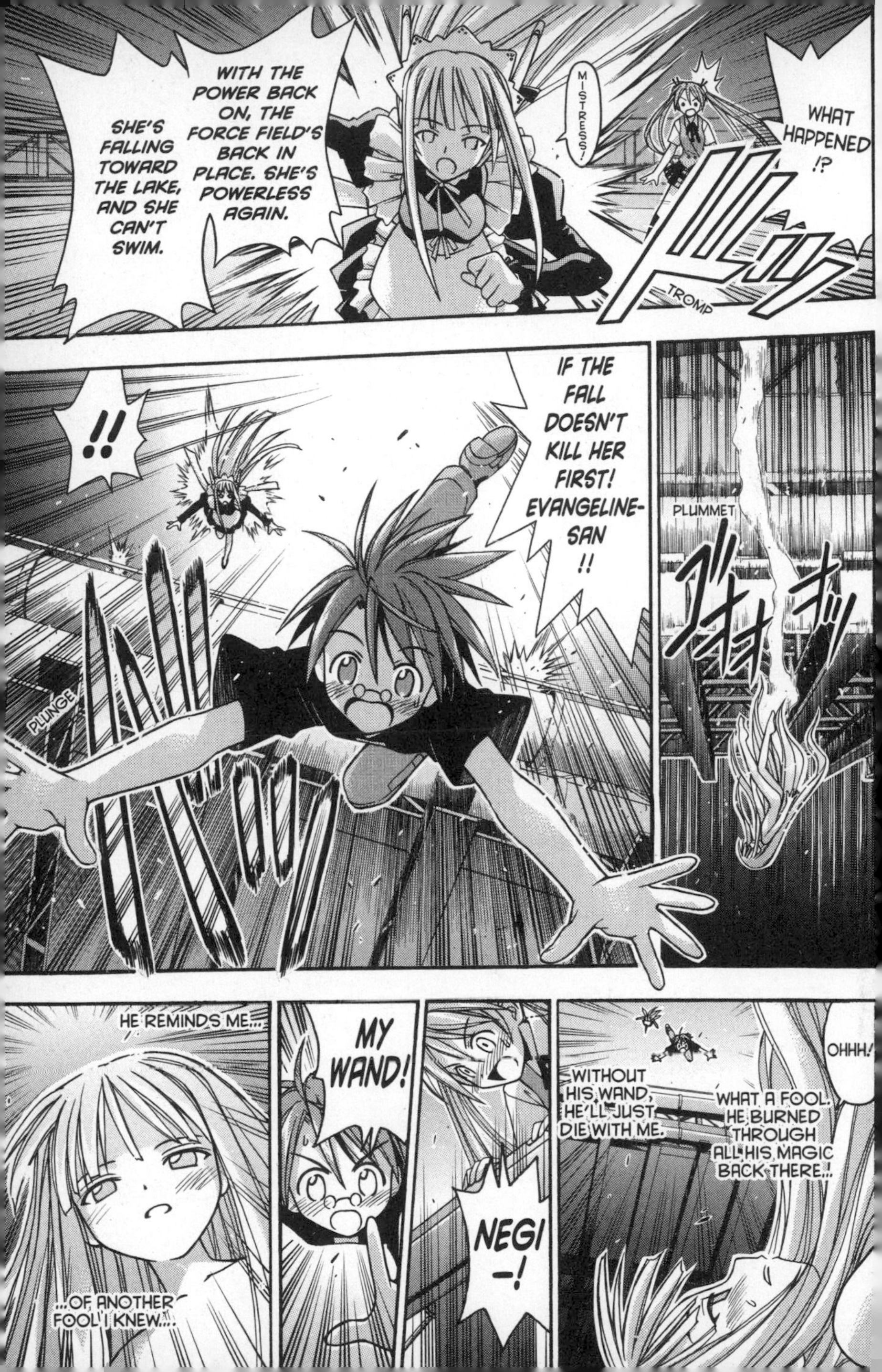
WHAT HAPPENED!?
MISTRESS!
TROMP
WITH THE POWER BACK ON, THE FORCE FIELD'S BACK IN PLACE. SHE'S POWERLESS AGAIN.
SHE'S FALLING TOWARD THE LAKE, AND SHE CAN'T SWIM.
PLUMMET
IF THE FALL DOESN'T KILL HER FIRST! EVANGELINE-SAN !!
!!
PLUNGE
OHHH!
WHAT A FOOL. HE BURNED THROUGH ALL HIS MAGIC BACK THERE...
WITHOUT HIS WAND, HE'LL JUST DIE WITH ME.
MY WAND!
NEGI-!
HE REMINDS ME...
...OF ANOTHER FOOL I KNEW...

I FELT LIKE IT. EAT UP. IT'S TASTY.

CRACKLE

WHO ARE YOU?

WHY DID YOU HELP ME?

THAT WAS CLOSE...

...KID.

CLASP

. . . .

CHOMP

HEY, COME ON NOW.

HEY YOU. WILL YOU BE MINE?

CLANK CLANK

. . . . . .

EVEN IF YOU RUN, I'LL FOLLOW YOU TO THE ENDS OF THE EARTH... AND BEYOND.

NO.

C'MON, EVA. YOU'VE BEEN FOLLOWING ME AROUND FOR A MONTH. IT'S ENOUGH ALREADY. SCRAM.

SAME THING!

ACK! I'M IN SCHOOL! I'M IN HELL!

NOO!

ACTUALLY, I LIKED YOU.

SSSHHHH

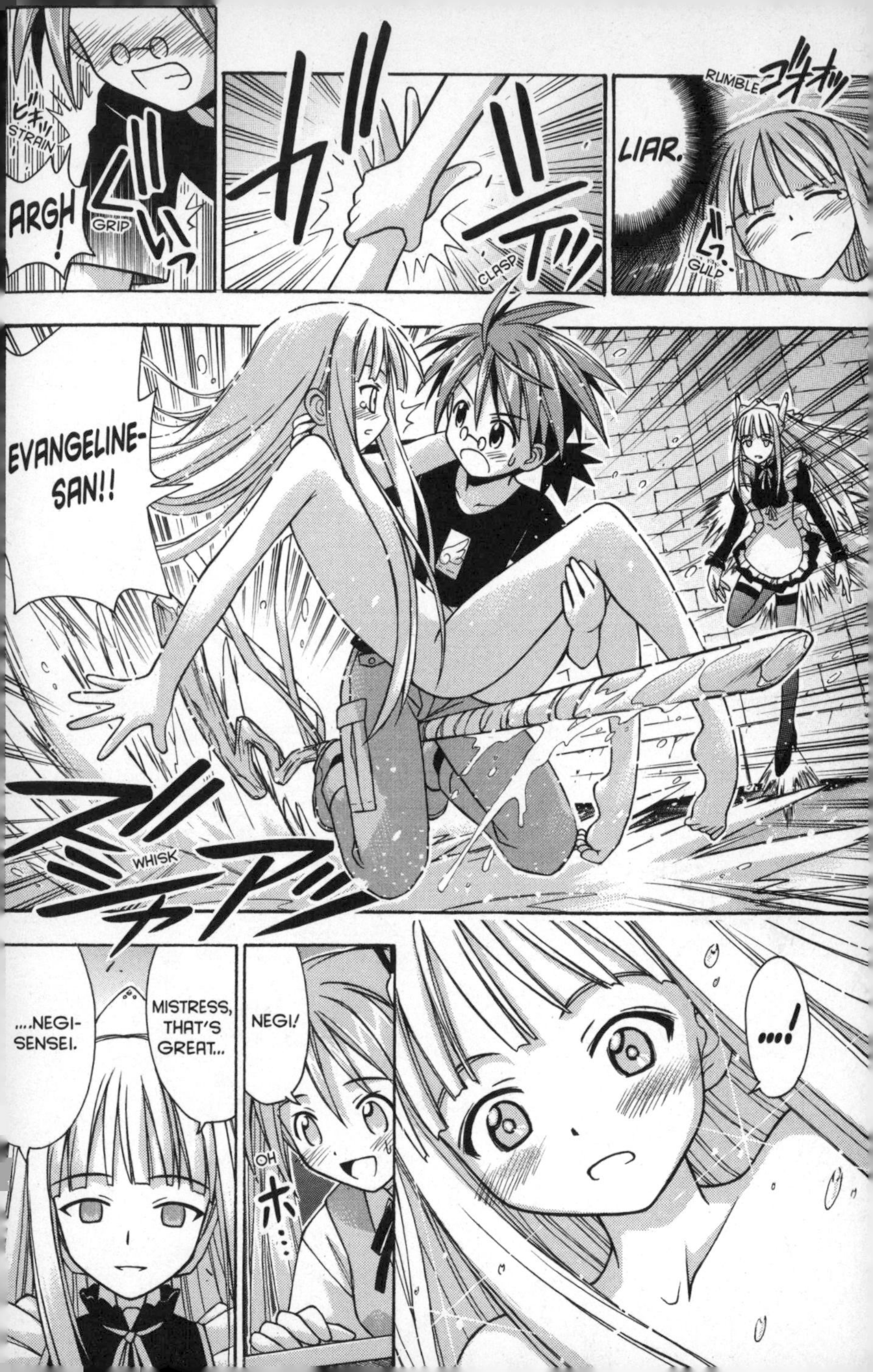
RUMBLE
LIAR.
GULP
CLASP
STRAIN
ARGH!
GRIP
EVANGELINE-SAN!!
WHISK
....!
NEGI!
OH
MISTRESS, THAT'S GREAT...
....NEGI-SENSEI.

UM...

BECAUSE ...

WHY DID YOU HELP ME?

HMPH.

...WITHOUT YOUR POWER... YOU WERE MY STUDENT AGAIN.

NOW, KNOCK OFF THE EVIL STUFF!

COME TO CLASS!

GRRR

EH HEH HEH! WELL, I GUESS THAT MEANS I REALLY WON.

FOOL.

WHAT!?

DOO DOO DOO キュッ キュッ♪

YES! I'LL WRITE, "I WON" IN YOUR PART OF THE CLASS REGISTER.

I CERTAINLY OWE YOU ONE FOR TODAY.

ALL RIGHT.

NOTHING'S "SAFE" WITH HER AROUND.

UM, IS IT SAFE TO SAY THEY'VE MADE UP!?

YOU KNOW, SEVEN MORE MINUTES OF BLACKOUT AND I'D HAVE WON!

EH? BUT...

WHAT ARE YOU DOING? CUT IT OUT, YOU. BETTER YET, GET LOST.

SHRIEK SHRIEK ギギッ

AW GREAT!

AND IF I CAN BECOME A MAGISTER MAGI, I'LL LIFT IT FOR YOU.

I'LL STUDY UP ON THE CURSE,

PINCH ムギギ

R-REST EASY, EVANGELINE-SAN.

NO. ACTUALLY SHE'S MELLOWED SINCE NEGI-SENSEI SHOWED UP.

WAS EVANGELINE ALWAYS LIKE THIS?

LISTEN UP, BOY. I HAVEN'T GIVEN UP! WATCH YOUR BACK ON THE NIGHT OF THE FULL MOON!

DON'T IGNORE ME!!

THAT REMINDS ME: I GOTTA CURE MAKIE-SAN AND THE REST.

SHRIEK

Y'KNOW, IF I JUST DRINK YOUR BLOOD, I LIFT IT IMMEDIATELY.

AND HOW MANY YEARS IS THAT GONNA TAKE?

SHRIEK ギャ

CONTINUED IN VOLUME 4

- STAFF -

Ken Akamatsu
Takashi Takemoto
Kenichi Nakamura
Masaki Ohyama
Keiichi Yamashita
Chigusa Amagasaki
Takaaki Miyahara

Thanks To

Ran Ayanaga
Toshiko Akamatsu

About the Creator

Negima! is only Ken Akamatsu's third manga, although he started working in the field in 1994 with *AI Ga Tomaranai*. Like all of Akamatsu's work to date, it was published in Kodansha's *Shonen Magazine*. *AI Ga Tomaranai* ran for five years before concluding in 1999. In 1998, however, Akamatsu began the work that would make him one of the most popular manga artists in Japan: *Love Hina*. *Love Hina* ran for four years, and before its conclusion in 2002, it would cause Akamatsu to be granted the prestigious Manga of the Year award from Kodansha, as well as going on to become one of the best-known and best-selling manga in the United Kingdom.

Volumes 1, 2 & 3 of *Negima!* are available now.

LEXICON NEGIMARIUM DE CANTU

Negima! Glossary Of Spells

Sixteenth Period

Undecim spiritus aerials, vinculum facti iimicum captent. Sagitta magica, aer Capturae. ("11 wind spirits, become a chain that binds and capture my enemy.") Magic that uses the wind to restrain enemies. It is a weak attack and had little effect on the experienced Evangeline.

Reflexio. ("Ice Shield.") A magic shield that is conjured to repel the attacking magic from an enemy. Evangeline is skilled at ice magic so she conjured an "ice shield." *Reflexio* corresponds to the English *reflection.*

Seventeenth Period

Frigerans Exarmatio. ("Release freeze weapon.") Magic that, without causing any frostbite injury to the opponent, freezes the things attached to the body and shatters them, disarming the enemy. Control over complicated magic power is necessary to wield this spell. However, metal and other types of hard materials cannot be shattered, so the most you can do is buy some time against these types of items.

Evocatio valcyriarum, contubernalia gladiaria. ("I summon the wind spirit!! Sword-wielding brothers in arms!!") The word *walkyria* has been Latinized, but corresponds to the old Nordic *valkyrie,* referring here to a "person who chooses immortality." In short, what Negi is summoning is an immortal god. Odin's handmaidens, who appear in Wagner's opera, are popular valkryies, but throughout this work, the term is used as a neuter noun and not a proper entity. "Age capiant" is a form of address that means, "please capture."

Flans exarmatio. ("Wind flower, disarm weapon.") This is, in fact, the magic that appears most frequently in *Negima!* The incantation blows off with a powerful wind items attached to an opponent's body . Clothing and other light things are changed into flower petals. The sole purpose is to disarm an opponent of weapons, so no matter strong the wind is, it will not blow away the opponent herself. When Negi sneezes and blows off the clothes of Asuna and friends, this is the explosion of this magic. Refer to the First, Second, Fifth, Sixth, and Twelfth Periods. (From the Seventeenth Period on.)

Nineteenth Period

Practe bigi nar. This is the "magic release key" and is not a Latin language spell. The formal "release key" is created by each student individually upon graduation from magic school, but *practe bigi nar* is an apprenticeship key given to a schoolchild.

Pactio. ("Probationary Contract.") A spell to enter a probationary contract between a wizard (magus) and a partner (minister) that brings about ecstacy in order to draw out both parties' consciousness from within their egos. A ceremony is necessary for the spell to work. The word *pactio* itself does not indicate that the spell is probationary; this is the same as the proper, permanent contract spell. However, stronger contract magic is used for the so-called real contract. When a wizard enters a probationary contract, certain powers are attained.

Twentieth Period

Sis mea pars per decem secundas. Ministra Negi, Asuna Kagurazaka. ("Contract executed in 10 seconds. Minister Negi, Asuna Kagurazaka.") A spell that sends a wizard's own magic power to the person with whom that wizard has entered a probationary contract; in this case, from Negi to Asuna. *Sis mea pars* means *you are a part of me.* If the contract is incomplete, there are restrictions on the magic powers sent, and it appears that with Negi and friends they were able to use the contract's power only during the first 10 seconds. If the contract is renewed correctly, the magic powers can be used for another 90 seconds (*per nonaginta secundas*).

Undecem spiritus lucis, coeuntes sagitent inimicum. Sagitta magica, series lucis. (11 spirits of light, come gather [shoot the enemy]; Magic Archer, consecutive bursts, 11 arrows of light) A basic battle spell. Light spirit version. *Serius lucis* means "range of light."

Twenty-Second Period

Nympha somni, regina Mab, portam aperiens ad se me alliciat. ("I invoke Queen Mab, the Dream Fairy, open the door and invite me into dreams.") Magic that lets you see into sleeping people's dreams. Mab is the name of a queen who appears in a Celtic myth. She is thought of as a fairy who controls dreams.

Manmanterroterro. The Thousand Master's "release key." A style that's changed considerably.

Infernus scholasticus. (School hell.) A very strange curse. In the past, it was used for making dropouts go to school. This curse has tormented Evangeline for over 15 years.

Twenty-Third—Twenty-Fifth Periods

Aer et aqua, facti nebula illis somnum brevem. Nebula hypnotica. ("Atmosphere. Water. White fog, seep. Give them repose, make them sleep.") Magic that conjures a fog that makes your opponent sleep.

Lic lac la lac lilac. Evangeline's "release key." Lilac thrives where things are difficult to grow, and when a flower is brought inside the house, it brings evil with it. In the language of flowers, the incantation refers to "purity" and "first love."

Septendecim spiritus glaciales, coeuntes inimicum concidant. SAGITTA MAGICA, SERIES GLACIALIS. ("17 Ice Spirits, come gather and rip apart my enemy"; "Magic Archer. Consecutive bursts. Eleven ice arrows.") The ice version of the "Magic Archer." Several sharp ice pillars attack the enemy.

Nivis casus. ("Ice explosion.") Magic that makes large volumes of ice appear in the air and attacks the opponent with both frosty air and a blast of wind. *Nivis casus* means "avalanche".

Veniant spiritus aerials fulgurientes, cum fulgurationi filet tempestas austrina. Jovis tempestas fulguriens. ("Ice spirits on high, fill the sky. Tundra and Glaciers on the run from the land of midnight sun"; "Frozen earth.") Attacks with huge ice pillars that come from the earth in an instant. If not dodged effectively, your feet become frozen to the ground and you aren't able to move. For enemies that can't fly, this magic is very effective to use before an attack.

Septendecim spiritus aerials, coeuntes...Sagitta maigca, wries fulguralis. ("17 Wind Spirits. Come gather..."; "Magic Archer, Consecutive blasts, 17 arrows of thunder.") The lightning version of "Magic Archer." If the user's power becomes too weak it also can be used to stun.

Undetriginta spiritus obscuri...Sagitta magica, series obscuri. ("29 Spirits of Darkness..."; "Magic Archer, consecutive blasts, 29 arrow of darkness.") The dark version of "Magic Archer." It's unknown what kind of power is in the flying dark bullet.

Undetriginata spiritus lucis...Sagitta magica, series lucis. ("29 spirits of light..."; "Magic Archer, consecutive blasts, 29 arrows of light.") Constitutes the opposite of the magic written above. Besides the fact that one is obscuri (dark) and one is lucis (light), they are parallel spells.

Veniant spiritus aerials fulgurientes, cum fulgurationi flet tempestas austrina. Jovis tempestas. ("Come wind, thunder spirits. Blow violently with thunder, Storm of the South Seas.") Magic that conjures a strong whirlwind and lightning that attacks the enemy. *Jovis* is another name for the king of Roman gods, Jupiter, who is thought to use lightning as a weapon. In short, *Jovis tempestas* means "Jupiter's storm that unleashes lightning."

Veniant spiritus glaciales obscurants, cum obscurationi flet tempestas nivalis. Nivis tempestas obscurans. ("Darkness obey, a blizzard, ice and snow of the night."; "Blizzard of darkness.") Magic that conjures a strong blizzard and darkness that attacks the enemy. As you might have noticed, there are several similar points with the spell above. It seems that Evangeline chose the same type of spells in order to fight Negi. Nivis tempestas obscurans means "snowstorm that brings darkness."

Mea virga. (My wand.) The words used to call the wand that Negi received from the Thousand Master. Mea means "my" and virga means "wand."

COMPILATION OF MATERIAL FOR THE BEGINNING SETTINGS OF NEGIMA!

THE ORIGINAL CHARACTER SKETCHES

WELL, THIS IS THE ORIGINAL CHARACTER SKETCH OF EVANGE-LINE. KINDA SAYS "WHAT THE HECK?" (HA HA.) I WANTED TO SEE HOW THE DARK VERSION WOULD LOOK, TOO. AROUND THE STUDIO, WE CALL HER "THE MASTER."

"EVANGELINE A.K. MCDOWELL" SERIOUS WIZARD. AGE UNKNOWN. SHORT.

THERE'RE ALSO 51 DARK VERSIONS.

DETECTIVE, ASSASSIN FROM HER FATHER'S SIDE. CAN REALLY USE MAGIC. A WITCH HAILING FROM THE MIDDLE REGION OF EUROPE. WON'T TAKE HER HAT OFF DURING CLASS. DESPISES THE MAIN CHARACTER.

FLUFFY HAIR IS PARTICULAR TO GIRLS' COMICS. I'LL RESEARCH THAT LATER.

GREMLIN

DUN DUN DUN!

YOU'LL DIE

UH, EVA-KUN, TAKE YOUR HAT OFF DURING CLASS.

NO.

RULER (MADE OF WOOD) INSTEAD OF A MAGIC WAND.

NEGI MAGI

MAGISTER

MAHORA MAGISTER

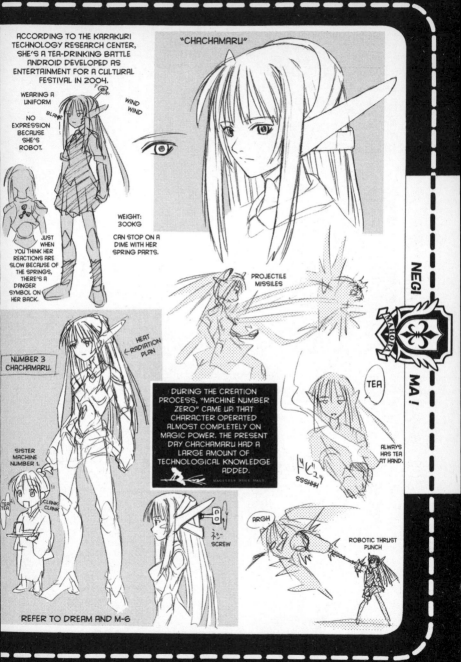

ACCORDING TO THE KARAKURI TECHNOLOGY RESEARCH CENTER, SHE'S A TEA-DRINKING BATTLE ANDROID DEVELOPED AS ENTERTAINMENT FOR A CULTURAL FESTIVAL IN 2004.

"CHACHAMARU"

WEARING A UNIFORM

NO EXPRESSION BECAUSE SHE'S ROBOT.

BLANK

WIND WIND

JUST WHEN YOU THINK HER REACTIONS ARE SLOW BECAUSE OF THE SPRINGS, THERE'S A DANGER SYMBOL ON HER BACK.

WEIGHT: 300KG

CAN STOP ON A DIME WITH HER SPRING PARTS.

PROJECTILE MISSILES

NUMBER 3 CHACHAMARU.

HEAT RADIATION PLAN

DURING THE CREATION PROCESS, "MACHINE NUMBER ZERO" CAME UP. THAT CHARACTER OPERATED ALMOST COMPLETELY ON MAGIC POWER. THE PRESENT DAY CHACHAMARU HAD A LARGE AMOUNT OF TECHNOLOGICAL KNOWLEDGE ADDED.

TEA

ALWAYS HAS TEA AT HAND.

SISTER MACHINE NUMBER 1.

TEA TEA

CLANK CLANK

SCREW

ARGH

ROBOTIC THRUST PUNCH

SSSHHH

REFER TO DREAM AND M-6

NEGI MA!

MAHORA

☆ SHE'S A TALL, GENTLE GIRL IN THE MIDST OF NINJA TRAINING WHO FORGETS SKILLS QUICKLY.

KAEDE NAGASE

UM, HOW DID THAT ATTACKING CICADA TRICK GO AGAIN?

DESCENDANT OF A NINJA WHOSE IDENTITY IS UNKNOWN. HOWEVER, THAT BRANCH OF THE FAMILY HAD ALREADY QUIT NINJA TRAINING. HER PARENTS TOLD HER SHE WAS A GENERATION TOO LATE, AND TOLD HER TO STOP, TOO.

UH, SARUTOBI'S SPIKE IS...RIGHT LEG GOES SOME-THING LIKE THIS...DON'T SAY A WORD, MOM.

HOW ABOUT STOP-PING THE FOOLISH-NESS, YOU.

PARENTS WEREN'T PRACTICING ANY-MORE SO THEY SAID ENOUGH ALREADY WITH THE ART OF THE NINJA

LIKES HATS.

TALL AND GENTLE. OPERATES AT ONE SLOW TEMPO.

LIKES CUTE AND FRIENDLY THINGS.

CHEEP

HEIGHT: 175CM

BLOOD TYPE: O.

JERSEY. →

HERE GOES. NINJA SKILLS.

OOH

WHAT A FORGETFUL PERSON.

UHH, HOW DID IT GO AGAIN?

LIKES AND IS GOOD AT TREE CLIMBING (THE ART OF SARUTOBI). THOSE ARE THE ONLY ARTS SHE CAN DO.

CONTINUED

CERTAINLY A TREE OR SOMETHING CAN TAKE YOUR PLACE?

YOU'RE RIGHT. THAT'S RIGHT. THAT'S RIGHT.

UM...TREE ...TREE.

YEAH, I THINK SO.

KAEDE HAS CHANGED CONSIDERABLY. THE FIRST VERSION WAS PORTRAYED AS SOMEONE WITH A LOT OF ABILITY. IT LOOKS LIKE SHE'LL BE PLAYING A ROLE HENCEFORTH. IN THE NEXT VOLUME 4, THE SCHOOL FIELD TRIP FINALLY STARTS. THAT'S EXACTLY THE BEST PART OF NEGIMA! EXPECT QUITE A STORY! --AKAMATSU

MAGISTER NEGI MAGI

Translation Notes

Japanese is a tricky language for most westerners, and translation is often more art than science. For your edification and reading pleasure, here are notes on some of the places where we could have gone in a different direction in our translation of the work, or where a Japanese cultural reference is used.

Sweet sake, page 15

We've used the phrase *sweet sake* here, instead of the actual Japanese term that appeared in the original, *amazake*. *Amazake*, which most Japanese are familiar with, is a drink brewed from rice and malt usually drunk in the spring or summer.

Ane-san, page 65

Ane-san is a generic term for a girl, usually older, that means sister. It can be construed as rude or too informal, although it's more likely in this case that Albert Chamomile is just trying to ingratiate himself with Asuna so she won't kick him out.

Garbage, page 66

Chamo may be destroying the evidence, but at least he's conscientious about it. Dividing garbage in Japan can be a complicated business. Trash is usually divided into burnables, nonburnables, and recyclables.

Karaage, page 67

Chamo rushes in to tell Negi that Nodoka is being attacked by *karaage*, which is Japanese-style fried chicken. Chamo's next comment in the original text is that he's really got to work on his Japanese—remember, he's from Wales, like young Negi. Problem is, the joke doesn't really work in English so we modified it a wee bit.

Tsujigiri, page 89

In the original text, Asuna says that she doesn't like what they're doing because it reminds her too much of *tsujigiri*. *Tsujigiri* refers to a time when samurais would sharpen their swordsmanship skills on people on the street, a clearly dishonorable act.

Sessha, page 107

Remember this term from volume 2? Just in case you don't: *Sessha* is a condescending word that samurai used to refer to themselves. It also refers to a character from a book written in the seventeenth century who assisted women down on their luck.

Char, page 107

A char is a fish you might catch in a mountain stream in the summer in Japan or China.

WANT TO GO FISHING? THE CHAR ARE PLENTIFUL THIS TIME OF YEAR.

MIGHT BE A GOOD WAY FOR YOU TO LEARN SELF-SUFFICIENCY.

Baths, page 111

As you might know, baths and hot springs are very popular in Japan. Outdoor baths, not necessarily in this style, can be found in the forests and mountains in resorts towns such as Gerou, in Gifu Prefecture.

WOW, AN OUTDOOR BATH.

FAN FAN

YEP. ♥

RUSTLE

LET'S BEGIN THE ENGLISH LESSON.

MAN, I LOVE THAT CUSTOM.

BOW.

Bowing, page 140

Note that all of the girls are bowing as Negi takes his place at the front of the classroom. This is a daily custom in Japanese primary and secondary schools, and is intended as a sign of respect and gratitude to the teacher.

Preview of Volume 4

Here is an excerpt from Volume 4, on sale in English in September 2006.

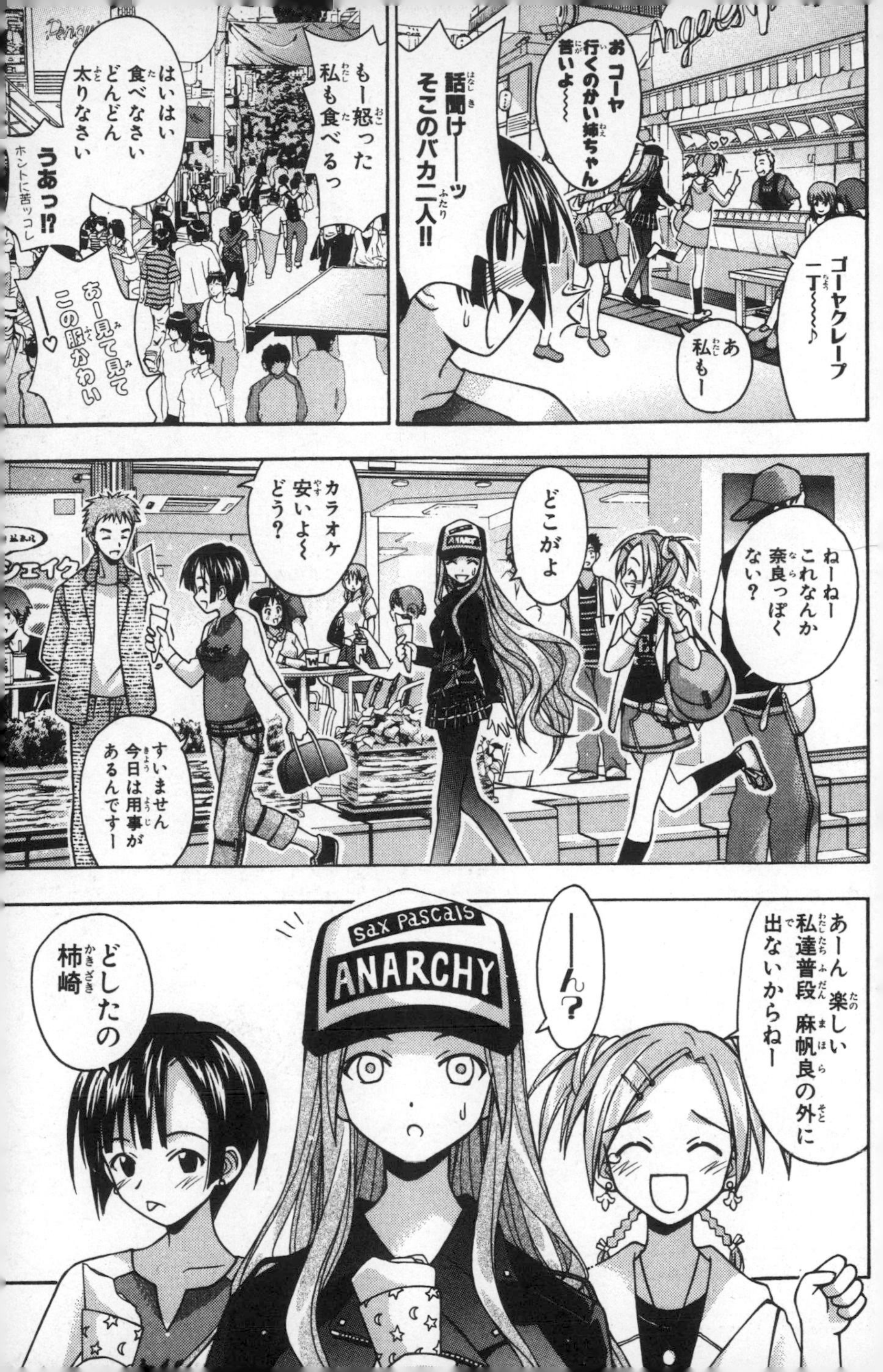
ゴーヤクレープ一丁〜〜〜♪
あ 私もー
おコーヤ 行くのかい姉ちゃん 苦いよ〜〜〜
話聞けーーッ そこのバカ二人!!
もー怒った 私も食べるっ
はいはい 食べなさい どんどん 太りなさい
うあっ!? ホントに苦ッコレ
あー見て見て この服かわいー♡
ねーねー これなんか 奈良っぽく ない?
どこがよ
カラオケ 安いよ〜 どう?
すいません 今日は用事が あるんですー
sax pascals ANARCHY
あーん 楽しい 私達普段 麻帆良の外に 出ないからねー
ーーん?
どしたの 柿崎

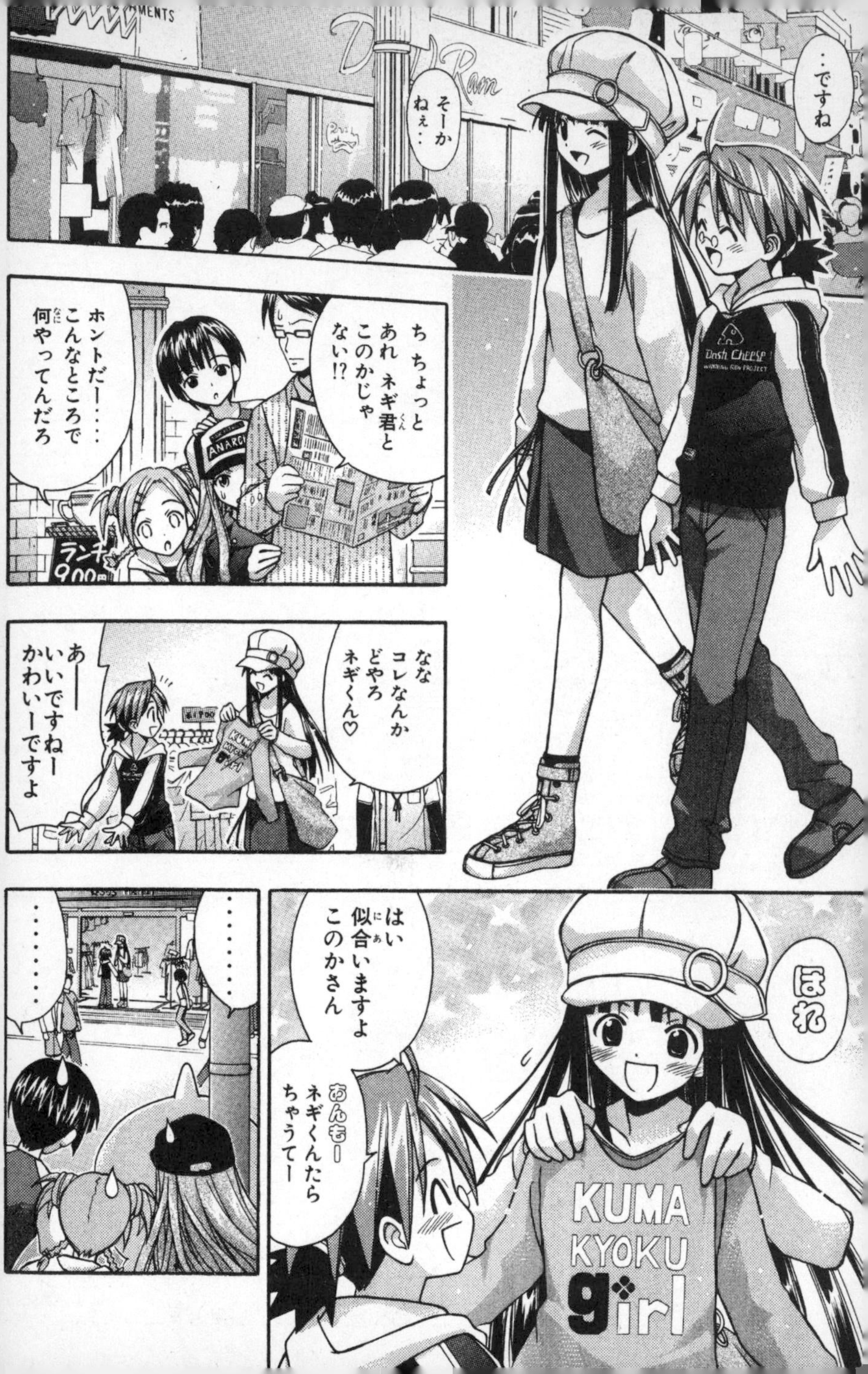
‥ですね
そーか ねぇ‥
ちょっと あれ ネギ君と このかじゃ ない!?
ホントだー‥‥ こんなところで 何やってんだろ
ランチ 900円
なな コレなんか どやろ ネギくん♡
あー いいですねー かわいーですよ
ほれ
はい 似合いますよ このかさん
あんもー ネギくんたら ちゃうてー
KUMA KYOKU girl
‥‥‥
‥‥‥

こ…
これって…・

もしかして
デートじゃ
ないの…・!?

でもネギ君10歳だし
…ちょっと姉弟感覚で
買い物に来ただけじゃ

それで
わざわざ
原宿まで
出てくる!?

ネギ君は
ただの10歳
じゃないよ〜

あーわわわ
たた
大変かもーっ

誰かに
知られたら
マズいよ これ

キャー──ッ!!

生徒に手を
出すなんて
ネギ君
クビだよクビ〜

いーいや待って
落ち着いて!

この場合
手を出したのは
ネギ君というより
多分このかなんじゃ
…・?

確かに
それっぽい
感じよね…・

おーっ
なるほど

コクリッ…

大体 このかと
ネギ君って
同じ部屋で
暮らしてるんだ
もんね〜

禁断な…・
もん♡

いろんな意味で
もん♡

この面倒見が
いいから母性本能
くすぐられて
いつしか恋愛感情
が…・

ネギ君〜
ああ♡♡

ホラ
アスナは寝るの早いし

この子に手を出すなんて

そして ある昼下がり

とにかく
当局に連絡
しなくちゃ

とっ
当局って!?
職員室!?

ととっ

バカ んなとこ
連絡したら
即クビ＆退学
でしょ

ギャッ

ひゃっ

トゥルルル
トゥルルル

BY OH!GREAT

Itsuki Minami needs no introduction—everybody's heard of the "Babyface" of the Eastside. He's the strongest kid at Higashi Junior High School, easy on the eyes but dangerously tough when he needs to be. Plus, Itsuki lives with the mysterious and sexy Noyamano sisters. Life's never dull, but it becomes downright dangerous when Itsuki leads his school to victory over vindictive Westside punks with gangster connections. Now he stands to lose his school, his friends, and everything he cares about. But in his darkest hour, the Noyamano girls give him an amazing gift, one that just might help him save his school: a pair of Air Trecks. These high-tech skates are more than just supercool. They'll enable Itsuki to execute the wildest, most aggressive moves ever seen—and introduce him to a thrilling and terrifying new world.

Ages: 16 +

Coming in October 2006!
Special extras in each volume! Read them all!

Air Gear © 2003 Oh!great / KODANSHA LTD. All rights reserved.

School Rumble

BY JIN KOBAYASHI

SUBTLETY IS FOR WIMPS!

She . . . is a second-year high school student with a single all-consuming question: Will the boy she likes ever really notice her?

He . . . is the school's most notorious juvenile delinquent, and he's suddenly come to a shocking realization: He's got a huge crush, and now he must tell her how he feels.

Life-changing obsessions, colossal foul-ups, grand schemes, deep-seated anxieties, and raging hormones—School Rumble portrays high school as it really is: over-the-top comedy!

Ages: 16 +

Coming soon in Jan 2006!
Special extras in each volume! Read them all!

School Rumble © 2003 Jin Kobayashi / KODANSHA LTD. All rights reserved.

BY CLAMP

Watanuki Kimihiro is haunted by visions. When he finds himself irresistibly drawn into a shop owned by Yûko, a mysterious witch, he is offered the chance to rid himself of the spirits that plague him. He accepts, but soon realizes that he's just been tricked into working for the shop to pay off the cost of Yûko's services! But this isn't any ordinary kind of shop . . . In this shop, Yûko grants wishes to those in need. But they must have the strength of will not only to truly understand their need, but to give up something incredibly precious in return.

Ages: 13+

Special extras in each volume! Read them all!

xxxHOLiC © 2005 by CLAMP. All rights reserved.

TSUBASA

VOLUME 1
BY CLAMP

SAKURA AND SYAORAN RETURN!

But they're not the people you know. Sakura is the princess of Clow—and possessor of a mysterious, misunderstood power that promises to change the world. Syaoran is her childhood friend and leader of the archaeological dig that took his father's life. They reside in an alternate reality . . . where whatever you least expect can happen—and does. When Sakura ventures to the dig site to declare her love for Syaoran, a puzzling symbol is uncovered—which triggers a remarkable quest. Now Syaoran embarks upon a desperate journey through other worlds—all in the name of saving Sakura.

RESERVoir CHRoNiCLE
1
TSUBASA
by
CLAMP
NEW FROM THE CREATORS OF CHOBITS!

Ages: 13+

Includes special extras after the story!

tanoshimi

Basilisk

ORIGINAL STORY BY FŪTARO YAMADA
MANGA BY MASAKI SEGAWA

THE BATTLE BEGINS

FOR MATURE AUDIENCES
Basilisk
1
THE KOUGA NINJA SCROLLS
ORIGINAL STORY BY FUTARO YAMADA
MANGA BY MASAKI SEGAWA

Mature: Ages 18+

The Iga clan and the Kouga clan have been sworn enemies for more than four hundred years. Only the Hanzo Hattori truce has kept the two families from all-out war. Now, under the order of Shogun Ieyasu Tokugawa, the truce has been dissolved. Ten ninja from each clan must fight to the death in order to determine who will be the next Tokugawa Shogun. The surviving clan will rule for the next thousand years.

But not all the clan members are in agreement. Oboro of the Iga clan and Gennosuke of the Kouga clan have fallen deeply in love. Now these star-crossed lovers have been pitted against each other. Can their romance conquer a centuries-old rivalry? Or is their love destined to end in death?

Special extras in each volume! Read them all!

tanoshimi

FREE

wallpapers

icons

previews

downloads

competitions

visit

www.tanoshimi.tv

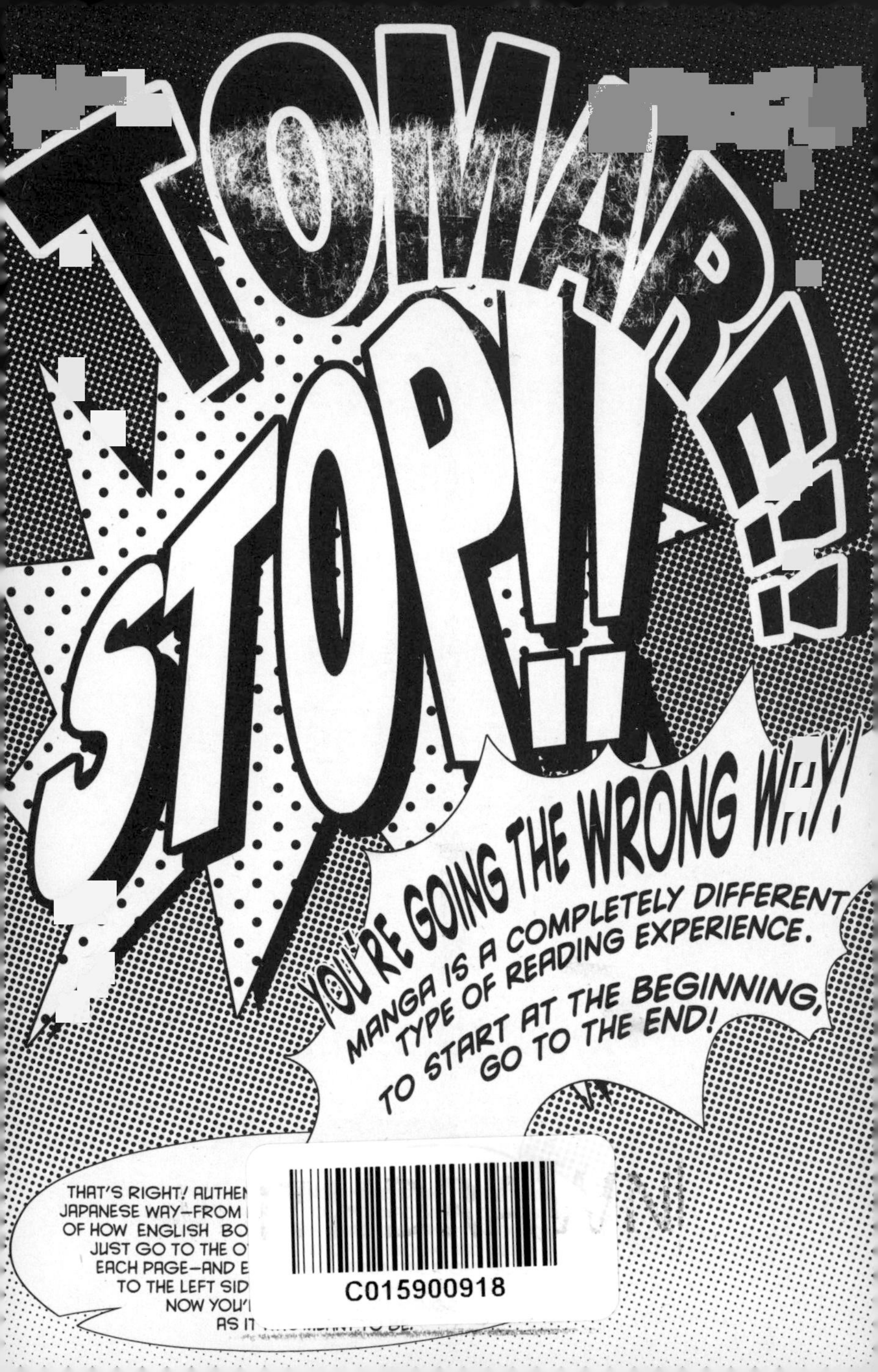
TOMARE!!
STOP!!
YOU'RE GOING THE WRONG WAY!
MANGA IS A COMPLETELY DIFFERENT TYPE OF READING EXPERIENCE.
TO START AT THE BEGINNING, GO TO THE END!
THAT'S RIGHT! AUTHEN
JAPANESE WAY—FROM
OF HOW ENGLISH BO
JUST GO TO THE O
EACH PAGE—AND E
TO THE LEFT SID
NOW YOU'
AS IT